The Iraq War

The Middle East in the International System

Anoushiravan Ehteshami and Raymond Hinnebusch,
SERIES EDITORS

"Pariah" States and Sanctions in the Middle East
Tim Niblock

The Foreign Policy of Middle East States
edited by Raymond Hinnebusch and Anoushiravan Ehteshami

Islam, the Middle East, and the New Global Hegemony
Simon W. Murden

The United Arab Emirates
Christopher M. Davidson

The Iraq War: Causes and Consequences
edited by Rick Fawn and Raymond Hinnebusch

The
Iraq War

Causes and Consequences

edited by
Rick Fawn and
Raymond Hinnebusch

LYNNE
RIENNER
PUBLISHERS

BOULDER
LONDON

Published in the United States of America in 2006 by
Lynne Rienner Publishers, Inc.
1800 30th Street, Boulder, Colorado 80301
www.rienner.com

and in the United Kingdom by
Lynne Rienner Publishers, Inc.
3 Henrietta Street, Covent Garden, London WC2E 8LU

Library of Congress Cataloging-in-Publication Data
The Iraq war : causes and consequences / edited by Rick Fawn and Raymond
Hinnebusch.
        p.   cm. — (Middle East in the international system)
    Includes bibliographical references and index.
    ISBN-13: 978-1-58826-413-8 (hardcover : alk. paper)
    ISBN-10: 1-58826-413-0 (hardcover : alk. paper)
    ISBN-13: 978-1-58826-438-1 (pbk. : alk. paper)
    ISBN-10: 1-58826-438-6 (pbk. : alk. paper)
1. Iraq War, 2003—Causes. 2. Iraq War, 2003—Influence. I. Fawn, Rick.
II. Hinnebusch, Raymond A. III. Title. IV. Series.
DS79.76.I7292 2006
956.7044'3–dc22

                                                            2006002386

British Cataloguing in Publication Data
A Cataloguing in Publication record for this book
is available from the British Library.

Printed and bound in the United States of America

  The paper used in this publication meets the requirements
of the American National Standard for Permanence of
Paper for Printed Library Materials Z39.48-1992.

5   4   3   2   1

Contents

Preface

While the war in Afghanistan saw most industrial countries not only rhetorically back the US-led campaign but also offer material assistance, the subsequent war in Iraq has profoundly divided opinion and represents a likely watershed in the post–Cold War international order. This volume seeks to examine the causes and explanations, official and otherwise, for the war and its consequences for the Middle East, for relations among key international actors, and for the future of the international system itself.

The Iraq War has had wide implications for the conduct of international relations. It marks a major break in the behavior of the world hegemon and in the norms of conduct that have governed international relations since World War II. It was the first preemptive war in a century and the first waged on the basis of so-called intelligence reports.[1] It carries implications for the nature of warfare, the "war on terror," the relevance of international law, and the United Nations. It is likely to have major long-term consequences for the Western alliance, the stability of the Middle East, and the role of oil in the world political economy.

It also has implications for the study of international relations. The widely varying reactions of states to the war permit and require analysis of the relative weight of various determinants—external constraints versus domestic politics, norms and ideology versus material interests—that govern foreign policy outcomes. The war carries implications for the competing schools of international relations: while some would say it validates realism's stress on power against liberalism's belief in the efficacy of law, multilateralism, and international organization, constructivists could point to the significance of identity and ideology in the construction of threats, particularly by the United States. While we do not systematically address these issues in the book, they are touched upon in the last two chapters, and it is hoped that the empirical content and the analysis provided by country specialists on major actors in the conflict will help to provide important grist to this necessary debate.

◼ Plan of the Book

Following a narration of key events leading to the Iraq War and its conduct, the volume examines the war's causes and consequences in four parts. The first analyzes the foreign policy making of the key powers that determined the terms of the crisis and its evolution, notably the belligerents, their allies, and the major powers that opposed the war. Here the authors explore what policies were adopted; how they came to be made, including against what domestic and international opposition; what state interests were served or compromised in so doing; and what the longer-term consequences might be of each country's position. Part 2 turns to the reaction of and consequences for Middle Eastern states and actors most strongly affected by the war, including Turkey, Syria, Jordan, Israel, Iran, and the Palestinian Authority. In Part 3 the authors focus on the context and consequences of the war, examining the impact of the war for Iraq itself, as well as the relation of the war to the United Nations, international law and ethics, and the world oil market. Finally, the implications of the war for international relations theory and foreign policy analysis are considered in Part 4.

◼ Orientation of the Book

The Iraq War has more sharply split the world's states, global public opinion, and scholarly discourse than any event in recent times. Communist-era dissident intellectuals, who physically suffered under totalitarianism, supported the war; and East Timorese Nobel Peace laureate José Ramos-Horta wrote, "If the antiwar movement dissuades the US and its allies from going to war with Iraq, it will have contributed to the peace of the dead." By contrast, Nelson Mandela accused the United States of creating a "holocaust" and John Pilger called the George W. Bush presidency the "Third Reich of our times." In diplomacy, US secretary of defense Donald Rumsfeld controversially recast Europe into "old" and "new," while French president Jacques Chirac told postcommunist states that supported Washington to keep quiet and that they were "badly brought up."

The staggering intellectual and diplomatic divides that emerged from the advance to war and the unraveling of the original justifications for war, even by the White House's own subsequent admissions, prompt examination of the mainsprings of war. Hence, one objective of this book, congruent with the study of international relations, is to uncover the realities beneath the discourse of the dominant elites in the world hegemon. We also aim to identify and explain, in largely positivist mode, how other states have tried to adapt to and been affected by the hegemon's actions. And in a more interpretative mode, we seek to marshal evidence to make arguments about the implications of the war for the debates among the various schools of IR theory. Whatever their aims and approaches, all the authors have backed their arguments with rigorous empirical research. While we have tried to avoid bias, ensure that our arguments conform to the canons of logic, and marshal accumulated evidence from a wide variety of sources, our findings are necessarily interpretative. We believe, however, that, even if readers disagree with some of these interpretations, the arguments and evidence to which they will be exposed will allow them to acquire an enhanced understanding of the war and its consequences.

We wish to thank Lynne Rienner and Elisabetta Linton for their interest in this work and their assistance in its publication, Jason Cook for careful copyediting, and Karen Williams for seeing the book through production.

—*Rick Fawn and Raymond Hinnebusch*

Note

1. Dilip Hiro, *Secrets and Lies,* p. xx.

1

The Iraq War:
Unfolding and Unfinished

Rick Fawn

V ictors may write the history; they certainly choose the dates. For its ini-
tiators, the Iraq War started and finished in 2003. Even the start of the
war is taken as 19 March, by US time, rather than a day later, when ordi-
nance hit Baghdad targets on 20 March, by Iraqi time. For others, the war
started before that date, and continued past George W. Bush's chosen date
of 1 May 2003 as the end of hostilities.

The events one considers important are inseparable from one's perspective. Developing any narrative of this war risks subjectivity, and even more
so as official Anglo-American explanations and justifications for it have
unraveled. Facts are also casualties of war, and the major media have been
caught out. The *New York Times* conceded that it wished it "had been more
aggressive in re-examining the claims [supporting war] as new evidence
emerged—or failed to emerge."[1] Even so, the major events can be adum-
brated, and this chapter provides a broad narrative chronology, within which
the more partial, focused, and explanatory approaches of the following
chapters may be located.

■ A Drumbeat for War?

The 2003 Iraq War has been mooted as a continuation (and conclusion) of
the unfinished 1990–1991 Gulf War. Advocacy of a war for regime change
in Iraq by the neoconservatives, whom George W. Bush brought into office,
predate his administration. According to Paul O'Neill, Bush's secretary of
the treasury, a plan to attack Iraq was even discussed at the first meeting of
the president's senior staff, on 30 January 2001.[2] Some believe Bush sought
to finish his father's earlier war, and sought revenge for an Iraqi plot to
assassinate the elder Bush in Kuwait in April 1993.[3] Regardless of an exact
or a singular motivation for war against Iraq, several of Bush's staff advo-

cated military action against Iraq within hours of the 9/11 attacks, including Secretary of Defense Donald Rumsfeld, Deputy Secretary of Defense Paul Wolfowitz, and Vice President Dick Cheney.[4]

The Bush administration prepared the US public and, to an extent—though immeasurably less successfully—the world, for war in advance of open fighting. On 29 January 2002, Bush made his first State of the Union address, including Iraq in his "axis of evil." This axis, he claimed, linked "the world's most dangerous regimes" threatening the United States with "the world's most destructive weapons." On 2 June 2002, Bush announced the doctrine of preemption, arguing that the United States might strike first to prevent a potential attack from materializing. In August 2002, Vice President Cheney asserted that Saddam Hussein sought a nuclear weapon with which he "could be expected to seek domination of the entire Middle East, take control of a great portion of the world's energy supplies, directly threaten America's friends throughout the region and subject the United States or any other nation to nuclear blackmail." Perhaps reflective of differences within the administration, the State Department denied that the United States was beating the drums of war.[5] But on 7 October, Bush claimed that Saddam's regime had trained Al-Qaida operatives "in bomb-making and poisons and deadly gases"—a claim that was later withdrawn. The preparation of the US public for war moved further on 11 October, when Congress voted to authorize Bush to attack Iraq if he decided it necessary.

Meanwhile, Bush had been persuaded by Secretary of State Colin Powell and British prime minister Tony Blair to seek UN approval for a war by making the case to the world that Saddam had weapons of mass destruction (WMDs). Addressing the UN General Assembly on 12 September 2002, Bush condemned what he deemed Iraq's "flagrant violations" of UN Security Council (UNSC) resolutions and indicated that if the UN did not fulfill its resolutions concerning Iraq (the language of which was arguably ambiguous), then the United States would act unilaterally. Bush's speech encouraged many to believe that the US government would try to deal with the Iraqi threat within the framework of the UN. Britain was solidly behind the United States and began producing its own evidence of Saddam's WMD efforts. Even Saudi Arabia, which had cautioned against a war, indicated it would allow use of its territory for a war if the UN sanctioned military action against Iraq.

But orchestrating such explicit UN authority would ultimately fail. Unusually, other key US allies began resisting the US push for war. Germany emerged as the major challenger to US policy when Chancellor Gerhard Schröder, facing a strong election challenge, won reelection on 22 September on the basis of his rejection of what he called US "adventures" in Iraq. He also rejected German participation in a war even if backed by UN authorization. Bush pointedly did not call him to offer the customary congratulations on his reelection. The French and Russian governments similarly announced that they were unconvinced of the grounds for war.

A key watershed, which could be said to be a compromise between the United States and those unconvinced of the danger posed by Iraq, was the unanimous passage of UNSC Resolution 1441 on 8 November, which put the onus on Iraq to prove it did not have WMDs by allowing the admission of UN inspectors and submitting all its records on the matter to the Security Council. The resolution observed that the Security Council had already "repeatedly warned Iraq that it will face serious consequences as a result of its continued violations of its obligations." Iraq had hitherto dragged its feet on admitting inspectors, giving credence to US claims that it had something to hide, but the regime appears to have belatedly become aware that only through compliance with UN demands could it hope to avoid an invasion. On 16 September 2002, Baghdad said it would "unconditionally" allow the return of inspectors, and on 18 November, after nearly four years of absence, the International Atomic Energy Agency (IAEA) and the UN Monitoring, Verification, and Inspection Commission (UNMOVIC) were permitted to resume their inspection efforts. On 3 December, Iraqi officials were seen to cooperate significantly with inspectors when the latter made an unannounced visit to a presidential palace. Saddam's regime then delivered 12,000 printed pages and related material, such as CDs, on 7 December, one day ahead of the deadline. One of Saddam's generals declared Iraq to be "empty" of WMDs. Saddam made a televised apology for his 1990 invasion of Kuwait.

Within days of the Iraqi submission, British and US officials were questioning its reliability. Following comments by Chief Inspector Hans Blix that the Iraqi declaration contained little new information, US officials indicated the course of US policy by saying Baghdad was in material breach of Resolution 1441. The Iraqi government responded by saying that the CIA could search Iraq for the alleged WMDs. Addressing the UNSC on 19 December, IAEA head Mohamed El-Baradei reported, "We still need much more cooperation from Iraq in terms of substance, in terms of providing evidence to exonerate itself that it is clean of weapons of mass destruction." On that day the United States and Britain declared Iraq to be in material breach of the resolution. Yet Blix had also said that access to the suspected weapons sites had been unhindered and that Iraqi cooperation had been forthcoming.[6] By the end of December, UN inspectors in Iraq declared that they had found nothing and also were not receiving sufficient help from Western intelligence. In one month, inspectors had visited 150 sites throughout the country, and had made surprise visits to 13 sites identified by Anglo-American intelligence as being of concern.[7] Rumsfeld, however, asserted that "any country on this earth with an active intelligence pro-gramme knows that Iraq has weapons of mass destruction."

US military deployments around Iraq continued throughout the second half of 2002, but January 2003 is taken as the period in which Bush decided to pursue war and the French government to oppose it.[8] UNMOVIC and the IAEA gave the Security Council their opinion on 9 January 2003 that, as Blix put it, no "smoking gun" had yet been found, although the Iraqi declaration was inadequate and incomplete and Iraq had not surrendered the names of scientists believed to be working on weapons programs.

On 13 January, Blair warned that the United States and Britain might move against Iraq without a second (specific) Security Council resolution authorizing war. On 19 January, Washington offered Saddam immunity from prosecution if he were to leave Iraq, as a means to avert war. On 21 January, French foreign minister Dominique de Villepin declared at the UN that "today nothing justifies considering military action."[9] With diplomatic lines being drawn, inspections still continued in Iraq. On 27 January, Blix, under intense US pressure, reported to the UNSC that "Iraq appears not to have come to a genuine acceptance—not even today—of the disarmament which was demanded of it and which it needs to carry out to win the confidence of the world." El-Baradei, however, gave a more favorable impression of Iraqi compliance with inspections, and asked for additional months to continue them. In his State of the Union address on 28 January 2003, Bush noted that the British government had learned that Saddam "recently sought significant quantities of uranium from Africa"—a charge that the White House retracted after the war. This claim was used to justify an attack on Iraq without UN authorization. Bush also repeated later-withdrawn assertions of Iraqi cooperation with Al-Qaida; even the *New York Times,* which supported the war, called these assertions "sweeping, if unproven."[10] Two days later, senior State Department officials advised senators that "clear evidence" existed that Iraq was hiding biological and chemical weapons, and sheltering members of Al-Qaida,[11] all claims that would prove false or remain unsubstantiated.

The US position received significant support when the leaders of eight European countries gave their backing in a letter published in several newspapers. Ten postcommunist countries followed with a similar letter. While each declaration appealed to Euro-Atlantic values and unity, French president Jacques Chirac, in one of the greatest verbal exchanges of the crisis, lambasted the postcommunist countries with remarks to the effect that they were "badly brought up" and had missed an opportunity to keep quiet. The Czech foreign minister gave a sense of postcommunist dissatisfaction, declaring that his country was not joining the EU to be told to remain silent.

With international differences on Iraq deepening, Powell presented the US case against Iraq to the Security Council on 5 February. He used satellite images and intercepted phone conversations between Iraqi officers to demonstrate Iraqi intentions to proceed with development of WMDs and to deceive inspectors. Powell made particular reference to mobile biological weapons laboratories. While this presentation was aimed at securing international support, "All accounts of the preparation of this speech convey[ed] a growing sense that the case lacked a hard core of fact, and in key respects relied on inference and innuendo."[12] In Iraq, UNMOVIC could find no corroboration of Powell's claims (and a year after his Security Council appearance, Powell admitted that his presentation had relied on bad intelligence and that his references to mobile chemical weapons laboratories had appeared solid then).[13] The UK government had also released an "Iraq dossier," the claims of which included that Iraq could launch WMDs, which were implied to have a range sufficient to reach Britain, in forty-five minutes. It would concede after the war that this was incorrect, the threat referring only to battlefield weapons, and the government was also embarrassed by revelations that parts of its report had been plagiarized from an outdated graduate student thesis. A day after Powell's presentation, weapons inspectors reported they were having "very substantial" meetings with the Iraqi government.[14] A Franco-German proposal on 9 February to increase the number of inspectors infuriated the Bush administration, which saw it as an effort to halt its war preparations. The next day the Belgian government joined the French and Germans in blocking NATO preparations to protect alliance member Turkey by sending it Patriot missiles in case of war, provoking probably the alliance's gravest crisis. Rumsfeld called their stand "inexcusable" and "beyond comprehension."[15]

On 12 February, weapons inspectors announced that they had found Iraqi Samoud-2 missiles that slightly exceeded the range permitted by the 1991 cease-fire. Saddam consented to destroy them, but London and Washington rejected his offer as meaningless. By 14 February, Blix could report to the Security Council that there was no serious evidence that Baghdad was failing to comply with the inspections; indeed, 177 inspections, which took some 300 samples from 125 locations, showed consistency with Iraqi declarations.[16] Blix's report also cast doubt on the intelligence behind Powell's earlier submission to the Security Council.

Opposition was mounting to the Anglo-American position. De Villepin told the UNSC—to applause—"In this temple of the UN we are the guardians of an ideal, the guardian of a conscience. This message comes to you from an old country, France, from a continent like mine, Europe, that has known wars, occupation and barbarity." At a televised Security Conference in Munich in February, German foreign minister Joschka Fischer told Rumsfeld of the US case for war: "Excuse me, I am not convinced." Thereafter, the French and German governments proposed to increase the number of inspectors to counter US skepticism of Iraqi intentions, but this was rejected by the Bush administration. On 15–16 February, antiwar protests were held in numerous cities worldwide; millions were estimated to have partaken, including an unprecedented 1 million in London, where Blair faced added difficulties. Some in his party were opposed to war per se, and others insisted on explicit UN authorization of war. However, UN Secretary-General Kofi Annan said that military action would not conform to the UN Charter.

The US and UK governments then argued that they did not need a second UN resolution to go to war and could do so on their own claims that Iraq was in breach of its obligations under UNSC Resolution 1441. Since the other permanent members of the Security Council—as well as much of world opinion—contested this view, Washington and London began canvassing support for a war resolution. In later February and the first half of March they sought support from nonpermanent members of the Council, with only the Spanish and Bulgarian governments being immediately receptive. This sparked a competition to secure the votes of other nonpermanent members; de Villepin toured African states, with Britain's junior foreign minister Baroness Amos attempting the same. Mexican president Vicente Fox perhaps summarized the dilemma for these smaller states when he told Chirac that he preferred the resolution to be vetoed by permanent members to avoid blame for an Anglo-American defeat. On 1 March the Turkish parliament further dumbfounded Washington by voting (marginally)[17] to refuse US access to its territory for a second front against Iraq. Russia's foreign minister intimated on 3 March that his country would veto a resolution. British hopes that Iraq would be shown to be in breach of UNSC Resolution 1441 were dashed when, on 7 March, Blix and El-Baradei reported that Iraqi cooperation had increased since January and said full inspections would require several months. Powell responded by taking this as evidence of an Iraqi breach of Resolution 1441, in that Iraq had refused "immediate, active and unconditional cooperation." On 10 March, Chirac said on French television that "insofar as disarming Iraq goes, the Americans have already reached their objective." He declared that no cause to attack Iraq existed and that, on the contrary, so doing would set a dangerous precedent and unleash a clash of civilizations. He added categorically that France would not participate in such a fight.[18] France would thereafter oppose a second resolution for war, proposing instead to allow the inspectors 120 days to finish the job, after which the UNSC would meet to decide what to do. Chirac would be accused by his detractors of thereby making a war more likely and of having the "blood of American and British soldiers on his hands."[19] A major turning point was the 15–16 March summit of Bush, Blair, and the prime ministers of Spain and Portugal in the Azores, where they announced that the UN had twenty-four hours in which to enforce Iraqi disarmament or war would occur. Knowing they lacked the votes for a second resolution, the United States and United Kingdom did not put it to the test, blaming France for threatening a veto.

The war was launched on the basis of US and UK claims about Saddam's WMDs and connections to Al-Qaida, but after the war these would be largely discredited. As early as May 2003, BBC reporter Andrew Gilligan reported on discontent in the intelligence services that the prime minister's office had, as the phrase famously became known, "sexed up" its 2002 dossier on the threat posed by Saddam's WMDs, and knew that its central claim that Iraq could launch WMDs within forty-five minutes was misleading. Clare Short, a Labour minister at the time of the war, accused Blair of lying to the cabinet over the war. In June 2004, Blix lambasted the intelligence given to weapons inspectors by the United States and Britain, saying it showed no evidence of WMDs. He went further, in accusing the United States of systematically trying to undermine his attempt to conduct an honest inspection. On 18 September 2004 he said that he thought Iraq had destroyed most of its WMDs a decade ago and charged Britain and the United States of spin regarding Iraq's threat. David Kay, the chief US weapons inspector, finally had to admit that "we were almost all wrong" to believe Saddam had WMDs. Condoleezza Rice seemed to suggest the same, stating, "I think that what we have is evidence that there are differences between what we knew going in and what we found on the ground."[20] The White House also conceded in September 2003 that Saddam had no connection to the 11 September 2001 terrorist attacks, and the 9/11 Commission report of 16 June 2004 reaffirmed that there was "no credible evidence that Iraq and al-Qaida cooperated on attacks against the United States." But by then, of course, the war had not only been waged, but also been considered officially over.

■ The Military Campaign

In what has been considered a de facto prewar paralleling the diplomacy at the UN, air attacks by the United States and United Kingdom against a variety of Iraqi air defense and command targets had crippled Iraq's limited air capacity. On 19 March a rain of missiles began exploding in Baghdad in an attempted "decapitation strike" aimed at Saddam; it failed, and Saddam made a defiant television appearance. Thereafter, Operation Iraqi Freedom began as US and British troops poured into southern Iraq from across the Kuwaiti border. Meanwhile, a "shock and awe" air campaign was aimed "across . . . a broad spectrum of capabilities [in the expectation] that [Saddam's] military would suffer systemic collapse."[21] In the south, British forces seized Iraq's second city, Basra, though the anticipated Shia uprising in support of the invasion did not materialize—indeed, paramount Shia leader Ayatollah Ali al-Sistani called for resistance. The coalition also encountered resistance in the port of Umm Qasr, which lasted several days.

US forces faced still greater resistance in the southern city of Nasiriya. Otherwise unopposed, US ground forces achieved the swiftest land advance in history.[22] In the north, about 1,000 US paratroopers landed to support a second Kurdish front against the Baghdad government. By 6 April, US forces had claimed control of the main routes into Baghdad as air and artillery attacks continued against the city. Resistance around the capital collapsed when Republican Guard commanders told their troops to go home, since without air cover the city could not be defended; some may have been suborned by the CIA, while others decided to save themselves and Baghdad from block-by-block destruction.[23] The official fall of Baghdad and ousting of the Hussein regime was taken to be 9 April, when a statue of the leader was symbolically torn down by a group of Iraqis with the assistance of US military equipment. Within two days, the major northern cities of Kirkuk and Mosul had been secured by Kurdish fighters. On 13 April, facing resistance, US troops reached Saddam's birthplace of Tikrit.

Whatever euphoria was expressed by some Iraqis at the fall of the regime, it was quickly displaced by the widespread looting and chaos that followed. In March 2005 the postwar Iraqi deputy minister of industry said that "sophisticated looting" of key weapons installations also occurred during that time.[24] As basic services collapsed and unruliness spread, aid workers exhorted the coalition to avert a humanitarian catastrophe. The worst claims of looting after the attack, on the National Museum, caused great worldwide damage to the image of the Anglo-American coalition. Rumsfeld dismissed the extensive pillage and chaos as "stuff happens." Meanwhile, the United States had taken care to secure the Ministry of Oil.

The conventional phase of the war, at least, could be said to have ended when, on 1 May, President Bush landed triumphantly on the deck of the aircraft carrier USS *Abraham Lincoln* and, in front of a banner proclaiming "Mission Accomplished," declared the war over. The militarily successful strategy to remove Saddam's regime, however, was damaged by the obvious lack of adequate planning for postwar rehabilitation. This was partly because the occupation administration was run exclusively by the Pentagon, which deliberately ignored the considerable preparation that had been done by the State Department, and partly because Rumsfeld, against the advice of his generals, declined to deploy the troop numbers deemed necessary to provide for postconflict security.

■ The Occupation of Iraq

Reconstituting Authority

The United States set out to establish its control over Iraq, to demolish the remnants of the ancien régime, and to reconstitute a new Iraqi authority with which it could work. On 21 April, retired US general Jay Garner arrived as Iraq's postwar administrator, but his failure to deal with the postwar chaos resulted in his replacement in less than a month by presidential envoy L. Paul Bremer, an antiterrorism expert with no experience in Middle Eastern affairs. Bremer quickly made two marks on the country. First, he dissolved the Iraqi army and purged 50,000 Baath Party members from public office, instantly creating 450,000 unemployed and thus disaffected men, some of whom still retained their weapons and knew where more munitions were stored. The United States would soon have to reverse this "de-Baathification" in order to reconstitute even the rudiments of the bureaucracy. Second, Bremer launched plans for privatization of Iraq's economy, making numerous utilities, telephone networks, and large companies available for purchase by Western buyers. While even most of the co-opted Iraqi politicians rejected this, Bremer insisted that "everybody knows we cannot wait until there is an elected government here to start economic reform."

Despite thousands of US troops on the ground, the struggle for Iraq was not finished and the balance of forces in fact remained fluid. From the outset, however, the coalition forces faced rising guerrilla resistance, which they attributed to die-hard Saddamists whose capture became a high priority. Before long, several individuals on the US list of "most wanted" Iraqis were arrested or handed over, including, separately, two of Saddam's half brothers. On 22 July, Uday and Qusay, Saddam's sons and lieutenants in ruling Iraq and now directing resistance to the occupation, were killed in Mosul by US missiles; their location was believed to have been disclosed to the United States by an informant who may have been rewarded with $30 million. The coalition made much of the capture, on 21 August, of "Chemical Ali," Saddam's leading weapons official. Finally, on 13 December, Saddam himself was found hiding in a hole near his birthplace of Tikrit. US forces aired footage of the captured Saddam to underline to his supporters that insurgency was futile. However, the seizure or death of these pillars of the old regime appeared to make little difference in quelling what was becoming a broadening nationalist resistance to occupation (see Chapter 17 and below).

Simultaneously, a provisional Iraq ruling group was being constituted. Ahmad Chalabi, the Iraqi exile picked by the Pentagon to run postwar Iraq, had arrived on 18 April. July saw the creation of the Iraqi Governing Council (IGC), with an appointed membership representative of Iraq's many communal groups. But US plans for consolidating a new Iraqi authority were soon contested. Bremer reached agreement on 15 November 2003 with the IGC that power would be given to an unelected interim government, to assume office on 30 June 2004, that would be charged to write the constitution that would allow for elections. Bremer's adviser, Noah Feldman, said the reason for not electing the new Iraqi authority was that "if you move too fast, the wrong people could get elected."[25] Iraqi opinion, however, increasingly mobilized behind Shia religious leader Ayatollah Ali al-Sistani, who demanded in November 2003 that the proposed interim government instead be directly elected. Nevertheless, the matter was finessed and on 28 May 2004 the IGC unanimously nominated secular Shia and former exile Iyad Allawi to be prime minister of the interim Iraqi government. A Baathist who left Iraq before Saddam's rule, Allawi was known to have strong ties to the CIA, yet was also "a strong critic of key US-imposed policies in post-war Iraq," including de-Baathification of the government and armed forces.[26] Three days later, Sunni Ghazi al-Yawar was appointed to the largely figurehead post of president, after the candidate favored by the United States was rejected. The interim government replicated the IGC, and about two-thirds of its members possessed foreign, primarily British or US, passports.[27] On 28 June 2004, two days ahead of the scheduled date, Bremer handed over power, boarded a plane, and flew out of Iraq, but not before laying the ground for a permanent US presence: he ordered the new Iraqi army to be subordinate to the US commander, while the Pentagon started building fourteen bases to garrison 100,000 troops. The interim government was expected to agree on a "status of forces treaty for permanent stationing" of coalition forces, which a US general called "a blueprint for how we could operate in the Middle East."[28]

The new government was thus in place, with powers that were to lapse with elections scheduled for January 2005. However, while this government may have ruled the Green Zone in central Baghdad, it faced mounting insurgency in the country at large, having military and police resources that were a fraction of those Saddam had commanded.[29] The threat of the defense minister to behead rebels personally had no effect on the insurgency. Meanwhile, the standing of the previous key US ally among exiled Iraqis, Ahmad Chalabi, rapidly deteriorated in August when an Iraqi court produced an arrest warrant for him for counterfeiting, his son was then accused of involvement in a murder, and a relative, Salem Chalabi, in charge of the legal proceedings against Saddam, had an arrest warrant issued against him for murder. All rejected the charges, but the coalition offered them no support.

In spite of various zigzags, the United States had managed to put together a core of Iraqi elites who were prepared, to various degrees and for various motives, to collaborate or conditionally cooperate with it in the hopes of influencing the rebuilding of Iraq or inheriting real power in future.

Extracting International Support

Despite having gone to war in defiance of the UN and some of its key allies, the United States came to believe that international acquiescence and UN legitimation were crucial to establishing its authority in Iraq. It enjoyed considerable success in acquiring this backing. On 22 May, UNSC Resolution 1483 was passed unanimously, providing legal authority for the occupation of Iraq, allowing oil exports, and removing previous restrictions on foreign economic activity in Iraq. In explaining France's support for the resolution, de Villepin said, "France remains true to its principle—the text does not legitimize the war, it opens the way to peace which we must all build together." The resolution also appointed a UN special representative to Iraq, a post filled by Sergio Vieira de Mello. Subsequently, France and Germany attempted to extract some time limits on and international authority over the occupation; Washington declared its authority in Iraq to be temporary and that its forces would remain in Iraq formally as "allies" rather than occupiers, but kept real power in its hands. Nevertheless, Resolution 1551, passed on 16 October 2003, accepted the legitimacy of the IGC and, in effect, recognized regime change. Subsequently, the Allawi government also received international legitimacy on 8 June 2004, when the Security Council voted to transfer sovereignty from the Coalition Provisional Authority.

On the other hand, US draft resolutions asking for multilateral military participation under US command were obstructed by France and Germany, although Japan agreed to Washington's request by making its largest deployment of soldiers since World War II. Bush and Blair's request for expanded NATO engagement in the country was also rebuffed by France. Some international support for the reconstruction of Iraq was demonstrated in October at the Madrid conference, at which $13 billion was committed over five years. But France and Germany pledged no funds, and on 10 December 2003 the US government announced that it was excluding companies from countries that opposed the war, such as France and Germany, and also ones deemed not to have supported Washington, notably Canada, from reconstruction contracts in Iraq. While this limitation was rescinded for a later round of contracts, more would be needed to close the cleavage among Western allies caused by the war.

Insurgency and Counterinsurgency

An antioccupation insurgency can be said to have begun, not long after the formal end of the fighting, in the Sunni stronghold of Fallujah with a demonstration that US troops forcibly dispersed, leaving scores of casualties. This action led to the first clamor among some Iraqis for wide-scale revolt against the coalition, which was soon taken up more broadly in the country. While concentrated in the Sunni heartland, Shia areas were not immune. Thus the British had to resort to antiriot measures to deal with disorder provoked by shortages in Basra, while six British soldiers were killed on 24 June 2003 in southern Iraq, hitherto a calm part of the country.

Initially the insurgency mostly aimed at US, and to a lesser degree UK, forces, but its attacks would steadily widen to include any target deemed likely to aid the occupation. Insurgency became bolder toward the end of 2003. US deputy defense secretary Wolfowitz narrowly missed becoming a casualty during a visit to the country on 26 October 2003 when a rocket blasted the Al-Rashid Hotel. Bremer also admitted that he had missed assassination. Insurgent attacks targeted a US Defense Intelligence base in Irbil, and the Baghdad hotel where CIA and Mosad operatives apparently stayed (the latter reportedly instructing US commanders on their experiences in counterinsurgency). Several US helicopters were also shot down by SAM-7 missiles.[30]

In June 2003, two attacks on oil pipelines demonstrated that insurgents were also able to strike high-value targets; in the middle of August, insurgents twice attacked oil pipelines in northern Iraq, causing severe disruptions. By mid-2004, sabotage of pumping stations had resulted in an 80 percent fall in oil production. The point was to dry up the revenue base of the occupation and what the resistance saw as its puppet government. Rumsfeld conceded in July 2003 that the US military presence in Iraq was costing Washington $3.9 billion per month, twice the original estimate.[31]

There was considerable debate over the sources of the insurgency. Bremer blamed much of the violence on the terrorist group Ansar al-Islam, which had links to Al-Qaida. Its leader, Mullah Mustapha Kreikar, compared the fighting against Americans in Iraq to Islamic resistance against the Soviets in Afghanistan. The coalition also routinely asserted that outside militants, crossing into Iraq from Syria or Iran, were responsible for the violence, although US commanders on the ground played this down and the numbers of foreign fighters captured remained small compared to the numbers of Iraqi nationals. Arab satellite television aired broadcasts believed to have been made by Saddam, encouraging anticoalition resistance. Bush proclaimed on 2 July: "There are some who feel the conditions are such that they can attack us there." To that he said, "My answer is: bring them on."

However, indiscriminately targeted counterinsurgency measures by the occupation authorities were themselves responsible for precipitating much resistance activity. For example, US soldiers killed several members of a family in Baghdad as they raced home to meet the curfew. Iraqi leaders in many towns accused US soldiers of randomly spraying gunfire that killed civilians in operations and firefights against insurgents. This came on top of findings by groups such as Human Rights Watch that the coalition had improperly targeted its firepower. Far from ending the insurgency, these measures appeared to embitter Iraqis against the occupation and recruit new activists to the resistance.

The insurgents began systematic targeting of those they considered collaborators with the occupation. Toward the end of August 2003, Shiite

Ayatollah Mohammed Baqir al-Hakim was killed by a car bomb in Najaf. He had fled Saddam's persecution and had recently returned from Iran and seemed moderate toward the coalition, even proposing cooperation. A subsequent broadcast purportedly by Saddam denied responsibility. Baqir's funeral became a vehicle to express opposition to the coalition for its failure to establish security. Among those assassinated by insurgents were Akila al-Hashemi, a female representative on the Iraqi Governing Council who was slated to represent Iraq at the UN, and Izzedin Salim, head of the council. Scores of middle-level officials, such as the deputy police chief of Mosul, were also killed.

On 9 October 2003 the car-bombing of a Baghdad police station that killed eight recruits and injured dozens was the beginning of a campaign by insurgents to deter Iraqis from joining the security forces that the coalition needed to pacify the country. On 10 February several dozen were killed by a car bomb while applying for jobs as policemen, and a similar number died the next day at an army recruitment office. In mid-June 2004, dozens more were killed by a car bomb. On 3 December 2004 about thirty people, over half of them Iraqi police, were slain in attacks on a Baghdad Shia mosque and a police station. Between 3 and 5 December over seventy Iraqis, mostly working in the security forces, were killed in insurgent attacks. On 2 January 2005 a car bomb blew up a bus of Iraqi national guardsmen outside Baghdad, killing twenty-six. Such attacks by largely Sunni insurgents on those they considered to be collaborators, mostly either Kurds or Shia, threatened to unleash a sectarian civil war in Iraq, but this potential cleavage was crosscut by the general cross-sectarian opposition to the occupation.

Concerted cross-sectarian opposition emerged in April 2004. Supporters of Shia cleric Muqtada al-Sadr rose up in several cities, including "Sadr City" (formerly Al-Tharwa) in Baghdad, Najaf, Nasiriya, and Basra, in response to attempts to repress his antioccupation propaganda. The United States declared that it would "kill or capture" Sadr and by the first week of August reported having killed as many as 300 of his followers. After three weeks of intensive fighting, a cease-fire was brokered by Grand Ayatollah Ali al-Sistani. A second form of major resistance to the coalition emerged in Fallujah, where 2,000 Sunni rebels, some believed to be foreign, held out against encirclement by the coalition. By the end of April, US forces had resorted to aerial bombardment of the city. After a pause in which a cease-fire held, on 8 November 2004, US forces again assaulted the city in strength, using air bombardments to pulverize it, a campaign that resulted in emptying the city of its population; a modern city of 1.9 million people was destroyed. An uprising ensued in Mosul; the police fled, leaving only Kurdish militias to confront the insurgents. This underlined the difficulty of recruiting reliable security forces; some joined to earn a salary but lacked motivation to fight their own countrymen, while others infiltrated on behalf of the insurgency. Similarly, when US forces withdrew from cites like Samrra and Ramadi after pacification campaigns, Iraqi army forces could not control these areas.

On 19 August 2003 an explosives-laden truck rammed into the Canal Hotel, site of UN headquarters in Baghdad. The attack, later claimed by an unknown group, left twenty-three dead, making it the largest murder of UN staff in its history. Among the victims was Sergio Vieira de Mello, the UN Secretary-General's envoy to Iraq and an esteemed veteran international civil servant. He was probably targeted because his lobbying for a UNSC resolution welcoming the Iraq Governing Council was seen as an attempt to legitimize the occupation; his murder was a message that all countries that sent personnel would be treated as part of the occupation.[33] While Kofi Annan initially said the United Nations would remain in Iraq, UN operations were curtailed and most staff withdrew, followed by other intergovernmental and nongovernmental organizations.

These ups and downs in the intensity of insurgency merely punctuated an ongoing battle between Iraqi resistance and US forces. The 139th US soldier was killed on 26 August 2003; that death gained particular significance, as it exceeded the number of US soldiers killed before the watershed of 1 May, when Bush declared hostilities concluded. In August 2004, US forces were suffering an average of eighty-seven attacks per day. By 7 December 2004, 1,000 US soldiers had been killed in Iraq since the start of the war. In 2005, despite the pacification of Fallujah and the end of Sadr's defiance in Najaf, one US official called southern Baghdad, where US forces had suffered ninety-four consecutive attacks, "enemy territory."[32]

The insurgents began targeting any foreign presence that they viewed as complicit in the occupation in an effort to drive them out of Iraq. The office of the International Red Cross as well as some police stations fell victim on 27 October to suicide bombers who took 35 lives and wounded over 200, marking the worst day of violence since the official end of Saddam's regime. At the end of March 2004 four US contractors were kidnapped, their bodies burned and dragged publicly before finally being hung from a bridge in Fallujah. At the end of June 2004 five foreign employees of General Electric were killed. A South Korean was beheaded by captors demanding the withdrawal of South Korean troops; Seoul nevertheless reiterated its intentions to deploy another 3,000 soldiers to bolster its current 600. In a recording believed to be genuine, Osama bin Laden offered rewards to those who killed US or UN officials or citizens of any state providing personnel to the coalition. Later, US contractor Nick Berg was videotaped being beheaded in what his kidnappers called direct retaliation for the abuses at Abu Ghraib. On 16 November 2004, Margaret Hassan, a British-born aid worker, living in Iraq for decades with Iraqi citizenship and married to an Iraqi, was believed to have been killed by gunmen after the release of a video depicting an execution.

The Battle for Legitimacy

The battle for Iraq was also a contest over legitimacy both in Iraq and at the international level. With the failure to find WMDs, the US and UK governments sought to advance other justifications for the war. In mid-May 2003, discoveries of mass graves of Saddam's victims at a site near Baghdad were used to bolster the case for the invasion. UK foreign minister Jack Straw said WMDs were not essential to the case for war, since the regime's wrongdoing was unquestionable. However, the cost of the war was high for an Iraqi population who had supposedly been liberated. Monitoring groups had recorded around 12,000 Iraqi casualties based on hospital and other reports, but another report, published in the respected medical journal *Lancet,* used extrapolation to make the explosive contention that up to 100,000 Iraqi civilians had been killed since the start of the war. This assertion was denied by coalition governments, though they had declined to keep records of Iraqi casualty figures and had discouraged the Iraqi Ministry of Health from doing so.[34] The coalition powers suffered a major legitimacy loss with the May 2004 revelation of sexual abuse and torture at Abu Ghraib, a major prison (notorious under Saddam), now holding captured Iraqis.[35] The images of abused captives provoked worldwide revulsion and condemnation. In Washington, Arthur Schlesinger's report on Abu Ghraib for the Pentagon indicated not only "brutality and purposeless sadism" but also concluded that the violations could not simply be blamed on individual miscreants: the US military as an institution was being questioned. Defense Secretary Rumsfeld was widely blamed for permitting the abuses. However, he would weather the crisis and was reappointed secretary of defense in Bush's second term. It was important for the Pentagon to be seen as acting on the abuses, and on 24 August an army reservist, one of seven US personnel accused of mistreatment of prisoners, said he would plead guilty. Revelations of abuse by British soldiers similarly emerged. The coalition suffered a further legitimacy setback in early June 2004 when the Pope attacked the mismanagement of Iraq, condemning the "deplorable" abuse of detainees and urging an international settlement. In September 2004, UN Secretary-General Kofi Annan, interviewed by the BBC, bluntly called the war "illegal," and on 21 September in the General Assembly he reprimanded states that "shamelessly disregard" international law and reiterated the centrality of international law to world stability.

While the coalition remained confident about defeating the insurgency, fifteen leading US military and diplomatic staff warned that insecurity was wrecking the attempt to transfer overt authority to reliable Iraqis; they also noted that the new Iraqi armed forces had been infiltrated by insurgents.[36]

Coalition leaders attempted to underscore their commitment to Iraq. On 21 December 2004, Blair flew into Iraq, and Rumsfeld made an unannounced trip on Christmas Eve 2004, declaring to US forces that the insurgency could still be defeated. However, even key allies seemed to be wavering. In mid-March 2005, Silvio Berlusconi announced that Italy's 3,200 soldiers and police assisting the United States in Iraq would be withdrawn by the end of the year, starting in September, though he subsequently said the date could be amended. The decision, which he said he discussed with Blair, was what public opinion expected. Though denied officially, the move was also believed to have been prompted by increased Italian casualties but especially by the accidental shooting by US forces of Italy's leading intelligence officer in Iraq as he drove a freed Italian hostage to safety.

Seeking Electoral Legitimacy

The occupation forces agreed to the holding of Iraqi elections on 30 January 2005 in an attempt to create an authority that had enough legitimacy to resist the insurgency and legitimize their presence internationally. The insurgents recognized the threat and Abu Musab al-Zarqawi, wanted by the United States for his militant opposition, pledged a bitter war of violence to undermine them. Despite continuing violence, Interim Prime Minister Allawi insisted that elections had to proceed, as they were the key to defeating the insurgency. On 27 December the main moderate Sunni Muslim party withdrew from the election, citing violence as inhibiting a fair vote. The party headquarters of Allawi and several polling stations were bombed. Despite these attacks, the election began on 28 January, with Iraqis living abroad being first to cast ballots in the country's first free election in five decades. The elections were greeted in the West as an immense achievement, even by those abroad who had opposed the war, and Western analysts saw the Iraqi outcome as encouragement for democracy across the region.

■ Outcome of the War

Was the invasion of Iraq a success in the war on terrorism and against proliferation of WMDs in hostile hands, the basis on which it was ostensibly waged? Bush asserted that Iraq was a key front in the war on terrorism, but critics claimed the invasion had actually turned Iraq into a haven for terrorists and enabled them to target US troops in a way that would otherwise have been impossible. The International Institute for Strategic Studies issued a report concluding that the Iraqi situation had encouraged Iran and North Korea to increase their resistance to international demands to stop their alleged nuclear weapons programs.

Simultaneous bombings occurred against public transportation in

Madrid on 11 March 2004 and in London on 7 July 2005, with a repeated attempt in the latter two weeks later; while the bombings were reviled, they were also widely seen as responses to these governments' support for the Iraq War.

The long-term consequences of the war cannot yet be known, and the story is far from over. As the second anniversary of the invasion approached in spring 2005, Bush announced that 120,000 US soldiers would remain in Iraq for another two years.

■ Notes

References to public quotations that were widely cited in the media and form part of official speeches that remain available on websites are not reproduced here.

1. "The Times and Iraq," *New York Times,* 26 May 2004, p. 10. The editorial said that the paper has provided solid journalism but that controversial information went insufficiently qualified or challenged, and that many of its articles relied on information from Iraqi informants whose credibility had been increasingly questioned.

2. Paul O'Neill's account was recorded in Ron Suskind's *The Price of Loyalty.*

3. See David Von Drehle and R. Jeffrey Smith, "U.S. Strikes Iraq for Plot to Kill Bush," *Washington Post,* 27 June 1993, p. A1.

4. This is documented in Bob Woodward's anecdotal account of executive planning after 9/11, *Bush at War.* For similar assertions, see Richard A. Clarke, *Against All Enemies.* These views are reinforced in secondary works such as by Anatol Lieven, *America Right or Wrong,* especially p. 142.

5. Cited in "Putting His Cards on the Table," *The Economist,* 31 August 2002, p. 33.

6. Hiro, *Secrets and Lies,* p. 111.

7. Ibid., pp. 113, 115.

8. See Lawrence Freedman, "War in Iraq," p. 31.

9. William Shawcross, *Allies,* p. 125.

10. Todd S. Purdum, "As Bush Prepares Public for War, He Covers His Domestic Flank," *New York Times,* 29 January 2003.

11. James Dao, "U.S. May Give the U.N. Data on Iraqi Labs," *New York Times,* 30 January 2003.

12. Freedman, "War in Iraq," p. 32.

13. See also Glenn Kessler, "Powell Says New Data May Have Affected War Decision," *Washington Post,* 3 February 2004, p. A1.

14. See, for example, Suzanne Goldenberg, Ed Vulliamy, Jason Burke, and Helena Smith, "Hope As Iraq Gives Ground over Arms," *The Observer,* 9 February 2003.

15. See *The Guardian,* 10 February 2003.

16. Hiro, *Secrets and Lies,* p. 143.

17. More votes were cast in favor than against, but Turkish parliamentary practice is to count abstentions as negative votes, which resulted in the resolution failing.

18. *International Herald Tribune,* 11–12 March 2003.

19. *Independent,* 2 June 2003; Shawcross, *Allies,* p. 149.

20. Commented on NBC television's *Today,* 29 January 2004.

21. Murray Williamson and Major General Robert H. Scales Jr., *The Iraq War,* p. 92.

22. Anglo-American losses in the first three weeks numbered about 70 (and many of these were due to accidents), while it was estimated that over 5,000 Iraqi soldiers were killed. International Institute for Strategic Studies (IISS), *Strategic Survey 2002/3* (London: IISS, 2003), p. 155.

23. See Hiro, *Secrets and Lies,* pp. 257, 394.

24. See James Glanz and William J. Broad, "Looting at Iraqi Weapons Plants Was Systematic, Official Says," *New York Times,* 13 March 2005. His statement came a week after a UN agency reported that some 90 significant sites had been raided or destroyed.

25. See Hiro, *Secrets and Lies,* p. 435.

26. James Drummond and Roula Khalaf, "Iraq Council Backs Former Exile with CIA Links as Interim Leader," *Financial Times,* 29 May 2004, p. 1.

27. Hiro, *Secrets and Lies,* pp. 484–485.

28. Ibid., pp. 458–459.

29. Saddam had 70 divisions. The interim government had 1 division of 8,000 men, a 40,000-strong National Guard, and a total of 16 helicopters. *The Economist,* 26 June 2004, p. 29.

30. As reported in Hiro, *Secrets and Lies.*

31. *The Economist,* 12 July 2003, p. 6.

32. Quoted in John F. Burns, "Across Baghdad, Security Is Only an Ideal," *New York Times,* 27 January 2005, p. 13.

33. See Hiro, *Secrets and Lies,* p. 350.

34. "Iraq Body Count," for example, at http://www.iraqbodycount.net. In April 2005 it put the Iraqi civilian death count between 20,117 and 22,851.

35. Abu Ghraib was reportedly overcrowded under Saddam's rule, with up to 5,000 prisoners; it was holding some 7,000 under the coalition.

36. Eric Schmitt, "In Iraq, U.S. Officials Cite Obstacles to Victory," *New York Times,* 31 October 2004.

Part 1

Key Global Actors

2

The United States: Belligerent Hegemon

Stephen Zunes

The 2003 invasion of Iraq was a US war. Unlike the Gulf War (1990–1991), this was not simply a matter of pulling together, leading, and dominating a multinational military force that had been effectively deputized by the UN Security Council (UNSC) to enforce its resolutions. The invasion not only had no legitimate basis under international law or the UN Charter, but also was a largely unilateral action in which only the British contributed a substantial number of combat forces, with the United States contributing close to 85 percent of the troops. The idea of invading Iraq would not have even been an issue before the international community were it not for the determination of the United States that the Baghdad regime be overthrown and replaced by a new government more to its liking.

■ The Construction of an Iraqi Threat: Dissecting Official US Policy

In the wake of the terrorist attacks of 11 September 2001, the main security threat perceived by US officials was a combination of terrorism and weapons of mass destruction (WMDs). The official US justification for war on Iraq was that Saddam Hussein's alleged development of WMDs and ties to terrorist groups combined to create an imminent threat to the United States. It appears that the decision to invade Iraq took place as far back as February 2002.[1] In July of that year, notes of a meeting between Prime Minister Tony Blair and leading cabinet members and security officials reveal that, at this point, a US-led invasion of Iraq was "now seen as inevitable." The justification that President George W. Bush wanted to utilize was "the conjunction of terrorism and WMD." Since there was little evidence to support this argument, however, the memo noted that "the intelligence and facts were being fixed around the policy."[2] Whether or not what would later prove to be grossly exaggerated claims about Iraq were believed at all by the administration, its success in "constructing" a sense of threat was the immediate cause of the war.

The initial focus of the Bush administration's campaign to justify an invasion was Iraq's refusal to allow UN Special Commission (UNSCOM) weapons inspectors back into Iraq to verify that the regime had destroyed its proscribed weapons, weapons programs, and delivery systems. Despite administration claims that Saddam had "kicked out"[3] the UNSCOM inspectors in December 1998, they had actually been voluntarily withdrawn by the commission's chairman, Richard Butler, under pressure from the Clinton administration in anticipation of the intensive four-day US bombing campaign that followed. As most analysts predicted at the time, this gave Saddam the excuse—along with revelations that the United States abused UNSCOM as a cover for spying—to refuse to allow inspectors from UNSCOM or the International Atomic Energy Agency (IAEA) to return. This refusal to allow the inspectors back in became a major focus of the Bush administration's case of why the United States should invade the country and overthrow its government, since it demonstrated, according to President Bush, that "this is a regime that has something to hide from the civilized world."[4]

Negotiations between the Iraqi government and the United Nations to allow a return of inspectors from the reconstituted inspections commission, known as the UN Monitoring, Verification, and Inspection Commission (UNMOVIC), began in spring 2002, with Iraq finally announcing late that summer that they would be allowed to return. At that point, however, the Bush administration began to denigrate the UN inspections process, which—as was widely suspected at the time and has subsequently been demonstrated—had been successful in disarming Iraq. For example, Vice President Dick Cheney, in a major policy speech at the end of August, claimed that "a return of inspectors would provide no assurance whatsoever of his compliance with UN resolutions."[5] Even Iraq's acceptance of a greatly strengthened inspections regime imposed by the Security Council that December (UNSC Resolution 1441), and the failure to find anything of significance in subsequent months, did not stop the Bush administration and congressional leaders of both parties from insisting that Iraq was somehow hiding massive stores of biological and chemical weapons, an advanced nuclear weapons program, and sophisticated offensive delivery systems.

This, of course, was utterly false. Despite extensive investigations, it has become apparent that Iraq had probably destroyed its WMDs and dismantled its WMD programs shortly after the 1991 Security Council resolution demanding that it do so. Most independent strategic analysts (this author included) had argued in the months and years prior to the invasion that it would have been virtually impossible for Iraq to have any remaining or reconstituted offensive WMD capability. The IAEA had concluded in 1998 that it appeared that Iraq's nuclear program had been completely dismantled.[6] Scott Ritter, the former chief weapons inspector of UNSCOM, estimated that as of December 1998, at least 95 percent of Iraq's chemical weapons program had been similarly accounted for and destroyed.[7] Despite extensive satellite and aerial surveillance, no signs of chemical or nuclear weapons–related activity could be found. The existence of a biological weapons program was a bigger question mark, since such a program would have been easier to hide. However, Iraq clearly lacked the sophisticated technology needed to weaponize biological agents through offensive delivery systems. In any case, UNSCOM noted in 1998 that virtually all of Iraq's offensive missiles and other delivery systems had been accounted for and rendered inoperable.[8] In addition, the shelf life of most biological and chemical weapons is quite limited. It was only as a result of the import of technology and raw materials from the Soviet Union, Germany, France, Britain, and the United States that Iraq was able to develop its biological, chemical, and nuclear weapons programs in the 1980s. There had been a strict international embargo on such exports to Iraq since August 1990, however, so there was no way Iraq could have reconstituted the programs destroyed under UNSCOM. While some countries, in part due to humanitarian concerns, were circumventing economic sanctions against Iraq, the embargo on military-related items was holding solid.

Moreover, at the time of the US invasion, Iraq's armed forces were barely one-third their 1991-war strength. Even though Iraq had not been required to reduce its conventional forces, the destruction of its weapons and the country's economic collapse had led to a substantial reduction in its armed forces. Iraq's navy was virtually nonexistent, and its air force was just a fraction of what it was before the 1991 war. Military spending by Iraq was estimated at barely one-tenth of what it was in the 1980s.

Another assumption pushed by the administration was that, if Saddam somehow did have an arsenal of dangerous weapons and means to deliver them, he would use them in an offensive operation against the United States and its allies. In short, deterrence theory—which had worked for decades against far more powerful nuclear-armed adversaries—somehow did not apply to Iraq.[9] However, Hussein had demonstrated repeatedly that he cared first and foremost about his own survival. He presumably recognized that any attempt to use WMDs against the United States or any of its allies would inevitably lead to his own destruction. Thus, while Saddam had used chemical weapons against an isolated Iran and against Kurdish civilians who could not fight back, he did not use them during the Gulf War, even when subjected to one of the most intense bombing campaigns in world history.

A second major rationale involved Iraq's alleged ties to international terrorism, particularly charges of links with Al-Qaida. Few independent observers thought it possible that the decidedly secular Baathist regime—which had savagely suppressed Islamists within Iraq—would be able to maintain close links with Osama bin Laden and his followers. Saudi prince Turki bin Faisal, his country's former intelligence chief, noted how bin Laden viewed Saddam "as an apostate, an infidel or someone who is not worthy of being a fellow Muslim."[10] Much of the money trail for Al-Qaida had come from US ally Saudi Arabia; none had been traced to Iraq. Fifteen of the nineteen 9/11 hijackers were Saudi; none were Iraqi. Admitting that there was no evidence of direct links between Iraq and Al-Qaida, the best that CIA director George Tenet could come up with in testimony before Congress was that the "mutual antipathy" that Iraq and Al-Qaida have for the United States "suggests that tactical co-operation between the two is possible."[11] The State Department's own annual study, *Patterns of Global Terrorism,* did not list any serious act of international terrorism by the government of Iraq.[12] The last clear example that US officials could cite of such Iraqi-backed terrorism was an alleged plot by Iraqi agents to assassinate former president George H. W. Bush when he visited Kuwait in 1993, a full ten years before the US-led invasion. Iraq's previous terrorist links had largely been limited to such secular groups as Abu Nidal, a renegade Palestinian organization that had been moribund since the late 1980s. The CIA reported that the Iraqis had actually been consciously avoiding any actions against the United States or its facilities abroad.[13] Investigations by the CIA and others have shown no evidence that Saddam's regime ever supported Jordanian-born terrorist Abu Musab al-Zarqawi—a major figure in the anti-US resistance in Iraq following the 2003 invasion—because they saw this radical Islamist as a threat. All indications are that his very brief visits to Baghdad were clandestine and that he did not have any major operations there prior to the US invasion. Al-Zarqawi's camp was located in a far northeastern corner of Iraq within the Kurdish safe area and well beyond the control of Saddam's government. Journalists who visited the camp where US officials claimed he was conducting ongoing chemical and biological experiments prior to the US invasion found nothing remotely resembling such activity, a fact confirmed by US Special Forces that seized the area a few weeks later.[14] Finally, given Saddam's distrust of others, few independent observers believed that he would go to the risk and expense of developing weapons of mass destruction only to pass them on to a group of terrorists, particularly radical Islamists who could easily turn on him.

Still, the Bush administration was somehow able to convince most of the US Congress, the news media, and the US public that even though Saddam Hussein's regime had only a tiny percentage of his once-formidable military capability still intact, Iraq was sufficient a threat that it was necessary to invade the country and replace its leader—the same leader Washington had quietly supported during the peak of Iraq's military capability. A month before the invasion, a public opinion poll showed that 72 percent of Americans believed that Saddam was personally involved in the 9/11 attacks against the United States.[15] During the initial phase of the war, the House of Representatives voted in favor of a resolution—with only a dozen dissenters—that the invasion of Iraq was "part of the global war on terror."[16] Similarly, as recently as September 2004, with only sixteen dissenting votes in the 435-member body, the House passed a resolution claiming that under Saddam's rule "the al-Zarqawi terror network used Baghdad as a base of operations to coordinate the movement of people, money, and supplies."[17]

As a result of the insurgency that followed the US conquest of Iraq, President Bush has subsequently declared that a successful US-led pacification of the antioccupation resistance in Iraq would be an "essential victory in the war on terror"[18] and that continued US military involvement in Iraq is necessary because "we must recognize Iraq as the central front in our war on terror."[19] In a nationally televised address less than six months after the invasion, President Bush declared that "the surest way to avoid attacks on our own people is to engage the enemy where he lives and plans. We are fighting that enemy in Iraq . . . today so that we do not meet him again on our own streets, in our own cities."[20] There appears to be no evidence, however, that those Iraqis currently fighting US occupation forces in their own country actually want to somehow sneak into the United States to kill American civilians. Indeed, no Iraqis have ever been known to commit an act of terrorism against Americans on US soil. Though Iraq was not a hotbed of terrorism for the last dozen years of Saddam's rule, it is now. The destruction of his tightly controlled police state by US forces opened up the country as a haven for the world's terrorists. The US invasion resulted in the replacement of a highly centralized authority by the kind of weak state that the Bush administration noted, in its September 2002 national security strategy (NSS), as being a breeding ground for terrorists: an inability to meet the basic needs of its citizens or control its borders.[21] Furthermore, a senior US counterterrorism official has acknowledged that "an American invasion of Iraq is already being used as a recruitment tool by al-Qaida and other groups."[22] Similarly, Richard Clarke, a former senior White House counterterrorism official, noted, "Fighting Iraq had little to do with fighting the war on terrorism, until we made it so." According to Jessica Stern of Harvard University's John F. Kennedy School of Government, "We're inspiring terrorism. The Bush administration didn't seem to have anticipated the extent to which terrorists would be drawn into Iraq and the extent to which they would be inspired by our occupation to attack elsewhere."[23]

■ Searching for Explanations

Since the threat Iraq supposedly posed appears not to have provided credible grounds for war, and certainly not more so in 2003 than in earlier years, one must suppose that it was not Iraqi behavior but a qualitative change in US foreign policy under the Bush administration that supplies a deeper explanation for the war. Indeed, this policy departs in significant ways from the norm since World War II.

From Multilateralism to Ideological Unilateralism
In the decades following World War II, US administrations—to varying degrees—saw US dominance as exercised though multiple independent centers of power, such as the United Nations and other intergovernmental organizations, with increasing emphasis in more recent years on the role of international financial institutions, such as the World Bank and the International Monetary Fund (IMF). International law was seen as a vehicle that would help facilitate use of the preeminent military and economic power of the United States in the interest of world order. While certain elements of international law could occasionally be stretched or quietly undercut, the prevailing view in Washington was that the UN system allowed for a relatively stable world order in which the United States and its allies could usually get its goals accomplished, and one that was far less dangerous than a more anarchic system.

Now, however, as a result of the emergence of the United States as the world's sole remaining superpower, with US military spending higher than that of the rest of the world's governments combined, and with US commercial and cultural influence far greater than that of any other country, the view among leading policymakers appears to be that the United States can now go it alone. The UN system is now seen as a constraint and an anachronism. The US no longer has to play by the rules and has the right and the ability to impose a kind of Pax Americana on the rest of the world.

This has manifested itself in a number of other policy shifts, such as the broad bipartisan consensus in Washington in support of Israeli prime minister Ariel Sharon's colonization and incipient annexation of large segments of the occupied West Bank and Golan Heights, the abandonment of the referendum process in Moroccan-occupied Western Sahara, and efforts to sabotage the Millennium Development Goals and other aspects of the world body's agenda at the UN World Summit in September 2005.

This is underlain by an intensified belief in US exceptionalism within the Bush administration. In his introduction to the 2002 National Security Strategy, President Bush asserted that the United States represents "a single sustainable model for national success."[24] The president declared: "I believe the United States is *the* beacon for freedom in the world. And I believe we have a responsibility to promote freedom that is as solemn as the responsibility is to protect the American people, because the two go hand-in-hand."[25] Historian Margaret Macmillan wrote, "Faith in their exceptionalism has sometimes led to a . . . tendency to preach at other nations rather than listen to them, a tendency [to believe] that American motives are pure where those of others are not."[26] Journalist Eric Zuesse observed how Bush "made clear right at the start that the United States had to be accepted by other nations as being not merely the first among equals, but a role apart, which simply mustn't be judged like other countries."[27] Furthermore, noted Zuesse, Bush "gives every indication that he hates Man-made international law, and really believes he's serving God through his campaign to destroy and replace it by his standing *above* it."[28]

Paul Wolfowitz, in an interview in the magazine *Vanity Fair,* emphasized that WMDs were never actually the primary reason for war, but that the president saw himself in an epochal struggle against evil and wanted to reorder the Middle East.[29] Part of this may be a reflection of the Protestant fundamentalism embraced by President Bush and others in the administration who believe in a kind of Manichean moralism that sees the world in simplistic terms of good versus evil. A revealing glimpse at the religious underpinning of the US leadership's view of the destiny of the United States through the invasion of Iraq could be gleaned from the Cheneys' 2003 Christmas card, which contains the quote, "If a sparrow cannot fall to the ground without His notice, is it probable that an empire can rise without His aid?"[30] President Bush was even blunter in a conversation with Mahmud Abbas in June of 2003, when he reportedly told the Palestinian prime minister that "God . . . instructed me to strike at Saddam, which I did."[31]

Perhaps it is no accident that a number of the neoconservative intellectuals who pushed for the invasion of Iraq were Trotskyists in their youth. Now, as then, they have embraced a kind of vanguard mentality that an ideal system destined by history sometimes needs to be imposed by force, which will surely be embraced by the vast majority of the population grateful for their liberation, while the minority who do not will have to be dealt with harshly. Whether the premise was religious or secular, however, the evidence seems strong that the US decision to invade Iraq was in great part driven by ideology.

Preventative War: The Return of Interventionism
For ideologues, the struggle with evil justifies exceptional means, in this case "preventative war." To be sure, the United States has violated international legal norms regarding foreign intervention and the use of force against sovereign states on many past occasions. However, most of these cases were either through covert actions, such as CIA involvement in military coups (Guatemala, 1954), or through overt military interventions done

under the cover of a regional security pact, such as the Organization of American States (Dominican Republic, 1965). Moreover, such efforts were thought to be a thing of the past. Given the domination of the neoliberal "Washington consensus," enforced through international financial institutions such as the World Trade Organization (WTO) and the IMF, such crude forms of hegemonic supremacy were no longer deemed necessary. For example, the debt crisis and the resulting structural adjustment programs imposed on many developing countries have made it difficult for their governments to pursue economic or other policies the US government might find threatening to its interests, enabling the United States to impose legally and openly what in previous decades had to be accomplished by cruder forms of intervention. What was exceptional about the invasion of Iraq, however, was its sheer brazenness: the vast majority of the world's governments, UN Secretary-General Kofi Annan, and a broad consensus of international legal scholars saw it as a clear violation of the UN Charter.

The formal shift in US attitudes was declared and codified in the 2002 national security strategy, in which it was argued that the United States should strike preemptively at any country it believes is developing biological, chemical, or nuclear weapons: "America will act against such emerging threats before they are fully formed."[32] This underscores the basis of the Bush administration's postinvasion rationale that, while Iraq may not have actually had any WMDs, offensive delivery systems, or WMD programs, even just having the potential to develop such weapons programs and weapons systems sometime in the future was enough to justify the invasion.[33] The invasion of Iraq, therefore, was not a "preemptive" war but a "preventative" war. The 2002 NSS blurs the distinction, arguing that since it is hard to know when or how terrorists might strike, it is therefore justifiable to attack any country that might be developing a weapons potential that might someday be used against US interests. But there is reason to believe that the change in policy toward the use of force is even more radical than this: in both public speeches and in private discussions, administration officials began to justify the Iraq War as a means of spreading democracy to the Arab-Islamic world. In effect, the United States now sees invading and occupying sovereign nations as a means of social and political engineering.

Why Iraq? Oil and Defiance

Why should Iraq have so rapidly become the focus of Bush's new foreign policy despite the meager evidence that it had anything to do with 9/11 or posed much threat to the United States? The triumph of neoliberal global economics has contributed in part to the end of the left-leaning nationalism that was once common in the Arab world, with most countries in the region now embracing what are euphemistically referred to as "free market reforms." Despite growing popular anger at US policies, most Arab states have substantially reduced their anti-Western rhetoric, support for terrorists, and other behaviors that were so disturbing to Washington in previous decades. Baathist Iraq was the only Arab state to largely resist such trends. Combining a sizable educated population, large oil resources, and adequate water supplies, Iraq was able to maintain a truly independent foreign and domestic policy. Even twelve years of draconian sanctions could not overthrow the government or make it more cooperative with Washington's strategic and economic agenda.[34]

As a result, the Bush administration was apparently determined to impose a new order whereby this important Middle Eastern country would have no choice but to play by US rules. Since simply appending a conquered nation to its conqueror's territory is not considered acceptable behavior anymore (US allies Morocco and Israel notwithstanding), a less formal system of control needed to be established. So Washington adopted a plan for Iraq that bore a striking resemblance to the British strategy in the Middle East following the collapse of the Ottoman Empire: rather than formally annexing Iraq, Britain occupied the country just long enough to establish a kind of suzerainty, where Iraq was made nominally independent within a few years, but Britain could effectively veto the establishment of any unfriendly government and could dominate the economy.[35] The invasion of Iraq, therefore, could be considered the military side of US-led globalization.

Skeptics of claims that the Bush administration invaded Iraq simply for its oil correctly observe that the United States is less dependent on Persian Gulf oil than are European or East Asian countries. However, controlling Iraq—which is the largest Arab country in the Gulf region, contains the world's second largest oil reserves, and borders three of the world's five largest oil producers—gives the United States enormous leverage. In dominating Iraq, the United States would not only control that country's oil reserves, but also be able to establish a permanent military presence in the heart of the Middle East. In the coming decades, in the event of a trade war with Japan or the European Union or a military rivalry with an ascendant China, effective control over Gulf oil is a trump card that Washington could play to its advantage. The invasion of Iraq, then, may represent not just a repudiation of the post–World War II international system embodied in the UN Charter, but also a return to the nineteenth-century great power politics of imperial conquest undertaken to control key economic resources.

Evidence that Iraq is seen as colonial spoils is the way US occupation forces have restricted investment and reconstruction efforts almost exclusively to countries that supported the US invasion—in direct contravention of WTO regulations that Washington insists upon rigorously enforcing against other nations. Similarly, following the US conquest in March 2003, US contractors and their employees were given preference over Iraqi companies and Iraqi nationals in procuring lucrative reconstruction assignments. From power stations to telecommunications, US infrastructure designs are replacing Iraqi and European systems. The Bush administration's initial economic designs for Iraq appear to resemble a kind of mercantilism.[36]

■ The Policy Struggle

War was not made without a political struggle. Bush apart, a number of key players were pushing for war, notably Vice President Cheney, whose intense focus on the alleged threat of the Iraqi regime was considered by some of his colleagues as "a disquieting obsession."[37] Defense Secretary Donald Rumsfeld, who as President Ronald Reagan's personal envoy to Iraq during the 1980s had pushed for more US support for Saddam Hussein's regime, was also a major advocate for war. A number of prominent neoconservative intellectuals, who throughout the 1990s had advocated a US takeover of Iraq—such as Paul Wolfowitz, Douglas Feith, Lewis Libby, and Richard Perle, among others—had landed important posts in the Defense Department and elsewhere in the Bush administration and became key players in the decision to invade. Initially, National Security Adviser Condoleezza Rice thought the administration should focus on what she considered the most pressing issues regarding larger countries like Russia, China, and India, though she eventually became supportive of the hardliners.[38]

Within the top levels of the Bush administration, the primary opponent of war was Secretary of State Colin Powell, who correctly predicted many of the negative ramifications of the decision. As a career military officer, however, he played the role of the loyal soldier, keeping most of his reservations private. There were strong disagreements over whom the United States should install as leader of post-Saddam Iraq, with Pentagon neoconservatives strongly supportive of exiled Iraqi National Congress leader Ahmad Chalabi, whom many in the State Department and CIA considered corrupt, untrustworthy, and lacking any credibility or following within Iraq. A large number of career staffers in the State Department, Defense Department, and CIA also privately expressed serious concerns over going to war, as did some top military officers, who were particularly concerned about the stability of Iraq following Saddam's ouster. They viewed proponents of the war as dangerous ideologues who twisted the facts to fit their preconceived and exaggerated view of the Iraqi threat. For example, when the CIA, the Defense Intelligence Agency, and the State Department's Bureau of Intelligence and Research came up with assessments that minimized or discounted administration assumptions of Iraq's alleged military threat or ties to Al-Qaida, Rumsfeld set up the Office of Special Plans, led by handpicked supporters of a US takeover of Iraq, to find intelligence—largely provided by disreputable Iraqi exiles—that would back the administration's case. These would then be leaked to the media, while rebuttals from the more reputable intelligence units remained classified and therefore unavailable to the public. As a result, the administration—with the collaboration of influential journalists such as Judith Miller of the *New York Times*—was able to lead the vast majority of Americans to believe that Iraq was a threat to US national security, thereby stoking popular support for the invasion.[39] As one former intelligence official described it, "They were using the intelligence from the CIA and other agencies only when it fit their agenda. They didn't like the intelligence they were getting, and so they brought in people to write the stuff. They were so crazed and so far out and so difficult to reason with—to the point of being bizarre. Dogmatic, as if they were on a mission from God. If it doesn't fit their theory, they don't want to accept it." Similarly, Greg Thielman, the director of the State Department's Bureau of Intelligence and Research until September 2002, observed, "This administration has had a faith-based attitude. . . . 'We know the answers—give us the intelligence to support those answers.'"[40] Perhaps it is a sign of just how far to the right US foreign policy has moved that the CIA, the military brass, and the State Department—long maligned by critics of US interventionism in the third world—are now seen as relatively rational and moderate elements in the policy process.

Nevertheless, the congressional leadership of both major US political parties strongly argued in support of an invasion and succeeded in getting overwhelming bipartisan support for a resolution, passed in October 2002, giving President Bush unprecedented war-making authority. Despite the magnitude of the decision, there were only very brief hearings in Congress, and those testifying were largely restricted to supporters of the administration's view that Iraq was a clear and present danger to US national security. Similarly, there was relatively little debate on the floor of Congress in the weeks leading up to the vote and the war itself. Democratic Party leaders in Congress joined their Republican counterparts in backing the invasion and lobbied their members to do the same. Almost all congressional Republicans came out in favor of authorizing force. The majority of Democratic senators also voted in support of the war resolution, though a majority of Democratic members of the House of Representatives voted against it.

The US news media largely supported the Bush administration's preinvasion claims of the Iraqi WMD threat, while strategic analysts who had come to different conclusions (this author included) were largely excluded from coverage in the mainstream media. Fox News, the leading news network on cable television, was particularly vehement in supporting the case for war; some of its commentators and talk show hosts even questioned the patriotism of those who opposed an invasion. A number of prominent news outlets, including the two leading newspapers of the United States—the *Washington Post* and the *New York Times*—have since publicly apologized for their unwillingness to take a more skeptical view of what are now recognized as false prewar claims by the Bush administration.[41]

Despite the prowar bias in the media, there was much skepticism within the US public regarding the invasion in the months leading up to the war. In addition to pacifist and leftist groups that had opposed US policy toward Iraq for over a dozen years, most religious denominations, labor unions, and leading academics in relevant fields weighed in against the invasion, as did a number of retired generals and former national security officials. There were sizable antiwar demonstrations in major US cities, drawing upward of half a million participants, in the months just prior to the invasion, comparable in size to those protesting the Vietnam War in the late 1960s. Once the war began, however, protests subsided and Congress passed nearly unanimous resolutions in support of the war effort. US media coverage during the invasion was based upon embedded reporters with US fighting units, thereby giving very limited coverage to civilian casualties or to Iraqi perspectives. In the aftermath of the war, the overwhelming editorial opinion in the United States has been for the continuation of the US military presence in Iraq. Moreover, most elected officials who believed the invasion was a mistake have joined the administration in insisting that the counterinsurgency war should continue and US occupation forces should remain in Iraq indefinitely. Public opinion, however, remains divided regarding the wisdom of the United States continuing what is seen as an increasingly futile counterinsurgency war, and antiwar sentiment is growing.

■ Consequences of the Iraq War

The Costs of Occupation

Ideology is likely to have its costs, and they were soon apparent in the miscalculations made over the invasion and occupation of Iraq. The original invasion plan had called for a broad-based multinational coalition with anti-Saddam Iraqi groups playing an active role in the fighting. It was also assumed that there would be well over a quarter million US forces involved, with the active support from neighboring states to launch a multipronged attack. Despite none of this coming to pass and top military officials expressing concerns about potential problems, war plans continued unabated.

The surprising ease with which the United States had toppled the Taliban regime in Afghanistan in fall 2001 as a result of precision bombing, special forces commandos, millions of dollars of bribes to tribal leaders, and an impressive display of US military technology, led to a level of confidence within the administration that an invasion of Iraq would be similarly straightforward. There was also a strong belief that the Iraqis would immediately welcome the United States as liberators, though this was based less on empirical evidence than on an assumption of how the Iraqis *should* feel; this belief was reinforced by some opportunistic Iraqi exiles who had not lived in the country for decades.

There were no Iraqi experts on the staff of the National Security Council (NSC) or anywhere within the inner circle of those planning the invasion. Faith in the power of the US armed forces led administration officials to dismiss warnings by Middle Eastern scholars and others of a backlash against precipitous military actions. Such concerns were largely ignored as a result of racists stereotypes that Iraqis and other Arabs "only understand force" and that "they like winners, and will go with the winners all the time."[42]

Geoffrey Kemp, the NSC's ranking expert on the Middle East during the Reagan administration, noted in a 2002 interview that the Bush White House's premise was, "You deal with Iraq and everything falls into place. Syria comes to terms. The Saudis will conform. Iran will be surrounded by American forces, and the mullahs will have to make concessions to the moderates. There will be a settlement between Israel and Palestine. The end of Saddam will lead to an economic renaissance in Iraq." He added, however, "Iraq is a proud country that has been humiliated, and it's madness to think that these people, while hating Saddam, are in love with the United States."[43]

The Costs for US Global Leadership

A year following the invasion, a poll by the Pew Research Center for the People and the Press indicated that the war had softened international support for the US-led war on terrorism, increased anti-US sentiment in the Arab-Islamic world, and alienated Europeans from US leadership.[44] Since the terrorist attacks against the United States in 2001, the Bush administration—in large part as a result of its invasion and occupation of Iraq—has brought the United States from having unprecedented sympathy and support in the international community to unprecedented hostility and isolation. In the face of worldwide opposition to the invasion, the administration and its allies have helped cultivate a dramatic growth in xenophobia and national chauvinism, in relation not just to the Arab-Islamic world, but to Europe as well. These have included such token initiatives as renaming "french fries" on the menu in the US Capitol's cafeteria to "freedom fries," to more substantive efforts to delegitimize international organizations. For example, in July 2004, nearly 80 percent of the House of Representatives voted in favor of a resolution condemning the International Court of Justice for its nearly unanimous ruling (with the US judge the sole dissenter) reiterating the obligation of occupying powers to uphold the fourth Geneva Convention.

The Costs for World Order

The most serious damage may be in regard to the United Nations. The UN Charter, which the United States signed and ratified in 1945, must, under Article VI of the US Constitution, be treated as supreme law. The conflict regarding access for UN inspectors and possible Iraqi procurement of weapons of mass destruction was initially one involving the Iraqi government and the United Nations. Legally, the United States was interested in no more than being one member of the UN Security Council. Furthermore, Articles 41 and 42 of the UN Charter specify that Security Council resolutions cannot be enforced by military action unless the Security Council determines that the government in question is in material breach of the resolution, that all nonmilitary means of enforcement have been exhausted, and then specifically authorizes the use of force. This was reiterated in Article 14 of Security Council Resolution 1441, targeting Iraq, which was introduced by the United States in fall 2002: it states that the Security Council "remains seized of the matter." In other words, only the Security Council as a whole, not any single member state, has the right to determine what happens next.

The administration's claim that invading Iraq was somehow an effort to uphold the integrity of the United Nations and its resolutions was disingenuous from the start. Since Iraq had disarmed some years earlier and had allowed UN inspectors to return and was fully cooperating with them, there are serious questions as to whether Iraq was actually still in material breach of UN Security Council resolutions at the time of the US invasion. At the time Iraq was attacked, there were more than 100 Security Council resolutions being violated by governments other than Iraq. The Bush administration has opposed enforcing these resolutions by military or any other means, however, since the majority of violating governments are considered US allies.

According to the UN Charter, the only other circumstance in which military force is allowed is under Article 51, which permits a member state to use force in the event of "armed attack . . . until the Security Council has taken measures necessary to maintain international peace and security." In other words, the United States could legally make war on Iraq only if there were a direct attack by Iraq against the United States and only until the Security Council were to convene and decide what to do about it. Customary law provides a slightly broader definition of self-defense, to include a preemptive strike to repel a clear and imminent threat, such as troops massing along the border poised to invade. Neither Article 51 nor customary international law gives the United States or any other nation the right to launch a preemptive invasion of another country simply because it thinks that the other country might be developing weapons that it fears might someday be used against it. It was largely to prevent such offensive wars that the United States and its allies created the United Nations at the end of World War II. Now, however, President Bush—backed by leading Democrats, including his 2004 election opponent, John Kerry—have essentially decided to overturn these basic international legal tenets that were institutionalized over the past century through the efforts of such US presidents as Woodrow Wilson, Franklin Roosevelt, Harry Truman, and Dwight Eisenhower. In other words, the US-led invasion of Iraq demonstrates how these principles of multilateralism and the rule of law have effectively been replaced by the Bush Doctrine, based on unilateral military force.

■ Notes

1. Seymour Hersh, *Chain of Command,* p. 188.
2. "The Secret Downing Street Memo," *Sunday Times,* 1 May 2005.
3. George W. Bush, State of the Union address, Washington, DC, 29 January 2002.
4. Ibid.
5. Richard Cheney, speech before the annual convention of the Veterans of Foreign Wars, Nashville, Tennessee, 27 August 2002.
6. International Atomic Energy Agency, "Iraq Nuclear Verification Program," 16 December 1998.
7. Scott Ritter, "The Case for Iraq's Qualitative Disarmament," *Arms Control Today,* June 2000.
8. Ibid.
9. This skepticism over the validity of deterrence theory under the Bush administration appears to go beyond the US conflict with Saddam Hussein's Iraq, given the decision to pull out of the first Strategic Arms Limitation Talks treaty (SALT I) (also known as the antiballistic missile treaty) with Russia and threats against Iran and North Korea.
10. Cited in Robert Scheer, "President Bush's Wag-the-Dog Policy on Iraq," *Los Angeles Times,* 7 May 2002.
11. Cited in Conn Hallinan, "A U.S. Cabal Pulling America to War," *Foreign Policy in Focus,* 3 May 2002.
12. US Department of State, *Patterns of Global Terrorism, 2001.*
13. Paul Rogers, "The Coming War with Iraq," *Open Democracy,* 20 February 2002.
14. *ABC News,* "No Chemical Weapons Found at Al Ansar Base," 31 March 2003.
15. Cited in Hersh, *Chain of Command,* p. 209.
16. US House of Representatives, House Concurrent Resolution 104, 21 March 2003.
17. US House of Representatives, House Resolution 757, 9 September 2004.
18. George W. Bush, speech before the UN General Assembly, 23 September 2003.

19. George W. Bush, address before the National Endowment for Democracy, Washington, DC, 6 October 2005.

20. George W. Bush, address to the nation, 7 September 2003.

21. US National Security Council, *The National Security Strategy of the United States of America,* September 2002.

22. Jessica Stern, "How America Created a Terrorist Haven," *New York Times,* 20 August 2003.

23. Cited in Robert Steinback, "Occupation Not an End to Terrorism," *Miami Herald,* 25 November 2003.

24. George W. Bush, "Introduction," *National Security Strategy.*

25. Bob Woodward, *Plan of Attack,* p. 88.

26. Cited in Dilip Hiro, *Secrets and Lies,* p. 388.

27. Eric Zuesse, *Iraq War,* p. 121.

28. Ibid., p. 118, emphasis in original.

29. Cited in Richard Cohen, *Washington Post,* 20 April 2004.

30. Nicholas Kristof, "The God Gulf," *New York Times,* 7 January 2004.

31. *Ha'aretz,* 24 June 2003.

32. Bush, "Introduction."

33. Woodward, *Plan of Attack,* pp. 85–86.

34. This is not to imply that Saddam Hussein's rule was anything close to being a progressive model for third world development. Indeed, his brand of Baathism was arguably closer to true fascism than was any regime in the world in recent decades. However one defines his ideology, he was clearly failing to follow Washington's lead.

35. The United States followed a similar pattern with Cuba in 1898, heralding the process as "liberation" from the Spaniards but retaining it as a de facto protectorate. This governing system lasted for more than five decades, until it was overthrown in Fidel Castro's 1959 revolution, less than a year after nationalist military officers in Baghdad ousted the monarchy established by the British. Even forty-five years after US-backed dictator Fulgencio Batista fled Havana, Washington still cannot accept a truly independent Cuba and still withholds diplomatic recognition.

36. See Naomi Klein, "Baghdad Year Zero: Pillaging Iraq in Pursuit of a Neocon Utopia," *Harpers,* September 2004. See also the Open Society Institute's Iraq Revenue Watch website, at http://www.iraqrevenuewatch.org. This rather brazen promotion of US business interests in newly conquered Iraq parallels the more subtle shifts in the Bush administration's international trade policy away from the Clinton administration's enthusiastic embrace of a free trade agenda, to one more open to protecting parochial US business interests.

37. Woodward, *Plan of Attack,* p. 4.

38. Hersh, *Chain of Command,* p. 167.

39. See Michael Massing, *Now They Tell Us.*

40. *The Guardian,* 10 June 2003.

41. See Massing, *Now They Tell Us.*

42. Hersh, *Chain of Command,* p. 182, citing Richard Perle.

43. Cited in Hersh, *Chain of Command,* pp. 186–187.

44. Pew Research Center for the People and Press, "A Year After the Iraq War," 16 March 2004.

3

The United Kingdom: Fateful Decision, Divided Nation

Rosemary Hollis

■ Britain Opts for War

On 20 March 2003, Britain went to war alongside the United States to invade Iraq. The legal basis for the British resort to arms was cited by the UK attorney general as resting on UN Security Council Resolution 1441 of 8 November 2002, though only a summary of his advice was released to Parliament and the public, and other legal experts disputed the validity of this position.[1] For his part, British prime minister Tony Blair referred to Iraqi noncompliance with the requirements of Resolution 1441 as justification for war when he addressed the House of Commons on 18 March 2003: "Iraq has made some concessions to co-operation but no-one disputes it is not fully co-operating. . . . "Iraq continues to deny it has any WMD, though no serious intelligence service anywhere in the world believes them."[2] In the remainder of his speech the prime minister argued that the time had come for action, in the interests of both disarming Iraq once and for all and upholding the credibility and effectiveness of the United Nations. He accused France of blighting efforts to agree a follow-up resolution to 1441, specifically endorsing military action, by announcing it would use its veto, and claimed: "In a sense, any fair observer does not really dispute that Iraq is in breach and that 1441 implies action in such circumstance. The real problem is that, underneath, people dispute that Iraq is a threat; dispute the link between terrorism and WMD; dispute the whole basis of our assertion that the two together constitute a fundamental assault on our way of life."[3]

As revealed in government documents obtained by the press in 2005, Blair had privately committed to US president George W. Bush by early 2002 that Britain would support military action to effect regime change in Baghdad, though in the expectation that a legal case for this could and would be established via diplomacy at the United Nations and that public opinion would be "sensitized" accordingly.[4]

When it transpired that explicit UN backing for such action was not forthcoming, Blair had to argue his own case, based on his reading of intelligence[5] and on his assessment of how best to handle US unilateralism and to preserve the reputation of the United Nations. Following the invasion and the failure to uncover an Iraqi arsenal of weapons of mass destruction (WMDs), Blair would justify his decision in the name of bringing freedom to the Iraqi people and confronting dictators who might aid and abet terrorists.

■ Explaining the Path to War

The "Special Relationship"
Though never formally spelled out, Blair's calculation that British interests required an unequivocal commitment to the transatlantic alliance was undoubtedly a decisive factor in his policy. Regarding Iraq specifically, British policy had already become closely tied to that of the United States as of the Gulf War (1990–1991), though for most of the 1990s London was more active than Washington in trying to find a diplomatic way out of what became a failing policy. Under the cease-fire agreement that marked the end of the war to liberate Kuwait, UN sanctions were to remain in place until Iraq disarmed. When this pressure failed to deliver full Iraqi compliance and the revelations of Iraqi defector Hussein Kamal showed the extent of Iraqi deception, British policy was to maintain sanctions as an instrument of containment while relying on successive "oil for food" deals to relieve some of the adverse effects on ordinary people. As other Security Council members lost faith in this approach, Britain joined the United States in justifying the sanctions regime, notwithstanding corruption and leakage, blaming the Iraqi regime for manipulating the sanctions to reinforce its position at the expense of the general populace. After the US-UK air strikes of December 1998 deepened the impasse, a British diplomatic effort to find a more viable formula, enshrined in UN Security Council Resolution 1284 of December 1999,[6] foundered when neither the United States nor other Security Council members put any effort into its implementation.

Alerted to Washington's intentions on Iraq in the wake of 11 September 2001,[7] the British prime minister was apparently sympathetic to the need to deal with Iraq once and for all,[8] but advocated concentrating on Afghanistan first. By the time Iraq came up for serious consideration between Blair and Bush in spring 2002, the British prime minister had established a close personal rapport with the US president, notwithstanding their ideological differences and much to the consternation of so-called Old Labour members of his party. Blair's line with Bush was that Britain would support the United States on Iraq, but that there must be UN backing for the endeavor.[9] He apparently calculated that this would be the best way to temper US unilateralism and make any action a multilateralist endeavor.

In any event, Washington's unwillingness to be bound by the UN compromised British room for maneuver and had real costs. A related aspiration of the British government, under Blair's leadership, had been to combine a close relationship with the United States with a leading role in Europe. The intention was that Britain would act as a bridge across the Atlantic, and the calculation was that only by being a leading force in the European Union would Britain retain its clout in Washington.[10] However, given London's close coordination with Washington, few outside observers saw any distinction between them. Proximity gave Britain the ear of the US administration but no guarantee of influence over its policy. This feature of the "special relationship" between Britain and the United States became cause for contention on the British political scene as the Iraq crisis gained momentum in 2002,[11] while the British government ended up going to war as the only significant contributor to the military effort alongside the United States and thus gained the label of Washington's "poodle."

Giving his personal take on Blair's handling of the special relationship, former foreign secretary Robin Cook would write:

> It would never occur to Tony Blair that there might be more respect for a Prime Minister who had the courage to say no to someone as powerful as the President of the US. He is programmed to respect power not rebel against it. . . . I have no doubt that Tony Blair genuinely believed the world would be better without Saddam. I am certain that the real reason he went to war was that he found it easier to resist the public opinion of Britain than the request of the US President.[12]

The New Labour Worldview

The New Labour worldview also conditioned Blair's strategy on the Iraq issue in the year or so preceding the invasion. This view treated globalization (and economic interdependence) as an irresistible imperative. Within this setting, Blair argued the case for revising the convention against intervention in the internal affairs of sovereign states that had held essentially since the Treaty of Westphalia. In an interdependent world, he believed, it is no longer appropriate to ignore the ills of poverty, disease, and crimes against humanity such as genocide and ethnic cleansing if intervention is feasible and can spread the benefits of human rights, democracy, and equitable development.[13] Since allied intervention in Kosovo, he had advocated the desirability of ending brutal dictatorships, and in his March 2003 speech to parliament Blair linked the argument to Iraq: "I have never put our justification for action as regime change. We have to act within the terms set out in Resolution 1441. That is our legal base. But it is the reason, I say frankly, why if we do act we should do so with a clear conscience and strong heart."

He then itemized some of the oppressive characteristics of the Iraqi regime and cautioned those who would oppose taking the risks of war that by opting for inaction they would be choosing in effect to embolden Saddam Hussein and abandon the Iraqi people.

Policy Implementation

The Politics of Justifying War: A Country Divided

Through summer 2002, Blair was reassuring everyone, including the rank and file of the Labour Party and some anxious ministers, that no decision had been made. Maintaining public silence about their private concerns,[14] ministers resisted pressure for parliamentary debate until the autumn.[15] Nonetheless, a serious public debate surfaced in the British media. One of the opening shots came in the form of a letter to *The Times* on 29 July 2002 from Field Marshall Lord Bramall, former chief of the Defense Staff, who posited both a best-case and a worst-case scenario for the aftermath of a US intervention in Iraq. At worst, he wrote:

> Conflict in Iraq would produce, in that area, the very display of massive, dynamic, United States activity that provides one of the mainsprings of motivation of terrorist action in the region and indeed over a wider area. Far from calming things down, enhancing any peace process and advancing the "war against terrorism," which could and should be conducted internationally by other means, it would make things infinitely worse.[16]

Another senior figure in the British establishment, Sir Michael Quinlan, former permanent secretary at the Ministry of Defense,[17] questioned the moral case for military action in the absence of compelling evidence to link Saddam Hussein to international terrorism and said that the WMD threat was better dealt with through deterrence. In due course the head of the Church of England, the Archbishop of Canterbury, Rowan Williams, joined the Catholic Church in refuting the justification for initiating war on moral grounds. Regional specialists contended that even if military victory was feasible in Iraq, the aftermath would pose a monumental problem of state building. The British equivalent of the US neoconservatives countered that such views smacked of racism and, egged on by some Iraqi exiles, claimed that Iraq was ripe for liberation and democracy.

On 12 September Bush went to the United Nations, speaking the language of multilateralism, but challenging the UN to confront the "grave and gathering danger." A vital Blair requirement had been met. In further preparation of the ground, Parliament was recalled for an emergency debate on 24 September. Fifty-three Labour members rebelled against the government line but failed to force a vote on military action.

The same day, No. 10 released the now infamous dossier on Iraq's WMDs. Among the assertions in this dossier, based on intelligence estimates and cleared by the Joint Intelligence Committee (JIC), the one that drew press attention in September 2002 was the claim that Iraq could launch chemical weapons within forty-five minutes of an order to do so. Repeated three times in the text, including in the prime minister's own introduction, this claim was later found to be attributable to only one, uncorroborated source, and the government left unchallenged the assumption made in some newspapers that the weapons in question were strategic rather than battlefield armaments and could therefore threaten British forces in Cyprus. Thus the impression was given to the British public that Saddam Hussein's Iraq posed a direct threat to British nationals and interests. Indeed, Blair said in his introduction that Saddam was "a current and serious threat" to the UK national interest.

The Diplomacy of War: Gambling on the UN

From early 2002, the US military, with input from some allies, including the British and Australians, was making contingency plans, and by September 2002 the British had made provision for 20,000 troops to be ready for action. The United States began deploying to the Gulf.

Meanwhile, the combined efforts of Tony Blair and US secretary of state Colin Powell persuaded Bush to take the Iraq issue directly to the UN, against the inclinations of more hard-line members of the administration. Following Bush's UN speech of September 2002, to which UN members reacted favorably, the British delegation at the UN, led by Sir Jeremy Greenstock, worked assiduously to formulate Resolution 1441, which was passed unanimously by the members of the Security Council in November 2002. The achievement and the drawback of this measure was that all the members could read into it what they wanted. Those who saw it as a mechanism for avoiding war through renewed weapons inspections were later to find themselves at odds with those, notably US civilians in the Pentagon, who saw it as smoothing the path to a multilateral endorsement for military action. For the British government the passage of 1441 marked the formal end of containment, and Parliament was invited to give the resolution its seal of approval, which it duly did.

Thereafter, US force deployments to the Gulf began to pose a dilemma. The buildup enabled the politicians to argue that visible preparations for action served to turn up the heat in Baghdad and would help to persuade the regime to comply with UN demands. Iraq did indeed finally agree to accept a new team of UN weapons inspectors under the leadership of Hans Blix, who began work in December. At the same time, however, all the speculation was that such forces could not be rotated in and out of the Gulf indefinitely while new inspections in Iraq took their course. Plus the local climate dictated military action before spring or its postponement to the following autumn.

Britain was effectively committed to ensuring that the United States, which insiders knew was bent on war, would not end up going it alone, and since Blair had promised support, for his sake there had to be UN approval for the expected military action. Blair apparently told Washington that his political standing at home required UN cover for resort to force.[18] According to this logic, therefore, Blix had to come up with a casus belli.

However, when Blix reported back to the UN Security Council on 7 March 2003, he did not deliver a definitive judgment. The Iraqis were, if grudgingly, more or less cooperating. France appeared determined to insist on more time for inspections and was seeking to preserve mulitlateralism by obliging the United States to bow to the UN, even though that could mean war eventually. Tony Blair was acting on the assumption that such a strategy was doomed, since the United States would go it alone if the UN failed to be supportive. Hence he needed the other UN members to concede to this reality and thus, by giving the United States the cover of the UN, preserve multilateralism. In the background, personal rivalry between the key protagonists was turning ugly. According to one account, French president Jacques Chirac found Blair's ambitions to take a leading role in Europe and then deliver Europe in the Atlantic alliance too much to stomach.[19] Consequently, he was hoping to use the crisis to humble the British prime minister. In any case, Chirac was enjoying unprecedented popularity at home for his country's stance at the UN.

By contrast, Blair faced unprecedented criticism and unrest from within his own party, as well as public resistance.[20] On 15 February 2003, upward of 1 million marchers took to the streets of London and Glasgow to demonstrate against war, bringing together people from all walks of life, including many who had never before marched or contemplated marching. Greenstock was charged with a last-ditch attempt to reconcile the conflicting positions at the UN. Eventually, frantic British and US diplomacy failed to line up majority Security Council support for a new resolution sanctioning resort to force. Chirac's announcement that he would veto such a resolution was deemed the fatal blow. The British leadership seethed and Blair played the anti-French card[21] in his appeal to the House of Commons on 18 March.

Notwithstanding significant public opposition, Blair's government won its mandate for war in the House of Commons on that day, by a vote of 412 to 149. Eighty-four Labour members (one in five), the Liberal Democrats, nationalists, and some fifteen Conservatives voted against. A larger number of Labour members, 139, had earlier voted for an amendment claiming the case for war "is not yet made." The Conservative Party leadership accepted the threat assessment embodied in the September dossier and emphasized by ministers at the Foreign Office and Ministry of Defense. Consequently, the Tories gave broad though not total backing to the government line. The Liberal Democrats, having made support for military action dependent on explicit endorsement from the UN, voted against the government motion in March 2003, though once battle was joined they pledged support to British forces in the field. Within the Labour Party many members took the same line as the Liberal Democrats and some were openly critical of their leadership. On the eve of war, Robin Cook, Leader of the House and former foreign secretary, resigned, as did Claire Short, international development secretary, in the aftermath.

■ The War and Aftermath

Once launched, the invasion of Iraq proceeded swiftly to Baghdad. Though cases of abuse of Iraqi prisoners and civilians by British forces were subsequently revealed, they were generally commended for their cautious handling of pockets of opposition inside Basra in the center of what became the British zone of occupation. By contrast, US troops were accused of being heavy-handed and incurring too many civilian casualties. While the predominantly Shia population in southern Iraq did not put up a fight, and along with others came out to celebrate the fall of Saddam Hussein, there was little of the joyful welcome for their liberators that would have made good publicity for Bush and Blair. Meanwhile, ignoring State Department preparations for "the day after the war," US officials fumbled the installation of a postwar administration. British officials assigned to the Coalition Provisional Authority found themselves unable to influence decisionmaking to any significant degree. British companies complained that they were not favored in the parceling out of contracts for reconstruction under US auspices.

A period of relative calm, sufficient for George W. Bush to declare the Iraq invasion a success, ended in the searing heat of August when the level of violence increased and suicide bombers attacked the UN headquarters in Baghdad. Thereafter, hope of turning the rebuilding into a manifestly multilateral endeavor was blighted and the insurgency swelled. More damaging for the British government, the occupiers found no sign of the vaunted weapons of mass destruction that had been key to the legal case for war. For months Tony Blair maintained that he still expected evidence of WMDs to be uncovered, but this was not to be the case.[22]

Meanwhile, No. 10 became embroiled in a fierce row with the BBC over the allegation of reporter Andrew Gilligan in May 2003 that the government had exaggerated the threat posed by Iraq and the September dossier had "sexed up" the intelligence assessment. Gilligan cited a senior intelligence source for his claim. In fact he had been briefed by former weapons inspector David Kelly, who was subsequently exposed and, though he denied using the words attributed to him by Gilligan, was so damaged by the exposure that he committed suicide on 17 July 2003. Blair set up an inquiry under Lord Hutton, who concluded that the government had not deliberately misled the public.[23] The evidence collected for the Hutton inquiry did reveal qualms among No. 10 staff, however, about the weakness of the case presented in early drafts of the dossier. Among the British public and press there was some surprise at how comprehensively Hutton exonerated the government and lambasted the BBC. While the corporation's chairman and director-general both resigned, no government heads rolled, and in effect there was not much public relations mileage for No. 10.

The subsequent Butler inquiry into the use of intelligence echoed Hutton in finding that the government's actions had not been deliberately misleading, though Butler did find that misjudgments had been made.[24] The Butler report exposed the flimsiness of the evidence on which some of the claims in the dossier were based, and revealed that the government had failed to revise its estimate of the danger posed by Iraq, in light of new evidence, in the run-up to the war.

■ The Fallout

The Iraq War did not turn out well for Tony Blair and, as he himself has lamented, lack of trust in his leadership became an issue. This did not mean his defeat in the 2004 election, but it contributed to the significant reduction in Labour's majority. Questions about the operation of key British institutions, including the intelligence services, the office of the prime minister, its publicity machine, government-appointed inquiries, the cabinet, Parliament, and the BBC have also left a mark.

The intelligence services clearly did not paint a correct picture of Iraq's capabilities, though some would claim that their findings were used selectively and raw intelligence was allowed to reach the No. 10 "spin doctors."[25] The fact that Alastair Campbell, communications chief at No. 10, was party to the ruminations of the JIC, was certainly a new departure. Also, apparently, John Scarlett, chairman of the JIC, became a personal friend of Campbell and was seemingly drawn into the heady atmosphere of politics at No. 10.[26] In the wake of Campbell's departure from No. 10, the prime minister downgraded his post to counter the impression of a leadership obsessed with "spin."

Blair has opted for a more presidential style than any of his predecessors, making the prime minister's office itself, rather than the cabinet, the source of policy decisions.[27] The problem is that the British system does not provide the appropriate safeguards for such an innovation, such as a vetting procedure for No. 10 appointees or their accountability to Parliament. The resignation of Claire Short led to revelations of the extent to which the prime minister's own cabinet could be kept in the dark about key policy decisions.[28] In Parliament, the process by which the "loyal opposition" is supposed to provide a check on the government failed to function because the Tories supported the government line and Labour back-benchers cannot fill the opposition role. In a sense it was the BBC that filled the gap in 2002–2003, only to incur the wrath of the government, hostility from Tory ranks, and damning criticism from Lord Hutton.

In terms of policy the Iraq War has not served well the objectives of the prime minister and New Labour. Tony Blair's strategy for bringing Bush to the UN ultimately failed to deliver the multilateral endorsement for the war that he sought and needed.[29] His ambition of combining a leadership role in Europe with a special relationship with the United States foundered: his position in Europe suffered and he received scant reward for his loyalty to Washington.[30] Most notably, Blair was disappointed in his quest to make Washington reinvigorate the Middle East peace process.[31] He personally seems to have understood that the credibility of the United States and then the United Kingdom in the region would depend on persuading the Israeli government to accept the importance of a viable Palestinian state for long-term peace and security. This goal was also a plank in his counterterrorism strategy. But Bush waited until his second term to make more than desultory gestures in this context.

Some observers, including members of the US Republican Party, think Blair sold his support for Bush too cheap. In fact, he may have sacrificed the place in history[32] he sought as a Churchillian figure leading his country to the right decision in the face of naysayers and skeptics.

■ Notes

1. See the resignation letter of Elizabeth Wilmshurst, deputy chief legal adviser at the Office of Foreign Affairs, dated 18 March 2003 and printed in *The Guardian,* 24 March 2005.

2. "PM Statement Opening Iraq Debate," 18 March 2003, http://www.number10.gov.uk.

3. Ibid.

4. Memo to Tony Blair from Sir David Manning, his foreign policy adviser, titled "Your Trip to the US," 14 March 2002, http://www.downingstreetmemo.com/manningtext.html; memo to Sir David Manning from Sir Christopher Meyer, UK ambassador to Washington, 18 March 2002, http://www.downingstreetmemo.com.meyertext.html.

5. To justify his interpretation of the legal position in the days preceding, the attorney general sought an assurance from Blair to this effect. Richard Norton-

Taylor, "The Attorney Who Passed the Buck," *The Guardian,* 3 March 2005; *Review of Intelligence on Weapons of Mass Destruction,* report of a committee of privy counselors, chaired by the Lord Butler of Brockwell (the Butler Report), HC 898, July 2004, paras. 365–387.

6. UN Security Council Resolution 1284 set the frame for a new weapons inspections regime (the UN Monitoring, Verification, and Inspection Commission [UNMOVIC]) and then conditional suspension of sanctions. In the meantime, so-called smart sanctions were supposed to replace the blanket boycott. Instead of denying Iraq all imports except certain designated items, the idea was to permit the entry of all civilian goods except specifically proscribed items. In the end, Resolution 1409 of May 2002 kept the onus on the UN to vet what Iraq could buy and Baghdad refused entry to UNMOVIC.

7. See Patrick Wintour and Martin Kettle, "Blair's Road to War," *The Guardian,* 26 April 2003; Bryan Burroughs, Evgenia Peretz, David Rose, and David Wise, "The Path to War," *Vanity Fair,* May 2004.

8. Burroughs et al., "Path to War."

9. See http://www.downingstreetmemo.com/manningtext.html; "Cabinet Office Paper: Conditions for Military Action," dated 21 July 2002 and published by *The Times,* 12 June 2005, http://www.globalsecurity.org/security/issues/iraq; transcript of "Iraq: Prime Minister's Meeting, 23 July," prepared by David Manning, http://www.downingstreetmemo.com/memoannote.html.

10. Ibid.

11. Roy Denman, "Blair Fails to Bond Britain to Europe or the U.S.," *International Herald Tribune,* 28 March 2003; David Leigh and Richard Norton-Taylor, "We Are Now a Client State," *The Guardian,* 17 July 2003.

12. Robin Cook, *Point of Departure,* p. 104.

13. "Doctrine of the International Community," speech by the Prime Minister, Tony Blair, to the Economic Club of Chicago, Hilton Hotel, Chicago, 22 April 1999, http://www.fco.gov.uk/news/speechtext.

14. Christopher Adams, "Prescott Says Cabinet Divisions on War with Iraq Are Not Serious," *Financial Times,* 17 August 2002; Michael White, "Blair Refuses Ministers Cabinet Debate on Iraq," *The Guardian,* 16 August 2002.

15. Glenn Frankel, "Blair Faces Rising Opposition to an Attack on Iraq," *International Herald Tribune,* 7 August 2002.

16. *The Times,* 29 July 2002.

17. Michael Quinlan, "War on Iraq: A Blunder and a Crime," *Financial Times* 7 August 2002.

18. Burroughs et al., "Path to War."

19. Philip Stephens, *Tony Blair: The Making of a Word Leader.*

20. Public opinion polls in the months preceding war showed a majority against, even if a second UN resolution was forthcoming. Krishna Guha, "The Gap in Support for War May Be Down to Britons' Distrust of President Bush," *Financial Times,* 28 January 2003.

21. Roy Hattersley, "Why We All Love to Hate the French," *The Guardian,* 21 April 2003.

22. Julian Borger, "The Inspector's Final Report," *The Guardian (G2),* 3 March 2004.

23. *The Hutton Inquiry, 2003–4,* extracts from the report that appeared on the Hutton Inquiry website on 28 January 2004 (London: Tim Coates, 2004), pp. 149–151; Michael White, Richard Norton-Taylor, and Ewen MacAskill, "A Litany of Failure—but No One to Blame," *The Guardian,* 15 July 2004.

24. Butler Report, pp. 152–153.

25. Brain Jones, "We Were Overruled, Says Former Intelligence Chief, and the Result Was a Dossier That Was Misleading About Iraqi WMD," *The Independent,* 4 February 2004.

26. Cathy Newman, "Campbell Exposes No 10 Manoeuvres," *Financial Times,* 20 August 2003; Max Hastings, "Blair Knew Better Than to Go to War on the Word of a Spy," *The Guardian,* 7 February 2004; Richard Tomlinson, "Who Was That at the Shredder?" *The Guardian,* 9 February 2004.

27. "Blair: President or Prime Minister?" leader column, *Financial Times,* 17 May 2003.

28. Christopher Adams, "Cook and Short Lead Cross-Party Assault on Blair over War in Iraq," *Financial Times,* 5 June 2003.

29. Andrew Rawnsley, "And Now for the Home Front," *The Observer,* 20 April 2003.

30. Philip Stephens, "The Choice That Was Best Avoided," *Financial Times,* 10 March 2003.

31. Sidney Blumenthal, "Bush and Blair—the Betrayal," *The Guardian,* 14 November 2003.

32. Nicholas Watt and Julian Borger, "Blair Tells Congress 'History Will Forgive Us,'" *The Guardian,* 18 July 2003.

4

France: Defender of International Legitimacy

Jolyon Howorth

The French approach to the crisis in Iraq went through several phases. From late summer 2002 until the voting of UN Security Council (UNSC) Resolution 1441 on 8 November 2002, it involved a campaign to rein in the perceived hawks in the George W. Bush administration by securing international agreement on two matters: the centrality of the UN, and the return of the weapons inspectors. From early November 2002 until early January 2003, France attempted to gather international momentum behind the inspections process. From early January until mid-February 2003, French officials, convinced the Bush administration was bent on war, fought to reinforce the inspections regime—as an alternative to war. From mid-February onward, in the context of a hypothetical second UNSC resolution authorizing the use of force, France attempted first to avert such a resolution, and then to create a majority against it: to block legitimization of force, and to avoid France's being obliged to use its veto. Once the war began, France's voice was temporarily silenced. After the war, France again became active in pressing the case for United Nations legitimization and oversight of the process of transition to democracy in Iraq.

■ Before War: Divergent French and US Approaches to Iraq

The reelection of Jacques Chirac in May 2002 was greeted with cautious relief in Washington. The outgoing Jospin government had vigorously criticized US foreign policy in general and the Bush administration in particular. Chirac's new foreign minister, Dominique de Villepin, signaled that France would adopt a less acerbic tone toward the United States. Paris had long been critical of UN sanctions against Iraq. Since the end of the Gulf War in 1991, French approaches had been driven by three factors: preserving the stability of the region, ensuring the authority of the UNSC, and avoiding a humanitarian disaster.[1] Colin Powell's moves toward a regime of "smart sanctions"—targeted more on the Iraqi leadership and less on the Iraqi people—narrowed the gap between Paris and Washington. In May 2002 the passage of UNSC Resolution 1409 effectively removed any major differences between France and the US over sanctions.[2]

. During summer 2002, as the Bush administration began to make more and more reference to preemptive regime change in Baghdad, the French government became alarmed. President Chirac, in a *New York Times* interview on 8 September 2002, formulated most of the arguments that all French spokespersons were systematically to deploy thereafter. Already, two key elements of French policy had emerged clearly. The first was that war should be an option of last resort. The second was that Saddam Hussein should and could be contained. France was in broad agreement with the United States on five points. First, Iraq under Saddam presented a danger, both to its neighbors and (especially) to the Iraqi people. Second, Saddam personally was a problem and his leaving power would be desirable. Third, any existing weapons of mass destruction (WMDs) must be declared and the weapons destroyed (in conformity with existing UNSC resolutions). Fourth, if necessary, military force should be used to bring about this result. And fifth, the global war on terrorism required the forging of a broad international coalition.

However, there was real disagreement on six issues. First, France insisted that the West did not know whether Iraq possessed WMDs. In order to find out, inspectors should return to Iraq. Second, despite the existence of ten previous resolutions, Iraq should be offered one final opportunity to comply with the UN. Third, while the United States advocated a single resolution authorizing both the return of the inspectors and military action in the event of any further "material breach," France insisted that recourse to military action should be the subject of a further UNSC resolution. Fourth, France was not opposed to preemptive war on principle, but rejected unilateral US preemption unsanctioned by the UN. Fifth, regime change as a policy objective was unacceptable, since it would open a Pandora's box in international law. The sole legitimate objective was to destroy any existing WMDs. Finally, France believed there had been no significant contact between the Iraqi regime and Al-Qaida.

The French government was concerned to respect three objectives. It was committed to the UN inspections process, stressing that more Iraqi WMDs had been destroyed by the inspectors between 1991 and 1998 than during the Gulf War. Second, while Iraqi disarmament was a legitimate objective, it had to be done in ways that bolstered rather than undermined regional stability. Third, if the international community was to insist on Iraqi compliance with UNSC resolutions, then it must apply this rule across the board—notably with respect to the Israeli-Palestinian conflict. At this stage, the international community in general and France in particular could have no certainty on two matters. First, *how* the Iraq regime would seek to respond to the UN challenge. France retained the military option if Saddam continued to obfuscate. Second, nobody yet knew *whether* the United States was determined to use military action come what may. Although there were both hawks and doves within the Bush administration, the latter seemed to be in the ascendant. But that might not last. The French position was clear—but open-ended. France would decide whether or not to join a military operation if and when one became imminent. Paris took a different line from that taken in 1990 when President François Mitterrand had reassured George H. W. Bush immediately that France would stand alongside the United States militarily if push came to shove. Several days later, he ordered the aircraft carrier *Clemenceau* to deploy to the Gulf. By contrast, no French troops were prepositioned in the region during the 2002–2003 crisis, although discussions did take place on a hypothetical French deployment. French strategy was largely dependent for its success both on Saddam's rational behavior *and* on Washington's willingness fully to explore avenues other than war.

The French position, unlike the positions adopted in some EU member states, enjoyed widespread public and political support. Polls consistently gave Chirac 65–75 percent approval ratings. Only Le Pen's National Front, the Communist Party, the Greens, and the populist movement of former defense minister Jean-Pierre Chevènement—in other words, the minority, extremist parties—were opposed to the basic thrust of the Chirac position. All these constituencies save the Greens had long-standing political sympathies for the Baathist regime.

The Ambiguities of Resolution 1441

The French approach challenged the United States at every stage to stick with the "international community," to eschew muscular unilateralism, to prioritize coalition building, and to engage in nation building for the long haul. It recognized the global preeminence of the United States as a political, diplomatic, and military power. France intended to articulate what it saw as an alternative approach to that of the US administration. Its chosen forum—the UNSC—offered maximum leverage. Throughout October and early November 2002, Paris pursued three objectives: the organization of a genuinely intrusive inspections regime, the rejection of automatic recourse to military action, and the principle of a second resolution to authorize the use of force. The ambiguities of UNSC Resolution 1441 will be analyzed repeatedly by historians. France can reasonably claim that 1441 did initiate a robust inspections regime; it did require further discussion in the Security Council in the event of Iraqi noncompliance; and it excluded any automatic recourse to military action. The United States and the United Kingdom can also legitimately argue that 1441 states clearly that "Iraq has been and remains in material breach" (Article 1); that any further noncompliance will constitute further material beach; that in such circumstances all that is required is that the UNSC should "convene . . . in order to consider the situation" (there is no explicit requirement for a second resolution); and that Iraq faces "serious consequences" in the event of further violations. Resolution 1441 can be read both as an *immediate alternative* to war and as an *eventual legitimization* of war.

That France saw it as an alternative to war is fundamental. A leitmotif in all French discourse at this time was the notion that the unity of the international community behind 1441 could achieve the desired objective without war. The hopelessness of an Iraqi standoff against the entire international community gave France confidence that Saddam *would* back down. This was the argument used by Chirac in pressuring Syria's Bashar al-Asad to vote in favor of 1441: the resolution, in effect "removed the triggers for war."[3] That was also the reading of 1441 that delivered the vote of Russia, China, and Germany. As late as the first week in January 2003, even the UK foreign secretary, Jack Straw, was reported as saying that the odds were then 60 to 40 against war.[4] However, throughout late November and much of December 2002, as US troop deployments to the Gulf intensified, "international attention continue[d] to focus on the planning for a potential invasion of Iraq aimed at achieving its forcible disarmament."[5] France seemed imperceptibly to be losing the battle to keep the international community focused on making the inspections work.

In early January 2003, the Quai d'Orsay became convinced that the United States was determined to go to war. This was confirmed on 13 January when senior French and US officials met in Washington. According to one analysis, the French got the reply: "Everything was impossible. The preparations for war must proceed."[6] France was thus faced with a clear strategic decision: either to find a diplomatic face-saver enabling it to step in line behind Washington, or to be prepared to engage in—and take the consequences for—all-out opposition.

Focused opposition to the US drive to war first manifested itself during a de Villepin press conference on 20 January 2003. The foreign minister faced a questioner who accused France of talking peace and inspections while secretly preparing to join the US war effort. It was well known in Washington that French liaison officers had been discussing with the United States the possibility of fielding up to 15,000 French troops as part of the coalition war effort. De Villepin was asked a straight question: Would France veto a second resolution? The implication was that it would not. De Villepin, visibly riled, replied: "France, as a permanent member of the UNSC, will assume its full responsibilities. . . . Believe me: when it comes to respect for principles, we will go the whole way." The words are ambiguous, but they were interpreted around the world as signaling a French veto.

Just two days later, President Chirac met Chancellor Schröder for the much-hyped fortieth anniversary of Franco-German reconciliation. Hitherto, Chirac had been careful to distinguish between the position of Germany (no participation in military action even if mandated by the UN) and France's position (wait and see). However, on 22 January he implicitly abandoned this nuance by speaking of a "common judgment" and a "common position" between the two countries. The Franco-German summit was universally interpreted as representing a shift in the French position. France, in its capacity as a veto-wielding member of the UNSC, had become the leading opponent of the US-led war effort. Not since Suez in 1956 had France and the United States found themselves at strategic odds in the UNSC. This was France's first diplomatic miscalculation. The problem, given the increasing evidence that the United States was going to go to war anyway, was precisely how to organize that opposition. France had three possibilities. The first was to try to mobilize outright international defiance of Washington—a position no French president could have contemplated. A second possibility was to persuade the European Union to adopt a common position. The Extraordinary European Council meeting in Brussels on 17 February 2003 did indeed produce a statement that was endorsed by all fifteen EU member states. The statement insisted on five main points, broadly reflecting the French approach:

1. EU determination to deal effectively with the threat of WMD proliferation.
2. Commitment to the UN remaining at the center of the international order.
3. Commitment to full and effective disarmament of Iraq in accordance with Resolution 1441.
4. Full support for the UN inspectors, who should be given the time and resources they need, without continuing indefinitely in the absence of Iraqi cooperation.
5. Force should only be used as a last resort.

Intensifying Inspections

Meanwhile, however, France selected a third course in order to keep the world's focus on the inspections. This was to intensify and enhance the inspections process. It built on the "time and resources needed" specification in the EU statement. Following Colin Powell's 5 February 2003 presentation to the UNSC of the "evidence" against Iraq, de Villepin proposed to the Security Council a reinforcement of the inspections regime. Over the next few days, this became a tripartite (French, German, Russian) proposal. France outlined in detail the requirements for inspections reinforcement: doubling or tripling the number of inspectors (from 110 to 240 or 360); dispatch of new types of inspectors—customs officers and accountants, archivists, translators; opening new regional offices in the western region of Iraq; sending mobile customs units to oversee import controls; dispatch of special units to keep permanent watch over suspect sites; reinforcement of intelligence and observation capacities (France offered to supply Mirage IV surveillance aircraft to this end); creation of a dedicated center in either New York or Vienna for the processing and coordination of all available data on Iraqi WMD, to be placed at the service of Hans Blix and Mohamed El-Baradei; and agreement on a precise timetable for the entire inspections process.

This was a robust move, but it came too late. Apart from the inexorable buildup to war, a massive US propaganda campaign had already been unleashed, denouncing France as an objective adversary of the United States and an objective ally of Iraq.[7] France's case was not helped by a parallel crisis over the issue of a NATO guarantee to Ankara in the event of an Iraqi preemptive strike against Turkey as the buildup to war continued. On 10 February, France, Germany, and Belgium refused to acquiesce in what they considered to be a US attempt to short-circuit the UNSC process by moving closer to war. This was France's second politico-diplomatic error in that it was now also cast as a saboteur of the alliance.

Yet France was not alone. It enjoyed widespread support within the Security Council. De Villepin's impassioned 14 February speech in favor of reinforced inspections was greeted with a spontaneous outburst of applause. On 20 February, the twenty-second conference of the heads of state of Africa and France issued a statement in support of the French proposals. The nonaligned movement and the Arab League issued similar statements. On 24 February, France, Germany, and Russia issued a joint memorandum, making further concrete proposals for an enhanced inspections regime and outlining a "credible" timetable. But by now the question of the timetable had become a central sticking point. On 14 February, there had been a widespread sense that de Villepin's suggestion of 14 March as the next deadline by which the UNSC should examine the report of the inspectors was unrealistic. Everybody knew that, by then, the key issue would be whether war had already broken out. The deadline mentioned in the tripartite memo of 24 February suggested "120 days" after adoption of the new reinforced regime—in other words, late June. This was a nonstarter. In any case, the French proposals were ignored by the very men to whom they were formally submitted: Blix and El-Baradei. The last chance to avert what was now seen throughout the world as an inevitable US-led war seemed to have slipped away.

Crisis over the "Second Resolution"

At this point, the spotlight focused on the proposed second UN resolution authorizing war. Tony Blair needed this second resolution for domestic political reasons. France argued that, since the inspections were still ongoing, there was no need for a second resolution. France went to extraordinary lengths to try to persuade the United States and the United Kingdom not to present a second resolution—given that this would inevitably lead to a crisis in the Security Council.[8] This became a trial of strength between Paris, confident of the support of wide sections of the "international community," and Washington, where the decision to go to war had already been taken. By early March 2003, the stakes were clear: France would be "punished" by the United States for its attitude. There was speculation that Chirac and de Villepin were reconsidering their line, and that there was still time to join the US crusade.[9] The defense minister, Michelle Alliot-Marie, reflecting a mood among France's military that regretted France's absence from the preparations, had announced on 29 January that France's armed forces were "ready to intervene." When the aircraft carrier *Charles de Gaulle* set sail from Toulon on 4 February, speculation mounted that France was preparing to align itself with the United States.[10] In reality, it is clear that, by the end of February, this was no longer a serious option. The inspectors' reports indicated that Saddam was cooperating—more or less. French leaders saw no reason to rethink their position.

This was made clear in Chirac's crucial television interview on 10 March. Asked how he would vote on the second resolution, Chirac initially took refuge in confidence that it would not muster the necessary nine votes. France, along with a majority of the Security Council, would vote no. Pressed repeatedly to say what France would do if, in fact, the US text produced a majority in the Council, Chirac finally crossed a Rubicon. France would still vote no. Technically, he conceded, the voting system of the UNSC meant that this would amount to a veto. But in reality, France would simply be voting the same way, irrespective of the votes of other UNSC member states. This was probably Chirac's most serious diplomatic miscalculation. It helped put an end to the increasingly futile US and UK efforts to create a Security Council majority for war. And, unintentionally, it gave Blair an alibi. On 18 March 2003, during the crucial debate in the House of Commons over war in Iraq, Blair cited France's threat to veto a second UN Security Council resolution authorizing military action as a decisive factor that had actually rendered war inevitable.[11]

■ War

As had been the case in 1991, war temporarily muffled whatever voice France had enjoyed in the international arena. On 19 March, President

Chirac issued a brief communiqué regretting this "action initiated without United Nations backing." He hoped that "these operations [would be] as swift and [would] cause as little bloodshed as possible" and looked to the future, which he saw as "fraught with consequences." He predicted that, in building the peace, it would be necessary to rebuild the alliance and argued that Europe should take a united position in this respect. France authorized full overflight rights to coalition aircraft and made no effort (as some had speculated it would) to draft a UNSC resolution condemning the US-UK action. When the Saddam regime fell, on 10 April, Chirac issued a new communiqué welcoming the fall of the dictatorship and noting that humanitarian assistance was now a priority. He also insisted that the United Nations should, "after the necessary phase of securing the region," be fully involved in restoring Iraqi sovereignty as soon as possible.[12] That position was premonitory of the attitude France was subsequently to adopt throughout the process of establishing peace, security, and transition in Iraq.

■ Evaluation

France did offer an alternative strategy to that of the United States, and it was one that carried the support of most of the countries and most of the peoples of the world (including the *peoples* of the countries—the United Kingdom, Spain, Poland—whose *leaders* supported the US approach). It was an alternative based on multilateral negotiations, United Nations legitimacy, a pragmatic process of weapons inspections, the primacy of international law, and above all the principle that war is the worst of all available options. Was the French alternative viable? In terms of establishing whether Saddam possessed WMDs and, if so, destroying them, it had much going for it. The inspections regime was inadequate, but France proposed reinforcing it. Above all, it was far too slow for US purposes. Given time, it might have achieved most of its stated objectives.[13] Time was not available. It now seems beyond question that the Bush administration had set an internal deadline of mid-March for the shift to war. In that context, the "viability" of the French alternative becomes almost irrelevant.

What were France's motivations? Arguments based on material interest do not hold water. France's trade with Iraq was minuscule. It had effectively written off the huge debt Saddam had built up in the 1980s. And if France had been genuinely interested in oil contracts, then self-interest would dictate bandwagoning with the United States rather than resistance. France's motives must therefore be understood in terms of a broader and longer-term concept of interest, involving a mix of principle and praxis. France believed that, since 11/9 (fall of the Berlin Wall in 1989) and especially since 9/11, the world was facing a dramatic choice: either continued development of a body of international law, forged multilaterally, framed through the United Nations, and applied consensually; or a return to the exclusivity of national interest. In that choice, the position of the United States was critical, since some of its leaders appeared to believe that it could benefit from the latter. One major role of the international community, in the French view, was to ensure that the United States stuck to multilateralism. France's position was based on the fear that precipitate, illegitimate, and perhaps even illegal US action in one of the world's most volatile regions (and the EU's "near abroad") would be a major strategic mistake.

Did France oppose the US "on principle" and/or out of some attempt to produce a counterweight that would help create a multipolar world? This question, so often put, is doubly misleading and inappropriate. The answer to the first part (on principle) is unquestionably no. France has repeatedly been the staunchest ally whenever push really came to shove (Berlin 1958–1961, Cuba 1962, Euromissiles 1983, Bosnia 1995). But it is not an unquestioning ally. Over this crisis, France genuinely felt a major difference of opinion on an issue of fundamental substance. France does not oppose the United States on principle. But it does occasionally oppose the United States. These are two very different issues. As to "counterweights" and "multipolarity," one has to distinguish between rhetoric and reality. It is almost received wisdom in the United States that France's policy is geared to "balancing" US power. However, few of those who use this argument make any attempt to say what it means in practice. Clearly, France does not aspire to act as a *systematic* rival of the United States, either alone or as part of a "pole." But Paris often speaks of "rééquilibrage." To US realists this sounds suspiciously like a classic case of smaller powers ganging together to "balance" against a hegemon. Yet "balancing" and "rééquilibrage" mean different things. "Rééquilibrage" in French discourse implies the creation of more *equality* within a community of values, either transatlantic or international. It implies the *sharing* of leadership rather than *disputes* over leadership. In advocating multipolarity, France was always careful to insist that this would not weaken the transatlantic relationship, which remained fundamental and special—but in need of greater "balance." However, the subtlety of France's position was lost on Washington and London.

What was the effect of the French position on the cause of European unity and on the EU's common foreign and security policy (CFSP)? Here the balance sheet is negative. By launching a crusade from within the United Nations, the one place where Paris can sit "eyeball-to-eyeball" with Washington, France short-circuited the EU. No serious attempt was made to forge an EU position. The Franco-*German* axis was mobilized, in ways that irritated other member states, and the Chirac outburst against the Central and Eastern European signatories of the Vilnius Letter was yet another diplomatic blunder. The assumption that France "spoke for" Europe smacked of arrogance and hubris. France was not alone in its neglect of the European card. The UK, which embarked early in 2002 on a unilateral campaign of support for the United States, can be deemed equally remiss in helping to foster European divisions.

Could France have played its cards differently? Yes, in three ways. First, by avoiding the specific diplomatic errors identified above. Second, instead of grandstanding in high-profile media interviews or under the public spotlight of the UN, French leaders could have made far more effort to meet bilaterally. Had Chirac met George W. Bush and Tony Blair (and even José María Aznar) on a one-to-one basis as often as he met with Gerhard Schröder and Vladimir Putin, some differences at least might have been ironed out. Third, a real and sustained effort should have been made much earlier in the crisis—as early as summer 2002—to forge European unity. France *is* potentially in a position to lead in European diplomacy. It has the expertise, the contacts, the creativity. But France can only do this in agreement with its partners. To speak "in the name of" Europe without first having consulted and forged a common position is counterproductive. The EU is capable of arriving at common positions on most issues of foreign policy. But it takes time, effort, and flexibility. France showed too little of that in the Iraq crisis. Only when Europe's leaders reach a point where, when faced with a crisis, their first instinct is to consult with one another (rather than to express personal or national preferences) will we see the development of a genuine CFSP. One redeeming feature of the Iraqi crisis is the apparent realization in both London and Paris that, on its own, the policy of either country toward the United States can achieve little. Only if the two can act together, jointly foster a genuinely united European position, and then jointly sell it to Washington, can the EU hope to have any influence. That may, yet, be the lasting lesson of the Iraq crisis.

◼ Notes

1. Jacques Beltran, *French Policy Towards Iraq.*
2. This resolution removed many previous restrictions on trade that were having deleterious effects on the Iraqi population.
3. Gareth Smyth and Roula Khalaf, "Pressure Brought Syria into the Fold," *Financial Times,* 9–10 November 2003, p. 4.
4. "War in Iraq" (pt. 1), *Financial Times,* 27 May 2003, p. 15.
5. International Institute for Strategic Studies, *Strategic Comments* 8, no. 10, "Invading Iraq: US Battle Plans Take Shape."
6. *Financial Times,* 27 May 2003. The French visitors were even told by Paul Wolfowitz that the window of opportunity for war would close in mid-March.
7. Richard Perle insisted in a speech in Washington, DC, on 4 February 2003 that France was no longer a US ally. Martin Walker, "Top Pentagon Adviser Says France No Longer US Ally," *Washington Times,* 5 February 2003. On 9 February,

respected columnist Thomas Friedman proposed replacing France on the UN Security Council by India. "Vote France Off the Island," *New York Times,* 9 February 2003.

8. For two weeks, it remained unclear whether the United States and the United Kingdom would muster the nine votes necessary for the resolution to pass. With hindsight, it is clear that only four countries were supportive.

9. *Time* magazine, in a special article on Chirac, "The French Resistance," as late as 24 February, still speculated that France would, in the end, join the war effort.

10. For the speculation about the French military's willingness to be involved, see Jacques Isnard, "Le 'Charles de Gaulle' va Quitter le Port de Toulon pour le Basin Oriental de la Méditerranée," *Le Monde,* 2 February 2003.

11. Prime minister's statement opening the Iraq debate, http://www.number10.gov.uk/output/page3294.asp.

12. For Chirac's statement, see http://www.elysee.fr/cgi-bin/auracom/aurweb/search/file?aur_file=discours/2003/c030410.html.

13. A very high-ranking UK official at the heart of the UN discussions believes that even one more month could have made the difference.

5

Germany: Solidarity Without Adventures

Graham Timmins

I n the days following the terrorist attack on the World Trade Center on 11 September 2001, the German government was quick to express its "unconditional solidarity" with the United States. But in doing so, German chancellor Gerhard Schröder sent out a warning to the George W. Bush administration in stressing the need for effective consultation between allies and ruled out any German involvement in "adventures."[1] This speech by Schröder turned out to be the opening statement in what became, over the course of 2001–2003, a hardening of Germany's position on military action against Iraq and that prompted the most serious crisis in German-US relations in the postwar period.

The German political psyche, which was shared by elites and the public, had throughout the Cold War been based around two statements: "never again" and "never alone."[2] The consequence of this attitude was a consistent preference manifested across the internal political spectrum to employ political solutions via multilateral organizations to address international conflict or what is commonly referred to as "civilian power."[3] It could be argued that this approach was a pragmatic response to the political constraints on military power and foreign policy decisionmaking placed on successive German governments after 1945. But even by the mid-1970s, once the Federal Republic of Germany had become a full member of the United Nations and the German economy was well on its way to becoming one of the most powerful in the world, the Genscherist tendency (named after the West German foreign minister from 1975 to 1992) of *sowohl als auch* (loosely translated as "neither one nor the other") prevailed and resulted in an aversion to the unilateral expression of German national interests and their representation through military means. Unification in 1990 restored German sovereignty to the full and provided the German government with the opportunity to develop and articulate its national interests in much the same manner as any other sovereign state. But while the center-right coalition under Chancellor Helmut Kohl hinted at a willingness to flex its political muscles, it was not until the election of the Social Democratic–Green coalition in September 1998 that an increased independence in the foreign policy sphere became apparent. Soon after the elections, Chancellor Schröder sent a clear message to his EU partners that Germans were Europeans "not because we have to be, but because we want to be."[4] This statement most vividly encapsulated not only the political but also the generational change that had occurred in Germany. The new government was made up of politicians who had no personal link to the historical burden of national socialism, and many had launched their political careers in the late 1960s campaigning for increased democratization of the German political system and as part of the left's protest movement against US military involvement in Southeast Asia and the arms race during the "Second Cold War" of the 1970–1980s.

The motivating factors that led to the willingness of the Social Democratic–Green coalition to pursue an independent foreign policy line against the United States, and the rupture this provoked in German-US relations, will provide the focus of this chapter. It will be argued that German policy during the Iraq crisis was a combination of political expediency and a new evolving international identity that stressed independence of decisionmaking. But despite the significance of the events during 2002–2003, it will be further argued that the political balance in the conduct and direction of German foreign policy remains firmly with continuity rather than change.

■ Domestic Politics and the Iraq Crisis

The long-standing elite preference for civilian power in Germany has been conducted within a context of mass public support. Mass opposition to militarism within German society could be witnessed by the high level of activism and the passive support it received in protesting the deployment of US cruise missiles on German territory in the 1980s, and again by mass protests opposing military action during the Gulf War in 1991. The deployment of a German military presence, albeit noncombat forces, first in the Balkans in 1992 and later in Somalia in 1993, provoked a negative public reaction, and in the latter case a legal challenge against the government by the Social Democratic Party. It was not until the "massacre of Srebrenica" in July 1995, when Bosnian Serbs killed a reported 8,000 people, that a fundamental shift in German mass and elite opinion occurred.[5] This event more than anything undermined the hitherto dominant postwar tradition of pacifism in society. It also prompted the political class and, in particular, the German left to revise their views on Germany's international role and supported the position that, given its historical legacy, Germany had a growing leadership responsibility in resisting aggression and human rights violations that would, if necessary, include military action. A Bundestag majority was subsequently obtained for a first-ever deployment of German combat troops in an out-of-area NATO operation in the Balkans in 1996. By the end of the decade the transformation in German military involvement in world affairs had progressed to an even more significant level, from peacekeeping to peacemaking, when in spring 1999 German combat troops participated in the NATO-led Operation Allied Force in Kosovo. But despite the international significance of this transformation, Anja Dalgaard-Nielsen has noted that, "while unconditional pacifism had lost the moral high ground, German anti-militarism has not disappeared, and there remains a distinct aversion to the early resort to military force."[6]

The events of 11 September 2001 represented a defining moment in the evolving post–Cold War international order and added further impetus to Germany's expanding international military role. Chancellor Schröder's promise of solidarity with the United States in combating international terrorism was honored in November 2001 when parliamentary support, with the aid of a vote of confidence, for German participation in Operation Enduring Freedom in Afghanistan was obtained, and by the end of 2002 approximately 8,500 German troops were deployed in various parts of the world, the second largest deployment for peacekeeping operations after the United States.[7] But in the case of Iraq, the German government had reservations from the outset regarding the alleged connections between Saddam Hussein and Al-Qaida. Following the federal elections in September 1998, the newly elected Social Democratic–Green coalition had been ambivalent regarding the US proposal to militarize the UN weapons inspection process, but by March 2001 had decided against supporting military action. When, as early as 19 September 2001, the US administration made its plans for military action against Iraq known to the German government, the response from Berlin was mixed.[8] Although willing to support the United States at a time of great tragedy, and although backing for military action under a UN mandate was not ruled out, the difficulty the government would have convincing Social Democratic and Green parliamentarians, not to mention the public, which was unconvinced by the search for weapons of mass destruction in Iraq and was set clearly against German participation in any military action, became a significant factor in its calculations. It was also the case that 2002 was an election year and the governing coalition was under pressure, having failed to have any impact on the growing problem of unemployment since its election in 1998. The government was therefore aware that a pro-US foreign policy line would have further damaged its electoral prospects.

The general approach taken by the German government at the start of

2002 in addressing this emerging dilemma was to play down the differences between Germany and the United States over Iraq, with the probable hope that military action could be avoided. But if Schröder had preferred to have kept the Iraq crisis off the electoral agenda, the launch of the new US national security agenda during the second half of 2002 and the plans outlined for a preemptive strike against Iraq, which formed part of the US-defined "axis of evil," put Washington and Berlin on a political collision course. The cracks between the US and European positions had been exposed in January 2002 when a NATO crisis management exercise was ended prematurely following disagreement on how best to deal with the threat of an attack using weapons of mass destruction.[9] When in August 2002 the German election campaign was launched, and given President Bush's increasingly belligerent position on Iraq, Schröder made a point of repeating the German government's position that it would be disinclined to participate in any "adventures." In early September, three weeks before the federal elections, Schröder moved to address the government's deteriorating electoral position by announcing that Germany would refrain from taking part in any military action against Iraq, even if a UN mandate were to be passed. In making this announcement, Schröder had taken a more radical position than even that of the French government, which was still prepared to consider its own involvement under a UN mandate. Soon after at an election rally in Cologne, Schröder went on the offensive in terms of electoral rhetoric and asked, "What kind of friendship is that if you are not free to state your opinion but instead have to stand there and click your heels together?"[10] In playing to the crowds in this manner, Schröder was fully utilizing public opinion survey data, which had consistently revealed a huge majority within German society who were against war in Iraq. But this use of rhetoric by Schröder had sent a political signal to his own party and, certainly in the minds of the US administration, had opened up an opportunity for the public expression of anti-US sentiment. Two examples of this were the analogy drawn by Ludwig Stiegler, the Social Democratic parliamentary leader, who compared President Bush to the Roman emperor Augustus, who had subordinated Germany to the Roman Empire in the twelfth century, and the analogy drawn by Herta Däubler-Gmelin, a member of Schröder's cabinet, who had compared Bush to Adolf Hitler in suggesting that the United States was seeking to deflect attention away from its domestic problems by launching an attack on Iraq.[11] Faced with what had been, until shortly before election day, an apparently certain victory for the Christian Democrats, opposition candidate Edmund Stoiber attempted to make political capital out of Germany's emerging international isolation and the growing rift in transatlantic relations by appealing to Germans to think back to the assistance the United States had provided in the postwar reconstruction of Germany. However, Schröder's position on Iraq, together with the handling of the flood catastrophe that hit the eastern states shortly before the elections, proved enough to save the Social Democratic Party's political life, and the governing coalition gained a narrow four-seat majority in the Bundestag.

Electoral expediency had therefore undoubtedly been a factor in the German position on Iraq. Schröder would have been unable to reconcile the demands being placed on Germany by the United States with the opposition he would have faced from his own party, coalition partner, and the electorate. In an attempt to rationalize the German foreign policy line and make a virtue out of a necessity, the idea of a "German way" gradually emerged as a central theme in the Social Democratic Party's platform in the course of the election campaign. Originally intended as an electoral tool to highlight the party's economic policies, the idea was gradually linked to foreign policy, but in a vague manner. The Social Democratic Party sidestepped any theoretical elaboration of the concept during the election campaign, and used it in pragmatic terms primarily as a metaphor for independence of decisionmaking. Since the elections and despite extensive academic discussion, any serious intention that existed to utilize the concept of a "German way" has died a silent death within government circles.[12]

Although tempting, to attempt to explain German foreign policy on Iraq during 2002 purely as a short-term electoral consideration would be too simplistic. As outlined earlier in this chapter, the generational change heralded by the 1998 election result had promised a more independent direction in foreign policy, what August Pradetto has referred to as a transformation from "tamed" to "normal" power.[13] The manner in which the newly elected government pursued an independent line as the Iraq crisis deepened would therefore be a genuine test regarding how far reality matched rhetoric as the German government wrestled with the challenge of developing a post–Cold War/postunification identity.

■ The Postelection Fallout in German-US Relations

The rift between Germany and the United States emerged fully into the open in January 2003 when the German government refused to sanction the deployment of German troops as part of a NATO force into Turkey, arguing that the only circumstances under which Turkey would require military assistance would be in the event of an attack on Iraq. The obvious concern within the German leadership was that German participation in a NATO force in Turkey would provide implicit approval for US policy. In taking this particular route, Schröder had signaled a new self-confidence in German foreign policy but also, as Schöllgen describes, "had unintentionally taken on the leadership role as a counterbalance to the US."[14] A Gallup poll in January 2003 revealed that 89 percent of Germans opposed a war against Iraq without UN support, and meant that, unlike the British and Italian governments, the Social Democratic–Green coalition had the luxury of widespread public support for its policy on Iraq.[15] But in coming out so clearly against German military involvement in Iraq, this public support had been purchased in exchange for its voice in Washington and undermined German attempts to moderate US policy following the Bush proposal to the UN Security Council for a second mandate in September 2002. Germany undertook a number of initiatives designed to rebuild links with Washington, including a willingness to take the lead for the International Security Assistance Force mission in Afghanistan. However, as Sebastian Harnisch argues, the narrow election victory and the "fragile" majority it produced in the Bundestag ruled out any question of Germany making a military contribution to operations in Iraq and removed any possibility in the short term of repairing the damage done to German-US relations.[16]

Unaccustomed to finding itself exposed in this manner and so far alienated from its traditional ally, Germany responded by linking into the French position more closely and seeking to develop a European response to the United States. Germany provided its full support for the French position, announced by Foreign Minister Dominique de Villepin at the UN Security Council session on 20 January 2003, that the French government would oppose the US-proposed military action in Iraq. Germany and France further cemented their joint position two days later during the celebrations to mark the fortieth anniversary of the Franco-German Elysée Treaty of Friendship on 22 January 2003, and in a joint statement the two declared that "Germany and France will strive in international organizations, including the UN Security Council, to reach common positions and to reach coordinated strategies towards third countries."[17] US defense secretary Donald Rumsfeld, in January 2003, responded to the Franco-German decision to coordinate their foreign policies by branding the two states as "Old Europe" and counterposed them against the pro-US states as belonging to "New Europe." The annual Munich Security Conference on 8 February 2003, with its traditional focus on transatlantic relations, provided the opportunity for Rumsfeld and German foreign minister Joschka Fischer to debate the differences in the US and German positions. Rumsfeld repeated his view that all NATO member states had an obligation to assist in the protection of Turkey. Fischer responded with probably the most passionate speech of his political career, in which he set out a defense of German foreign policy and heavily criticized the rationale for military action against Iraq: "I am not convinced. That's my problem. I cannot go to the public and say that these are the reasons because I won't believe them."[18] That no official transcript of the speech has appeared on the German foreign ministry website is indicative of its spontaneity and the extent to which it was driven by Fischer's personal political convictions as much as it was by government policy.[19]

The approach taken in Berlin and Paris was that the UN weapons inspection team should be given more time and that a tougher line should be taken against any obstruction by the Iraqi regime. This strategy was pursued at the EU level, and on 17 February 2003 a EU declaration was agreed, stating that "war is not inevitable" and that "force should be used only as a last resort."[20] The EU declaration, however, was an attempt to paper over the cracks that had emerged yet again within the European Union's common foreign and security policy between the Franco-German axis and the transatlanticist nations, led by the United Kingdom and Spain. As John Peterson and Mark Pollack argued, "it was easy—far too easy—to blame the rift [in transatlantic relations] on the behavior of the most aggressive, undiplomatic and unilateralist US administration in modern history. Simplistic or not, Rumsfeld's old v new Europe distinction encapsulated a basic split that appeared and then reappeared within the EU's common foreign and security policy (CFSP), NATO, and the United Nations Security Council with remarkable consistency."[21]

As well as strengthening Franco-German cooperation, Schröder looked to coordinate its position with Russia and to utilize the new "strategic partnership" that had been launched in April 2001 and included a regular governmental consultation process.[22] Both the French and Russian leaderships had become increasingly nervous of the US post–Cold War foreign policy agenda and in broad terms favored a multipolar perspective on international relations. Following his election as president in March 2000, Vladimir Putin had launched Russia's new foreign policy concept in June 2000, which was noticeable for its more distanced approach toward relations with the United States.[23] Furthermore, Jacques Chirac's election victory in May 2002 had provided the French leadership with a mandate for a more assertive foreign policy in enhancing France's position in the world. Quite unintentionally Germany found itself part of this Franco-Russian "multipolar alliance" by default. Faced with growing US pressure for a second UN mandate that would set Iraq an ultimatum requiring full cooperation with the arms inspection process or face military consequences, Germany, France, and Russia issued a joint statement on 5 March 2003 that was unambiguous in declaring that the three states would block any attempt in the UN Security Council to pass a mandate sanctioning the use of military force against Iraq.[24]

With the outbreak of war imminent, both Schröder and Fischer underlined their commitment to maintaining Germany's independence of decisionmaking. In his State of the Nation speech to the Bundestag on 14 March 2003, Schröder argued, "We must have the courage to fight for peace as long as there is a scrap of hope that war can be avoided,"[25] and at the UN

Security Council meeting on 19 March 2003, one day before the outbreak of the Iraq War, Fischer condemned the use of military action and restated his opinion that "the [UN] Security Council had not failed" in its attempt to disarm Iraq and that there was "no substitute for its functions as a guardian of peace."[26]

In the six months following its election victory the German government had thus attempted to minimize the consequences of the damage done to German-US relations with a closer coordination of policy on a bilateral level with France and Russia and using these joint positions to influence multilevel policy inside the European Union and the United Nations. Rather than representing a new style and direction in German foreign policy, the behavior of the Social Democratic–Green coalition was highly reminiscent of the traditional Genscherist approach. The overriding significance of German foreign policy on Iraq is the fact that Germany found itself on the opposing side of the political divide to the United States in such a polarized manner. Germany's deeply ingrained foreign policy perspective of "never alone" had traditionally contained the caveat of "and never without the US." What was new in this respect was Germany's willingness to detach itself from the US line in a hitherto unparalleled manner.

■ Conclusion: German-US Relations Beyond the Iraq War

It remains in general terms unclear what lessons can be drawn from the Iraq crisis regarding German foreign policy. Hanns Maull, on the one hand, suggests that "German foreign policy has changed fundamentally in recent times and has started to loosen itself from the old constraints and has set out on a new but as yet undefined course."[27] On the other, Harnisch argues that German policy during the Iraq crisis represented more the political calculations of a beleaguered Social Democratic leadership seeking to navigate a course between the obligations of international alliances and the domestic party debate than the formulation of any "new thinking" in German foreign policy.[28] There is probably some truth in both interpretations. While the Social Democratic–Green coalition was in all likelihood sincere in its intention to develop a more independent line on international affairs, alliance obligations and domestic politics undoubtedly reduced the political leadership's scope for maneuver. However, there is little evidence to suggest that Germany is seeking to move away from a consensual model of international relations, has any intention of developing its military capacities independent of NATO and the EU, or is reordering its alliance preferences. This argument therefore suggests that modified continuity rather than any fundamental change in German foreign policy making and outputs is most likely in the future. In the period leading up to the Christian Democratic election victory in 2005, opposition policy was focused on addressing what it viewed to have been the inconsistencies of application rather than the need for any reorientation of foreign policy objectives.[29] It appears from this position that the Social Democratic–Green coalition has done little if anything to undermine the cross-party consensus on foreign policy.

The impact of the Iraq crisis on the future of German-US relations and, in more general terms, for EU-NATO relations, European security and defense policy, and the "EU voice" inside the UN Security Council, is also far from clear. Condoleezza Rice's threat to punish the French, ignore the Germans, and forgive the Russians has been tempered by the postwar political situation in Iraq, but the political damage incurred by Germany's position is unlikely ever to be fully erased in the collective minds of the Bush administration and will undoubtedly influence the thinking of future administrations, both Republican and Democrat, for some time into the future. Willy Brandt famously remarked on the night the Berlin Wall fell, in November 1989, that "nothing will ever be the same again." Much the same comment can be made regarding the aftermath of the Iraq crisis and its impact on German-US relations. But even if the consequences prove permanent, they are unlikely to be fatal for the long-term relationship, such is the underlying interdependency of the transatlantic alliance.

◼ Notes

1. "Regierungserklärung von Bundeskanzler Gerhard Schröder vor dem Deutschen Bundestag zu den Anschlägen in den USA, am 19 September 2001," quoted in Sebastian Harnisch, "Bound to Fail? Germany's Policy in the Iraq Crisis 2001–2003," paper presented at the twenty-seventh annual conference of the German Studies Association, New Orleans, 18–21 September 2003; also available in *German Politics* 13, no. 1 (2004).

2. Hanns W. Maull, "Normalisierung oder Auszehrung? Deutsche Außenpolitik im Wandel," p. 19.

3. For a discussion of the civilian power concept, see Hanns Maull, "German Foreign Policy Post-Kosovo."

4. *New York Times,* 12 December 1998.

5. Martin Walker, "A Continent Stands Transformed," *The Guardian,* 7 June 1999.

6. Anja Dalgaard-Nielsen, "Gulf War," p. 110.

7. Gregor Schölligen, "Die Zukunft der Deutschen Außenpolitik Liegt in Europa," p. 9.

8. Harnisch, "Bound to Fail?"

9. Ibid.

10. "Foreign Policy Works for Schroeder," *BBC News,* http://news.bbc.co.uk1/hi/world/europe/2261878.stm.

11. "Germany/US: Roots of Dispute Go Deeper Than Campaign Rhetoric," *Radio Free Europe/Radio Liberty,* http://www.rferl.org/features/2002/09/25092002160700.asp.

12. Interview with Social Democratic adviser on foreign affairs, Berlin, 19 July 2004.

13. August Pradetto, "From 'Tamed' to 'Normal' Power."

14. Schöllgen, "Die Zukunft," p. 10.

15. Gallup poll data quoted in Sylvia Kritzinger, "Public Opinion in the Iraq Crisis," p. 31.

16. Harnisch, "Bound to Fail?"

17. Gemeinsame Erklärung zum 40. Jahrestag der Elysée-Vertrags, Paris, den 22.01.2003 in Forschungsinstitut der Internationalen Wissenschaftlichen Vereinigung Weltwirtschaft und Weltpolitik (IWVWW) e.V., Berichte, März 2003, p. 81.

18. A summary report on Joschka Fischer's speech in Munich is available from the Deutsche Welle website, at http://www.dwelle.de/bscms_english/current_affairs/1.17399.1.html.

19. According to the official statement on the Munich Security Conference website, http://www.securityconference.de: "Joschka Fischer [held] a free speech [at] this year's conference. Due to this, his notes cannot be published on this site. A typed version of his speech will also not be available."

20. Conclusions from Extraordinary European Council on Iraq, 17 February 2003. Statement available at the EU website, http://europa.eu.int/comm./external_relations/iraq/intro/ec170203.htm.

21. John Peterson and Mark A. Pollack, "Conclusion," pp. 135–136.

22. Gerhard Schroeder took the unusual step of publishing the German policy line on Russia in the form of an article in *Die Zeit,* 5 April 2001. The article has since been reproduced on the German government's website, http://www.bundesregierung.de/interview,-35312/bundeskanzler-schroeder-deutsc.htm.

23. A translated version of the foreign policy concept of the Russian Federation can be found at http://www.bits.de/index.html.

24. See *Internationale Politik* 58, no. 4 (2003) for the Gemeinsame Erklärung Russlands, Deutschland's und Frankreichs zu Irak, veröffentlicht am 5. März 2003 in Paris.

25. Full text available in German at http://www.bundestag.de/bic/plenarprotokolle/pp/2003/index.html.

26. United Nations, *Security Council Minutes,* 4,721st meeting, S/PV.4721, 19 March 2003, p. 4.

27. Maull, "Normalisierung oder Auszehrung?" p. 17.

28. Harnisch, "Bound to Fail?"

29. Interview with CDU special adviser on foreign policy, Berlin, 15 July 2004.

6

Russia: Diminished Power

Stephen White

R ussia entered the twenty-first century as a diminished power. It had, most thought, lost the Cold War. It had lost almost half of the population who had been resident in the USSR in its final years, and had fallen behind Indonesia and Brazil among the world's most populous nations. Its population, moreover, was continuing to fall, by about a million a year; on United Nations projections it would have a population of just 101 million by 2050, less than the projected population of much smaller developing nations like Egypt or Uganda. The national territory was only three-quarters of that of the USSR. And the economy had been contracting steadily since the end of communist rule, reducing gross domestic product to not much more than half of its level in 1990. There was a serious danger, Vladimir Putin warned, in his first address as acting president, that Russia would slip not into the second but into the third rank of world powers if these tendencies continued.[1]

Foreign as well as domestic policy reflected this diminished status. The new national security concept, adopted in January 2000, identified two divergent trends: one that pointed toward the formation of a multipolar world in line with Russian interests, and another that assumed a rather different structure, based on the domination of the Western countries and of the United States in particular. Russia was still a global power, with centuries of history and rich cultural traditions. But there had been disturbing developments, both at home and abroad. Russia's own scientific base had weakened, the economy had contracted, and there were separatist tendencies in some of the regions. Abroad, NATO's new willingness to act outside the territory of its own members threatened to destabilize the international system, and technological developments were likely to unleash a new stage in the arms race. Still more fundamentally, there were threats to Russia's "spiritual-moral legacy," including attempts by foreign sects to undermine its traditional religious allegiances.[2]

71

A new foreign policy concept, adopted in summer 2000, set out the country's priorities within this changing international environment. Russia's position in world affairs, it suggested, had generally strengthened, but there were still "negative tendencies." As the national security document had done, the foreign policy concept identified several new threats to Russian security, including a growing trend toward a unipolar world order dominated militarily and economically by the United States, and a tendency for the international agenda to reflect the wishes of Western bodies with a limited membership rather than the wider community of states that was represented in the United Nations. Efforts were being made to justify the actions of these more limited groups of states in the name of "humanitarian intervention," on the basis of what was being described as "limited sovereignty." Russian policy placed greater emphasis on international law, and on the role of the United Nations and its Security Council; and Russian diplomacy would seek to strengthen a "multipolar system of international relations that would genuinely reflect the diversity of the contemporary world with its varied interests." That, in turn, involved an "optimum mix of efforts in every direction," given that Russia had a spread of priorities across Europe and Asia and that limited resources were available to achieve them.[3]

■ Russia and the Iraqi Conflict

There was no direct reference to Iraq in the foreign policy concept, but Russian policy was set out authoritatively elsewhere, in a study by the minister of foreign affairs, Igor' Ivanov, that was published in 2001. As Ivanov explained, Russian policy aimed to turn the Persian Gulf area into a "zone of peace, security and cooperation" of a kind that would avoid any repetition of wars and conflict. The situation around Iraq must be normalized, and regular relations must be established among the states of the region. It was essential to reduce levels of armaments, to reduce the foreign military presence, to develop trust, and to facilitate a broader regional cooperation. A component part of these efforts should be the establishment in the region of a zone free of weapons of mass destruction. The process of regularization could be strengthened by the establishment of a regional organization responsible for maintaining peace and stability with the participation, apart from the countries of the Gulf, of the permanent members of the Security Council of the United Nations and other interested parties. Russia, he claimed, took a leading role in such initiatives, and, acting through the United Nations, it was making every effort to accelerate the dropping of sanctions on the basis of Iraq's fulfillment of the resolutions of the Council.[4]

Russia had a variety of interests to defend as the region moved steadily toward confrontation in the early years of the new century. There was a long-standing friendship treaty, originally signed in 1972. But more than this, there were several thousand Russians living and working in Iraq, and substantial Russian investments that would be repaid only if relations were maintained with the Iraqi government. There was also a personal element, in that Evgenii Primakov, the Arabist who had been foreign minister and then prime minister during the late 1990s, was a long-standing friend of Saddam Hussein's and had acted as an intermediary in 1990–1991; he was in Baghdad again in February 2003. But the foreign ministry suggested more general grounds of principle for resisting Western action, including the danger that it might encourage Islamic terrorism and increase anti-US feeling in various countries, including Russia.[5]

When relations deteriorated once again in December 1998, following Iraq's failure to comply fully with the requirements of UN weapons inspectors, and the United States and Britain launched missile strikes against Iraqi targets, President Boris Yeltsin complained that they had "crudely violated the UN Charter and generally accepted principles of international law and the norms and rules of responsible behavior of states."[6] Primakov condemned the US action more directly, and condemned any attempt to "resolve problems unilaterally, from a position of strength."[7] Underlining the gravity with which it viewed the situation, the Russian government withdrew its ambassadors from London and Washington in a gesture of official dissatisfaction that had not been seen since the worst days of the Cold War.[8]

The Kremlin continued to speak out against the use of force against the Saddam Hussein regime in the early years of the new century, unless such action was taken with the explicit authorization of the Security Council, where as a permanent member Russia has a veto. But Russia, unlike France, did not explicitly threaten to use its veto to block a new resolution in the early months of 2003 as the United States and its British ally sought to obtain the backing of the Security Council for the use of military means against an apparently recalcitrant Saddam. A joint Franco-German-Russian statement, issued in February 2003 while Putin was in Paris, opposed the use of force so long as the weapons inspectors were continuing their work.[9] Meeting the German chancellor in Moscow two weeks later, Putin made clear that Russia would refuse to support a new UN resolution that opened the way to the automatic use of force.[10] And Foreign Minister Ivanov, in London at the beginning of March, insisted that there was "no real need for a new resolution" in existing circumstances.[11]

There was little more support for the British and US position among ordinary Russians, and little belief that military action was being contemplated for any other than the most self-interested of reasons. One poll, conducted by Russia's public opinion research center just days before the invasion began, on the night of 19–20 March 2003, found that 71 percent of the population viewed the United States as a danger to peace and international security, while only 45 percent saw Iraq as a comparable threat.[12] Just after the invasion had begun, 80 percent of Russians reportedly felt "indignation" about the US-led campaign, and just 3 percent approved of it.[13] What, it was asked, had the United States brought to Iraq, once the military operation had come to an end and Baghdad had been taken? For 45 percent, it was "anarchy," and for another 19 percent, "a regime more cruel than Saddam Hussein's"; just 10 percent thought it was "freedom." By December 2003 there was still strong public hostility to the US-led occupation: 74 percent regarded it as largely or entirely in negative terms, with just 9 percent taking the opposite view.[14]

There was an equal degree of skepticism about the motives for the campaign. What, Russians were asked on the eve of the invasion, was the main reason for the actions the United States and its partners were contemplating against Iraq? First of all, they thought, it was promoted by a US determination to seize control of Iraq's oil reserves (39 percent); a second reason was the US drive for world domination (29 percent). Iraq's support for international terrorism, which was the ostensible casus belli, was identified by no more than 17 percent.[15] Opinion was even more skeptical by the end of the year, in another survey conducted by the national public opinion research center. Almost half (49 percent) said the purpose of the war had been to secure US control over Iraqi oil, and another 27 percent thought it had been to "show everyone who's 'boss' in the world"; just 6 percent thought it had been to "stop Iraq making weapons of mass destruction."[16]

▪ The Kremlin's Response to the War

When war began the Kremlin was also sharply critical. As President Putin put it in an official statement, the US-led action was being taken in spite of global opinion and contrary to international law and the UN Charter. There could be no justification for such action, whether it was a charge that Iraq had supported international terrorism (of which the Kremlin had no evidence) or a wish to change the Iraqi government, for which there was no legal basis. Nor was there any need for such action—Iraq posed no danger to its neighbors or other countries, as it was weakened economically and militarily after a ten-year embargo, and international weapons inspectors were continuing their work. UN Security Council Resolution 1441, in the Russian view, had not sanctioned the use of force but was rather a means of allowing the inspectors to complete the task with which they had been entrusted. The action that had been taken, Putin went on, was a "major political mistake," not only in humanitarian terms, but also in the threat it represented to the international order. If some states felt able to impose their will on others, without regard to the sovereign status, not a single state anywhere in the world could feel secure. Russia called for an early end to the hostilities, and for the conflict to be referred to the UN Security Council.[17]

A more differentiated response emerged a couple of weeks later when Putin met regional journalists in Tambov. "For political and economic reasons," he told them, "Russia does not have an interest in a US defeat. Our interest is in shifting efforts to solve this problem to the floor of the UN." It was not, commentators remarked, a popular choice—public opinion would have preferred more forthright support of a long-standing Russian ally. At the same time, it did not imply that Russia had accepted the new doctrine of preemptive war. However, it did reflect the fact that Russia had a considerable stake in any post-Saddam regime. The total value of Russian oil contracts with the former regime was estimated at about $30 billion, Iraqi debt to Russia amounted to an estimated $8 billion, and Russia had apparently been making $1–2 billion a year from the UN's oil-for-food program. The United States would clearly be taking responsibility for the allocation of rights for oil production in post-Saddam Iraq, so Russia could "lose everything" unless it maintained reasonable relations with the US government. Even if the United States and its partners lost the war, Saddam would be unable to fulfill the terms of Iraq's oil contracts with Russia, if only because international sanctions would still be in effect. So the only scenario under which Russia could count on some presence in the Iraq energy industry of the future was a US victory. It was, commented *Izvestiya,* an "utterly pragmatic" decision.[18]

Russians themselves had a mixed view of Putin's response. Very few (2 percent) thought he had actually supported the US-led campaign; rather more thought he had "stayed on the sidelines" (39 percent), or that he had "criticized US actions" (52 percent), based on a national opinion poll conducted in April 2003. As for their own assessment, a plurality (45 percent) thought Russian action had been "reasonable and correct" in the circumstances; a substantial proportion (38 percent) thought they should have "opposed the US more decisively," but only 3 percent thought Russia "should have supported the US."[19] The State Duma, which had strong Communist representation, characterized the campaign as "aggression," and suspended its consideration of the Strategic Offensive Reduction Treaty, which had been signed in May 2002 and eventually ratified by the US Senate in June 2003. There were demonstrations in many Russian cities as the war began; the one in Moscow on 9 April, with about 20,000 participating, was the largest that had taken place since the end of Soviet rule.[20]

■ Russian Opinion and the Iraqi Issue

My own investigation, undertaken with Margot Light and Roy Allison, of Russian opinion in early 2004 (see appendix to this chapter) showed considerable continuity with the attitudes that had been apparent immediately after the conflict in Iraq began. What, first of all, were the reasons for the war? Very few, on the evidence of our survey, accepted the justifications that had been offered by the US-led coalition. No more than 12 percent identified one or another of the coalition's own justifications of its actions as the primary reason for the conflict, and no more than 16 percent opted for one of these justifications as a secondary reason. Much more often, it was the US drive to secure control of Iraqi oil that was identified as the main cause (about two-thirds offered this as either a primary or a secondary reason for the war), followed by the US determination to establish its geopolitical ascendancy in the region (more than half identified this as a primary or second reason) (see Table 6.1).

We were also concerned to establish the consequences that the war would have, in the view of ordinary Russians (see Table 6.2). Again, there was little agreement with the assumptions on which the coalition had been conducting its campaign. Few thought the position of ordinary Iraqis would improve, or that stability in the region would be enhanced, or that the authority of the United Nations would be strengthened. Above all, there was little confidence that weapons of mass destruction would become less likely to fall into the hands of terrorists.

Table 6.1   Russians and the Reasons for War

	First Reason	Second Reason
To enforce UN resolutions	2	2
To destroy Iraqi weapons of mass destruction	6	5
To remove Saddam Hussein from power	15	16
To strengthen the influence of the US in the Near East	25	29
To establish democracy in Iraq	1	4
To obtain control of Iraqi oil reserves	37	28
To prevent terrorists obtaining access to weapons of mass destruction	3	5

Source: 2004 Russia survey (see appendix to this chapter). Figures show percentages of individuals who identified the options shown; answers of "don't know" and lack of response account for residuals. Question wording was: "There are different views about the reasons that led the US and its allies to begin war against Iraq. Here is a list of reasons that other people have suggested. [Show card; read out.] Which two of these reasons, do you think, were the most important?"

Table 6.2 Russians on the Consequences of the Iraq War

	Agree	Disagree
The life of ordinary Iraqis will improve	17	58
The Middle East will become more stable	18	57
The authority of the United Nations in the resolution of international conflicts will increase	19	51
The risk that weapons of mass destruction will fall into the hands of terrorists will become less	24	48

Source: 2004 Russia survey (see appendix to this chapter). Figures show percentages of individuals who identified the options shown; answers of "don't know" and lack of response account for residuals. Question wording was: "Tell me please what you think of the consequences of the war in Iraq. Do you agree or disagree that . . ." (Read out; one answer to each question.)

▧ Iraq and Russia's Security Environment

Russian responses rested on a rather different view of their security environment than in the Western countries. Russians share the Western view that terrorism and Islamic fundamentalism are more serious threats than those from other states. They did not think it was very likely, on our evidence, that another country would attack Russia in the coming five years. And if there was a threat to Russian security, it was more likely to come from an organized force of some kind than from another state. Russians shared the concern of many in Western countries about international terrorism: for 95 percent it was a serious threat to Russian security, and for 93 percent the drug trade was a comparable threat. For 73 percent transnational crime was a serious security concern, and for the same proportion Islamic fundamentalism was a serious threat of this kind.

Iraq, however, ranked relatively low among the challenges that confronted postcommunist Russian society (see Table 6.3). On the evidence of our survey, Russians see their security challenges in terms that would have been very familiar in the Soviet period: by a considerable margin, the United States is seen as Russia's main security threat, followed by NATO and China (predictably, 92 percent of those who thought NATO was a threat to Russian security took the same view of the United States, and 71 percent of those who thought the United States was a threat to Russian security took the same view of NATO). There is little threat from other European countries, in the view of our respondents, including Germany and the EU as a whole. But there is least threat of all from Iraq and from Ukraine, another Slavic republic with which there are close human and diplomatic relations.

Table 6.3   Russia's Security Environment

	Some or Large Threat	Little or No Threat
China	31	56
Germany	19	66
Iraq	9	78
United States	48	40
EU member countries	13	67
Ukraine	6	82
NATO	32	48

Source: 2004 Russian survey (see appendix to this chapter). Figures show percentages of individuals who identified each option; answers of "don't know" and lack of response account for residuals. Question wording was: "What do you think, what threat to the security of our country might the following countries or organisations represent?" [Show card.]

We asked a series of open-ended questions that allowed our respondents to give their own account of the threats to Russian security that they could envisage over the coming years. By a considerable margin, "terrorism" was the most important; but 37 percent had no idea, and Iraq as such did not rate a mention. We asked similarly about threats to world security over the coming five years, allowing respondents again to volunteer their own opinions: once more, "international terrorism" was more frequently cited as a potential threat than any other. We asked more pointedly which countries or organizations represented a threat to Russian security over the coming years: more than half (55 percent) had no idea, but among those who offered a definite response it was above all the United States (23 percent), followed by NATO and China (both about 4 percent). Just under 3 percent suggested the Middle East or Chechnya; fewest of all (less than 2 percent) suggested Iraq.

We asked another and rather larger question, about which countries were disposed in a friendly way toward Russia and which in an unfriendly way (as our respondents perceived it). A part of this list is reproduced in Table 6.4. In every case, our respondents thought foreign countries were more friendly toward Russia than unfriendly. But there were some clear differences. Among the "friends," India, Germany, France, and Finland stood out, as indeed they have done in other investigations.[21] Countries such as Norway and Sweden, China and Vietnam, and Canada and Australia were seen as scarcely less positively disposed. Attitudes toward another group of countries were rather more reserved, including the United Kingdom, Japan (where a territorial dispute continues), Israel, and the Republic of Korea (North Korea was thought to take a more friendly view of its northern neighbor). Iran and Iraq were seen as still less favorably disposed, although the balance of opinion was still strongly positive. Most hostile of all was the

Table 6.4 Russia's Friends and Foes

	Very or Fairly Friendly	Very or Fairly Hostile
India	85	2
Germany	81	5
France	81	4
Finland	80	3
Sweden	76	3
Canada	73	5
China	73	12
Japan	69	14
United Kingdom	67	11
Israel	67	10
Iran	59	18
Iraq	57	19
United States	46	36

Source: 2004 Russia survey (see appendix to this chapter). Figures show percentages of individuals who identified the options shown; answers of "don't know" and lack of response account for residuals. Question wording was: "Tell me, please, which countries have a friendly attitude towards Russia . . . And which, in your opinion, have a hostile attitude?" (Show card.)

United States, and this was the only country where popular attitudes were thought to be not much less hostile than they were friendly.

■ The Limits of Russian Power

It is difficult not to conclude that Putin used the resources at his command with considerable skill, but equally difficult not to conclude that those resources were very limited. Russia had a stake in the crisis, for reasons of propinquity as well as its interest in the Iraqi energy markets of the future. But its influence was greatest within the United Nations, particularly within the Security Council, which left it marginalized when the US-led coalition took action without a further resolution that would have explicitly authorized the military option. Russian representatives insisted that the US-led action was illegal, and demanded that the whole issue be brought back to the Security Council; this strained relations with the United States, but helped to maintain Russia's position within the Arab world, where it had a whole series of interests, and improved Russia's image in continental Europe, especially in France and Germany. At the same time, Russia avoided exercising its veto, which might have precipitated a break with the United States that would have damaged Russian interests in a post-Saddam Iraq, and made it clear that once the war had begun, it favored the cause of the United States and its coalition partners. As rapid victory gave way to a costly and contentious occupation, Russia could hardly be blamed for the difficulties it encountered; but Russian insistence on the primacy of international law began increasingly to appear a well-chosen option, and Putin himself felt able, by 2005, to call for the occupying armies to be withdrawn as part of a wider settlement.[22]

Appendix

The primary source of Russian public opinion is a national representative survey conducted by Russian Research in association with the project "Inclusion Without Membership? Bringing Russia, Ukraine, and Belarus closer to 'Europe,'" directed by Stephen White, Margot Light, and Roy Allison and funded by the UK Economic and Social Research Council under grant RES-000-23-0146. Fieldwork took place between 21 December 2003 and 16 January 2004. The number of respondents was 2,000, selected according to the agency's normal sampling procedures; it was representative of the Russian population aged eighteen and over, using a multistage proportional representation method with a random route method of selecting households. Interviews were conducted face-to-face in respondents' homes; the response rate was 57 percent. The sample was then weighted in accordance with sex, age, and education in each region. There were 97 sampling points, and 150 interviewers were employed, whose work was checked by field supervisors according to the agency's normal practices.

Notes

1. *Rossiiskaya Gazeta,* 31 December 1999, p. 4.
2. *Sobranie Zakonodatel'stva Rossiiskoi Federatsii* no. 2 (2000), pp. 691–704.
3. *Rossiiskaya Gazeta,* 11 July 2000, p. 5.
4. Igor' Ivanov, *Novaya Rossiiskaya Diplomatiya,* p. 169.
5. *Nezavisimaya Gazeta,* 17 March 1998, p. 6.
6. *Rossiiskaya Gazeta,* 18 December 1998, p. 3.
7. *Rossiiskaya Gazeta,* 19 December 1998, p. 1.
8. *The Guardian,* 19 December 1998, p. 2.
9. *Vremya Novostei,* 13 February 2003, p. 2.
10. *Keesings,* pp. 45, 253.
11. *Kommersant,* 5 March 2003, p. 10.
12. *Izvestiya,* 15 March 2003, p. 3.
13. Russian public opinion research center data, consulted at http://www.russiavotes.org.
14. Ibid.
15. *Vremya MN,* 21 March 2003, p. 2.
16. See http://www.russiavotes.org.

17. *Rossiiskaya Gazeta,* 21 March 2003, p. 2.

18. *Izvestiya,* 4 April 2003, p. 1.

19. Ibid., at http://www.russiavotes.org.

20. *Vremya MN,* 10 April 2003, p. 2.

21. See V. A. Kolosov, ed., *Mir Glazami Rossiyan,* pp. 116–126.

22. *Trud,* 20 August 2005, p. 1. See also Galia Golan, "Russia and the Iraq War."

7

Central and Eastern Europe: Independent Actors or Supplicant States?

Rick Fawn

In describing a divergence of policies among European states on going to war against Iraq, US defense secretary Donald Rumsfeld produced one of the most striking geopolitical terminologies of that crisis—"Old Europe" and "New Europe." French president Jacques Chirac equally generated the surliest reply of the predicament: he called the postcommunist democracies "badly brought up" and declared them to have "missed a good opportunity to keep quiet."

While the whole Euro-Atlantic region (and beyond) was united after 9/11 and agreed and generally offered practical assistance for the US-led military intervention in Afghanistan, the Iraq debacle divided these closest of allies.

The postcommunist Central and Eastern European (CEE) states[1] faced a dilemma: all have sought the most favorable relations with major Western powers and membership in both NATO and the European Union. For these countries, the ideal has been to see, and be part of, a unified Euro-Atlantic community. In that community a happy, if unspoken, division of labor was seen to exist: the EU would be the soft security provider of socioeconomic benefits, and NATO, even with a modified post–Cold War mandate, would provide a traditional hard security guarantee.

The ultimate geopolitical disaster for these states would be if a rift occurred between these two organizations. Not only would that shatter the Central and Eastern European post–Cold War iconography of Europe, but such a scenario would also render them vulnerable to precisely the polarities of interwar Europe that forced these smaller countries—with horrendous consequences—to try to choose among lesser evils and that scuttled their security.

The political landscape was further complicated by timing: while three of the CEE states had already joined NATO in 1999 (the Czech Republic, Hungary, and Poland), at the time of the Iraq War none of them had yet entered the EU and several more were only expecting to join NATO. We have the hindsight now that seven joined NATO on 4 April 2004,[2] and eight successfully entered the EU on 1 May 2004.[3] But if we consider the rhetoric provoked by the Iraq War, nothing could be taken for granted, and these EU and NATO hopefuls could have rightly felt in 2003 that their accession projects—the entirety of their post–Cold War foreign policies—were at risk. At the same time, postcommunist states see themselves as great friends of the United States and staunch believers of its centrality to European security. They were seemingly caught in the proverbial middle, between the United States (and some key West European states) and other West European powers. How did CEE governments behave during and after the Iraq crisis? What were the motivations and costs in supporting the Anglo-American position?

■ The Actions of the CEE States

Thirteen postcommunist governments gave some form of written support that deemed Iraq already to be in violation of UN Security Council (UNSC) resolutions and that gave backing to a US war. The most important expression of this support was the Letter of Eight, which was followed by the Letter of Ten. Each will be considered in turn.

The Letter of Eight, as it became known, appeared in the *Wall Street Journal Europe* on 30 January 2003. Originally titled "United We Stand: Eight European Leaders Are One with President Bush," the opinion piece was cosigned by the prime ministers of five West European states (Britain, Denmark, Italy, Portugal, and Spain), as well as by the prime ministers of Poland and Hungary and the president of the Czech Republic.[4] Slovak premier Mikuláš Dzurinda apparently also wanted to sign it, and the Latvian government endorsed it upon its publication. The letter deemed Iraq to pose a threat and that its regime was already in breach of UNSC resolutions and that UN inspectors confirmed such findings. Among its declarations was that "Resolution 1441 is Saddam Hussein's last chance to disarm using peaceful means. The opportunity to avoid greater confrontation rests with him. Sadly this week the U.N. weapons inspectors have confirmed that his long-established pattern of deception, denial and noncompliance with UN Security Council resolutions is continuing."

The leaders of ten postcommunist countries—Albania, Bulgaria, Croatia, Estonia, Latvia, Lithuania, Macedonia, Romania, Slovakia, and Slovenia—then signed a letter, which became known as the Vilnius Letter. This letter appeared the day after US secretary of state Colin Powell made his presentation to the UN Security Council intended to show Iraq's violations of resolutions. The ten signatories stated in the letter that Powell had given compelling evidence at the UNSC of Iraq's intentions and that they deemed Iraq to be in violation of Resolution 1441. If Iraq did not comply, the countries declared themselves "prepared to contribute to an international coalition to enforce its provisions and the disarmament of Iraq."

These statements gave significant moral and political support to Washington. Among CEE states, Bulgaria featured politically important by holding a rotating seat on the UN Security Council in 2003 as the issue of a second resolution on Iraq came to the fore. Bulgaria became one of the Council members to side clearly with the United States and Britain. (By contrast, Slovakia was apparently relieved to end its rotating membership in the beginning of 2003, with an official saying, "Thank God we got off the Security Council in time.")[5]

Some of the CEE governments also lent direct military assistance to the war effort. The United States, Britain, and Australia engaged in direct military action, but Poland also gave direct military assistance to the operation, including the assignment of several dozen special forces for use in the war itself. The Czech Republic, having a specialization in antichemical warfare, dispatched a nuclear, chemical, and biological unit to Kuwait (as it did in 1990–1991), though the government said it would not enter Iraq without a UN resolution, and ultimately it was not deployed in the invasion of Iraq. Hungary lent its Taszar airbase to the United States before the war for the training of some 4,000 Iraqi opposition soldiers.[6] Many more CEE governments assisted the war by giving use of their airspace or bases to US forces.

In addition, Serbia, which was not a signatory of either letter, provided Washington with information before the war on the sites and plans of Yugoslav-made bunkers in Iraq. When Zoran Živković, prime minister of Serbia and Montenegro, was in Washington in August 2003, he offered 1,000 troops for Iraq. These measures have been seen as ways by Belgrade to gain favor with Washington, possibly with particular regard for the future of Kosovo, and more generally to repair relations.[7] Indeed, in the Serbian case not only was the country seeking to recover from the pariah status given it by the West due to the actions of the Milosevic regime, but also the successor government was accused of supplying arms to Iraq.[8] Among the charges was that Serb companies were upgrading Iraqi MiG fighters and supplying solid fuel propellant to be used in Iraqi missiles. Serb prime minister Vojislav Koštunica claimed ignorance and established a commission to investigate those and all Yugoslav foreign arms sales. Western officials eventually accepted that the sales were made by "rogue" dealers connected to the Milosevic regime.[9]

Ukraine also deserves particular mention. It provided some 1,500 peacekeepers for the postwar administration of Iraq. This measure, like that of Serbia's, may have been an effort to improve the country's standing with

Washington. Relations between Ukraine and the United States (as well as Britain, and other Western powers) had become so strained that Ukrainian president Leonid Kuchma was unwanted at the Prague NATO summit. This was in part because of Ukraine's questionable democratization, marred by such acts as the disappearance of journalists, and also by the government's apparent contravention of UN resolutions against Iraq by supplying Saddam's regime with a proscribed radar system. The Czech government, host of the NATO summit, even sought to enact the alliance's objection to Kuchma by intending to deny him a visa to the country, an unusual diplomatic slight that ultimately went unimposed. When Kuchma insisted on coming, the seating arrangement of countries—planned in alphabetical order in English—was changed to French so that the US and UK delegations would not be seated next to him. In these circumstances, therefore, the Ukrainian dispatch of troops can be (and was) interpreted as an overture to the West. This motivation, however, does not fit the pattern of other CEE states whose trajectory of integration—the disruption of the Iraq crisis notwithstanding—seemed complete.

The CEE governments showed substantial support for the postconflict situation, giving peacekeepers. Most significant, Poland accepted an invitation from Washington to become a coadministrator of postwar Iraq, taking charge of a south-central section of the country and command of troops from a dozen other countries. Poland "temporarily" relinquished this command as tensions flared to open fighting around Fallujah. To be sure, in such cases, CEE governments often ensured that their troops were officially referred to only as "peacekeepers" and not soldiers, in order to draw a distinction between activities in the war and thereafter. In sum, the CEE states can be seen—in words and deeds, but with small qualifications—as staunch supporters of the US position.

As ever in the study of foreign policy, a distinction between the actions of the state and the views of society needs to be made. Throughout many of the countries that adopted policies supportive of the United States, public opinion was often radically different. It is important, therefore, to note that the majority of CEE populations did not support the war.[10] The positions taken by these governments—and all thirteen of the signatories are functioning democracies—should seem all the more significant.

Why did CEE leaders lend this support? Was it pragmatism, a calculated move to secure benefits from Washington? Or did the CEE leaders act out of obligation to it? Did postcommunist leaders believe, based on their experiences of communist rule, that it is morally defensible, even necessary to apply military force against a malevolent dictator? Or did the CEE leaders, partly out of their genuine trust in the United States, believe in a credible and imminent threat from Iraq? These explanations need not be mutually exclusive.

◾ Why the CEE Governments Acted as They Did

Pragmatism

Did the CEE states support the US position only or primarily to serve their own interests? While "small" in gross domestic product or armed forces, these countries added substantially to the numerical list of those supporting the US stand. In addition, some CEE political leaders carry a particular aura of morality from their communist-era dissent, a legacy that the US government appreciated and mobilized. Indeed, the region was portrayed as providing evidence of the costs of not confronting authoritarian regimes. For example, upon the entry of seven CEE states to NATO, George W. Bush said their history of communist rule meant that they had "a fresh memory of tyranny. And they know the consequences of complacency in the face of danger."[11] Certainly media analysts saw the Bush administration as reading this history to account for "their strong support for the U.S. position on Iraq,"[12] and their induction into NATO in April 2004 was described as "bolstering" the US position on Iraq.[13]

CEE government support of the US position on Iraq lent the comfort not only of numbers but also of an understanding of American values generally and for waging the Iraq War in particular. *New York Times* writer Thomas L. Friedman said he found in the region "the cure to anti-Americanism." He observed, "After two years of traveling almost exclusively to Western Europe and the Middle East, Poland feels like a geopolitical spa. I visited here for just three days and got two years of anti-American bruises massaged."[14]

And the CEE states could be seen to gain some favor from the Bush administration for the support they lent. Bush was reported as increasing the "White House effort to reward his allies" in the war while ignoring others. Hence the foreign ministers of Bulgaria, Estonia, Latvia, Lithuania, Romania, Slovakia, and Slovenia were granted private audiences with him in the Roosevelt Room of the White House in May 2003.[15] Similarly, Senator George Voinovich of Ohio said of the seven NATO applicants: "They've acted as de facto allies. In fact they've acted as better allies than some of the members that are currently in NATO."[16]

The idea that mutual gains were sought between CEE and the US governments was suggested in the region. When, for example, the Estonian parliament voted overwhelmingly in 2004 to extend its presence in Iraq for another year, Trivimi Velliste, deputy of the opposition party Pro Patria Union, explained: "If we are trustworthy allies today, then tomorrow and the day after tomorrow our allies will also be loyal to us."[17] Even those who adopted a moralistic line in favor of war against Iraq, like former Polish dissident and newspaper editor Adam Michnik, also advocated the need to show allegiance: "Poland is an ally of the United States. It was our duty to show that we are a reliable, loyal, predictable ally. America needed our help, and we had to give it."[18] Such thinking was already being operationalized in early 2003, during which Poland's ambassador to Washington declared that his country was emerging "as an excellent ally of the United States."[19] Those who took a moral stand in opposing the war also demonstrated pragmatic considerations. Another leading former Polish dissident, Jacek Kuroń, condemned the war as "making enemies for ourselves."[20]

Apart from generating untold controversy, Rumsfeld, in describing "Old" and "New" Europe, was acknowledging the geopolitical arrival of the CEE states. That statement, in which he defined "Old Europe" as Germany and France, received universal attention. His next sentence, however, received little: "If you look at the entire NATO Europe today, the center of gravity is shifting to the east and there are a lot of new members." The geopolitics of this—the relative strategic and economic weight of these countries—can be debated, although they certainly added a considerable number of new voices to official European security debates. Regardless of the criteria used to measure this putative new "center of gravity," Rumsfeld's comment was a significant nod to their escape from relative foreign policy invisibility and their emergence instead on the Euro-Atlantic stage. If NATO is meant to act on the basis of sovereign egalitarianism—that each state has an equal say regardless of size—then a further ten states out of twenty-five taking a view discordant with some of the others is to be expected.

Rumsfeld's comment was followed by the suggestion of military and strategic benefits to the postcommunist states. Using the same metaphor, Rumsfeld declared in early February 2003: "We are reviewing our bases . . . the centre of gravity is shifting in the [NATO] alliance. The interest and the enthusiasm that the countries that had lived under repressive regimes previously [have for NATO] is a good thing for NATO."[21] In this context, the CEE leaders were perceived by US officials as generating opportunities for both parties. Romania was not only a "paradise" of pro-US sentiment, but also a country for which Iraq presented an opportunity to cooperate with the United States. Its reward could be the stationing of US troops.[22]

Talk continued of a shift, possibly permanently, of US military facilities from Germany to some postcommunist states. Doubtless some skeptics of the United States in Western Europe would applaud the departure of existing US military forces. Central European officials, however, responded to this talk positively. A Czech official acknowledged the CEE states to be in "a very difficult situation." He said, however, that if the situation "leads to the Americans withdrawing from Germany, we and the Poles will welcome them. We need NATO."[23]

If they sought such, did Central and Eastern European governments gain practical benefits from their pro-US stance? Even for those critical of

Poland's presence in Iraq, "it was an unquestionable honor for Poland—so recently a Soviet satellite state—to be asked by the Americans to assist after the war."[24] In practical terms, Poland's status in the region was (conceivably) elevated when the Riga Initiative was launched during Polish president Aleksander Kwaśniewski's July 2002 visit to Washington, which would make Poland the regional leader. Indeed, by one reckoning Polish leaders decided to augment Poland's standing *before* the Iraq War and intended that support of the United States during the war could make Warsaw "the chief U.S. ally in Europe."[25] Such thinking may have been prevalent in Warsaw; such analytical reasoning, however, needs to contend with the continuing importance to Washington of other allies, particularly the United Kingdom.

It can also be reasoned that the CEE states knew better than to expect direct payoffs from the United States. Postcommunist governments officially supported NATO's war against Serbia over Kosovo in 1999 because they deemed the actions of the Milosevic regime to be in contradiction of human rights. Postcommunist support for NATO during that conflict can be read as a case where postcommunist states backed the war—against the will of the majority of their populations—to gain NATO entry. True, several of these states gained that by 2004. But considering the demands made by CEE governments and the promises offered by Western leaders at the time, a five-year delay in membership did not fulfill regional expectations. For Albania and Macedonia, profoundly affected by the war and thoroughly supportive of the United States and NATO during the 1999 crisis, NATO membership did not materialize at all.[26] Lending support in 2003 over Iraq for the sake and the expectation of a tangible strategic gain seems unlikely behavior. Mere pragmatism as an explanation for CEE official behavior seems questionable.

Nevertheless, postcommunist support for Washington in the Iraq War can be construed as a move to improve the prospects of entry into NATO for those not members at the time of the war. Entry into the alliance, of course, requires the approval of all existing members, so impressing only one member, no matter how seemingly influential, does not in itself secure membership. That said, on 2 May 2004, Powell visited Albania to thank the country for its support in the war. With the foreign ministers of Albania, Croatia, and Macedonia, Powell also signed the US-Adriatic Partnership Charter, which is meant to hasten their admission into the alliance.[27] It may be that postcommunist countries outside the immediate circle of those expecting EU and NATO accession—such as these three—lent their support also to accelerate at least NATO membership. But if that was a calculation, surely they would jeopardize their relations with the EU. For countries further from the EU/NATO fold, those unlikely to have even the prospect of accession negotiations, or those that have had strained relations with the United States, support for US action in Iraq might have served to gain better relations. Supporting the United States during and after the war may have been a means for previously ostracized Serbia and Ukraine to attempt rapprochement.

Even CEE governments on close terms with the United States could not secure all they sought, further suggesting limitations (or miscalculations) to a pragmatic motivation behind policy. For example, parts of the Polish political establishment advocated that the requirement of visas for Poles to visit the United States be lifted as an express repayment for their support of the war. Tadeusz Iwinski, a senior adviser to Polish premier Leszek Miller, said this measure would have a "psychological and symbolic importance." He added, "We are America's true friends and we have shown it many times, and there should be some sort of concrete steps from the US to back that up."[28] But as some Czech members of parliament experienced when they similarly sought lifting of visas to the United States in exchange for Czech military contributions to Afghanistan, the position of the US government was that visa regimes are unrelated to other policies.[29] It may be true that visa regimes are beyond such deals (though they can be lifted without prior public notice and often as just such a gesture of "goodwill").

And where other public disagreements occurred in the region with Washington, US diplomats attempted, apparently successfully, to smooth differences. Thus, in the Czech Republic, US ambassador Craig Stapleton was reported to have "clashed" with President Václav Klaus over support for the war. Suggestions followed in the Czech media that, as a result, Klaus would not be granted an invitation to the White House.[30] The newly appointed US ambassador to the Czech Republic, William Cabaniss, however, prioritized improving relations over the issue, and especially Czech prospects of contracts in reconstructed Iraq. Immediately upon installation as ambassador, he traveled with Czech foreign minister Cyril Svoboda to Iraq with the express purpose, in his words, to "jump right in to try to help these Czech businesses do business with the American side of the Provisional Authority."[31] The practical gains to the CEE countries of backing the US position on Iraq seem very small. Indeed, to raise such an argument at all requires the question of potential costs, and these are seen in the region's relations with the European Union.

As lauding as it was of postcommunist states' support for the United States, even the generally prowar *New York Times* warned, "Eastern European leaders must also take into account that deepening military friendship with the United States could jeopardize economic integration into Europe."[32] In the lead-up to EU accession, even Poland, considered instinctively Atlanticist, was "anxious not to alienate the EU."[33]

The reaction to the Letter of Eight by the president of the Greek parliament, Apostolos Kaklamanis, now seems mild: he declared the impending war was "undermining the course of Europe toward integration."[34] For countries hoping to enter the EU, that could sound ominous. But if they had any doubts, Chirac declared their position to be "not really responsible behaviour" and added that the CEE countries "missed a good opportunity to keep quiet." He went even further, warning the CEE states that their stand could be "dangerous" because their accession into the EU had yet to be ratified. Asked why he seemed to treat existing EU member states differently, Chirac frankly replied: "When you are in the family . . . you have more rights than when you are asking to join and knocking on the door." He gave Bulgaria and Romania his most fierce attack: "If they wanted to diminish their chances of joining Europe, they could not have found a better way." The varying intensity of Chirac's remarks to states corresponds to concentric circles of their place in the EU accession process: existing member states of the EU in the Anglo-American coalition received no criticism; those about to join the EU received some; and Bulgaria and Romania, furthest outside the EU due to their accession negotiations being unfinished, were thus the most vulnerable and also the most castigated.

CEE leaders, unsurprisingly, reacted negatively (but generally politely) to Chirac's chastisement. Romanian president Ion Iliescu stated, for example, that Chirac's comments were "inappropriate" and that he should regret them as outside "the spirit of friendship and democratic relationships." A Czech minister stated that Chirac was bullying these states while a Polish deputy foreign minister reasserted his country's right to make decisions and called on Chirac to respect that.[35]

Despite Chirac's comments, the practical fallout seemed limited, though the postcommunist governments could not have known that at the time. On a smaller level, ten postcommunist countries were excluded from the EU dinner in February 2003. On a more significant level, a bloc of EU countries began meeting separately on military matters. But this cannot be seen as a slight against (only) the Central and Eastern European governments, as major existing member states such as Britain, Italy, and Spain were also excluded. The CEE governments could not predict the EU reaction, which now seems negligible; with so much at stake, why did the CEE governments adopt a position that risked derailing hard-won relations with the EU? Did they, perhaps, face insurmountable obligations to the United States?

Obligations to the United States?

Polish president Kwaśniewski's comment "if it is George Bush's view, then it is mine" suggests knee-jerk obligation to follow US policy. Suggestions have been made that "old habits of obedience die hard," making comparison to the Soviet period, when East European divergence from Soviet foreign policy risked military reprisal.[36]

But such a view risks downplaying how the CEE governments genuinely see the United States as the only "clean" power in Europe, one that has not trampled on their history and security and instead is even seen as a liberator. It also cannot explain the tremendous costs postcommunist states faced. The timing of the Iraq War overlapped with the final stages of NATO accession for several CEE states and EU accession for all of them. This can be read in two broad ways. First, CEE governments were overly sensitive to US needs and, for the sake of NATO entry and generally pleasing the hegemon, they gave support. But if this type of analysis is at all relevant, then surely CEE concern about jeopardizing EU membership must also have been fundamental to their foreign policy calculations.

Second, if the CEE governments were thinking in terms of trade-offs, then they must have thought that there were key supporters of either position in both NATO and the EU (i.e., the British, Spanish, and Italian governments for war; the German and French against it). They could be rewarded or punished in roughly equal measure.[37] If this thinking is relevant, then it suggests the CEE governments generally adopted the position they did because they could and wanted to, rather than their policies being a knee-jerk response to US policy. Some CEE leaders may be seen to have tried a Machiavellian balancing act. As mentioned, the letters of support referred to several European and international intergovernmental organizations. Romania and Bulgaria both signed the Letter of Ten, but also the more moderate conclusions of the European Council asking that force be a last resort and asking for UN inspectors to be allowed more time. The behavior of these two states may well be explained by their particular vulnerability. They were not included in the 2002 EU announcement of accession for 2004. And they were subsequently treated to the harshest of Chirac's collection of verbal abuses. Chirac himself differentiated this treatment by stating that those in the family were to be treated more leniently. It may be, therefore, that the postcommunist countries that most attempted to appeal to all sides were those also most vulnerable in the enlargement process by being further outside of it: Bulgaria and Romania (EU candidates for the second wave of postcommunist enlargement); Albania, Croatia, and Macedonia (as EU accession hopefuls). The French reaction to them underscores that vulnerability.

Though the Letter of Eight was often seen as a British-Spanish initiative, it can also be criticized for having been written by US activist Bruce Jackson. And while the Vilnius Letter was composed by those countries' ambassadors to Washington, Jackson was apparently involved in it as well. Not holding any official US position, Jackson contacted or traveled to some of the leaders who signed it. The tongue-in-cheek "Observer" column in the *Financial Times* pointed out that the letter was not inspired by the postcommunist countries themselves but by Jackson, who, the column explained, was "officially known as president, Project on Transitional Democracies, and president, US Committee on NATO." The satirical column added that Jackson is "close to Lockheed, the US aerospace company, and is a staunch supporter of NATO enlargement."[38] A decidedly more sober and lengthy article in the same publication referred to Jackson as "a former military intelligence officer and ex-Wall Street banker" who "is a sort of freelance US envoy to the former Soviet bloc."[39] Regardless of its origins and contending interpretations of its content, the Letter of Eight was taken both in Europe and the United States as positioning several European leaders with the US government's stand.

In perhaps one case did a CEE state feel an obligation to sign a letter of support. Dimitry Rupel, Slovenia's foreign minister, was unhappy with the Vilnius Letter and said his country was being pulled between the two organizations. By his own admission, however, he was alone in questioning the content of the letter: "I did not want to sign the letter. I wanted some changes. But what could I do. One lone voice?"[40] At the same time, Rupel's sentiments had no palpable negative effect on Slovenia's admission in NATO, entering the alliance in April 2004 with seven other postcommunist states. And when Bush thanked CEE states for their support in the Iraq War on the occasion of the US Senate approving NATO enlargement, he made (unsurprisingly) no mention of Slovenia's lack of backing.

What can be deduced is that CEE governments in fact sought the best position possible. They seemed heavily motivated by fear of Saddam's regime and by their communist-era appreciation of the need to use credible threats or even force against tyrants. That said, their political statements of support to the United States—the Letter of Eight and the Vilnius Letter—were also crafted to *foster* Euro-Atlantic harmony. This surely came from the CEE's genuine belief in the value of a coherent "West," while also being motivated by sense of threat.

Consider the two letters in turn. The Letter of Eight can be read as saying very little, by reiterating a position that had already been agreed in international consensus, including that Saddam had to comply with Resolution 1441. Other than Saddam's general breaches of UNSC resolutions, which for some was sufficient, the letter did not explain what exactly would constitute the grounds for war. The letter's intention was to reinforce Euro-Atlantic relations and not to allow the Iraq issue to divide countries united by their history and political culture. The letter also therefore could be seen to be speaking to both the United States and "Europe," by making reference not only to the UN and to the NATO Prague summit, but also to the Copenhagen European Council. Indeed, the letter could have been in breach of the Amsterdam Treaty, which pledges signatories not to disrupt common foreign and security policy. Regardless, the leaders of member states that signed did not consult, as commentators have pointed out, with any of the other member states, or Javier Solana of Greece, which held the

EU presidency at the time.[41] Indeed, Greek diplomats were "appalled" that they were not consulted or even advised in advance of the letter's publication. President of the Greek parliament Apostolos Kaklamanis said, "The ideal of the European Union has suffered a severe blow."[42]

While some European powers felt the CEE states acted "unilaterally" by siding with the United States, it is relevant to note postcommunist reservations about how the French and German leaders delivered their own positions. Jacques Chirac and Gerhard Schröder issued their foreign policy statements on the looming war without multilateral consultations within the EU. Aspiring EU members were startled by the Franco-German approach to the war. Alexandr Vondra, a former communist-era dissident, who became a senior Czech foreign policy official, explained: "They warned nobody in advance" and consequently "We were all taken by surprise."[43]

The Vilnius Letter was arguably also ambiguous. While it stated that Iraq was already in breach of UN Security Council Resolution 1441, it pledged the commitment of the signatories in the event of Iraqi noncompliance. The exact terms of what Iraq had and had not done were not specified, and the entirety of the debate about enacting war seemed to hinge on this interpretation.

To the extent that CEE governments might be accused of having it both ways, this demonstrates freedom in foreign policy decisionmaking. This seems hardly a fair accusation in the tough arena of world politics; it is simply good diplomacy.

Apart from risking reprisal from France or the EU as a whole for their stand, the postcommunist states had opportunities to withdraw their material support for the United States if they had doubts about the position they had adopted. This could have been when the situation in Iraq turned increasingly grim with growing unrest and specific attacks on coalition forces. Indeed, CEE governments could reasonably have been expected to waver in the face of increased violence in Iraq. By early April 2004, five Bulgarian soldiers, three Ukraine soldiers, two Polish soldiers, and one Estonian soldier had been killed.[44] In addition, these countries perceived the threat of terrorism at home—heightened by the Madrid attacks of March 2004, which took nearly 191 lives—which would have served as an excuse to change policy, just as it seemingly swung the Spanish population against the incumbent Aznar government. Poland, for example, feared a terrorist attack in Warsaw—an apparent plot was discovered, targeting the city's synagogue, the Czech embassy, and the airport. Reports ran that Poles were "concerned that they might become a target because of the presence of their troops in Iraq."[45]

Instead, CEE forces in Iraq and their governments at home held up against the strain. Some Hungarian soldiers, for example, asked to return home after 10 of their 190-soldier unit were injured in an attack on 18

February 2004.[46] Attacks on CEE forces in Iraq and the threat of terrorism at home could have given these governments the excuse to withdraw, as the Philippines had done.

But when, for example, several Hungarian soldiers were injured in early April 2004, Prime Minister Peter Medgyessy said in France that his soldiers would remain, because withdrawing them would "mean terrorism has won."[47] At the same time, the Estonian parliament voted fifty-one to three to renew its military presence until 2005. Similarly, Ukraine reiterated its commitment to keeping its 1,650 troops in Iraq.

Osama bin Laden's offer of a "truce" with European states prompted the Dutch and Poles to state jointly on 15 April 2004 that their troops were present for peacekeeping in Iraq and not for war. Polish defense minister Jerzy Szmajdzinski said the stabilization force was not offensive and fired only in self-defense.[48] The same day, Romania's Supreme Council of National Defense resolved that its forces would remain in the coalition in Iraq, although it requested the Ministry of Defense to enhance their security.[49]

CEE governments could have been encouraged by Washington to adopt a pro-US position. Regardless, they did so at some cost. In addition, an argument of acting out of obligation to the United States, not least because of structural constraints imposed by the international system, seems to discount major considerations in postcommunist foreign policy thinking.

Morality and Resistance Against Authoritarianism

In the case of Iraq, some CEE leaders felt that a moral case for war existed. Having recently emerged from communist rule, many CEE leaders believed (rightly) that they understood authoritarianism. The view of how to deal with existing abusive regimes was, of course, hardly universal within and across CEE societies. But some public and official rhetoric clearly called for military action—within certain contexts—against Saddam's regime, and these leaders invoked their experience of communism in doing so. The letter of the Vilnius Ten made this view clear: "Our countries understand the dangers posed by tyranny and the special responsibility of democracies to defend our shared values. The trans-Atlantic community must stand together to face the threat posed by the nexus of terrorism and dictators with weapons of mass destruction."

Even two years after the war, and with no evidence of existing Iraqi weapons of mass destruction (WMDs), the Albanian ambassador to Washington wrote: "Unlike people in other countries in Europe and elsewhere, the Albanian people have not forgotten what it is like to live under tyranny and repression. The Albanians for more than 40 years were held in thrall by the repressive forces of the communists, living like prisoners without rights in their own country. It was to the United States that freedom-loving Albanians looked for inspiration during those dark years, and the Americans have not let us down."[50] Similarly, former Estonian prime minister Mart Laar wrote that because of the experience of both fascism and communism, "the Central and Eastern Europe approach to foreign policy is today based more on values than that of Western Europe. They are more receptive to 'moral arguments' on Iraq and a host of other issues and less understanding of 'European realpolitik.'"[51] Martin Šimečka, son of a leading communist-era Slovak dissident, wrote that the United States was a "dissident power" that supported democracy, even alone. And former Czech dissident Václav Havel—a Nobel Peace Prize nominee and recipient of numerous international awards for, inter alia, his moral character—signed the Letter of Eight.

Former dissidents such as Havel do not use words frivolously. They suffered personally under communism and believe in the power and integrity of language and of truth. Detractors of someone like Havel might argue that having been "moral" before does not automatically make every stand moral thereafter. Indeed, other former dissidents opposed the war. Leading Solidarity activist Jacek Kuroń, for example, condemned both the morality and pragmatism of the war, calling it "a shameful adventure" that was "making enemies for ourselves."[52] Indeed, this is another reminder that communist-era dissidence was hardly homogeneous, but often composed of intellectuals and industrial laborers, the religious and the agnostic, the divergent communist and the anticommunist. So in the Czech Republic, communist dissident Petr Uhl publicly protested against the war. Again, President Václav Klaus was apparently so angered with US actions that he refused to meet with the US ambassador and looked likely to scuttle a planned meeting with Bush in Washington.

One can also attack—as has been implied—the circumstances in which respected dissidents signed the Letter of Eight. As journalists showed, Havel signed the letter on the hop—while attending the theater in Bratislava. There is also some suggestion that, in signing the letter at the very close of his presidency, he was forsaking responsibility or even bequeathing an awkward diplomatic legacy to his successor and rival, Klaus. These accounts do not document closely, however, that Havel signed the letter on the advice of his dissident-era friend and long-standing and trusted foreign policy adviser Alexandr Vondra. More importantly, Havel and other Central European former dissidents had discussed the Iraq crisis and had a common position.[53] Their positions can be criticized on many counts; frivolity is not one of them. They therefore presumably had important motivations for their standpoint. This may have been that they expected a substantial gain from the United States that outweighed the enormous importance (and social and financial benefits) of EU membership, although this morality cannot and should not be reduced to crass pursuit of "national

interests." It may also have been that they genuinely believed a threat existed and that their moral outlook motivated them to resist the apparent noncompliance of the Iraqi regime to international demands of disarmament.

A Final Reason for Supporting
the US Position: Threat Perceptions

Running through the above discussion is a postcommunist belief in the
United States and a willingness to show solidarity generally, particularly
against a leader whose domestic tyranny was compared to communism. Still
another reason for the CEE stand was that these governments—like many
elsewhere—believed that Saddam's regime posed a serious military threat,
including, especially, the use of weapons of mass destruction. If Iraq was
taken to be a threat, the dissident thinking, for example, ran that one had to
stand up not only to authoritarian, murderous dictators as a principle, but
also, especially, when their malevolence went potentially beyond their borders. Thus much of the language of the CEE governments and of notable
intellectuals was to resist this behavior. Polish president Kwaśniewski's
comments of March 2004 become telling. Speaking in Polish to a Warsaw
audience of predominantly French journalists (who could be taken to be
antiwar and/or anti-US), he said what was reported as: "Naturally, I feel
uncomfortable due to the fact that we were misled with the information on
weapons of mass destruction." The phrase was then translated again from
French to English. The president was then being quoted even as having said
that he had "been taken for a ride."[54] The implication of this wording, of
course, was that he was taken for a ride by Washington.

The Polish presidential press agency sought to clarify the matter: subsequent news releases deliberately omitted the word "misled." He also thereafter said that Britain, Spain, and the United States were themselves "misled" by Saddam's intentions, implying that Saddam had deliberately
produced deceptive signals on his WMDs. In addition to the verbal amplifi-
cation, Kwaśniewski made policy reiterations, including at that time that
Polish troops would remain in Iraq,[55] and denouncing the Spanish withdrawal as a victory for terrorists. He also left no doubt regarding his view of
the outcome, insisting, "I personally think that Iraq today without Saddam
Hussein is a truly better Iraq than with Saddam Hussein."[56] It may be that
Kwaśniewski felt—or was—pressured to make these amendments. In any
case, Polish policy ultimately stood alongside US policy.

■ Conclusion

Rumsfeld's rhetorical empowerment of the "New" Europe was welcomed
by many in the postcommunist world. As former Estonian prime minister

Mart Laar declared: "The new Europe has arrived with its own aspirations, ideas and hopes."[57] For the most part, though, it has divided. Rumsfeld's categorization dividing Europe into old and new was "not only intellectually false, but also politically offensive," as the "New" Europe was a result of Franco-German efforts. Witness one French commentator: "To assume, as some Americans do, that a country's degree of modernity is determined by its standing with Washington is misguided and narcissistic in the extreme."[58] If not creating them, Washington increased divisions within the Euro-Atlantic area that the CEE states would not have wanted. And the CEE stand with Washington reaffirmed for those in "Old" Europe already so predisposed that the postcommunist states are US Trojan horses inside the European Union. If anything, the CEE position over Iraq will ensure that common and foreign security policy of the twenty-five (or more) EU states will only occur on bland issues. This perhaps unintended influence already shows the power of the CEE states in Europe. They are also not losers in this process—CEE governments always favored NATO over "Europe" to provide meaningful hard security. And even in supporting the United States on Iraq, all postcommunist states slated to join the EU in 2004 did so, with others remaining on the same trajectory as before.

If the CEE states have regrets, it is likely for the same reason that supporters elsewhere may have faced: that the "evidence" made in favor of war has increasingly unraveled into indefensibility. Otherwise, CEE foreign policies do not seem to have suffered permanently. They may also be taken more seriously—if begrudgingly—by European powers skeptical of US policies.

■ Notes

1. Central and Eastern Europe here excludes post-Soviet republics except for the Baltic republics of Estonia, Latvia, and Lithuania, and also includes Bulgaria, the Czech Republic, Hungary, Poland, Romania, Slovakia, and Slovenia. The chapter will also make some reference to other Yugoslav successor states, to Albania, and to Ukraine. Some post-Soviet states also contributed to the stabilization efforts in Iraq, such as Georgia, but the emphasis remains on the aforementioned postcommunist states.

2. Bulgaria, Estonia, Latvia, Lithuania, Romania, Slovenia, and Slovakia.

3. The Czech Republic, Estonia, Hungary, Latvia, Lithuania, Poland, Slovenia, and Slovakia. Bulgaria and Romania, while admitted to NATO in 2004, were not admitted to the EU but are expected to enter it by 2007.

4. The letter was signed by Spanish prime minister José María Aznar, Portugese prime minister Jose-Manuel Durão Barroso, Italian prime minister Silvio Berlusconi, British prime minister Tony Blair, Czech president Václav Havel, Hungarian prime minister Peter Medgyessy, Polish prime minister Leszek Miller, and Danish prime minister Anders Fogh Rasmussen.

5. Cited in Philip H. Gordon and Jeremy Shapiro, *Allies at War,* p. 151.

6. "Taszar: US Army Is Believed to Be Training up to 4,000 Iraqi Opposition Troops at This Hungarian Air Base," *The Middle East,* February 2003, p. 23.

7. See "Cuddling up to the Americans," *The Economist,* 23 August 2003, p. 31. In response to the Serb offer of soldiers, Kosovan president Ibrahim Rugova said that, while not having an armed forces, he was "happy to offer a police force for Iraq and Afghanistan." See Julia Geshakova, "Belgrade Offers Washington Soldiers for Afghanistan," http://www.rferl.org/features/2003/10/08102003160259.asp.

8. This was according to a report by the International Crisis Group, itself apparently based on US government reports. See Jimmy Burns, "Belgrade Anger at Report of Link to Baghdad," *Financial Times,* 26 November 2002, p. 9.

9. Richard Beeston, "Koštunica Promises to Stamp Out Illegal Arms Trade," *The Times,* 7 November 2002, p. 21.

10. See, for example, Eugen Tomiuc, "Do Citizens of Vilnius 10 Support Action Against Iraq, or Only Their Governments?" *Radio Free Europe/Radio Liberty,* 7 February 2003, http://www.rferl.org/features/2003/02/07022003192525.asp.

11. "President Bush Meets with Central European Foreign Ministers: Remarks by the President with Central European Foreign Ministers—the East Room," Office of the Press Secretary, 8 May 2003, http://www.whitehouse.gov/news/releases/2003/05/20030508-8.html.

12. Brian Knowlton, "U.S. Approves Adding 7 Countries to NATO; Alliance Made 'Stronger,' Bush Declares," *International Herald Tribune,* 9 May 2003, p. 3.

13. Christopher Marquis, "7 Nations Join NATO, Bolstering U.S. on Iraq," *New York Times,* 3 April 2004, p. A3.

14. Thomas L. Friedman, "Where U.S. Translates As Freedom," *New York Times,* 28 December 2003. Other such comments were to be found in the US press. Marine captain Kurt Sanger called Romania a "paradise" where people really like Americans; quoted in Ian Fisher, "U.S. Eyes a Willing Romania As a New Comrade in Arms," *New York Times,* 16 July 2003.

15. David E. Sanger and James Dao, "Bush Hails New Friends and Omits Some Old Ones," *New York Times,* 9 May 2003, p. 16.

16. Quoted in Knowlton, "U.S. Approves Adding 7 Countries to NATO," p. 3.

17. Quoted in *RFE/RL Newsline* 8, no. 70 (15 April 2004).

18. Thomas Cushman, "Anti-Totalitarianism as a Vocation: An Interview with Adam Michnik," *Dissent* magazine, Spring 2004.

19. Quoted in "Polish Pride, American Profits," *New York Times,* 12 January 2003.

20. Quoted in "Haniebna Awantura," *Życie Warzawy,* 4 September 2003, cited in Ray Taras, "Poland's Diplomatic Misadventure in Iraq," p. 4.

21. Quoted in Ian Traynor, "Washington to Cut Bases in Germany As Its Forces Head East," *The Guardian,* 11 February 2003.

22. Fisher, "U.S. Eyes a Willing Romania," p. 1.

23. Quoted in Traynor, "Washington to Cut Bases in Germany," 11 February 2003.

24. Taras, "Poland's Diplomatic Misadventure in Iraq," p. 4.

25. Ibid., p. 5.

26. Some of the reactions of six postcommunist countries to the Kosovan conflict are considered in Rick Fawn, "Perceptions in Central and South-Eastern Europe," pp. 135–155.

27. See Barry James, "U.S. and Albanians Sign Accord on Court; Powell Thanks Tirana for Aid on Iraq," *International Herald Tribune,* 3 May 2003, p. 4.

28. Edward Alden and Jan Cienski, "Poland Angered at US Failure to Waive Visas," *Financial Times,* 28 January 2004, p. 11.

29. The Czech foreign ministry said the proposal was unrealistic and the US embassy countered that visa regimes were particular rules and recommended that Czech officials inform the public. See "Èeska Diplomacie Odmitá Tlak na USA," *Lidové Noviny,* 26 January 2004.

30. *Mladá Fronta Dnes* reported on 31 July 2003 that Bush told former president Havel that he was not interested in meeting Klaus during a planned visit to Washington.

31. "William Cabaniss: The New United States Ambassador to Prague," Radio Prague, 3 February 2004.

32. Fisher, "U.S. Eyes a Willing Romania."

33. Marcin Zaborowski and Kerry Longhurst, "America's Protégé in the East?" p. 1018.

34. Quoted in Barry James, "Iraq Letter Splits Europe: Action 'Appalls' Greece," *International Herald Tribune,* 1 February 2003.

35. Comments are summarized in "'New Europe' Backs EU in Iraq," *BBC News,* https://newsvote.bbc.co.uk.

36. See Jacques Rupnik, "Why Are the Eastern Europeans Pro-American?" p. 69.

37. One may contend that the CEE governments arguably may have felt that their interests in the EU were protected, or at least not jeopardized, because some major EU states adopted the same policies on war (such as Britain, Spain, and Italy). If we are speculating about trade-offs, however, then presumably the postcommunist states would have calculated that *any* single member of the EU could cause difficulties for postcommunist accession.

38. "Lock Horns," *Financial Times,* "Observer" column, 10 February 2003, p. 12.

39. Gerard Baker, Tony Barber, Judy Dempsey, James Harding, Joshua Levitt, and Quentin Peel, "The Rift Turns Nasty: The Plot That Split Old and New Europe Asunder," *Financial Times,* 28 May 2003, p. 19.

40. Quoted in "Lock Horns," p. 12.

41. See Quentin Peel, "The President Who Speaks for Europe," *Financial Times,* 4 February 2003, p. 23.

42. Quoted in James, "Iraq Letter Splits Europe."

43. Martin Woollacott, "The Split Loyalties That Now Define the New Europeans: Disputes Between the Larger Members over America Pain the East," *The Guardian,* 19 September 2003.

44. *The Times,* 8 April 2004, p. 15.

45. Ian Fisher, "3 Held Amid Heightened Fears," *New York Times,* 23 March 2004, p. 14.

46. *RFE/RL Newsline* 8, no. 38, pt. 2 (27 February 2004).

47. *RFE/RL Newsline* 8, no. 67 (9 April 2004).

48. *RFE/RL Newsline* 8, no. 71, pt. 2 (16 April 2004).

49. Ibid.

50. Fatos Tarifa, "Albania Stands with U.S. in Iraq," *Washington Times,* 27 March 2005.

51. Mart Laar, "The New Europe Has Arrived, and It Is Time to Change the Old Ways," *The Scotsman,* 20 February 2003, p. 17.

52. Quoted in "Haniebna Awantura."

53. See Adam Michnik, "We the Traitors," *Gazeta Wyborcza.*

54. See, for example, Paul Krugman's article of the same title in the *New York Times,* 19 March 2004. The related publication *International Herald Tribune* ran his op-ed the following day with the title "Taken for a Ride by Bush."

55. Plans for the withdrawal of Polish troops from Iraq were announced later, as were those for other states.

56. Quoted, for example, in Thomas Fuller, "President of Poland 'Deceived' on Iraq; but Kwaśniewski Will Try to Persuade the Spanish to Stay," *International Herald Tribune,* 19 March 2004, p. 1.

57. Laar, "The New Europe Has Arrived," p. 17.

58. Dominique Moisi, "Reinventing the West."

8

Japan: A Bandwagoning "Lopsided Power"

Yukiko Miyagi

J apan gave active support to the United States in the Iraq War: condemning the Iraqi regime and seeking UN legitimization of US policy before
the war; and afterward providing reconstruction assistance, including the
dispatch of its Self-Defense Forces (SDF) to Iraq. This was the first time
since World War II that the Japanese military had been deployed in an area
of overseas combat, causing a nationwide controversy over its constitutionality. The issue at stake in 2003 was not some remote Iraqi threat, but rather
a test of Japan's fidelity to its US alliance, the very centerpiece of its security against threats from East Asia. It also reflected a decision to rely on US
hegemony in the Middle East to secure Japan's access to energy supplies.
And the war was seen as an opportunity to normalize the use of Japanese
military power as a step in throwing off the constraints that made Japan a
lopsided power with an abnormal asymmetry between its economic and
political/military power.

■ Japan's Position on the War

Prewar Policy
Until early March 2003, Japan's official stand was the search for a peaceful
resolution of the Iraqi weapons of mass destruction (WMD) issue.
Ostensibly working toward this end, Prime Minister Junichiro Koizumi
demanded the Iraqi regime's unconditional acceptance and full cooperation
with the UN Monitoring, Verification, and Inspection Commission
(UNMOVIC) inspections and sent special envoys to the leading Arab states
to increase pressure on Iraq for acceptance. In reality, aware of the US determination on war regardless of Iraq's behavior, Japan tried to convince
Washington to secure a UN resolution on the basis of the WMD threat Iraq
supposedly posed, rather than acting unilaterally with the aim of regime

change. This, Japan advised, would frame the issue as one of the international community against Iraq rather than as a US attack on Iraq. A UN resolution was also important to gaining Japanese domestic support for the dispatch of its Self-Defense Forces, in that it would legitimize it as a contribution to Japan's international obligations.[1] To give the appearance of exhausting all peaceful means of resolving the crisis, special envoys were sent to Iraq urging compliance. Iraq asked the Japanese prime minister's special envoy, sent on 3 March 2003, to make a sincere effort for a nonmilitary resolution of the crisis, as Japan was doing in the case of North Korea, but Japan contented itself with the mere delivery of demands on Iraq.[2] As the US intention to launch a military attack even without a UN resolution became apparent during US secretary of state Colin Powell's visit to Tokyo on 22–23 February 2003, the Japanese government advised the United States to use twelve-year-old Resolutions 678 and 687 as the legal basis for war.[3] It also stepped up its efforts to get support for the US draft resolution authorizing war through bilateral contacts with states on the Security Council and, in particular, by offering economic assistance to undecided nonpermanent members of the council.

Wartime Policy

Japanese prime minister Junichiro Koizumi expressed his government's support for the US announcement on 17 March 2003 that it would go to war without a UN resolution. Japan immediately began diplomatic efforts to secure a UN resolution on postwar Iraq. It also tried to defuse Arab anger by promising humanitarian assistance for Iraq and economic assistance for the Palestinian refugees and Jordan. The absence of a UN resolution made it impossible for the government to offer financial and logistical support for the US military attack itself, but it enlarged its support for US-allied forces in the Indian Ocean established during the 2001 war in Afghanistan; this included the dispatch of an Aegis-equipped naval vessel that could be used to give intelligence support for US military operations, an act that potentially breached the constitutional prohibition on participation in offensive military actions.[4] The contradictions in Japan's policy were exposed by its stands during the war. It rejected the appeal of the Iraqi deputy ambassador for Japanese intervention to halt the indiscriminate US missile attacks and cluster-bombings on civilian residences and hospitals while claiming to adhere to a policy of peaceful conflict resolution and ostentatiously offering "humanitarian assistance" to the Iraqi people.[5] Japan's initiatives were, in contrast to the Gulf War (1990–1991), quickly formulated and implemented, having been preplanned since the time a US military attack on Iraq appeared on Washington's agenda.

Postwar Policy

Japan's first priority after the war was to secure a UN resolution on postwar reconstruction that would secure the passage of domestic legislation allowing the dispatch of the SDF.[6] Following the passage of UN Security Council Resolution 1483 of 22 May 2003, on the reconstruction of Iraq, Japan passed the Iraq Reconstruction Law in July 2003, enabling the dispatch of about 1,000 SDF troops to Iraq to carry out reconstruction assistance. The Japanese government was determined to send the Japanese troops despite a high risk of casualties and despite Al-Qaida's threat to attack Tokyo, and was not deterred by the murder of two Japanese diplomats. To reduce domestic reaction, it incrementally staged the troops' dispatch beginning in December 2003. However, domestic skepticism over the legitimacy of SDF activities in Iraq forced the government to shift its initial emphasis on the SDF mission from one of providing logistical support for the occupation forces to one focused on rehabilitation and reconstruction. Also, keen to show leadership in undertaking the reconstruction of Iraq, Japan cochaired the US-led international donor conference held in Madrid on 23–24 October 2003 and itself pledged $5 billion, the second largest financial contribution after the United States and representing nearly 10 percent of the total sum called for by the United States.

In the wake of the war, the Japanese government, anxious to protect the flow of Middle Eastern oil to Japan and to ward off terrorist attacks in retaliation for its support of Washington, redoubled its efforts to appease Arab opinion. Viewing support for the Middle East peace process as an effective means to counter Arab and Muslim perceptions of Japan as totally aligned with the United States, Japan called for a return to the internationally backed "roadmap" peace plan in opposition to the Bush administration's support for Sharon's policy of Jewish settlements in the Occupied Territories; Japan also broke ranks with the United States in condemning the Israeli government's assassinations of Palestinian leaders. To secure the safety of the SDF in Iraq, Japan assured Middle Eastern governments and publics (via Al-Jazeera) of its purely nonmilitary mission, and sought friendly relations with local Iraqi communities (by providing assistance and some employment). The Iraqi population, however, largely interpreting Japan's role as participation in the US occupation of Iraq and believing Japan to be partly motivated by the hope of economic gain from Iraq's reconstruction, had an increasingly ambivalent view of Japan—a client of the United States that had supported the military attack but also a source of much needed assistance in the reconstruction of Iraq.[7]

Japan's Position Explained

Systemic Structural Determinants

Japan's security dependence on the United States. Global structural factors, and specifically Japan's position in a US-dominated unipolar world order, provided the context of its support for the United States in the Iraq

War. Japan's lop-sided combination of large economic resources with only limited military capability—dictated by its US-designed 1947 Peace Constitution—had generated a dual policy of relying on international institutions for global security and on the United States for its military security in East Asia. Japan's stake in its security alliance with the United States had increased with its perception of a growing threat from North Korea and, to a lesser extent, China. As the United States—especially under George W. Bush—tried to make its military power the basis of global order at the expense of liberal institutions centered on the UN, Japan was made more dependent on the United States for its security and correspondingly more vulnerable to US demands to use its substantial resources in support of US policy. At the same time, a world order based more on military power generated a powerful incentive for Japan to recover a more "natural" balance between economic and military power, without which its global political influence remained limited. The Iraq War was perceived as an opportunity to both reinforce the US security alliance and to redress this lopsidedness by deploying military forces abroad. Also, Japanese policy was shaped by the desire to gain influence in Washington in the hope that US policy would be more sensitive to Japan's interests: notably that it would tolerate Japan's stake in Iran's Azadegan oil field, that it would back Japan's ambition for a UN Security Council seat, and that it would heed Japan's counsels to avoid a war over North Korea's nuclear capability. One could say Japan was prepared to support a war in the Middle East in order to avoid one in East Asia.[8]

Economic dependence on the Middle East. Japan's deep dependence on Middle Eastern oil, for which it had long relied on good relations with Middle Eastern countries, was another structural constraint potentially shaping its policy; but dependence by itself does not determine the means pursued to address it. While in the 1973 Arab-Israeli war Japan had distanced itself from US policies (particularly its pro-Israeli biases) that might antagonize Middle Eastern oil-producing states, by the time of the Iraq War this constraint had eased. For one thing, Japan's former important oil relationship with Iraq was now negligible due to the damage of the Iran-Iraq War (1980–1988), the Gulf War (1990–1991), and the effects of subsequent US sanctions against Iraq.[9] After the Gulf War, Iraq became for Japan mainly a card to play in bargaining with the United States over Japan's wish to continue its much more important oil relation with Iran despite US attempts to isolate the latter.[10] While alignment with the United States in a war opposed by the Arab and Muslim public was a risk,[11] most of the oil producers were bandwagoning with the United States, not opposing it as in 1973; Japan had also reached agreements with Saudi Arabia, the United Arab Emirates, and Iran in September 2001 to guard against any short-term interruption in oil supplies. And bandwagoning with the United States in the Iraq War might, on the other hand, permit Japan to share in the economic spoils of the war and to secure a share of Iraqi oil under the umbrella of US hegemony in the region.

The Domestic Policy Process

Elite goals. Elite-specific norms and interests were the immediate driving force in policymaking. Japanese policymakers' experience of growing international demands for Japan's financial contributions in international crises, which when given did not earn Japan due respect from the other great powers, fueled an urge to regain the full power, influence, and respect they felt Japan deserved.[12] Additionally, the value of the US security umbrella was largely unquestioned in elite circles. The elite had been traumatized by the heavy US criticism of Japan's "too little, too late" response during the Gulf War;[13] the solution, it believed, was a proactive and visible response to international crises, both to satisfy the United States and as an opportunity to deploy military force abroad. On the other hand, there was also some fear among the elite that US power might be exercised in ways damaging to Japanese interests; specifically, Koizumi, having personally initiated attempts at normalization of relations with North Korea, had a strong stake in sustaining the influence with the United States that was needed to avoid a US war against Pyongyang or a crisis that would stir up Japanese fears of North Korea to the detriment of the government. The elites' policies were also tempered by some disagreement among themselves over how far to go along the path of total alignment with Washington and by the antimilitary national norms dominant among the mass public.

The inner policymaking circle: the ruling party and senior bureaucrats. The ultimate decisions in the Iraq War were made by the top political leaders, primarily by Prime Minister Koizumi, who was the main driver behind Japan's initiatives, including the major break with precedent: deployment of the SDF to a combat zone.[14] Koizumi's particular political position in some ways explains this. On the one hand, lacking a strong personal faction within the ruling Liberal Democratic Party (LDP), Koizumi was keen to show himself indispensable to the US-Japan relationship; on the other hand, his ability to impose his views owed much to his extraordinarily high public popularity rating, upon which the LDP depended to stay in power.[15] Giving key backing to the prime minister was the rising group of pro-US military activists within the LDP leadership fostered by his cabinet appointments; the foreign ministry, whose top ranks were imbued by a pro-US culture; and the national defense agency, which had been established in close affiliation with US counterparts and whose rising status within the government paralleled Japan's attempt to expand its military role. Given his personal public standing, his privileged access to the United States, and his support within the military-industrial complex, Koizumi was able to centralize sufficient power in the cabinet institution to override elite and mass opposition.[16] The exceptionally powerful political position of the Koizumi cabinet also encouraged bandwagoning by senior bureaucrats seeking his support for their favored policies.[17]

The prime minister was not completely free from intraparty opposition. There were two opposing tendencies within the ruling LDP, one that was resentful of the way his policymaking style bypassed traditional consensus building within the party,[18] and one that objected to his evasion of any discussion of the constitutionality of the government's policy and that believed involvement in the war carried more costs and risks than opportunities. When policymaking required Diet approval, the government had no choice but to seek intraparty consensus through compromise as well as intimidation of internal opponents in order to ensure passage of the needed legislation. However, the government's relative success in pushing through its policy exposed how far the coming of Koizumi had eclipsed the influence of the traditional mainstream Diet members who favored more cautious, self-restrained, and moderate policies, particularly regarding the use of the SDF, in favor of promilitarist Diet members pushing for rapid recovery of Japanese military power.

The ruling coalition. When the war crisis occurred, the LDP governed in coalition with two much smaller parties, the New Conservative Party and the Komeito. The New Conservative Party, having split from the LDP, had no significant policy differences with it over the Iraq War. The Komeito had originally stood for a UN-centered and antimilitarist policy but followed the LDP line, even to the point of risking its main public support base.[19] It was motivated by the urge to survive in a slowly emerging two-party system, and this was believed to require being more accountable to establishment interests than to its original political base, the mass public, and middle-sized and small business; additionally, there was a trade-off agreed between Komeito and the LDP in which the Komeito received concessions on tax legislation for its constituents in return for support of Koizumi on the Iraqi issue.[20] Moreover, the coalition parties received certain concessions on Iraq from the LDP—such as the delaying and phasing of the SDF dispatch and refraining from logistical support for US forces in postwar Iraq. In effect, the coalition parties added a number of Diet seats to the support of the LDP while providing a very minimal check on its policy.

The Diet and the opposition parties. The LDP-led coalition's absolute majority in the Diet allowed it to suppress the proper consultative and debating functions of parliament. This could be seen in the passage of the Iraq Reconstruction Law, in which only a short time was allowed for deliberation and in which voting took place in the absence of opposition protesters. The largest opposition party, the Democratic Party, stood against a war without a UN resolution, and therefore against the government's pro-US stance and against SDF participation in the US-led reconstruction of Iraq. But it lacked the intraparty policy cohesion to translate its relatively large number of Diet seats into effective opposition. While the smaller opposition parties, the Communist Party and the Socialist Democratic Party, were staunchly against the war, their seats had declined to the point where the LDP could ignore them in the policymaking process.

Business interests. As a part of "iron triangle" dominating Japanese policymaking, the business community has close ties with and great influence on policymakers, although public criticism of this relation had made it more circumspect. Most business leaders expected a war in Iraq to have a negative effect on the economy and their businesses from increased oil prices and reduced investment and exports.[21] However, viewing the US determination on war as unchangeable, they focused on how to minimize the negative effect and how to make profitable use of it. The business sectors most enthusiastic for participation in the US war coalition were Japan's overdeveloped construction industry, which hoped for contracts,[22] and the general business companies that had had business in Iraq in the 1980s or, having a military industry section, welcomed increases in defense spending along with the SDF's future expanded role. They believed clear support of the United States and the early dispatch of the SDF would gain a substantial share in the postwar reconstruction contracts allocated by the United States, and there was some impatience among them at the government's delay in deploying the SDF in the face of public opposition.[23] On the other hand, the Japanese oil business was relatively more cautious and reluctant to engage in Iraq, seeing investment there as highly risky.[24] The failure of the United States to stabilize Iraq has made all Japanese firms more cautious, but many remain optimistic about longer-run opportunities.

The normative disjuncture between policymakers and the mass public. The ruling elites' main dilemma was that their foreign policy priorities, including their policy in Iraq, pursued in defiance of long-standing national norms, enjoyed little or only reluctant public support. To legitimize their agenda they attempted to stretch existing normative constraints and to use global crises, of which the Iraq War was a major opportunity, to promote fait accompli embodying new norms they hoped the public would come to accept.

In the Iraq War, the Koizumi government could not initially exploit the justification for involvement in war employed at the time of the Gulf War, namely the need of Japan to contribute to the international community as embodied in the UN, since no UN resolution was forthcoming justifying an attack on Iraq and about 78 percent of the Japanese public were against the US attack on Iraq.[25] Instead the government emphasized the importance of the US-alliance for Japan, exploiting the growing national sense of regional insecurity (particularly from North Korea), while playing down, for fear of provoking a nationalist backlash, US pressures on Japan. There was no alternative for Japan, the government insisted, and to oppose the United States would undermine Japan's national interests. The public, while reluctantly acknowledging this, did not abandon its basic preference for liberal international institutions. UN legitimization, however, was provided for Japan's participation in Iraq's reconstruction,[26] and the public was prepared to tolerate Japan's financial contributions (which were only constrained by budgetary considerations) and humanitarian assistance, even outside a UN framework. Koizumi wanted more, however, namely the dispatch of the SDF to postwar Iraq. To this end, he tried to stretch the interpretation of the Japanese Peace Constitution, claiming that the preamble's stated "aspiration [of Japan] to occupy an honored place in an international society striving for the preservation of peace" meant that Japan should gain international respect by sending Japanese troops for the purposes of international cooperation.[27] However, this reinterpretation of the constitution did not win public acceptance. The public did not support military involvement, constraining how far the SDF could be used in Iraq, although the government was able incrementally to shift their views toward its own. Thus, before the Iraq War started, about 70 percent were against SDF dispatch,[28] initially making it impossible to obtain a Diet majority for it. After the postwar SDF dispatch (facilitated by the reconstruction resolution), however, a May 2004 opinion poll showed that supporters of the dispatch briefly eclipsed opponents by 42 to 41 percent, and 43 percent of respondents thought the SDF was making an important international contribution, even though 52 percent still opposed the government's political support for the war. But in December 2004, opponents of the extension of the SDF mandate reached 58 percent, compared to 31 percent in support.[29] As it was difficult to shift public opinion to the point government leaders wanted, they tried to muffle debate,[30] claiming it was "against the national interest to tell the public in advance" what the government intended.[31] In dispatching the SDF, the prime minister expressed his determination to risk his political career for what he believed was right, and added that he was certain that the public would in the future understand his actions.

Yet while the public remained skeptical throughout of government policy, this translated into no political accountability of the government. One reason was the role of the media. The progovernment newspapers systematically promoted the government message, and although small in number, they included a powerful newspaper with the world's largest circulation.[32] In addition, national public television, while ostensibly neutral, relied heavily for its information on the Japanese and US governments.[33] Most newspapers and the widely watched, privately owned television news programs were in opposition to the US attack on Iraq and helped to maintain the critical domestic atmosphere. But the disproportionately heavy reporting on the US compared to that on the Middle East side tended to frame the issue in terms of Japan's relationship with the United States, limiting the scope of the debate so that media critics were unable to present a viable alternative to the government's policy.[34] Moreover, the "lack of investigative reporting" by the Japanese media[35] meant the public was not exposed to information on vital matters such as the doubtful credibility of the WMD allegations made against Iraq or of the consequences of the war for international law and institutions. The government also promoted sympathetic reporting of the personal experiences of SDF troops in Iraq, generating public sympathy for their presence there and diluting public opposition to it.

Second, the active expression of public opposition over the Iraqi issue was ineffective, as public street protests, resolutions by local assemblies in opposition to the military attack, protests by local governors, a lawyers' lawsuit against the government, and a "human shield" of Japanese traveling to Iraq were all ignored by the government. In the end, the government prevailed because, while a majority opposed its policies on Iraq, this did not necessarily turn that majority against the government per se; thus an opinion poll showed that 26 percent of those who opposed the US invasion of Iraq nevertheless supported the government, with the majority of such supporters saying that there was no credible alternative to Koizumi.[36]

Third, the government actively manipulated public opinion. For example, when three Japanese citizens were kidnapped in Iraq, the government contrived to deflect attention from its own share in a war that had generated such insecurity in Iraq by blaming the victims for irresponsibly putting themselves in harm's way.

■ Policy Outputs and Consequences

Koizumi's policy in the Iraq War signaled another step in the post–Gulf War shift in Japan's role in the Middle East and the world. Japan moved from its traditional pacifistic policy toward joining the international power game on the side of the United States, and from the traditional practice of seeking to protect its own Middle Eastern interests from US pressure within liberal international institutions, above all the UN, toward weakening this institution in pursuit of its interests in tandem with the United States. In addition,

Japan made a step forward on the road to become a "normal" great power possessing military projection capability. It did not, yet, wholly abandon its traditional reliance on the UN and the principle of multilateralism, but its collaboration with the United States may have contributed to consolidation of a world order in which force plays an increased role at the expense of law.

Whether this has served Japan's strong economic interest in sustaining oil supplies, gaining access to the Iraqi market, and maintaining its ties with the Arab world, however, seems questionable. Japan has burned many bridges with the Arab public while tying its regional role closely to US dominance in Iraq and the wider region. The government has sacrificed the historical benign image of Japan in the region, which had been earned by years of economic assistance and political neutrality.

Japan's drive for international respect may also not have been served by the war. Stark inconsistencies in Japan's policy—proclaiming commitment to the UN yet ignoring and manipulating it when it was expedient, projecting an image of a peaceful state while supporting an illegitimate military attack, depicting the dispatch of its military forces to the Arab and Iraqi people as a peaceful contribution while emphasizing the military nature of its cooperation to the United States—all risk damaging Japan's international standing, and not just in the Middle East. Japan's many bilateral diplomatic interventions in promotion of US policy, insofar as they were perceived as an effort to curry favor in Washington, have probably cost it international respect. For example, the Japanese elites' push for a UN Security Council permanent seat seems to have been harmed by this erosion of respect.

The effects of the Iraq War on Japan remain ambiguous, and it is too early to tell whether the new assertiveness pioneered by the Koizumi government will be consolidated as a new national norm. It is possible, however, that a strong political leader has sufficiently established as normal what was previously thought to be abnormal, so that, in a similar crisis in the future, a similar Japanese response will be a matter of uncontested bureaucratic routine.

■ Notes

1. *Chunichi Shinbun,* 16 March 2003; *Asahi Shinbun,* 9 March 2003, 23 March 2003. In order to enable the SDF dispatch overseas, it would have to be either as a part of a UN peacekeeping operation under the Peacekeeping Operation Law, or at least based on a UN resolution under a new law to be passed for this particular occasion.

2. *Asahi Shinbun,* 8 March 2003.

3. Interview with a researcher at the Middle East Research Institute of Japan, 20 September 2005.

4. *Shukan Zenshin* no. 2082 (16 December 2002), http://www.zenshin.org/f_zenshin/f_back_no02/f2082.htm.

5. *Asahi Shinbun,* 2 April 2003.

6. The resolution's call for contributions "by any means," including military assistance, was included at the specific request of the Japanese government. Interview with a researcher at the Middle East Research Institute of Japan, 20 September 2005.

7. *Tokyo Shinbun,* 16 January 2004, http://www.tokyo-np.co.jp/00/tokuho/20040116/mng_tokuho_000.shtml; *Weekly MDS (Movement for Democratic Socialism)* no. 825 (6 February 2004), http://www.mdsweb.jp/doc/825/0825_08a.html.

8. Interview with a retired high-ranking foreign ministry official, 28 September 2005.

9. Japan's oil imports from Iraq in the month before the Iraq War were 0.3 percent of its total oil imports, and Japan had no investment in Iraq. Energy Agency, "Iraku Kougeki go no Sekiyu Jousei" [The Oil Situation After the Attack on Iraq], 21 March 2003, http://www.enecho.meti.go.jp/oil/index.htm.

10. Interview with a researcher at the Institute of Developing Economy, Tokyo, 22 October 2003.

11. Japan's oil consumption in the early 2000s was 52 percent of its entire energy consumption, all imported and 85 percent from the Middle East. Agency for Natural Resources and Energy, http://www.enecho.meti.go.jp/english/energy/oil/policy.html.

12. For example, the elite thinks Japan is entitled to a permanent seat in the UN Security Council. *Chunichi Shinbun,* 14 March 2003; Foreign Minister Kawaguchi's speech to the 159th session of the Diet, 19 January 2004, http://www.mofa.go.jp/announce/fm/kawaguchi/speech040119.htm.

13. Naoto Amaki, *Saraba Gaimusho,* p. 78.

14. Conversation with a high-ranking Japanese foreign ministry official, 7 April 2004.

15. The Koizumi cabinet started with a popularity rating of around 80 percent, as opposed to the 20 percent typical of his predecessors, and remained above 40 percent even after his support for the US military attack, the passage of the Iraq Reconstruction Law, and the SDF dispatch to Iraq. Four months later, 73 percent of the respondents wanted Koizumi to stay in office, even though only 30 percent supported the LDP. *Asahi Shinbun,* 19 January 2004, 20 April 2004.

16. Tomohito Shinoda, *Kantei Gaiko,* pp. 34–50.

17. Amaki, *Saraba Gaimusho,* pp. 187, 218, 235, 249.

18. Shinoda, *Kantei Gaiko,* pp. 106–107.

19. *Rodo Shinbun,* 25 February 2003, http://www.jlp.net/syasetu/030225b.html.

20. Ibid.; Sadao Hirano, *Komeito-Soka Gakkai no Shinjitsu,* 2005, p. 56.

21. "Deflation, Management of Bad Credits, and Iraq: How Would the Business Leaders Confront the Accumulated Difficulty? Listening to Their Voices in the New Year," *Mainichi Shinbun,* 21 January 2003, http://www.mainichi.co.jp/life/family/syuppan/economist/030121/1.html.

22. The 21st Century Public Policy Institute, April 2003, http://www.geocities.jp/ntt21c/0351x34u.html; *"Iraku Fukkou Shien ni Kansuru Kinkyuu Youbou"* [Urgent Requests Regarding the Reconstruction Assistance for Iraq], Kaigai Kensetsu Kyoukai, Nihon Kensetsugyou Dantai Rengoukai, Nihon Doboku Kougyou Kyoukai, Kenchikugyou Kyoukai [Association of Overseas Construction

Business, the Japan League of Construction Groups, the Japan Association of Civil Engineering, and the Association of the Construction Business], June 2003, Japan Federation of Construction Contractors web page, http://www.nikkenren.com/comment/r_2003_6.html; interview with representatives of the Japan Business Federation, International Cooperation Bureau, Latin America, Middle East, and Africa Group, 16 September 2005; interview with a representative of Japan Petroleum Development Association, 21 September 2005.

23. Sakae Tsuda, "Iraku no Fukkou Jigyou to Nihon" [The Reconstruction Business in Iraq and Japan], *Japan Mail Media* no. 214 (14 April 2003), http://www.asyura.com/0304/war31/msg/1153.html; Kazuyuki Hamada, *Iraku Sensou Nihon no Wakemae: Bijinesu to Shite no Jieitai Hahei* [Japan's Share in the Iraq War: The SDF Dispatch as Business], http://www.esbooks.co.jp.

24. Interview with an executive in the Institute of Energy Economics, Japan, 21 October 2003; interview with a representative of Mitsui Co. Ltd., Tokyo Chamber of Commerce and Industry, 20 November 2003.

25. *Asahi Shinbun,* 25 February 2003.

26. In response to UN Secretary-General Kofi Annan's statement doubting the legitimacy of the Iraq War without a UN Security Council resolution, Foreign Minister Yoriko Kawaguchi rejected his authority to interpret "what the UN Security Council members decided." On the other hand, in order to get public support for the SDF dispatch in Iraq, Annan was invited to Tokyo to express his appreciation of it. *Asahi Shinbun,* 25 March 2003.

27. Prime Minister Koizumi's press conference, 9 December 2003, http://www.mofa.go.jp; Prime Minister Koizumi's New Year's reflection, 1 January 2004, http://www.kantei.go.jp/foreign/koizumispeech/2004/01/01syokan_e.html; Prime Minister Koizumi's speech to the 159th Diet session, 19 January 2004, http://www.mofa.go.jp/announce/pm/koizumi/speech040119.html.

28. Takasi Tachibana, "Iraku Hahei no Taigi wo Tou" [Questioning the Justification for the Dispatch to Iraq], *Gendai,* March 2004, p. 29.

29. *Asahi Shinbun,* 25 February 2003, 11 December 2003, 15 March 2004, 20 December 2004; *Yomiuri Shinbun,* 2 June 2004, http://www.yomiuri.co.jp.

30. Koizumi claimed that the public should not always be heeded, since it was often wrong in always preferring peace to war. *Asahi Shinbun,* 5 March 2003, 17 March 2003.

31. *Asahi Shinbun,* 14 February 2003.

32. Hiroshi Fujita, "Tayou na Iken wo Kousei ni Tsutaeta Ka: Yomiuri to Asahi, Mainichi, Sankei wo Hikaku, Bunseki Suru" [Did the Media Report the Various Opinions Fairly: The Comparison and Analysis of *Yomirui, Asahi, Mainichi,* and *Sankei*], *Ronza,* November 2003, pp. 86–94.

33. Japan Communist Party member Hiroko Yada's web page, http://www.hatta-hiroko.jp.

34. Fujita, "Tayou na Iken wo Kousei ni Tsutaeta Ka," p. 93.

35. Ellis Krauss, "The Media's Role in a Changing Japanese Electorate," p. 7.

36. *Asahi Shinbun,* 11 September 2003, http://www.asahi.com.

9

Canada: Outside
the Anglo-American Fold

Rick Fawn

How would a medium-sized state with some idealistic foreign policy aims and limited military capacity, strapped geographically and economically to the United States, and culturally and politically linked to it and the United Kingdom, react to *their* war against Iraq?

One approach to assessing Canadian foreign policy behavior during the Iraq crisis is systemic—how the country is constrained by its relative size and location in the international system. The country is too small to have a deciding influence on world politics. It is economically and militarily—if not routinely, at least ultimately—dependent on its superpower neighbor. This approach therefore suggests the Canadian stand instinctively would be highly supportive of its US counterpart. Indeed, Canadian foreign policy rhetoric often refers to the centrality and positive nature of US-Canadian relations. US president John F. Kennedy perhaps best summarized the inexorable nature of US-Canadian relations when he addressed the Canadian parliament on 17 May 1961: "Geography has made us neighbors. History has made us friends. Economics has made us partners. And necessity has made us allies. Those whom nature hath so joined together, let no man put asunder."

A second line suggests—especially in a potential era of foreign policy diversification after the straightjacket of the (necessary and beneficial) alliances of the Cold War—that Canada might take a different line from the United States, one that followed ideas and ideals rather than structural constraints or material interests. With elements of idealism in Canadian foreign policy—such as with its tradition of sovereign equalitarianism, on peacekeeping, on development, and more recently, on the promotion internationally of "human security"—and with little fear of real penalties from Washington, Canada might adopt policies at odds with the United States but that expressed these distinctive aspects of its foreign policy.

Instead, this chapter suggests that while Canada produced a contradictory position over Iraq that fulfilled neither of these predictive scenarios, this resulted not from any deliberate short-term calculation to satisfy contradictory domestic and international interests, but rather from an incoherent domestic policy process. Perhaps without lasting consequences, such indecision and incoherence nevertheless harmed short-term Canadian interests on all fronts. Canada forewent adopting an opportunistic foreign policy toward Washington (with concomitant material benefits),[1] but also failed to achieve some international status and prestige (and the fulfillment of the legalist-humanist dimensions of Canadian foreign policy) by adopting a principled, unflinching opposition to war without specific international authorization.

What occurred in Canadian policy, and why? The chapter considers the Canadian government's diplomatic stand, then its military policies, assessing in each case key ambiguities. It then considers domestic political developments and constraints and, finally, US reactions to determine costs to Canada of its varied positions.

◼ Canadian Foreign Policy and the Iraq War

While doubtlessly partisan, in January 2003 former prime minister and leader of the opposition Conservative Party Joe Clark echoed the views of many that Canada lacked a stance on the impending war against Iraq: "the prime minister is being dangerously ambiguous as to what Canada's position would be. . . . No one knows where Canada stands. Our allies don't know, our citizens don't know, [prime minister Jean Chrétien's] own government doesn't know."[2]

Diplomacy and Multilateralism
In a seemingly firm statement in November 2002, Canadian minister of foreign affairs Bill Graham said: "Canada should not be intimidated to enter into an alliance to attack Iraq. Instead, Canada should be able to speak frankly to the U.S. in defence of the principles and Canadian values as expressed in our foreign policy." As events progressed, Graham was accused of "backtracking." By 24 March 2003, with war under way, he declared full support to the US terms and interpretation of the conflict with Saddam Hussein: "We as a government are supportive of the United States' desire to get rid of Saddam Hussein, to deal with the weapons-of-mass-destruction issue around the world, and we'll continue to work with the United States in terms of non-proliferation, in terms of the war on terrorism." In reply to questions the next day, however, he announced, "No, Canada has never been in favour of regime change."[3]

While the Canadian foreign minister appears to have changed policy wholesale, prime minister Jean Chrétien can be said to have first offered ambiguity, then similarly an about-turn. Like many leaders, even those who came to oppose the use of force by the United States, Chrétien maintained that Saddam needed to fulfill UN resolutions and that the failure to do so could result in (unspecified) measures being taken against him. Thus, for example, Chrétien explained in November 2002: "We are telling [Saddam] collectively that we are standing together, telling him that if he does not respect that [UNSC Resolution 1441], there will be consequences."[4] While Chrétien threatened "consequences," at no point was he deemed to have categorically ruled out military participation in the war if no explicit resolution was passed.[5] If anything, Chrétien's desired outcome, as expressed to the Chicago Council on Foreign Relations on 13 February 2003, was for a UN-brokered solution. He said, "If it must come to war, I argue that the world should respond through the United Nations," and stated that this was "the best way to give legitimacy to the use of force in these circumstances." Once Bush announced that the United States would forgo submitting a second resolution to the Security Council and was prepared to attack Iraq, Chrétien announced in parliament (receiving applause), "If military action proceeds without a new resolution of the Security Council, Canada will not participate." Indeed, ultimately Canada did not officially participate militarily, although the country seemed to have been preparing to send a battle group of up to 800 soldiers to Iraq until the war started. They were then "suddenly" redirected to peacekeeping operations in Afghanistan.[6] Chrétien's views on the legitimacy of the war, irrespective of Canadian participation, varied markedly. On 17 March 2003 he said the war was "not justified" but three days later asserted that the United States had a "right" to invade Iraq and that Canadians should "respect that."[7]

Ambiguities in Canadian foreign policy continued under Chrétien's successor, Paul Martin. When US forces located Saddam in an underground shelter, Martin declared, "On behalf of all Canadians, I want to congratulate the Iraqi people, the Governing Council, and coalition forces on the capture of former Iraqi dictator Saddam Hussein." He lauded the event, declaring that "ultimately Saddam Hussein being brought to justice, will enhance the prospects for early reconciliation while paving the way to allow Iraq to rejoin the community of nations." Significantly for this argument, Martin concluded: "Canada will continue to work with the coalition, and the United States, as well as international institutions to support the reconstruction effort in Iraq."[8] To be sure, some countries that opposed war have agreed to work with Washington in postwar reconstruction. But apart from the overall congratulations to the United States, Martin also referred expressly to the "coalition."

If a Canadian policy can be determined, it was a middle position that favored diplomacy and mediation, particularly through the UN Security

Council, which threatened some action against Iraq for noncompliance. This interpretation explains Canada's actions toward the Security Council. Even though it was not a member of the Security Council in 2003, Ottawa nevertheless submitted a proposal to extend the deadline by which weapons inspectors could search in Iraq to 15 April. This contradicted US intentions to foreclose on any role for the Security Council by 17 March, which was widely read as a move toward war. The White House brushed aside the Canadian proposal. Nevertheless, Canada's UN ambassador, Paul Heinbecker, stated: "We are convinced that Iraq is contained and that if it co-operates the disarmament of Iraq can be had without a shot being fired."[9] Such efforts fit with what several powers sought to do. But even these efforts at diplomacy have been charged with indecision. When the Commons Committee on Foreign Affairs held an emergency session in September 2002 on the looming war, it could not reach agreement on whether the country should act as an impartial mediator.[10] Chrétien became confident of the principles of inspections, telling the House of Commons on 3 March that UN inspectors could have secured Saddam's cooperation if allowed more time.

Ultimately, Canadian diplomatic policy was not to support the war. While statements caused uncertainty over that policy, the country's apparent military policy regarding Iraq created further misunderstanding, and even led the United States (perhaps willingly) to count Canada officially as a combatant member of its coalition.

Military Policy

Several coalition partners of the United States do not possess armed forces—the political value of simply having states as allies was important. But the United States was said to be "impressed" by the combat performance in Afghanistan of Canada's highly trained specialist unit Joint Task Force 2 and "had its eye on the unit for its campaign in Iraq."[11] A further benefit to the United States—and a complicating factor for Canadian policy—was that significant parts of Canadian military capacity had been deployed in the Gulf in advance of the Iraq War. Defense Minister John McCallum ignored concerns that the Canadian military would be involved. The plan to deploy Canadian officers to the regional command center in Qatar in February 2003, before the looming war, also caused difficulties for the government. McCallum brushed this aside, explaining: "It's a change in time zone. It's not a change in policy."[12]

This did not remain rhetorical; the risk that Canadian forces deployed in the Gulf could be used in war, by default, materialized. Canadian military personnel were serving, by virtue of exchanges, in the Iraq theater with coalition forces. These personnel were also wearing Canadian uniforms, though many would not be immediately visible, instead serving in support and logistics, such as airborne warning. Once the issue was public, Chrétien told the House of Commons that if Canadian troops were present, they were not in combat roles. But a British military spokesperson confirmed for the CBC that Canadians were on the front lines. Unsurprisingly, right-wing opposition Canadian Alliance leader Stephen Harper seized on this inconsistency to demand that Chrétien come out in support of the Canadian troops, thereby seeking to draw the prime minister into a declaration of support for the war. By contrast, the left-wing New Democratic Party (NDP) pounced on the contradictions created for the government's position and called for the soldiers to be recalled. The NDP's brash leader, Jack Layton, consequently demanded: "Whether it's the troops on exchange who must be withdrawn . . . ships escorting vessels of war . . . or planes supplying data to the US fifth fleet . . . let me be clear, Jean Chretien must ensure that Canada in no way is supporting Bush's war on Iraq."[13] Instead, by default, the forces remained in place, but the Canadian government issued no elaboration on what that meant for Canadian policy on the war.

An added question was the remit of Canadian naval forces that were already in the Gulf. Apart from questions concerning their direct role in a potential war (which could be made clear), the Canadian position remained unclear on the fate of intercepted Iraqis. With some public opinion concerned about the fate of any Iraqis captured by Canadian forces, McCallum explained that it was "highly unlikely" that Iraqis would be allowed to escape, and said that Canadian forces would contact Ottawa in such an event. A clear line again seemed absent.

In addition to not having a mechanism to determine the role of Canadian personnel in the Gulf, Canada appears to have forgone an overall position on the war. With the war under way, Defense Minister McCallum noted, "The terrorist risk will, if anything, be greater than before as a consequence of war." But this prompted him to say, "So for us to cut and run when the terrorism risk is greater would not be compatible with Canadian traditions." Unsurprisingly, the CBC considered the minister "elusive" on Canada's military role once war started.[14] Apart from enunciating its position, the government seemed to make its remaining forces unavailable so as to be unable to act. This occurred, according to media analysts, by the government's efforts to increase Canadian participation in the postconflict mission in Afghanistan. Indeed, McCallum did not want to suggest that Canada was militarily indifferent, and upon sending troops for peacekeeping in Afghanistan, said Canada was "a peaceable kingdom, never a pacifist kingdom."[15] Nevertheless, the lack of a moral stand was illustrated by the comments of a military analyst: "The Canadian decision to commit to ISAF [International Security Assistance Force, in Afghanistan] apparently was made out of domestic political considerations, proving to be a very convenient excuse for our government not to send troops to Iraq."[16] Such criticism would have been unnecessary if a distinct policy had been issued. It may also have helped to prevent Canada from being officially classed as a military participant in the coalition.

This occurred when the US Department of Defense listed Canadian contributions of three Hercules military transports (a modest contribution, but perhaps all the more believable in view of Canada's smaller facilities). Canadian officials insisted that Canadian forces took no part in the Iraq War and said the United States confused this with Canada's supply of Hercules transports to the Afghan operations.[17] Additionally, secondary studies of the war assert that Canada made military contributions. Anthony Cordesman, for example, lists Canada has having supplied three transport planes and thirty-one personnel.[18] After the start of the war, US ambassador to Canada Paul Cellucci noted that while he was disappointed that Canada had not been part of the coalition, Canadians had indirectly provided more support for the United States in Iraq than the majority of coalition states. He was right to comment, "It's kind of an odd situation."[19] Perhaps recognizing the need to differentiate Canadian military policy from that of the United States, Chrétien rebuked claims that new increases in Canadian defense spending were in response to US criticisms or requests. Chrétien said defense spending increased by C$2.5 billion over three years and that other expenditures also had importance: "We have medicare which is on the table, we have infrastructure on the table, we have our children's agenda, native problems, environmental problems, they are all on the table."[20] The variations in Canadian policy might suggest that the government was balancing—rather unsuccessfully—contending domestic and foreign pressure.

■ Domestic Views

Canadian public and media discourse represented a spectrum of support for and against the US-led war. Some mainstream media supported the US position. Leading columnist Robert Fulford endorsed the Anglo-American bypass of the UN Security Council: "Had the Americans and the British waited for the French, the Russians and the rest, Saddam would have maintained his power while his terrified people starved and he played infinite variations on the game of UN arms inspection."[21] US views were reproduced in the Canadian press, such as that of Frank J. Gaffney Jr., assistant secretary of defense under Ronald Reagan and president of the nonpartisan Center for Security Policy, when he wrote in August 2003: "President Bush has done the American people and the world a great service by re-establishing a principle very nearly obscured by recent practice: The legitimacy of an American foreign policy initiative derives from its justness, wisdom, and congressional approval, not from the vagaries of UN Security Council resolutions. Now is no time to go wobbly on that principle."[22]

Support for the war also came from Canada's best-known (liberal) intellectual Michael Ignatieff, albeit based at Harvard: "What I felt was disappointing about a lot of Canadian opposition to the war was that very few people seemed to give a damn about the human-rights situation." He added: "Very few seemed to care that peace had the consequence of leaving 26 million people inside a really odious tyranny."[23]

But high-profile opposition existed as well. Lloyd Axworthy, Canadian foreign minister from 1996 to 2000, condemned US expediency in allying with disreputable regimes, writing in 2003: "All one had to do is join the anti-terrorist parade and all sins are forgiven."[24] Some politicians were more blunt. A member of parliament and of the governing Liberal Party, Carolyn Parrish, exited a party meeting on 26 February 2003, and was overheard saying: "Damn Americans. Hate those bastards."[25] She was obliged to apologize, though further anti-Bush comments resulted in her being expelled from the party caucus. While some public figures adopted strident positions, public opinion was split; in December 2002, 41 percent opposed war while 40 percent supported it. French-speaking Quebec gave the lowest support for war of all the provinces, at 23 percent.[26]

The government was faced with two different forms of challenge by opposition parties. On one hand, as indicated above, the socialist NDP opposed the war outright and accused the government of complicity and deceit, particularly over Canada's unclear military contributions to the coalition. When the United States listed Canada as a military partner, NDP leader Jack Layton, whose party asked about Canadian deployments in the Gulf throughout the war, would not accept—remarkably—that any error lay with the United States. Instead, he charged: "Either the Minister [of Defense] did not know what his troops were doing, or he simply wasn't telling us the truth; and it's up to him to prove to us that this American report is wrong."[27]

On the other hand, right-wing Alliance Party leader Stockwell Day also demanded access to Canadian military records, but for different reasons. His party supported the war and wanted to discredit the government for not exalting the work of Canadian personnel. He exclaimed: "If it [the report on Canadian military deployments] is accurate, first I would say that I am very proud of our troops for being willing to put themselves in harm's way for this cause. And if it's true, then all Canadians should be able to share in that pride, a pride which has been shrouded by our government's hypocrisy, and that's a tragedy."[28]

It could be said, therefore, that the Canadian government faced a dilemma in accommodating balanced but divided opinion. Equally, Ottawa may have faced (or expected) pressure from Washington, and both official and popular US responses to Canada's lack of support suggest such.

▨ Consequences:
US Reactions to Canadian (Non)Policies

Canadians were stung when George W. Bush failed to include Canada in his list of countries that had aided the United States after 9/11.[29] Perhaps as a result, the Canadian media particularly seized on how, by contrast, the White House mentioned Canada negatively for declining to join the war against Iraq. Noted widely was presidential spokesman Richard Boucher's comment: "We're disappointed that some of our closest allies, including Canada, do not agree on the urgent need for action."[30] Among the diplomatic rebukes Canada received from the United States were statements by its US ambassador, Paul Celluci. A week into the war, on 25 March 2003, he pronounced that Americans "are so disappointed" and "upset" that "Canada is not fully supporting us."[31]

Popular attacks on Canada and Canadians occurred during the Iraq conflict. It happened to be Canadian-born ABC correspondent Jeffrey Kofman to whom haggard US troops of the Third Division, stationed in Falluja, expressed their frustrations. One division member, quoted by Kofman, stated: "If Donald Rumsfeld was here, I'd ask him for his resignation." This degenerated into right-wing web stories declaring: "ABC News Reporter Who Filed Troop Complaints Story—Openly Gay Canadian." This was amended shortly after to: "ABC News Reporter Who Filed Troop Complaints Story Is Canadian." *New York Times* columnist Maureen Dowd noted that the new title left "readers to discover in the body of the story what the Bush provocateur apparently felt was Mr. Kofman's other vice."[32] The Canadian newspaper *Globe and Mail* reported that Internet journalist Matt Drudge was tipped by the White House that Kofman was "not only gay, but also Canadian." Kofman said he tried to hide his Canadian-ness, but that his Canadian pronunciation of "o-u-t" in words such as in *about* had caught up with him.[33] ABC backed Kofman's story.

Otherwise, Canadian media reported various, but unquantified, grassroots activities that registered dismay at Canada's stand, such as Canadian truckers in the United States being refused the sale of gasoline. One of the world's leading oil-well firefighters, Canadian Mark Badick, said he was told by US contractors not to expect contracts because of Canada's nonparticipation in the war.[34] That became official policy in December 2003 when the Bush administration bracketed Canada with France, Germany, and Russia—the latter three having unambiguously opposed Washington at the

Security Council—in denying them the right to bid for postwar reconstruction contracts in Iraq.[35] Even when the Canadian government indicated, while the war continued, that it wanted to be involved in postconflict reconstruction, Foreign Affairs Minister Graham had to concede in April 2003, "we are willing to look at all requests, all offers. We have not exactly got a request yet."[36]

■ Conclusion

This brief sketch of competing—and irreconcilable—domestic pressures suggests the Chrétien government might have been motivated to secure a best-fit policy. Similarly, the importance of the United States to Canada cannot be overstated, and with that might be an expectation of Canadian accommodation of US desires.

Yet no policy strategy emerged from the government that could, or did, satisfy *any* constituency. Perhaps it was too demanding a situation. As one prominent commentator colloquially suggested, "Maybe he [Chrétien] is out of his depth on this one."[37] Regardless, Canada gained no policy benefits and suffered some setbacks from the Iraq crisis. It could have adopted lines similar to those of France, Germany, and Russia (and at one point seemed to be doing exactly that), but did not. Neglecting that option meant forgoing the prospect of prestige and perhaps of self-perceived morality.

Despite the dominance of the United States over Canada, Ottawa has broken ranks with Washington on important foreign policy matters, particularly involving the use of force, such as Cuba, Vietnam, and Grenada. On that basis, it is conceivable that Canada could have also outright opposed US policy over Iraq. Instead, Canada came to be perceived as not standing with the United States in 2003 and was both castigated and punished economically. Rather than having a coherent policy on the Iraq War, the Canadian government could be said to have had a nonpolicy that put the country into a no-man's land where it achieved little.

To be sure, Canada did not go to war, but as suggested, its policy was vague, and it did not adopt a strident position opposing the war, such as France did. To be equally sure, even with the foreign minister expressing pleasure at the capture of Saddam, many were happy that Canada was not participating in the postconflict management of Iraq. Wrote one columnist: "Hands up, all those who are really sorry that there are no Canadian troops now patrolling the hot dusty streets on Baghdad and Basra, taking fire from angry Iraqis."[38]

But that position was not so clearly arrived at, and ambiguities riddled other parts of Canadian policy. Canadian interests, particularly economic, are tied inexorably to those of the United States. But these were not strong enough to propel Canada into the coalition. Nor did the Canadian government seek substantially to appease the United States over the war, even rhetorically, as much as Bob Woodward could report that US national security adviser Condoleezza Rice secured such from her (unnamed) Canadian counterpart once the war began.[39] Rather, the belated Canadian position appears to have derived from a muddled policy process—not one resulting directly from either domestic or international pressures. In that way, Canadian policy may be an anomaly among states in dealing with the Iraq crisis.

■ Notes

1. A leading financial commentator wrote before the war began that had the government backed Washington, Canada could have expected preferential treatment on various economic issues. This prediction included that the soft lumber dispute would have gone in Canada's favor, and that "instead of a punitive duty of 27%," it would be reaping export taxes; "Canada would have already been exempt from the looming, and onerous, border-crossing requirements" of Homeland Security; and the "White House would have continued to promote a favourable image about Canada south of the border." That many Canadians surely feel that Washington ignores their country, let alone "promotes" it, is irrelevant. Diane Francis, "Chrétien Played His Cards Wrong," *National Post,* 11 March 2003, p. FP3. The commentary is an indication of views that Canadian economic interests require adherence to current US policy.

2. Widely quoted on 27 January 2003.

3. Jeff Sallot, "Graham Backtracks on Regime Change for Iraq," *Globe and Mail,* 25 March 2003.

4. Cited in Tim Harper, "Chrétien to Boost Cash for Military," *Toronto Star,* 22 November 2002.

5. See, for example, Adam Segal and Erik Missio, "Canada's Position," *CBC News Online,* 11 April 2003, http://www.cbc.ca/news/iraq/canada/canada_role.html.

6. Chris Wattie, "Ottawa Offered to Join Iraq War," *National Post,* 27 November 2003, p. A1.

7. See "Why We Didn't Fight," *National Post,* 28 November 2003, p. A19.

8. "Statement by the Prime Minister: The Capture of Former Iraqi Dictator Saddam Hussein," 14 December 2003, http://pm.gc.ca/eng/news.asp?id=11.

9. Cited in Steven Edwards, "Plan Gives April 15 Deadline, Clause to Authorize War," *National Post,* 12 March 2003, p. A1.

10. CBC summary, http://cbc.ca./news/iraq.

11. "JTF2: Canada's Super-Secret Commandos," *CBC News Online,* 2 March 2004, http://www.cbc.ca/news/background/cdnmilitary/jtf2.html.

12. *CBC News,* 11 February 2003.

13. Jack Layton, "Speech to the Ontario Bar Association," notes for an address by leader of Canada's NDP, Toronto, 20 March 2003.

14. Adam Segal and Erik Missio, "Canada's Position."

15. Quoted in, for example, Canadian Press, "Canada Ready for Afghanistan Casualties: Minister," *Toronto Star,* 17 July 2003.

16. Sean Maloney, "Canada's Ill-Conceived Mission to Kabul," *National Post,* 14 August 2003.

17. "U.S. Thanks Canada for Help in Iraq War," *Toronto Star,* 15 June 2003.

18. Anthony Cordesman, *The Iraq War,* pp. 15, 24.

19. Chris Spannos, "Canada Quietly Supported U.S. Iraq Invasion," 19 January 2004, http://newstandardnews.net/content/?action=show_item&itemid=128.

20. Cited in Harper, "Chrétien to Boost Cash for Military."

21. Robert Fulford, "The New American Era of Peace Through Power," *National Post,* 10 April 2003, p. 1.

22. Frank J. Gafney Jr., "Iraq Is Not a Place for 'Blue Helmets,'" *National Post,* 26 August 2003, p. A14.

23. John Geddes, "SMART GUY, EH? Harvard prof. TV star. Sex symbol. Michael Ignatieff is Canada's best-known intellectual—and supporter of George W. Bush's war," *Maclean's,* 23 June 2003, p. 20.

24. Lloyd Axworthy, *Navigating a New World.*

25. *CBC News,* 26 February 2003.

26. Ekos poll, reported in "Canadians Polarized on Support for War: Poll," 9 December 2002, http://www.cbc.ca/story/canada/national/2002/12/07/poll_sat021207.html.

27. Kate Jaimet, "Opposition Demands Proof on Planes," *CanWest News Service,* 15 June 2003.

28. Ibid.

29. After several senior US officials were prompted on this oversight by Canadian journalists, Bush belatedly replied that one does not thank family. Playing on that metaphor, during a visit to Halifax in eastern Canada on 1 December, he said: "Thank you for your kindness to America in an hour of need" and "Our two peoples are one family and always will be." For an overview of Canadian reactions to 9/11, see Rick Fawn, "Canada: Reluctant Moral Middle Power," in Mary Buckley and Rick Fawn, eds., *Global Responses to Terrorism* (London: Routledge, 2003), pp. 79–89.

30. See, for example, Canada's national news magazine, *Macleans:* Julian Beltrane, "Washington Is Watching," 31 March 2003, p. 36.

31. "Speech by the U.S. Ambassador to Canada A. Paul Cellucci to the Economic Club of Toronto," 25 March 2003, at the US embassy website, http://www.usembassycanada.gov/content/content.asp?section=embconsul&document=cellucci_030325.

32. Maureen Dowd, "Let's Blame Canada," *New York Times,* 20 July 2003.

33. Simon Houpt, "Canadian Targeted After Critical Iraq Report," *Globe and Mail,* 19 July 2003.

34. Stephen Handelman, "The Big Chill: Canada Could Pay a Hefty Price for the Government's Antiwar Stance," *Time International,* 7 April 2003, p. 57.

35. Canada was included in the subsequent round announced in January 2004.

36. Cited in Sheldon Alberts, "'We Have Not Exactly Got a Request Yet' to Help Rebuild Iraq, Graham Says," *National Post,* 11 April 2003, p. A6.

37. Andrew Coyne, "War Tomorrow, but Never War Today," *National Post,* 12 March 2003, p. A19.

38. Graham Fraser, "Intervention Hope Kept Alive by Chrétien," *Toronto Star,* 20 July 2003.

39. See Bob Woodward, *Plan of Attack,* p. 373.

Part 2

Key Regional Actors

10

Syria:
Defying the Hegemon

Raymond Hinnebusch

T he US conquest of Iraq threatened the Syrian regime's very survival. Washington's neoconservatives legitimized the war in terms of an Iraqi threat, but made little secret of their desire to remake the Middle East, and with the defeat of Iraq, only the submission of Syria and Iran would be needed to realize this project.[1] Yet even with US power poised to arrive on its doorstep, Syria refused to submit to Washington's demands for cooperation. Why did Syria give the neoconservatives an opportunity to paint it as a US enemy by opposing its invasion of Iraq?

■ Explaining Syria's Defiance

Failure of the Peace Process
President Bashar al-Asad's defiance of Washington, in striking contrast to the appeasement of Washington practiced by every other Arab leader, was no idiosyncratic choice. Syria's state formation, particularly the dismemberment of historical Syria and the Zionist colonization of Palestine, put the country on an Arab nationalist foreign policy tangent that has endured through countless leadership changes. The loss of the Golan Heights in the 1967 Arab-Israeli war further locked Syria into a struggle with Israel to recover this territory.[2]

Under Hafiz al-Asad, Damascus had seen the United States as both Israel's main backer and the one state that could restrain Israel and conceivably broker an acceptable Syrian-Israeli peace settlement. While Syria had traditionally sought to balance between the United States and the USSR, with the end of the Cold War it began to bandwagon with the US hegemon, partly in order to balance the greater threat from Israel: hence it joined the anti-Iraq coalition in the Gulf War (1990–1991) and the Madrid peace process, by which it hoped to recover the Golan. At the same time, the stagnation of the state-dominated economy, as oil prices and aid to Syria declined, required an opening to the world market and an influx of investment, which the regime sought through incremental economic liberalization—but which could not ultimately succeed without a regional peace settlement.

It was widely expected that these developments, combined with the leadership change at the death of President Hafiz al-Asad, might be the watershed that released pent-up pressures for change. Bashar al-Asad was seen as representative of a new generation with a vision of "modernization" entailing economic liberalization, a reduction of rent-seeking corruption, and an opening to the West. However, the external environment for domestic reform was soured by the failure of the Syrian-Israeli peace process, the outbreak of the second Palestinian intifada, and the rise of the hard-line Sharon government in Israel. With a peace settlement off the agenda and with it the prospect that economic liberalization might quickly rescue the economy, Bashar's regime opted to pursue alternative strategies, including a deepened opening to Iraq from which it hoped to secure the resources to stabilize the economy.

Rise of the Neoconservatives

What ultimately brought Syria and Washington into confrontation was the rise to power of the US neoconservatives who, intimately associated with the Israeli Likud party, had advocated the use of sanctions or force against Syria well before reaching governmental power.[3] The events of 11 September 2001 gave them new opportunities to paint the foes of Israel as foes of the United States and promote a pro-Israeli imperial project in the Middle East. While US moderates in the State Department and CIA were skeptical about aggressively confronting Syria, whose intelligence information was proving useful in the "war on terrorism," the neoconservatives, making no distinction between Israeli and US interests, aimed to destroy common ground between Syria and the United States.[4] As Damascus saw it, while Syria had been moving since the Cold War to link its security to international legitimacy and law, the invasion of Iraq signaled that the United States was now reverting to a policy of overt imperialism, in alliance with Israel, that threatened to overturn the rules of world order.

Syria and Iraq

Even as George W. Bush sought to isolate Iraq, preparatory to regime change, Syria was acquiring a deepening stake in its Iraqi alignment that was threatened by an invasion. Syrian interests in Iraq were partly economic: Syria's receipt of Iraqi crude oil, via the newly reopened Iraq-Syria pipeline, earned an annual windfall profit of around $1 billion in revenue for the government, a crucial buffer against economic crisis that allowed the regime to pursue economic reform at its chosen incremental pace. The monopolistic contracts in Iraq obtained by proregime businessmen (and their political patrons) refurbished the regime's clientele networks. Also, Iraq was a strategic hinterland for Syria in its conflict with Israel, which the neoconservatives sought to turn into a pro-Zionist client state; if they succeeded in Iraq, Damascus would, in one way or another, be next. Finally, the invasion was an egregious affront to the Arab nationalist values so ingrained in Syrian thinking: if in 1991 Saddam Hussein was the aggressor, in this instance, as Syrians saw it, an Arab state was the victim of a predatory imperialist power serving Israeli interests.[5]

Some pundits blame President Bashar al-Asad for inviting US hostility by his stand on the war, arguing that he sought to assume his father's legitimacy as leader of Arab nationalism yet lacked the acumen of Hafiz, who had managed to put Syria on the winning side of the first US-Iraq conflict.[6] But opposition to the invasion was a collective decision that would have been taken by any nationalist leadership in Damascus.

■ Syria's Response to the US War

The Failure of Syrian Diplomacy

Through its position on the UN Security Council (UNSC), Syria stood at a nexus between the regional and global arenas, from which it attempted to build a coalition against war. It acted in concert with Russia, France, and Germany in the Security Council, even voting in support of Resolution 1441, mandating the renewal of United Nations weapons inspections in Iraq, in the hope this might deprive the neoconservatives of their excuse for war.[7] Indeed, US secretary of state Colin Powell, seeking Syria's vote, sent a letter to Syria to the effect that the resolution would "serve to avoid a future military confrontation."[8] In his speech to the UN Security Council, Foreign Minister Farouk al-Sharaa argued that the disarmament of Iraq's alleged weapons of mass destruction was being achieved through Iraqi cooperation with UN inspectors, and demanded that international legitimacy be upheld against Washington's threat to launch an illegal war. Syria's UN ambassador, Mikhail Wehbe, said he believed that evidence presented by the United States to the Security Council on Iraq's weapons had been fabricated.[9] Syrian commentators explained that none of Iraq's neighbors felt it was a threat, and that weapons of mass destruction were a mere pretext for a war motivated by the interests of Israel and the US companies that hoped to profit from postwar reconstruction contracts.[10] In the Arab League, Syria invoked the Arab Collective Security Pact and urged that the war could be stopped if Arab states refused to allow their territory to be used to prosecute it (as Turkey impressed Arab public opinion by doing). However, although the Arab states passed resolutions against a war, those hosting US forces rebuffed Syria.

On the eve of the war, Syria's Grand Mufti, Ahmad Kaftaru, urged Muslims throughout the world "to use all means and martyrdom operations to defeat the American, British, and Zionist aggression on Iraq." Some half a million Syrians protested the war in Damascus.[11] Bashar, in his famous interview with *Al-Safir,* observed: "No doubt the U.S. is a super-power capable of conquering a relatively small country, but . . . the U.S. and Britain are incapable of controlling all of Iraq."[12] This was widely interpreted in Washington to put Syria on the wrong side of the "with us or against us" dictum laid down by the Bush administration.

Between Support for the
Resistance and Neoconservative Threats

Syria did little to actually oppose the US invasion, and to the extent it did, acted covertly and halfheartedly, and quickly backed away under US threats. Expecting that Iraqis would defend the regime for months, Syria allegedly facilitated arms smuggling and the movement of volunteers to Iraq to join the resistance. The regime was unwilling to stand against the tide of anti-US fury that swept Syria, and although the thousands of Arab volunteers that transited to Iraq came from all over the Arab world, many were from northern Syria. Business interests threatened by the invasion and the most militant Islamists ideologically aroused by it were concentrated there, while Syrian border tribes were extensions of those fighting the occupation in Iraq.[13] Once the Saddam regime fell, Syria apparently also gave refuge to some Iraqi officials fleeing Iraq. Amid Washington's initial military successes in Iraq, the neoconservatives launched a campaign of accusations against Syria that seemed a prelude to an attack on it. The United States bombed the Syrian trade center in Baghdad and shut down the revenue-earning oil pipeline to Syria. Asked whether US forces would invade Syria, Bush answered, "Each situation will require a different response, first things first; we expect co-operation from Syria."[14]

Under US threat, Syria officially closed its four official border posts with Iraq on 5 April 2003. After that, Syria claims it neither allowed volunteers to exit Syria for Iraq nor allowed fleeing Iraqi officials to enter Syria. Neither did it comply with US demands to extradite such officials, although some were evidently expelled. Syria was unwilling to either deploy troops to police its 500-mile border, or to dissipate its legitimacy through repression of the centers of resistance in the north of Syria. However, although the Syrians "were not going out of their way to stop" the movement of fighters into Iraq, the flow slowed to a trickle.[15]

At the outset of war, Syria announced that it would not cooperate with any puppet regime established in Baghdad, but in fact, caught between principle and pressure, it pursued a zigzag policy. Not wanting to be isolated from its Security Council allies at a time when it was under immediate US threat, Syria reluctantly adhered to UNSC Resolution 1483, which in effect legitimized the occupiers' control of Iraq's oil money. It even reached limited arrangements with the occupation authorities to provide electricity to Mosul and to trade Iraqi crude for Syrian petroleum products.[16] Syria refused to recognize the US-installed Iraq Governing Council (IGC), and there were conflicts over demands for the return of Iraqi assets that had been transferred to Syrian banks before the war, with Syria insisting it would only return them to a legitimate government.[17] Syria campaigned in vain to prevent the IGC's wider recognition, as both the Arab League and the Organization of Petroleum-Exporting Countries allowed it to assume Iraq's seats; yet Syria itself voted for UN Resolution 1511, which affirmed IGC's embodiment of the sovereignty of Iraq until an internationally recognized representative government could be established, and which called for action against "terrorist" infiltration of Iraq.[18] At the same time, Syria openly received delegates of Sunni groups overtly opposed to the occupation.[19] Defense Minister Mustafa Tlas insisted that Iraqi resistance to occupation was a legal right, and Bashar affirmed that Syria supported the people of Iraq against the US plan to efface its Arab and Muslim character. However, he added: "I do not mean we should support the resistance with weapons. I want to make this point clear so that it will not be misunderstood."[20]

By the end of 2003, as debate raged in Iraq over the transition to self-rule, Syria supported those demanding elections, notably the Shia, against the US attempt to manipulate representation to an Iraqi constituent assembly. Syria, Bashar affirmed, would recognize Iraq when elected and autonomous, not imposed, institutions were in place.[21] Yet keen to get the Iraqi government to acknowledge that it needed Syrian cooperation to stabilize the country (and desiring it to reopen the Kirkuk-Banyas oil pipeline closed by Washington), Syria later received interim Iraqi prime minister Iyad Allawi and signed a border security agreement with him: Syria's information minister declared that the more the Iraqi government liberated itself from US control, the more Syria would cooperate with it.[22] But in May 2005, Syria announced that diplomatic ties would be restored with Iraq after a twenty-five-year abeyance, although the Iraqi government remained dependent on the occupying forces.

This ambivalence reflected the fact that Syria was caught between its reluctance to acknowledge the principle of regime change and occupation, and its need not to be outside UN legitimacy, its desire to salvage some of its interests in Iraq, and its wish to use the US predicament in Iraq to extract concessions on US-Syrian relations. It was also torn between its revulsion at dealing with what it saw as collaborators working with the United States and its interest in rebuilding relations with Iraq's rulers, most of whom—the

Kurds, Shia, and anti-Saddam Baathists—it had supported in the Saddam Hussein era; alienating them risked the potential that Syrian influence in Iraq might (together with that of its ally, Iran) be able to counter that of the United States. Syria hoped it might yet salvage an acceptable Iraqi outcome: if the resistance were to continue unabated, the United States would be unlikely to take on Syria as well; if Iraq were to be democratized, Syria's relations with most key forces there might secure a friendly Iraq.[23]

■ Consequences of the War

Coping with Washington's "War of Nerves"

In the wake of the conquest of Iraq, sandwiched between Israeli military power in the east and the US occupation to the west, the Syrian regime's very survival required it to play its few remaining cards with the utmost skill. US secretary of state Colin Powell arrived in Damascus with a list of demands on Syria—to expel militant Palestinian factions, dismantle Hizbollah, withdraw from Lebanon, and cooperate with the occupation regime in Iraq. These demands struck at Syria's most vital interests—its cards in the struggle over the Golan, its sphere of influence in the Levant, its Arab nationalist stature in the Arab world. No Syrian government could accede to them except under the direst and most imminent threat. Moreover, US demands were presented in a triumphalist style certain to inflame resistance: Powell told the US press that "there are no illusions in [Bashar's] mind as to what we are looking for from Syria." A State Department remark ahead of the visit that "we're not coming bringing any carrots" brought foreign ministry spokesperson Bouthiana Shaaban to respond that Syria was willing to contribute to regional solutions but could not bear to be dictated to by the United States. Cooperation required "real engagement on a parity of dignity."[24]

Amid unprecedented external pressures and in the absence of Hafiz al-Asad's astute hand at the helm of state, decisionmaking by an untested president and a fractured collective leadership appeared to issue in ad hoc reactions uninformed by a coherent strategy. According to one critic, "It used to be [under Hafiz] that the president said something and it happened. Now you hear the president saying something, the foreign minister saying the opposite." The absence of Syria's delegate from the UN vote on Resolution 1483 may have been due to a dispute between the foreign minister, backed by much of the Baath Party, who opposed the resolution, and the president, who did not wish to put Syria outside the Security Council consensus and ultimately acted unilaterally.[25] Syria's ineffectualness in the Security Council and in response to an Israeli air raid in October 2003 suggested an inability to coordinate policy at the very top. Clearly the regime was being pulled in opposing directions: the public outrage at US behavior—from which the policy process was insulated under Hafiz's realpolitik—welled up through the fissures in the regime and made its legitimacy incompatible with submission to US dictates; yet the regime's survival required some accommodation with Washington.

Al-Sharaa reflected the despair of many Syrian officials at the seeming capture of US policy by what they saw as the extremist and anti-Arab "neoconservative gang that surrounds President Bush." He famously remarked that no US administration had ever displayed such violence and stupidity as Bush's.[26] On the other hand, President Bashar al-Asad wanted to prevent Syria from becoming incompatible with US ambitions in the region and hoped to exploit differences within the US administration by making some concessions. There were also those who advocated acquiescence to the regional policy of the United States if the latter lifted its threats to the regime and its pressure to liberalize internally.

Perhaps reflective of this internal balance, the regime attempted to steer a middle way between unrealistic defiance of US power and total surrender to US dictates. Syria would continue to distinguish between its real enemy, Israel, and the United States, which it hoped would return to its traditionally more balanced policy. It would use dialogue to convince the United States that unqualified support for Ariel Sharon and the invasion of Iraq, in actually inflaming terrorism, would damage its own national security. It would cooperate with the United States on shared interests, while refusing submission to demands that damaged its interests. Syria hoped Washington's difficulties in Iraq would bring it to the realization that its military power did not nullify its need for cooperation in the region, which depended on mutual respect based on sovereignty. The Syrian regime believed that it retained enough bargaining cards to sustain this policy, namely its centrality to an Arab-Israel peace, to regional stability, and to restraining Hizbollah with its proven ability to hurt Israel as well as the intelligence cooperation against terrorism that it offered the United States. Syrian elites also clung to the view that the United States could not readily resort to military force against Syria, because, unlike Iraq, Syria did not violate international legitimacy, was not subject to international sanctions, and did not suffer from the isolation of Saddam's regime.[27] Syria also tried to disarm the neoconservatives with a series of incremental concessions: closing its borders with Iraq, refraining from opposition to the so-called roadmap to Middle East peace, even though it was excluded at Israeli's behest, putting Hizbollah under heavy pressure to refrain from challenging Israel in southern Lebanon, closing the Damascus press offices of the militant Palestinian factions, and offering to unconditionally resume peace negotiations with Israel.

However, every concession Syria made to Washington merely whet the latter's appetite for more. Anders Strindberg reported that some diplomats in Damascus believed the United States wanted to humiliate Syria for its opposition to the war.[28] In June 2003, US forces clashed with and captured Syrian troops in a raid well inside the Syrian border. Washington charged that Syria had not complied with its demands, and levels of tension were described as reaching a "Syrian-American crisis."[29] In October 2003 an Israeli air raid on a Palestinian camp near Damascus was openly justified by Bush and widely seen as part of a US strategy to ratchet up the pressure on Syria. In November the so-called Syria Accountability Act passed the US Congress, allowing Bush to apply a combination of diplomatic and economic sanctions against Syria. William J. Burns, assistant secretary for Near Eastern affairs, opined that "Syria harbors the illusion that cosmetic steps will be enough to defuse our concerns . . . from a misplaced belief that U.S. engagement in Iraq and with the Israelis and Palestinians will prevent us from pursuing a robust agenda with Syria." Burns acknowledged that Syrian cooperation against Al-Qaida had saved American lives, but insisted that this was not sufficient to outweigh Damascus's continued support for other "terror groups"—that is, those contesting Israel's hold over occupied Palestinian territories.[30]

The Continuing Conflict over Iraq

Charges by the United States that Syria was facilitating the insurgency remained a continuous thread of contention and occasional engagement with Washington in the two years following the invasion. The neoconservatives, put on the defensive by the failure to find nonconventional weapons in Iraq and by the growing resistance to the occupation, sought to divert attention from these failures by blaming Syria. Empirically, we cannot ascertain the extent of Syria's role, with or without its government's connivance, in fueling the resistance in Iraq. Reportedly, 200 Syrian insurgents were captured in two years of occupation, but such foreign fighters make up no more than 3–5 percent of the total insurgency.

In order to undermine the neoconservative drive against it, Syria cracked down on the centers of Islamic militancy in Aleppo (confiscating passports, detentions), took further measures to seal the border (more troops, berms), tried to get US commanders to work with Syrian officers on border management, and requested, in vain, that the United States provide appropriate surveillance technology. The US military welcomed this stance, but cooperation was regularly squelched by its Pentagon bosses; thus in December 2004, at a time when the US military reported new Syrian checkpoints and arrests of jihadis, Secretary of Defense Donald Rumsfeld's response was to charge that Syrian meddling in Iraq was "killing Americans."[31] Bashar's orders to secure the border have perhaps only been partially implemented by rival security forces, which, for bribes or out of animosity toward the US occupation, may look the other way regarding jihadi activity. However, as Syria's tightened controls on its border during 2004 and it became obvious that there was no large-scale movement across it, and indeed, that infiltration via other countries was at least as significant,[32] Washington began to claim that, nevertheless, most of the suicide bombers came from Syria (although studies showed that over 50 percent of suicide bombers were Saudi)[33] and that militant cells inside Iraq drew on "unlimited money" from an underground financial network in Syria run by former Baath Party leaders and relatives of Saddam Hussein. In February 2005, Syria handed over a half brother of Saddam to the Iraqi authorities and deported to Tunisia and Morocco groups of their nationals involved in smuggling insurgents.[34] A telling episode was Washington's claim that Al-Qaida leader Abu Musab al-Zarqawi had traveled to Syria in April 2004 to meet insurgents based there. Later, some US officials covertly let it be known that this claim was bogus, based on a single source considered unreliable by intelligence officials but that had been quickly seized upon by the neoconservatives.[35] In May 2005 there was a major US counterinsurgency operation close to the Syrian border.

Underlying the unrelenting US demands on Syria was, in part, the fact that Washington can only avoid "imperial overreach" if it gets others to bear part of the burdens of policing the chaos in Iraq, exacerbated by its own dissolution of the Iraqi army and ultimately the responsibility of the occupier. The United States seeks to avoid the investment in money and manpower to secure the border by forcing Syria to undertake this task. What distinguishes the US moderates from the hard-liners is that the former would give Syria some incentives to do this while the latter prefer to use threats and coercion, or even to use the issue to demonize the country in preparation for regime change.

The Struggle for Lebanon

The neoconservatives had long seen Lebanon as a point of vulnerability for Syria.[36] If Syria could be forced out of Lebanon, a pro-Western Lebanese government could be brought to sign a peace treaty with Israel, and the Syrian regime, isolated and having suffered a major loss of prestige, might collapse. In 2004 a chain of events in Lebanon allowed Washington to strike a major blow at Syria, which seemingly fell into a trap being prepared for it. Apparently intent on heading off any challenges to its control over Lebanon, Syria engineered a change in the Lebanese constitution allowing its main Lebanese ally, President Emile Lahoud, to assume another term. Lahoud's rival, Rafiq al-Hariri, apparently enlisted France's President Jacques Chirac, a close friend who, perhaps seeking to heal the breach with Washington over Iraq, formed a tactical alliance with the United States in the Security Council. They engineered UNSC Resolution 1559 of September 2004, which called on Syria (without actually naming it) to withdraw from the country and for Hizbollah to disarm, despite the protest of the Lebanese government against this interference in its sovereign affairs. This change in French policy, from a buffer against, to a facilitator of, US threats against Syria, was a major diplomatic setback for Damascus.

Syria was taken wholly by surprise. It had misread US intentions over Lebanon (where Washington used to see Syria as a stabilizing force), believing its rhetoric on withdrawal was designed to obtain Syrian concessions over Iraq—which Syria at this time was delivering. It also had not expected Chirac's alliance with the United States on the issue. However, it was the assassination of Hariri that energized a convergence of forces against Syria's position in Lebanon. Europe and Washington were in accord against Syria. Faced with near-total isolation and fearful that defiance would make Damascus the target of selective enforcement of UN resolutions, Damascus apparently lost its nerve and withdrew its troops. If Syria hoped that this major concession would appease Washington, it was badly mistaken; it only whet the appetite of the neoconservatives and strengthened the position of the hard-liners, who argued that threats work better than compromise in dealing with Syria.[37] The United States now appeared committed to a policy of what Flynt Leverett called "regime change on the cheap."[38] Previously, fear of an Islamist takeover had been the main factor deterring Washington from an energetic push against the Syrian regime, but the neoconservatives were quite willing to risk what they called "creative destruction" in Syria. They were hoping that the Hariri assassination could be pinned on Syria and used to construct some international legitimation for action against it. In spring 2005, the Syrian regime, sensing the futility of appeasement, reversed its policy of concessions: intelligence and military cooperation with the United States over terrorism and the Iraqi border was ended.

Between Arabism and the West

Syria is in Washington's crosshairs largely because it is the last remaining voice of Arab nationalism that has stood up to Israel and opposed the Iraq War; the United States seeks to make an object lesson of Syria to convey the message that Arab nationalism is very costly. The final destruction of Arabism would help clear the way for a pro-Israeli Pax Americana in the region; conversely, Washington's failures in Iraq and Syria's resistance to its demands raise the prestige of the Syrian regime and its Arab nationalist ideology.[39] The United States and Syria seem locked in a zero-sum game. In this struggle, Washington has deprived Syria of some of the cards by which it exercised political leverage in regional politics and especially toward Israel, most notably its dominant role in Lebanon. Equally important, the Bush administration's devaluation of the traditional goals of US policy toward the Middle East, regional stability, and the peace process has correspondingly devalued the cards by which Syria could promise to deliver or obstruct these goals.

Unremitting US hostility made it all the more important for Syria to sustain alliances essential to block the neoconservative effort to isolate and demonize the country. Yet Syria's relations with other Arab states were strained by its criticism of their obeisance to Washington and even more so over the Hariri affair. Bashar's one success was his consolidation of detente with Turkey. His reformist image and good relations with Europe prior to the Iraq War, and Syria's impending adhesion to the Euro-Med partnership, had been seen in Damascus as a key shield against US hostility. However, in the year after the war, Washington succeeded in driving a wedge between Syria and several European countries that chose to obstruct the partnership agreement, first by making it conditional on Syria's unilateral renunciation of its nonconventional deterrent against Israel, and then by demanding its withdrawal from Lebanon. Washington was determined to make Syria pay dearly for its defiance.

■ Domestic Consequences of the War

The neoconservatives trumpeted the conquest of Iraq as a first step toward inspiring revolt against similar regimes across the region. In Syria, the war, coming at a time when reform was incrementally advancing, but when the reforming president had yet to consolidate his power, slowed domestic change. In the wake of the fall of Baghdad, Bashar sought to unjam the reform process by installing a new government of reformist technocrats, reserving only key security portfolios for Baathists. However, the party regional command, which must approve governments, refused to reduce the party's role at a time of intense external threat.

To be sure, US threats put the regime in a dilemma. "To stand up to the Americans you have to make internal changes and mobilize people around you," said one analyst. "If not, you have to follow the Americans. The regime . . . has not decided which way to go." Human rights campaigner Haitham al-Maleh and opposition figurehead Riyad al-Turk agreed that US pressures undermined reformers and enabled the regime to justify continued emergency powers.[40] Indeed, reformers "see no evidence of the Americans wanting democracy in Syria, rather they want to change the behavior of the regime in favor of the Israelis."[41] The regime faced criticism for the ineffectualness of its response to the Israeli attacks, but no opposition figure advocated submission to US demands to reduce support for Hizbollah or militant Palestinians. An exiled opposition figure famously said that not a single Syrian would accept returning to Syria on a US tank. Regime security baron Bahjat Suleiman acknowledged that the Syrian opposition was loyal, and

Bashar claimed that the small percentage of people who thought the war on Iraq would help democracy had been disillusioned by the disaster it inflicted on that country.[42] Syrians of all ages, sects, and classes seemed to share a profound dislike of Bush for having attacked Iraq, as they believed, on behalf of Israel and to seize its oil. Some favorably compared their president's stands to the failure of the "cowards who run the Arab countries" to stand up to Bush.[43] The Iraq War stimulated an Islamic revival and the regime tried to use it to strike a détente with Islamic forces that had long represented the main alternative to Baathist rule.[44] The secular loyal opposition asked to be included in a national unity government to strengthen Syria against the external threat, but an elite under siege from without declined to simultaneously risk political change from within.

The legitimacy of Bashar's regime might be thought to have greatly suffered from its post–Iraq War reverses, given that this has long rested on its claim to act for Syrian Arab nationalism. If Hafiz was respected for his effectiveness on behalf of this cause, Bashar has been humiliated by his inability to respond to US pressures or Israeli military provocations and his forced evacuation of Lebanon. To Arab nationalist-minded Syrians, Bashar may appear to have squandered the cards his father left him. For others, the mounting costs that the defense of Arabism is inflicting on Syria, combined with the me-first policies of the other Arab states and the recent anti-Syrian animosity displayed by many Lebanese, have stimulated a certain growth of a "little Syrian" identity at least partly divorced from Arabism. To the extent this is the long-term outcome, Washington will have won.

Yet there are counterforces and indicators. The very fact that Washington targets the regime for its stands on behalf of still popular *Arab* causes—its support of Palestine, its association with Hizbollah, and its opposition to the invasion of Iraq—generates a certain solidarity between regime and people—and conversely, concessions to the United States cost some of this legitimacy. Many Syrians, feeling victimized by the US-orchestrated global demonization of Syria over its presence in Lebanon, rallied around the government rather than turning against it. Additionally, the chaos and sectarian conflict in Iraq, together with the fear—ignited by the Kurdish riots of 2003 and the rise of Islamic militancy—that the "Iraqi disease" could spread to Syria, lead the public to put a high premium on stability. This generates for the regime what might be called "legitimacy because of a worse alternative."[45]

■ Notes

1. Patrick Seale, "Why Are the US and Israel Threatening Syria?" *Al-Hayat*, 18 April 2003.
2. Raymond Hinnebusch, *Syria*, pp. 139–164.

3. A 1996 document, "A Clean Break: A New Strategy for Securing the Realm," drafted by a team of advisers to Israeli prime minister Benjamin Netanyahu by current Bush administration officials, Richard Perle and Douglas Feith, called for "striking Syrian military targets in Lebanon, and should that prove insufficient, *striking at select targets in Syria proper*" "Is Syria Next?" *The Nation,* November 3, 2003. A report written in 2000 by Daniel Pipes and Ziad Abdelnour, who heads the US Committee for a Free Lebanon, strongly criticized Washington's policy of engaging Syria rather than confronting it, and called for a preemptive war on Syria using Israeli proxy forces in Lebanon and Israeli forces to strike at Syrian targets if needed. A way to win US support for a preemptive war against Syria, they suggested, was by "drawing attention to its weapons of mass destruction program." Immediately before the Iraq invasion, Undersecretary of State for Arms Control and International Security John Bolton traveled to Israel and promised Prime Minister Ariel Sharon that "it will be necessary to deal with threats from Syria, Iran, and North Korea afterwards." Tom Barry, "On the Road to Damascus: The Neo-Cons Target Syria," *Counterpunch,* 8 March 2004.

4. Jim Lobe, "Bush Stance on Syria Hit Shows Neocons Still Hold Sway," *Interpress Service,* 8 October 2003; *Middle East International,* 21 November 2003, p. 25.

5. *Financial Times,* 17 April 2003; Anders Strindberg, "Iraq Crisis Threatens Syrian Reforms," *Jane's Intelligence Review* 15, no. 1 (January 2003), pp. 38–41.

6. Eyal Zisser, "Syria and the War in Iraq."

7. Strindberg, "Iraq Crisis."

8. Dilip Hiro, *Secrets and Lies,* pp. 98–99.

9. Oxford Business Group, online briefing, 2 October 2003, http://www.oxfordbusinessgroup.com.

10. Steven Stalinsky and Eli Carmeli, "The Syrian Government and Media on the War in Iraq," Middle East Media Research Institute, Inquiry and Analysis Series no. 134, 21 April 2003, http://memri.org.

11. Ibid.; Oxford Business Group, online briefing, 31 March 2003, http://www.oxfordbusinessgroup.com.

12. *Al-Safir,* 17 March 2003.

13. *Middle East International,* 2 May 2003, p. 13; *Financial Times,* 26 August, 2003; *International Herald Tribune,* 16 July 2003, p. 6.

14. *Middle East International,* 4 April 2003, pp. 9, 25.

15. *Washington Post,* 29 October 2003; *Middle East Intelligence Bulletin,* June 2003; *Middle East International,* 25 July 2003, p. 7.

16. Oxford Business Group, online briefing, 22 August 2003, 6 September 2003, http://www.oxfordbusinessgroup.com.

17. *The Times,* 21 October 2003; *Middle East International,* 5 December 2003, pp. 19–21.

18. *Middle East Intelligence Bulletin,* November 2003; Oxford Business Group, online briefing, 22 August 2003, http://www.oxfordbusinessgroup.com; *Middle East International,* 24 October 2003, pp. 8–9.

19. *Financial Times,* 3 November 2003, p. 9; *Middle East Intelligence Bulletin,* November 2003.

20. Bashar al-Assad, interview with *Al-Arabiya* in Middle East Media Research Institute, Special Dispatch Series no. 527, 22 June 2003, http://memri.org.

21. See http://nytimes.com/2003/12/01.

22. *Al-Hayat,* 7 July 2004; *Daily Star,* 26 July 2004; Rime Allaf, "Point of No Return? American Relations with Syria," *World Today,* November 2004.

23. *Middle East International,* 13 June 2003, pp. 27–29.

24. *Financial Times,* 26 August 2003; *Federal News Service,* 18 June 2003.

25. *Financial Times,* 26 August 2003.

26. *Al-Hayat,* 29 July 2003.

27. Imad Fawzi Al-Shuaibi in *Al-Hayat,* 13 July 2003; *Al-Hayat,* 23 July 2003.

28. Anders Strindberg, "America's Nonsensical Syria policy," *Middle East International,* 25 July 2003, pp. 27–29.

29. Walid Choucair, "The Syrian-American Crisis," *Al-Hayat,* 1 August, 2003.

30. Statement before the Senate Foreign Relations Committee, Washington, DC, 30 October 2003. In regard to intelligence cooperation, Seymour Hersh reported that the CIA had told him that Syria passed on hundreds of files of crucial data regarding Al-Qaida and other radical Islamic groups in the Middle East and that "the quality and quantity of information from Syria exceeded the agency's expectations," but that Syria "got little in return for it" except neoconservative-inspired hostility. Seymour Hersh, "The Syrian Bet," *New Yorker* magazine, 27 July 2003. See also "Is Syria Next?" *The Nation,* 3 November 2003; *New York Times,* 6 February 2004.

31. Flynt Leverett, *Inheriting Syria,* p. 140.

32. *Daily Star,* 9 March 2004.

33. Anthony Cordesman, *Iraq's Evolving Insurgency,* pp. 47–48.

34. Oxford Business Group, Syria, 7 July 2005.

35. *SyriaComment.com,* 3 June 2005.

36. Leverett, *Inheriting Syria,* p. 144.

37. Joshua Landis reports on the triumphalism in the US embassy in Damascus at *SyriaComment.com,* Friday, 3 June 2005.

38. *Financial Times,* 2 May 2005, 17 June 2005.

39. Ashraf Fahim, *Daily Star,* 24 April 2004.

40. *Financial Times,* 26 August 2003.

41. *Financial Times,* 29 October 2003, p. 14.

42. See http://nytimes.com/2003/12/01.

43. Saul Landau, "A Report from Syria: Between Israel and Iraq . . . a Hard Place," http://www.counterpunch.com, 26 July 2003.

44. See http://www.csmonitor.com, 3 November 2003.

45. *Al-Ahram Weekly Online,* 16–22 June 2005, http://weekly.ahram.org/eg; David Hurst, *Los Angeles Times,* 7 June 2005.

11

Jordan:
Appeasing the Hegemon

Neil Quilliam

K ing Abdullah of Jordan advised Washington against the Iraq War but ended up bandwagoning with the United States, even giving the invaders covert and tacit support, in defiance of the overwhelming opinion of his own public. By contrast, during the Gulf War (1990–1991), Abdullah's father, Hussein, had remained neutral, although the US-led coalition considered him to be supportive of Iraq, thereby putting Jordan outside the "new world order." King Hussein's policy reflected the mood of his country, particularly Jordan's Palestinian communities who applauded Saddam Hussein's linkage of Iraq's withdrawal from Kuwait with Israel's from the occupied West Bank and Gaza. This earned King Hussein valuable political capital that he subsequently spent on concluding a peace treaty with Israel in 1994, the price exacted from Jordan for readmission to the international community.

King Abdullah, who succeeded his father in February 1999, was in a different situation and made different choices when it came to the 2003 US-led war on Iraq. He must have had in mind the high costs of his father's policies in terms of Western economic support. Moreover, lacking his father's broad domestic legitimacy outside his immediate circle, traditional supporters, and the armed forces, he opted to rely on outside powers, the United States and European Union, to shore up his position and strategy. If, during the Gulf War, King Hussein was unable to resist the pressure of the crowd, during the Iraq War, King Abdullah was unable to resist that of the United States. And he was able to weather the storm of protest at home with relative ease.

■ Government Policy Toward the War

Publicly, the Jordanian government opposed the war against Iraq. The king stressed to the United States and European Union that a diplomatic solution,

143

in accordance with UN Security Council (UNSC) Resolutions 1284 (1999) and 1409 (2002), was the only appropriate model for resolving the conflict between Iraq and the UN. In August 2002 he told the *Washington Post* that an attempt to invade Iraq would be a "tremendous mistake" and that it could "throw the whole area into turmoil."[1] Abdullah also tried to persuade the United States to put more energies into resolving the Palestinian-Israeli conflict. He was consistent in opposing the war, but also called upon Iraq to comply with UN resolutions; thus the king distanced himself from US policy, but placed the responsibility for the outcome firmly on the shoulders of Saddam Hussein. This caveat led some observers, at the time, to believe that the king had already reached an agreement to lend facilities to the United States during the war, on the condition that the United States would stand by the Jordanian regime, come what may. It was also the case that Abdullah had been strident in his support of the previous US war on Afghanistan and of the ongoing "war on terror," despite a groundswell of domestic opposition to both. As the prospect of war drew nearer, King Abdullah agreed to allow US military forces to be stationed in Jordan on the condition that their presence be kept as secret as possible. Prime Minister Abul Ragheb also stressed that Jordan would not take part in any military acts against Iraq and neither would it permit the use of its land or airspace for this purpose.[2] "The U.S. knows we're walking a very tight rope here," Foreign Minister Marwan Muasher told foreign journalists on 13 March 2003.[3] In reality, Washington did employ Jordanian-based forces against Iraq. The Jordanian monarchy has to perform a delicate balancing act between the often contradictory pressures of domestic, regional, and international arenas.

■ Determinants of Jordan's Policy

Domestic and Regional Pressures

No Jordanian leader can wholly ignore the views of the Jordanians of Palestinian origin, who constitute an estimated 60 percent of the Jordanian population, and although their loyalty to the Jordanian monarchy is more or less secured, their sympathies clearly remain with their brethren in Israel, the West Bank, and Gaza. This makes the monarchy's alignment with the United States, Israel's main backer, a domestic liability. The proposed attack on Iraq, paralleling George W. Bush's support for the massive Israeli repression against the Palestinian intifada, made a stand with the United States deeply unpopular. It was no less unpopular with the Transjordanian part of the population, who have had long-standing ties with and even admiration for the Iraqi regime as a bulwark of Arab nationalism. The Transjordanian residents of the southern city of Maan, who have frequently resisted the central authority of the state, had benefited from the sanctions imposed upon Saddam Hussein's regime, as they provided a lucrative transport service between Aqaba port and the Iraqi border; therefore the decision to align Jordan with the United States helped undermine Maan's primary source of income, trade, and employment. The decision was also unpopular among Islamists of both Jordanian and Palestinian background; the modus operandi established by King Hussein between the state and the Islamic Action Front nevertheless survived, providing Abdullah with sufficient autonomy to implement his preferred policy. However, more radical Islamists, such as Abu Musab al-Zarqawi, later joined the Sunni-led insurgency in Iraq.

At the regional level, Jordan had a relation of economic interdependence with Iraq. In 2002, Iraq was Jordan's principal trading partner. Bilateral trade between the two countries represented 20 percent of Jordan's $6 billion in external trade. Moreover, Iraq had a tradition of selling cheap crude oil to Jordan. For example, under a 2001 agreement, Jordan obtained half of its crude oil free of charge, and received a discount of 40 percent of the price above $20 per barrel on the other half. Thus Jordan needed strong guarantees from the United States that if Saddam Hussein's regime were deposed, it would still be the recipient of favorable trade with the new Iraqi regime. Jordan's decision to quietly endorse the Iraq War marked a break with its long-standing close ties with Iraq.

Economic Imperatives

Internal economic imperatives were crucial in explaining Abdullah's choices. King Abdullah's accession to the throne coincided with a growing perception that the rentier era was over and that globalization posed a significant challenge to Jordanian livelihood while also providing new opportunities if Jordan could position itself better in the global economy. At the same time, Abdullah's ambition, given his inability to play the nationalist card in a new world order profoundly hostile to Arabism, was to root the legitimacy of the monarchy in its ability to provide its citizenry with "economic security." Anticipating that the state would be unable to continue its traditional role as an allocator of rent, the government had embarked on a deepening liberalization of the economy. Jordanians would have to be encouraged to become competitive on the world market, taking advantage of their relative high levels of education and skills in which the government had been investing. This project involved increasing integration into the world market, facilitated by accession to the Euro-Med partnership and the World Trade Organization. It had its risks and downsides, however. The restructuring demanded by international economic institutions tended to penalize the poor, and its pursuit remained inexplicable to the average citizen. Thus Jordan would all the more require outside aid and understanding in helping it over this difficult transition. In the short term, at least, Jordan's economic dependency on the West was actually deepened by this project (especially as Jordan's stand on the war jeopardized the economic benefits from its Iraqi ties).

Jordan's predicament was understood by its Western patrons, and its foreign policy moderation had been earning it considerable political credit and economic aid even before the war. A free trade accord and a debt-rescheduling agreement with the Paris Club of creditors in July 2002 indicated the substantial rewards that close ties with the United States could bring. In any event, Jordan's strategic utility to Washington was rewarded in May 2003 when the United States agreed to pay $700 million compensation to mitigate the adverse effect of war on tourism, in addition to the normal $450 million annual economic, military, and food aid.[4] Additionally, the EU granted Jordan 35 million euros in emergency funds in November 2003.[5]

The US Alliance

The Jordanian regime cannot do without the United States—whether it is the protection of its security against both Israeli ambitions and Arab resentment, the annual subsidies its treasury needs to keep the government running, or the economic opportunities the US market can provide. Especially, given his economic project, Abdullah could not afford to replicate his father's choices and antagonize Washington. Although he sought to temper US policy toward Iraq (and the Palestinian-Israeli conflict), Jordan's king understood the missionary zeal of the US administration and its determination to remove Saddam Hussein. He calculated that Jordan's medium-term interests would be better served if they correlated with US policies in the region and the prevailing world order, which Washington dominated. For a resource-poor state, the war was an irresistible opportunity to demonstrate Jordan's loyalty to Washington in the hope of continuing economic and political rewards.

■ Controlling the Domestic Backlash

King Abdullah, having felt compelled to respond to international rather than domestic pressures, had perforce to control the potentially destabilizing domestic backlash. The day after the war started, he made an emotive speech on television. He insisted Jordan had done everything within its power to prevent the outbreak of war, and called for unity and stability, saying: "Let us all be one hand, one family, one heart and let us work in the spirit of one team in order to preserve our security and stability." Abdullah's speech was replete with references to maintaining domestic security. He advised that demonstrations in favor of Iraq should be "expressed in a civilized manner that will help to ease the anguish of our brothers . . . our expression should reflect the true belonging to beloved Jordan."[6]

The king's speech triggered a contentious public debate. Ninety-five well known political personalities signed a petition appealing to the king to declare the war illegal. They argued that "moral, national and legal duties oblige all Arab governments to clearly denounce the aggression on Iraq as illegitimate."[7] The signatories included four former prime ministers, Ahmad Obeidat, Taher Masri, Abdel-Raouf Rawabdeh, and Mudar Badran; courtiers, such as Adnan Abu Odeh; security barons, such as Samih Bino, former head of the Anti-Corruption Unit at the General Intelligence Department; along with former ministers and parliamentary deputies. The petition signaled the level of discontent felt toward the government's Iraq policy even among the king's traditional supporters. Seemingly coming from within the very state establishment, it was a unique challenge to the Hashimite monarchy. Moreover, the government's position was deeply unpopular among the Jordanian population. During the course of the war, over 100 demonstrations were held in the capital, Amman. The opposition, a loose collection of Islamists, Arab nationalists, and communists, was firmly opposed to the war. The country abounded with conspiracy theories about the US intent to subdue the region, impose democracy, capture energy resources, and serve Israel's interests.

Abdullah's response to the opposition to his policy was unequivocal. He responded firmly: "I am a Muslim, an Arab and a Hashemite. No one can outbid my concern for my people and nation."[8] However, it was the intact loyalty of state institutions, notably the armed forces and security services and the support of Jordan's largest tribal confederations, that enabled the regime to weather the crisis. The regime was able to mobilize counterpetitions, filling local newspapers with pledges of support for the king and praise for his efforts to prevent the war, and, in this, support came not only from the king's traditional supporters—the Transjordanians—but also from the Palestinian-dominated business community.[9] Additionally, the Jordanian government continued its "Jordan First campaign," which promoted loyalty to Jordan over other causes, such as sympathies with Iraq, pan-Islamism, pan-Arabism, Baathism, tribalism, and the Palestinian cause. It called for a new social contract in which, in return for citizen loyalty, the regime would negotiate the currents of international crisis and globalization in order to promote Jordanians' standard of living. For some, however, the campaign denoted Jordanian complicity with a US-led war on Iraq or promoted the interests of Transjordanians over Palestinians.

Important to the government's ability to contain and dominate the public discourse was the series of repressive laws it had already enacted, taking advantage of the 9/11 crisis and issued by decree after being rejected by parliament. Thus, public demonstrations could not be held without permission of the authorities. The government was authorized to close newspapers, impose heavy fines, and imprison journalists, for up to three years, for producing material offensive to the royal family or considered to be "harmful to national unity," or that might sow the seeds of hatred and malice or instigate acts of religious and racial fanaticism.[10] Owing to these press laws, the press became the mouthpiece of the government and sought to "nuance" the Jordanian position vis-à-vis Iraq. Where necessary, the king could still rely on the loyalty of his security services to sustain his foreign policy in the face of public opposition. The repression of the rebellion in Maan in November 2002 indicated that the special relationship between the monarchy and the traditional repressive levers of the state, oiled by patronage, nepotism, and *wasta* (intercession), had not been irreparably damaged by the crisis.[11]

Finally, a significant factor in the regime's ability to contain the fallout of the war was the rapid implosion of the Iraqi regime that stunned the Jordanian public. Demoralized, Jordanians no longer took to the streets and instead resigned themselves to another round of humiliation, silently attributing the cause to the failure of all Arab regimes.

■ Domestic Politics in the Shadow of Iraq: The 2003 Elections

The government's reputation was bruised by its policy on Iraq and it sought to restore confidence by reinstituting the democratic process and lifting press restrictions.[12] Although it surprised few when King Abdullah postponed the November 2001 elections, the decision to announce the dates of a new election during the US-led war on Iraq was met with disbelief. However, the 2001 Elections Law had been carefully crafted to curtail the Islamists' influence by increasing the number of seats in parliament from 80 to 110, and ensuring that the king's loyalists were awarded with a disproportionate number of them. Hence the elections produced a result entirely consistent with the king's wishes and his government's vision. The fourteenth lower house of parliament comprises seventeen Islamic Action Front (IAF) members, five Independent Islamists, and two Leftist Democrats, with the remaining seats held by tribal members. The Pan-Arabist and Baathist Parties failed to win a seat, as did the National Democratic Current and the Democratic Bloc. Twenty-six parliamentarians represent the business community.[13] The seventeen seats won by the IAF would have been far greater had electoral districts not been gerrymandered.[14] Although a more liberal chamber would have been more conducive to the economic reform program embraced by the king and government, a tribal-conservative chamber beholden to the king was the lesser of two evils—for the only realistic alternative, an Islamist parliament, would have both thwarted the king's reform agenda and challenged his legitimacy.

▪ The Impact of War on Jordan's External Relations

So far, King Abdullah has weathered the storm of regional unrest. On one level, his calculation has paid off. The US-led war swept the Iraqi regime aside and with the United States at the helm of Iraq, Jordan expected privileged access to contracts, decisionmaking, and a cheap supply of oil. If this were to be the case, and were the livelihoods of the Iraqi population seen to improve, and a legitimate government—accepted by the Iraqis and capable of ruling the country, restoring peace and order—put in place, then King Abdullah could claim his policy to be a resounding success, silencing his domestic critics.

However, the US neoconservative plan did not take into account the human and financial cost of occupying Iraq. As long as the occupying forces are unable to restore peace and provide security for Iraqis, Abdullah's decision will remain suspect in the eyes of the Jordanian public. Moreover, there are perceptible tensions between the Jordanian government and the Iraqi National Congress (INC), which constituted an important part of the Iraqi Governing Council. Members of the INC, a predominantly Shia organization, contend that Jordanian-Iraqi trade ties helped entrench the Baathist regime and helped perpetuate its rule of oppression. Moreover, 2005 Iraqi elections led to the creation of a Shia-led government, and this may place Jordanian-Iraqi relations under considerable strain.

The Iraq War also served to fully restore Jordan's relations with Saudi Arabia and Kuwait. King Abdullah's patient diplomacy has begun to bear fruit, and an oil agreement reached with Kuwait, thanks to strong US pressure on Kuwait, is an important testament to his efforts.[15] The current oil supply agreement with Kuwait will probably become permanent, and this should insulate the government to some degree from shocks associated with the global oil market. Similarly, the government can expect a growing tax take from the new and reformulated trade ties emerging with Iraq.

Most important, Jordan proved to be a reliable partner of the United States and demonstrated its strategic utility to the Bush administration. However, Jordan's tacit support of the Iraq War did not translate into blanket support for the United States. The Jordanian cabinet has continuously argued that the international community and the UN should play a central role in Iraq. Furthermore, they have called for a political system that empowers Iraq's diverse communities and safeguards the security of future Iraqi governments. In this context, the Jordanian government called upon the UN to play a supervisory role in Iraq's first post-Saddam elections.

▪ Conclusion

The Iraq war may have served the interests of the Hashimite monarchy and provided King Abdullah with enough latitude, money, and opportunity to reorient Jordan toward a liberal version of modernity. Both king and government took a considerable gamble and invested their political acumen in the prevailing international order, sacrificing nationalist and Islamic legitimacy. King Abdullah's legitimacy and domestic reputation now, therefore, rest wholly on his ability to produce a tangible increase in the welfare of the Jordanian population, and this, in turn, is dependent on continuing US support. One could characterize Jordan's foreign policy as conforming to the dependency school of thought, whereby it is constrained by the immediate political environment, but the state is awarded conditional autonomy by its international patrons. If the government's economic reforms start to bear fruit, and the United States remains a loyal and durable partner, Jordan can expect to transform its vulnerability—US clientage—into an asset. However, if the instability and insecurity in Iraq continues, the Jordanian monarchy and government may find themselves isolated, if the next US administration withdraws its military or cultivates a new strategic partnership with the Iraqi government. In both cases, Jordan may find out that its strategic value was overinflated.

▪ Notes

1. G. Kessler and P. Slevin, "Abdullah: Foreign Leaders Oppose Attack; Jordanian King to Urge Bush to Focus on Peace in Mideast, Not Invasion of Iraq," *Washington Post,* 1 August 2002.

2. "Abul Ragheb: Jordan Will Not Take Part in Any Military Act Against Iraq," 21 January 2003, http://www.arabicnews.com/ansub/daily/day/030121/2003012105.html.

3. V. Walt, "U.S. Troops Keep Quiet on Iraq's Western Front," 16 March 2003, http://www.usatoday.com/news/world/iraq/2003-03-16-iraq-border-usat_x.htm.

4. H. Azzam, "Jordan's Economic Growth Prospects for the Second Half of 2003," *Daily Star,* 24 June 2003.

5. "EU Gives Jordan 35 Million Euros to Help with Economic Fallout of Iraq War," 4 November 2003, http://www.eubusiness.com/afp/031104145254.ngyl3oib.

6. Speech by King Abdullah, 21 March 2003, http://www.jordanembassyus.org/hmka03212003.htm.

7. Muriel Mirak-Weissbach, "Arab Nations Changed, Shaken by the War," *Executive Intelligence Review* 30, no. 14 (11 April 2003), http://www.larouchepub.com/other/2003/3014arab_destabil.html.

8. *Petra News Agency,* interview with King Abdullah, 2 April 2003, http://www.jordanembassyus.org/hmka04022003.htm.

9. Economist Intelligence Unit, *Jordan Country Report.*

10. A. S. Hamzeh, "Jordan Press Association Assigns Lawyer to Contest Penal Code Amendments," *Middle East News Online,* 26 October 2001, http://www.mideastweb.org/mewnews1.htm.

11. For more details about Maan, see *Red Alert in Jordan: Recurrent Unrest in Maan,* International Crisis Group, February 2003, http://www.crisisweb.org/home/index.cfm?id=1824&l=1.

12. The government repealed the 2001 amendment to Article 150 of the penal code on 21 April 2003. Economist Intelligence Unit, *Jordan Country Report.*

13. K. Dalal, "1.3 Million Voters Elect New Parliament," *Jordan Times,* 18 June 2003.

14. The IAF won twenty-three out of eighty seats in 1989, and became the single largest bloc. It boycotted the 1997 elections, but participated in the 2003 elections.

15. Kuwait, Saudi Arabia, and the United Arab Emirates (UAE) have supplied Jordan with 100,000 barrels per day of oil at preferential prices since the suspension of the Iraqi oil supplies after the breakout of the war in March 2003, with Saudi Arabia providing 50,000 barrels per day and Kuwait and the UAE 25,000 barrels per day each. This agreement was initially concluded for three months, then renewed for successive periods. "Kuwait to Renew Oil Supplies to Jordan," *Jordan Times,* 6 August 2003.

12

Saudi Arabia: The Challenge of the US Invasion of Iraq

Madawi al-Rasheed

The US invasion of Iraq in 2003 was perhaps the most difficult challenge facing the Saudi government since the Gulf War of 1990–1991. The invasion was unprecedented, unprovoked, and lacking in wide Arab and international support and in the name of threats, specifically, weapons of mass destruction (WMDs) and links to Al-Qaida, that proved to have little credibility. Official Saudi Arabia wished to see Saddam Hussein and the Baath regime go, but feared the aftermath. It opted for an indecisive position, hiding behind a confused rhetoric of open objections to the war in regional Arab meetings and forums and implicit approval, even secret cooperation in allowing US military command centers to conduct the war from its own territory. The ramifications of the swift collapse of the Baathist regime as a result of military intervention without a UN Security Council resolution have set a precedent that could have serious consequences for Saudi Arabia and the whole of the Middle East.

■ The Determinants of Saudi Policy

Saudi Arabia and Iraq: An Uneasy Accommodation

The Saudi position vis-à-vis the war on Iraq has to be put in the context of the historical rivalry between the two states—rooted in sectarian differences between a predominantly Sunni Saudi Arabia and Shia majority Iraq; the al-Saud–Hashimite rivalry over leadership in the Arab world;[1] and the clash between the pro-Western Saudi orientation and the revolutionary rhetoric of the various Iraqi leaderships after 1958.[2] When Iran's revolutionary rhetoric threatened Saudi Arabia, Riyadh financed Saddam's war, but this was a temporary alliance of necessity, with Saudi Arabia hoping that the Iran-Iraq War would destroy both contestants for the position of "Gulf regional power." When Saddam invaded Kuwait, Saudi Arabia hosted the US operation Desert Storm against him, and in the 1990s supported international sanctions against Iraq, even allowing its territory to be used by the British and US military to monitor the no-fly zones over Iraq involving periodic attacks on Iraqi targets. Yet after 2000 the Saudi government began to pursue a policy of "rehabilitating" the Iraqi leader, now that he was exhausted and crippled by almost a decade of international sanctions,[3] a stance accelerated by the strains in its relations with the United States.

Domestic Consequences of the Gulf War

In the Gulf War, there had been an overwhelming consensus within the Saudi government over the need for the liberation of Kuwait, although public opinion was divided on the means to achieve this goal. Saudi Arabia cooperated fully in the US war effort and financed the military operations. However, this had undesirable consequences. It was a tremendous economic burden and resulted in mounting debt to the US government.[4] At the domestic political level, Saudi cooperation unleashed an indigenous Islamist opposition whose seeds had been sown in the country prior to Saddam's invasion of Kuwait.[5] The reason behind the strengthening of the Islamist opposition was Saudi Arabia's complete reliance on foreign troops, mainly Americans, to liberate Kuwait and defend itself against what was considered an imminent Iraqi attack. Saudi Islamists considered their government's acceptance of a US military presence to be religiously and politically unacceptable given Saudi Arabia's "sacred" status as the land of the two Holy Mosques.[6] Most Islamists regarded the presence of US troops as symbolic of the country's dependence on this superpower to the detriment of Saudi Arabia's independence and sovereignty.

Strains in the US-Saudi Alliance

Another challenge facing Saudi Arabia comes from the strains introduced into its long-standing strategic alliance with the United States by the attacks of 11 September 2001. That the attacks were sponsored by Osama bin Laden, a Saudi national, using fifteen young Saudis, stimulated US suspicion of and even hostility toward the Saudi regime. US pundits criticized not only individual princes but also the country's political structure, economic opaqueness, educational program, religious curriculum, social and cultural traditions, lack of religious freedom, and treatment of minorities and women.[7] This criticism was accompanied by open accusations of sponsoring terrorism, princely connections with charitable organizations listed as having connections to Al-Qaida, a lawsuit against several high-ranking Saudi princes by the families of the victims of the 11 September attacks, the expulsion of several Saudis with diplomatic status from Washington, and the imprisonment of more than 100 Saudis in Guantanamo Bay. Following the 9/11 attacks, the United States began preparing for a reduction in its military presence in

Saudi Arabia in favor of the small neighboring Gulf states.[8] Key US figures, researchers, and journalists accused Saudi Arabia of the abuse of human rights and lack of religious freedom. In the eyes of many Saudis, Saudi Arabia's main patron-protector was turning into a threat.

The US-led war on Afghanistan in 2001 caught Saudi Arabia between the need to appease its US patron and Islamic opinion. While Saudi Arabia was more than happy to see the demise of the Taliban regime and the weakening of bin Laden's Al-Qaida base, the government was reluctant to openly declare its full support for the onslaught on Afghanistan, although US military bases in Saudi Arabia were used as a launching ground for military operations throughout autumn 2001.[9] Support for the US war on Afghanistan was "implicit" at the official level as the government impatiently awaited the capture or killing of bin Laden, who more than any other opposition in the history of the Saudi state represented a serious threat to the continuity and stability of the Saudi regime.[10] Bin Laden's Islamic rhetoric and actions have combined to create a volatile political climate in Saudi Arabia, where his popularity was evident among some religious scholars and the youth of the country.[11]

■ The Official Saudi Position on the War

As the US invasion of Iraq became inevitable, the question of whether Saudi Arabia wanted the Baath regime replaced by a pro-Western government "pumping oil in greater quantities than Saudi Arabia" posed a dilemma for the Saudi government.[12] Furthermore, Saudi Arabia worried about the possibility of an Iraqi Shia pro-Iranian government installed at its doorstep, following the demise of Saddam's Sunni regime. Saudi Arabia's responses to the war had to be handled carefully so that the US-Saudi strategic alliance did not suffer, while at the same time maintaining the semblance of Arab solidarity against US aggression to appease its own indigenous population.

In summer 2002 the question of Saudi Arabia's cooperation with the United States in the war against Iraq became urgent. In an interview, Prince Saud al-Faysal, Saudi Arabia's foreign minister, confirmed that "it is . . . only wise to give the diplomatic solution a chance before going to war and this is what we are asking the United States to do." When asked whether Saudi Arabia would allow more US troops to be placed on Saudi soil, the foreign minister replied, "under the present circumstances with no proof that there is a threat imminent from Iraq, I don't think Saudi Arabia will join in."[13]

In October 2002 Saudi Arabia declared that his country would allow US use of Saudi military facilities to attack Iraq, provided there was UN approval for it; but on 4 November 2002, Faysal told CNN that it would not.[14] In the same month, during a televised address on Saudi television, Crown Prince Abdullah insisted that "our armed forces will, under no circumstances, step one foot into Iraqi territory" and added that "we do not accept that this war should threaten Iraq's unity and sovereignty or that its resources or internal security should be subjected to a military occupation." Abdullah called for "a united free and independent Iraq, a principle that we refuse to negotiate or discuss."[15] By March 2003 it had become clear that Saudi Arabia "will not play a pivotal role in case the US attacks Iraq. Saudi Arabia will play a secondary role. Saudi Arabia have been pressuring the US not to show to the outside world that they are using Saudi Arabia as a take off point for its attack."[16]

The contradiction and ambiguity of the Saudi position reflected the regime's desperation both to appease Washington and not be seen providing a territorial base for the US attack. It also reflected a lack of consensus among senior members of the royal family, mainly Crown Prince Abdullah; Prince Sultan, minister of defense and aviation; and Faysal. Saudi Arabia continued throughout the tense months before the war to call for a diplomatic and peaceful solution to the crisis, by allowing the inspectors more time and urging Saddam to cooperate with the UN inspectors team and implement UN Resolution 1441. This was in line with the formal Arab position in the 2002 Arab League Beirut summit, which declared that an attack on Iraq "would be an attack on the national sovereignty of all Arab states."[17]

This rhetoric was a direct response to Saudi domestic opinion, which was overwhelmingly antiwar and anti-US, following US accusations that Saudi Arabia had directly or indirectly "sponsored terrorism." The regime gave the green light to its own intellectuals, religious scholars, international lawyers, writers, and journalists to respond to the US media onslaught.[18] Hundreds of Saudis enthusiastically took up this window of opportunity after decades of being censored by the government as they evaluated US policies toward their own country, the US military presence in Saudi Arabia, and US bias in favor of Israel in the Israeli-Palestinian conflict.[19]

The official position was declared on 18 March 2003 by Prince Saud al-Faysal: "1-under no circumstances will the Kingdom participate in the war against the brotherly nation of Iraq, 2-we expect the war to end upon implementation of the Security Council Resolution 1441 to eliminate weapons of mass destruction, 3-we avoid engaging in a reckless adventure that endangers the safety of our country and people."[20] Yet, while no US troops directly arrived in Iraq from Saudi territory, the government let US forces use military bases for directing planes and monitoring war efforts. During the war Faysal proposed a cease-fire "that allows for diplomacy to work,"[21] while Saudi Arabia called upon Saddam to save his country by stepping down.

■ Saudi Society and the War

An accurate assessment of Saudi opinion on the war is difficult in the absence of opinion polls and given the ban on public protest. However, no less than in the rest of the Arab world, in Saudi Arabia the so-called Arab street was overwhelmingly antiwar and anti-US. The US justification for war—the threat of WMDs—lacked credibility, given Washington's endorsement of Israeli WMDs. Yet Saudis also remembered the Iraqi invasion of Kuwait in 1990 and the Scud missiles that landed in Riyadh as the liberation of Kuwait from Saudi soil began. The majority of Saudis rejected the US military intervention as a matter of principle, but agreed on the need for regime change in Iraq as long as this change was carried out by Iraqis. Saudis differed on the interpretation of the events and the means needed for achieving regime change in Iraq.

The US war on Iraq was rejected by a broad cross section of Saudi intellectuals, professionals, and writers, including nationalists, Baathists, Nasserites, leftists, liberals, and independents. A petition against the war was published by a group of liberal Saudis associated with the call for *islah,* or reform of the Saudi political system. The list of names also included Shia activists and religious scholars—for example, Sheikh Hasan al-Safar. On 13 March 2003, more than fifty Saudis signed and published a petition in the form of a letter to US president George W. Bush. They welcomed democratic change in Iraq and most definitely in their own country, but insisted that it could not be brought about by an "unjust war." They stated:

> We regard your threats to use force in countries like Iraq, Iran, Lebanon, North Korea, Indonesia and Palestine as reflecting the law of the jungle and [believe it] will undermine human civilisation. . . . We reject your foreign policy, which is based on . . . war and undermining the stability of governments and even overthrowing them. We object to your unilateralism and your inability to participate in the international community as an equal partner. . . . You are selective in your application of justice. Israel, a country which regularly challenges international law, kills Palestinians, and possesses weapons of mass destruction, does fit your description of a terrorist state. Your aggression in Iraq will bring on you the wrath of people not only in Saudi Arabia but also in the whole world.[22]

Yet some Saudi liberals who were critical of the United States, especially after its post–September 11 attacks on Saudi Arabia, and who were initially hesitant in supporting the war openly, applauded the capture of Saddam. Writing in English, a Saudi writer remarked that "President Bush, wrong on just about everything else, is right on this one."[23] Similarly, Abdul Rahman al-Rashid, editor (resigned in 2003) of the daily newspaper *Al-Sharq al-Awsat,* wrote fifty-six articles on the war, over a period of six months (December 2002–May 2003), which were highly critical of Saddam Hussein and appreciative of his removal.[24]

Perhaps the strongest antiwar attitude was expressed by Saudi Islamists. On this issue, groups ranging from radical jihadis to centrist Islamist reformers, religious scholars, and exiled Islamists converged on total rejection of the war, interpreted as a "Christian-Zionist imperialist plot" and a "New Crusade."[25] There was also an overwhelming rejection of Saddam Hussein, whom they saw as the "other face of American imperialism." One Saudi religious scholar, Nasir al-Omar, wrote an extended essay titled "Waylun lil Arab min Sharin qad Iqtarab" (Arabs, Beware of an Approaching Evil). He raised seven points relating to the Iraqi crisis:

1. The war is not [just] between Bush and Saddam [but] is yet another episode in the series of crusades announced by Bush. The first of such episodes took place when America used Saddam to hit Iran, followed by the Gulf War of 1990, followed by the American invasion of Afghanistan.
2. Our enmity with Saddam and his atheist regime is not a justification for the war.
3. The war on Iraq is an unjust crime and Sunni Iraqis will bear the heaviest loss.
4. It is an Islamic obligation to support our brothers in Iraq rather than support the regime.
5. A serious disaster stems from the relationship between the Muslim umma and its illegitimate governments, which have supported American interests throughout the modern period.
6. The responsibility for resisting this invasion falls on Muslims, who should abandon their preoccupation with trivial matters and concentrate on the real issues, that is, resisting the invasion.
7. American strategic plans for the Muslim world are long-term. America will use all means available to dominate the Muslim world. Therefore, Muslims should resist by applying all means, including education, military confrontation, economic pressure, and social and psychological force.[26]

Similar to the statement of the Saudi liberals, mentioned earlier, Saudi Islamists issued a joint declaration whose signatories included Muslim scholars and professionals from Pakistan, Sudan, Yemen, Morocco, and Palestine. The declaration summarized their position: "America's objective in this war is to destroy the Muslim identity of the region and replace it with American culture. America seeks to control the economic wealth of the country to cover up its failure in Afghanistan. It also aims to occupy the region with more war and unrest to protect the security of Israel and destroy the Palestinian uprising."[27]

The overwhelming Islamist consensus concealed latent divisions within the outspoken groups over whether religious scholars would issue a fatwa (religious opinion) supporting jihad in Iraq, as was done against the Soviet invasion of Afghanistan. Hard-line Islamists, often working abroad or clandestinely, exposed contradictions in the official Saudi position and among the established ulama (religious scholars), none of whom called publicly for a jihad in Iraq. A Saudi affiliate of Hizb al-Tahrir argued that "the American invasion of Iraq will drag the US into the heartland of the Arab world and will eventually lead to fierce resistance by the Islamists and eventual expulsion of Americans."[28]

A survey of official Saudi print media between December 2002 and May 2003 indicates that 90 percent of articles published during a period of three months before the war started supported the Iraqi people against outside aggression by the United States, while 73 percent of the articles were against Saddam Hussein and the Baath regime. Ninety-one percent of articles published in one daily newspaper *(Al-Sharq al-Awsat)* were extremely negative in their evaluation of Saddam and the Baath Party. In general, 90 percent of articles were anti-US, reaching a 100 percent level in weekly magazines *(Al-Majala, Al-Yamamah, Iqra)*. As the war started, 98 percent of published articles in one newspaper *(Al-Yum)* adopted a positive tone toward Iraq. Negative opinions of the United States and Britain also reached a high level of 95 percent in some publications.[29]

◼ Conclusion: A Confusing War like No Other

An understanding of the confused and some would say contradictory official Saudi responses to the war on Iraq needs an assessment of the local historical moment of Saudi Arabia, both state and society. Long regarded as one of the most stable countries in the region and one of the most resilient monarchies in a turbulent area, Saudi Arabia entered the twenty-first century with severe domestic problems, compounded by an unprecedented and overtly hostile US attitude. If the government fully supported US war efforts, it risked antagonizing its own local population, who were increasingly becoming impatient not only with US policies, but also with their own leadership, seen by many Saudis as corrupt, unjust, lacking political wisdom, and totally under the influence of the United States. If the government openly rejected the war, it risked antagonizing a US administration already critical and even hostile. These dilemmas explain the contradictory statements of the Saudi government before and during the war.

Since the official cessation of US military operations in Iraq in May 2003, followed by the beginning of the Iraqi resistance against the coalition forces, the Saudi position has reflected a desire to "live with" the occupation of Iraq, hoping it would be short. Official Saudi Arabia feared several outcomes: a spillover (i.e., a wave of internal instability and increased demands for internal reforms); increasing demands for religious freedom and equal rights from the Shia community in the Eastern province; and increased terrorist attacks and low-intensity warfare with Al-Qaida activists and sympathizers, motivated not only by local grievances but also by Saudi "impotence" during the Iraqi crisis. Unfortunately for the Saudi government, these fears materialized. Saudi liberals and Islamists intensified their activities and demanded greater and substantial reforms. In April 2003 the Saudi Shia issued a petition demanding reform of their minority status. Finally, two major terrorist attacks (May and November 2003) targeted residential compounds inhabited by foreign and Arab residents, while a low-intensity warfare between security forces and Al-Qaida was ongoing in almost all major cities. The discovery of hidden weapons and several cells resulted in Saudi Arabia publishing several lists of the names of most-wanted terrorists, with financial rewards offered for information leading to arrests. If the Gulf War had crystallized outspoken Islamist opposition, advanced the politicization of citizens, and led to serious economic difficulties, the invasion of Iraq in 2003 only deepened the crisis. It coincided with the maturity of Saudi opposition forces and confirmed the government's confusion in coping with an increasingly volatile constituency at a time when Saudi Arabia cannot take for granted its status as a strategic ally of the United States.

■ Notes

1. See Haifa al-Angari, *The Struggle for Power in Arabia;* Madawi al-Rasheed, *A History of Saudi Arabia,* pp. 103, 116–117.

2. On Iraq, see Charles Tripp, *A History of Iraq.* In the 1970s, Baathist Iraq welcomed Saudis who shared its ideological orientation. On this phase of the Saudi-Iraqi relationship, see Falah al-Mudayris, *Al-Baathiyuun fi al-Khalij wa al-Jazirah al-Arabiyya,* pp. 51–60.

3. On sanctions against Iraq, see Sarah Graham-Brown, "Sanctioning Saddam."

4. On this turbulent episode in Saudi history, see Anthony Cordesman, *Saudi Arabia.*

5. See Madawi al-Rasheed, "Saudi Arabia's Islamist Opposition"; Madawi al-Rasheed, "La Couronne et le Turban." See also Hrair Dekmejian, "The Rise of Political Islam in Saudi Arabia"; Mamoun Fandy, *Saudi Arabia and the Politics of Dissent.*

6. The Saudi government secured a fatwa from the highest religious authority in the country at the time, Sheikh Abd al-Aziz ibn Baz, legitimizing the invitation to foreign troops. However, several young religious scholars regarded the invitation as illegitimate. For further details, see al-Rasheed, *History of Saudi Arabia,* pp. 163–187.

7. On current challenges facing Saudi Arabia, see Daryl Champion, *The Paradoxical Kingdom;* Pascal Menoret, *L'Enigme Saoudienne.*

8. Details of US policy vis-à-vis Saudi Arabia after 11 September 2001 are outlined in Gregory Gause, "The Approaching Turning Point: The Future of U.S.

Relations with the Gulf States," Brookings Project on U.S. Policy Towards the Islamic World, Analysis Paper no. 2, May 2003, p. 2.

9. Before the US war on Afghanistan, Saudi religious scholars expressed objection to the war and to their government assisting the United States in its war efforts. The fatwa of Sheikh Humud al-Oqla al-Shuaybi on the illegitimacy of "assisting the US against the Muslim Afghans" was one such reaction. See http://www.aloqla.com/mag/index.php/sections.php?artld=42.

10. Bin Laden's attitude toward the Saudi regime became more radical in the second half of the 1990s. This was also reflected in the increase of terrorist attacks on Saudi soil. Two devastating attacks (the May and November 2003 bombings in Riyadh) took place after the US occupation of Iraq.

11. Several opinion polls conducted after 11 September 2001 indicated that bin Laden's popularity was very high immediately after the attacks. Some sources hinted that as many as 90 percent of young Saudis admired bin Laden.

12. Simon Henderson, *Weekly Standard,* 13 May 2002.

13. Interview with Saudi foreign minister Prince Saud al-Faysal, Iraq Watch, 11 August 2002.

14. See http://cnn.worldnews.printthis.clickability.com/pt/cpt?action=cpt&ti.

15. Ibid.

16. Interview with John S. Fakianakis, *ABC News Online,* 4 March 2003, http://www.abc.net.au/cgi-bin/common/printfriendly.pl.

17. Iraq Watch.

18. In response to US media hostility toward Saudi Arabia, the government used a US public relations company to polish its image in the United States.

19. Throughout 2003 Saudi Arabia witnessed a quasi–press freedom that allowed journalists writing in newspapers owned by the state or individual princes to attack the United States for its support for Israel. This openness was mistakenly understood by local and foreign observers as "freedom of speech."

20. Statement by Prince Saud al-Faysal, Saudi Ministry of Foreign Affairs, 18 March 2003.

21. Interview with Prince Saud al-Faysal, Saudi Ministry of Foreign Affairs, March 31 2003.

22. The full Arabic text of the petition is in *Shuun Saudiyyah* no. 3 (April 2003), p. 14.

23. Muhammad al-Rasheed, "We Are the Problem and Not America," *Saudi Gazette,* 30 November 2003.

24. *Al-Sharq al-Awsat,* 11 January 2004, p. 16.

25. For a Saudi Islamist view on the war, see "Bayan Hawla al-Tahdidat al-Amrikiyyah lil Mintaqah," http://www.islamtoday.net/iraq2/byan.htm.

26. Nasir al-Omar, "Waylun lil Arab min Sharin qad Iqtarab," http://www.islamtoday.net/articles/show_articles_content.cfm?i.

27. See "Bayan Hawla al-Tahdidat al-Amrikiyyah lil Mintaqah," http://www.islamtoday.net/Iraq2/byan.htm.

28. Interview with Muhammad al-Masari, London, 24 November 2003.

29. Ibid.

13

The Palestinians: Finding No Freedom in Liberation

Rex Brynen and David Romano

M uch has been made of the connections between the war in Iraq and the Palestinian issue. On the one hand, many Palestinians—faced with the grinding realities of occupation—lionized Saddam Hussein as a hero willing to stand up to Israel. They also often turned a blind eye to his aggressions and repressions. In the aftermath of US intervention, many attributed almost mythic anti-imperialist qualities to anticoalition violence in Iraq, seeing it as a sign of weakening US hegemony. For their part, many Israelis (and supporters of Israel) sought to tar the Palestinians with a Saddamist brush as a way of currying favor in Washington. Enthusiasm for the war often led them to argue that the removal of Saddam and demonstration of US resolve would somehow facilitate Arab-Israeli peacemaking by removing an outside source of support for violence and by rendering the Palestinians more amenable (or vulnerable) to US pressure.

All of these perceptions were far more rooted in Palestinian (and Israeli) desperation at their continuing conflict than in an accurate reading of the situation in Iraq. Indeed, in many ways, the war in Iraq has had only relatively minor effects on the Palestinian-Israeli relationship, which continues to be driven by its own predominantly local dynamics.

■ Context: Iraq, Saddam, and the Palestinians

The Palestinian movement had a long, complex, and often troubled relationship with Iraq, the Iraqi Baath, and Saddam Hussein. In the 1970s, Iraq had provided financial support for Palestinian organizations, sponsored and controlled its own (the Arab Liberation Front), backed the Palestine Liberation Organization (PLO) in its conflict with Syria in Lebanon, and been a supporter of PLO radicals opposed to Yasir Arafat. It had engaged in a covert war of assassinations against PLO moderates at one point through its support for the Abu Nidal organization, but in the 1980s the Iran-Iraq War had seen considerable rapprochement between the PLO and Baghdad as the latter reached out to Arab allies.

There was widespread popular support among many Palestinians for Iraq during its 1990–1991 occupation of Kuwait, with Saddam seen as the only leader willing to stand up to the United States, Israel, and the conservative forces of the Arab status quo. Iraq's wartime Scud missile attacks against Israel further strengthened this view. The PLO, aware of sentiments on the street, was unwilling to either support Kuwait or condemn Iraq. After the war, this stance cost Palestinians dearly: most of the once 400,000-strong Palestinian community in Kuwait were expelled or denied reentry, and conservative Gulf states cut their financial contributions to the Palestinian movement. The financial weakening of the PLO and the growing US postwar influence in the Middle East were among the reasons why the Palestinian movement subsequently embarked on the Middle East peace process at Madrid in 1991.

Throughout the 1990s, support for Iraq under sanctions was strong among Palestinians. One 1998 survey in the Occupied Territories showed that some 94 percent of Palestinians expressed support for the following reasons: sympathy for the Iraqi people (72 percent), followed by opposition to US policies (64 percent), with only 29 percent expressing support for Saddam and his policies as a reason.[1] Palestinian journalist Daoud Kuttab would later comment:

> When Saddam invaded Kuwait, many hailed this move as a possible contributor to the shake up of the Arab leaders, especially in the Gulf and Saudi Arabia, that may get them to genuinely help the Palestinians. And when Saddam made true on his threats to attack Israel, he was quickly applauded as the first Arab leader who didn't restrict his support to lip service. . . .
>
> None of this blind support was logical. . . . Most Palestinians realized that they had been duped. . . . They were able to understand the level of suffering that he was causing to his own people and the corruption of his authority and its dictatorial ways. But a sinking Palestinian community wanted to clutch at any straw.[2]

Iraqi policy sought to reinforce this connection as a way of burnishing Saddam's Arab nationalist credentials. Despite crippling international sanctions, Iraq provided financial support for the Palestinians, especially after the eruption of the Al-Aqsa intifada in fall 2000. According to officials of the (small, Iraqi Baath-controlled) Arab Liberation Front, $10,000 was paid to the family of each Palestinian "martyr" (including relatives of suicide bombers), with some $35 million dispensed in this way by March 2003.[3] While this sum was very small in relation to the development assistance and budget support being provided by the Gulf states, it received sympathetic notice in the territories and hostile commentary from Israel.

■ Palestinian Perspectives on the War

For many Palestinians, the drumbeat of approaching war in Iraq was part of a broader plot against Palestinian self-determination, the Arabs, and Islam. Officially, the Palestinian Authority tended to refrain from substantial comment, for fear of antagonizing Washington. However, an official editorial by Arafat's ruling Fateh movement indicated a common view:

> President Bush believes that the Palestinian people can only be overpowered after the US liquidates the Iraqi regime that stands firm against the blockade. Despite international protests, Bush believes the US is going to achieve its dream of imposing its leadership on the world. It is then that Sharon can play a role different from that of 1991. . . . Bush, the son, can [get] revenge for his father's failure to put into effect the new world order, and Sharon will be able to remove the effects of the psychological defeat Israel had brought upon itself during the second [1990–1991] Gulf war. . . . Israel and the US are [seeking to] settle old scores with, first, Iraq and, then, the Palestinian people, as a prerequisite for plotting against Arab and Muslim countries.[4]

Arafat himself warned Arab leaders that "the government of Israel is the first instigator of this war on brotherly Iraq and considers this war its own war against the Palestinian people, their National Authority, entity, independence and against the whole Arab nation from the [Atlantic] ocean to the [Persian] gulf."[5]

There was little difference between these views and the Palestinian opposition. Hamas spiritual leader Sheikh Ahmad Yassin warned, "The battle America is undertaking is designed to allow Israel to remain in the Palestinian homeland." In his view, "America is implementing Zionist Israeli policy to serve the Zionist project in Palestine" through a "war of crusaders against Muslims that began in Afghanistan and today in Iraq and tomorrow in another country."[6] Ahmad Sadat, the imprisoned general secretary of the leftist Popular Front for the Liberation of Palestine, warned that "the U.S. intends to control and re-shape the region, with Israeli partnership, to acquire long-term security for its imperialist interests." Thus, he suggested, "the American military occupation of Iraq represents the central point of attack on the Arab and the Palestinian liberation scheme."[7] Statements by Israeli officials and politicians supporting US military action against Saddam reinforced this perception. The role of US pro-Israeli neoconservatives in pressing for the war confirmed it still further.

In this context, when US-led intervention finally came, Palestinian public opposition to the war was universal. In a public opinion survey conducted in the West Bank and Gaza in early April 2003, before the fall of Baghdad, fully 99 percent opposed US military action: 58 percent felt that Washington sought to control Iraqi oil and 32 percent believed the war was intended to help Israel. Only 2 percent believed that alleged Iraqi weapons of mass destruction were the real reason for US policy. Most felt that the war would increase the desire of Palestinians to conduct attacks against Israelis (78 percent) and would reduce the prospects for peace (61 percent), and a plurality feared that Israel would use the war as an opportunity to expel Palestinians from the territories (46 percent).[8] Also, fully 61 percent of Palestinians believed that Saddam would ultimately win the conflict.

It didn't turn out that way, of course. News of the fall of Baghdad in April 2003, the obvious joy of most Iraqis at the toppling of the Baathist regime, and the humiliating capture of a meek and disheveled Saddam by US troops in December, were all greeted with shock by many Palestinians who had come to believe accounts (often received via Arab satellite television news) of steadfast Iraqi resistance. The words of one Ramallah taxi driver were typical of the reaction to Saddam's capture: "It's a black day in history. . . . I am saying so not because Saddam is an Arab, but because he is the only man who said 'no' to American injustice in the Middle East."[9]

◼ Consequences of the War

Political Effects

The actual political effects of the war were more modest than many Palestinians had predicted. There were no mass expulsions of Palestinians from the territories. Violence and counterviolence continued, but largely due to local decisions and circumstances. The war in Iraq did hasten the formal release by the Quartet (the United States, the European Union, Russia, and the United Nations) of its "Performance-Based Roadmap to a Permanent Two-State Solution to the Israeli-Palestinian Conflict" in April 2003.[10] This called for the ending of violence, normalizing Palestinian life, and rebuilding of Palestinian institutions (phase 1), to be followed by a transition to "an independent Palestinian state with provisional borders and attributes of sovereignty" in the latter half of 2003 (phase 2), and negotiations that would ultimately lead to full Palestinian statehood and a permanent peace (phase 3) in 2004–2005.

While development of the roadmap had been under way for almost a year, Washington had been in no hurry to launch the initiative. Since assuming office, most senior members of the Bush administration had tended to see the Arab-Israeli conflict as a no-win game, one that had consumed the time of President Bill Clinton to little positive political or diplomatic effect. It was argued that conditions were not yet ripe for a US initiative. The war against terrorism, and intervention in Afghanistan and Iraq, were seen as more pressing priorities. Finally, for those in the administration who believed that the toppling of Saddam and the demonstration of US "resolve" in Iraq would help to remake the Middle East, it was still too soon to act. The situation in Iraq would need to be consolidated before US attention could be turned elsewhere.

However, the EU lobbied for the release of the roadmap. Washington's chief ally in Iraq, British prime minister Tony Blair, pressed particularly hard on the issue, arguing that an initiative was needed to counter Arab criticism of US/Western policies and demonstrate a commitment to Palestinian-Israeli peace. In this view, far from Palestine being a distraction, movement on the Palestinian issue would foster a better regional atmosphere for progress in Iraq too. Washington was swayed, and on 30 April 2003—three weeks after the fall of Baghdad—the roadmap was formally released, accompanied by a terse three-paragraph statement by President George W. Bush.[11]

The roadmap soon stalled. Israeli prime minister Ariel Sharon seemed committed to retaining Israeli control over large portions of Palestinian territory, despite his formal acceptance of the roadmap. Occupation and violence continued in the West Bank and Gaza, each contributing to the other in a vicious cycle. Periodic terrorist attacks against civilians within Israel also occurred. Arafat seemed both unable and unwilling to control the violence, a stance that further alienated Washington and strengthened the Israeli right. Efforts to reform the Palestinian Authority, which itself began what appeared to be a process of gradual disintegration, failed. Despite substantial sections of both publics being in general agreement on the basic elements of a negotiated resolution of the conflict, trust between the two sides had evaporated—and, with it, hopes for negotiations.[12]

Throughout, Washington's support for its own roadmap was lackluster, with little sign of active and robust engagement. The lack of progress (and the general view in the Bush administration that most of the blame for this accrued to the Palestinians, and to Yasir Arafat in particular) created a context in which Israel was better able to put forward its own plan for unilateral disengagement. In August 2005, Sharon withdrew troops and settlers from all Gaza (except its border envelope) and from a small number of settlements in the West Bank. This, coupled with the continued construction of a separation wall within Palestinian territory, would reduce Palestinian-Israeli interaction and leave Israel more secure from terrorist attack. It also would leave Israel in control of large areas of the West Bank. While unilateral disengagement and the route of the wall were billed as an interim arrangement pending a return to negotiations, the danger loomed that such "temporary" arrangements would eventually become permanent. Similarly, while Sharon expressed his willingness to see a Palestinian state established, the truncated area that seemed to be on offer was not likely to be acceptable to the Palestinians.

The Palestinians in Iraq

While the war in Iraq may not have had a fundamental effect on the Palestinian-Israeli conflict, it did fundamentally reshape the lives of one group of Palestinians: the Palestinian community in Iraq itself. On the eve of the war, there were between 30,000 and 90,000 Palestinians resident in Iraq. Of these, by far the largest group was in Baghdad, with much smaller communities found in Mosul and Basra. The original core of this population comprised some 4,000 refugees who had left Palestine in 1948, along with Iraqi military units, in the closing stages of the 1967 Arab-Israeli war. Others had moved to Iraq in 1967, during the 1970–1971 Jordanian civil war, or to work or study.[13]

Although Palestinians in Iraq were not eligible for refugee services from the UN Relief and Works Agency for Palestine Refugees in the Near East, they were provided with some benefits by the Iraqi state. In particular, a majority (63 percent) of Palestinians in Iraq received state-subsidized rental apartments (although, in many cases, they were thus consigned to state-designated and inferior accommodations). Since 80 percent of Palestinians in Iraq were in the low-income category (16 percent middle-income, and 4 percent high-income), relatively few could afford to live independently of such state housing assistance.

With the approach of the war, some Palestinians sought to flee Iraq for Jordan or elsewhere. The Jordanian authorities, anxious to prevent a refugee influx, held all refugees in camps at the border unless they could show Jordanian citizenship.[14] Those who remained in Iraq suffered all of the challenges facing others in the country: the war itself, postwar looting and criminality, the collapse of public utilities and services. To these, however, could be added additional difficulties. Saddam's attempt to identify himself with the Palestinian cause left a postwar stigma on the Palestinian community, now viewed with suspicion because of their past (involuntary) association with the hated dictator. As Arabs and (overwhelmingly) Sunnis, Palestinians could be viewed with particular suspicion by Kurds and Shiites, especially amid the growing ethnic and sectarian polarization of postwar Iraq.

Lacking large tribal and clan connections, Palestinians could not rely on the sort of community self-defense mechanisms and supports that other Iraqis were able to turn to. Finally, many Iraqi property owners, chafing under years of Baath rent controls, suddenly saw the opportunity to increase rents or evict tenants. The Palestinians, bereft of protections and having enjoyed past government subsidies, were particularly vulnerable to this. Many were forced into the Al-Awda temporary refugee camp, where the UN High Commissioner for Refugees provided tents for 350 or so families (others were later found more permanent housing).[15]

In the immediate aftermath of the war, reports in Israel suggested that a future Iraqi government might be favorably disposed to Israel.[16] This seemed to be little more than wishful thinking, as indicated by the continuing propensity of many Iraqi Arabs to attribute US occupation, acts of violence, or other events to some form of "Zionist conspiracy." Following the Iraqi elections of January 2005, and the formation of a new government, Foreign Minister Hoshyar Zebri noted that Iraq "supports the Palestinian people and backs the Palestinian Authority in its efforts to establish a Palestinian state with Jerusalem as its capital."[17]

However, it is also clear that years of support for Saddam by Arab states, or inaction at his brutal rule, had severely soured many Iraqis on Arab nationalism, and not only the Iraqi Kurds for whom it had never held any appeal. The attribution of terrorist attacks in Iraq to "foreign" (Arab) militants further strengthened this view, as did periodic reports of the involvement of individual Palestinians in such attacks. All of this threatened to create further ill will toward the Palestinian community in Iraq, especially when many of the most heinous attacks against Iraqi civilians were linked to Palestinian-Jordanian (Sunni) Islamist militant Abu Musab al-Zarqawi. Officially, the Iraqi government stated that "there was no intention to increase the suffering of the Palestinians in Iraq whom we consider our dear brothers. . . . Reports of the involvement of some members of the Palestinian community in terrorist operations are no more than individual cases that cannot be used to generalize all the Palestinians living in Iraq."[18] Unofficially, many Iraqis (especially Shiites and Kurds) undoubtedly held much less positive views.

■ Conclusion

The medium- and long-term consequences on Palestinians of the US-led intervention in Iraq are unclear. Even if Iraq becomes a model US ally and ascendant US power secures greater regional cooperation and compliance, Palestinians seem unlikely to accept a Sharon-like agenda. If Iraq all goes horribly wrong, the resultant damage to US prestige will have negative effects on the search for Arab-Israeli peace.

Overwhelmingly, however, the future of the Palestinian issue will be far more shaped by developments closer to Palestine: Arafat's death in November 2004 and the new policies adopted by his successor, Mahmud Abbas; the twists and turns of Israeli politics; the ramifications of Israeli unilateral disengagement; the potential cycle of occupation, violence, revenge, and retaliation; and the willingness of the international community (and especially Washington) to press the parties to move toward a mutually acceptable negotiated outcome. While the Gaza disengagement provided some limited opportunities for moving forward, one cannot yet be optimistic that Palestinian statehood and a full end to Israeli occupation will be forthcoming anytime soon. In the interim, Palestinians in Iraq will continue to try to secure a place for themselves in a very unstable Iraqi sociopolitical milieu.[19] They will distance themselves from a fallen regime that adopted their cause, but that they never really embraced.

■ Notes

1. Jerusalem Media and Communications Center, *Public Opinion Poll #25*, February 1998, http://www.jmcc.org/publicpoll/results/1998/no25.htm.
2. Daoud Kuttab, "Saddam and Palestine," *Jordan Times*, 19–20 December 2003.
3. *Associated Press*, 13 March 2003.
4. Fateh, "Iraq and Palestine: The Tale of a Plot," http://www.fateh.net/e_editor/02/150202.htm.
5. "Arafat: Israel Is the First Instigator of War on Iraq," *Palestine Media Center*, 2 March 2003, available at http://www.palestine-pmc.com/details.asp?cat=1&id=624.
6. Quoted in *Palestine Chronicle*, 30 January 2003, http://www.palestinechronicle.com/article.php?story=20030130100403414.
7. "Interview with Imprisoned PFLP General Secretary Ahmad Saadat," http://www.fightbacknews.org/2003-3-summer/pflp.htm.
8. Palestinian Center for Policy and Survey Research, *Public Opinion Poll #7*, 3–7 April 2003, http://www.pcpsr.org/survey/polls/2003/p7a.html. Another April 2003 poll, conducted by the Jerusalem Media and Communications Center, also found a majority of Palestinians in the West Bank/Gaza (56 percent) fearing negative effects of the war in Iraq on the Palestinian issue. Jerusalem Media and Communications Center, *Public Opinion Poll #48*, 5–9 April 2003, http://www.jmcc.org/publicpoll/results/2003/no48.htm.
9. *Ha'aretz*, 15 December 2003.
10. The text of the roadmap can be found at http://www.state.gov/r/pa/prs/ps/2003/20062.htm.
11. One effect that the war in Iraq did have was to fan the flames of Palestinian anger at US policy (as among many in the Arab world). One manifestation of this may have been an October 2003 bombing of a US diplomatic convoy in Gaza, the first attack of its kind. The attack was criticized by all major Palestinian groups, and appears to have been conducted by a local activist cell acting on its own rather than reflecting a change in strategy by one group or another.
12. The 2003 release of the "Geneva Accord"—an unofficial draft peace agreement drawn up by Palestinian and Israeli peace activists—showed both how close and how far the two sides were from peace. Polls suggested that up to 39 percent of Palestinians and 47 percent of Israelis supported the contents of the accord. Some 85 percent of Palestinians supported a cease-fire with Israel. Some 77 percent of Palestinians and 80 percent of Israelis favored mutual reconciliation after a peace agreement was reached. However, polls also showed 87 percent of Palestinians supporting attacks on Israelis within the territories, 48 percent supporting attacks on Israeli civilians, and 58 percent believing that the roadmap was "dead." Fifty-two percent of Israelis felt that there was no serious partner for peace among the Palestinian leadership, and only 29 percent favored an immediate resumption of negotiations. For the text of the Geneva Accord, see http://www.heskem.org.il/

heskem_en.asp. For survey data, see Palestinian Center for Policy and Survey Research, *Joint Palestinian-Israeli Public Opinion Poll,* 16 December 2003, http://www.pcpsr.org/survey/polls/2003/p10ejoint.html, and *Public Opinion Poll #10,* 4–9 December 2003, http://www.pcpsr.org/survey/polls/2003/p10a.html.

13. Unless otherwise noted, data on the prewar situation of Palestinians in Iraq are drawn from the Palestine Liberation Organization (PLO), Department of Refugee Affairs, *Palestinian Refugees in Iraq* (1999), translated by *FOFOGNET Digest* 2003-159, 14–15 July 2003. The lower estimate of 30,000 Palestinians (1999) is drawn from the PLO. While the UN High Commissioner for Refugees reported immediate postwar estimates of 80,000–90,000, later reports are much closer (22,000) to the PLO figures. Ben Granby, "Iraqi Palestinian Update: Refuge and Death," *Electronic Iraq,* 5 February 2004, http://electroniciraq.net/news/1359.shtml.

14. "270 Palestinians, Other Nationals Allowed into Kingdom," *Jordan Times,* 23 April 2003.

15. Granby, "Iraqi Palestinian Update."

16. "Iraq to Weigh Returning Jewish Property," *Jerusalem Post,* 26 December 2003.

17. "Question and Answer with Foreign Minister Hoshyar Zebari," *Al-Sharq al-Awsat,* 2 August 2005, http://aawsat.com/english/news.asp?section=3&id=1066.

18. Ibid.

19. After decades of living in Iraq, many Palestinians feel as Iraqi as they do Palestinian. One Palestinian woman in Al-Awda camp in Baghdad stated that she "doesn't see a solution for Palestine, it's been so long." In the meantime, she would like to see "stability return to Iraq, development for the country, and a departure of U.S. forces." She insisted, "We feel Iraqi." David Romano's interview with Rasmeeya, fifty-five-year-old Palestinian resident of Al-Awda Camp, 24 November 2004, Baghdad.

14

Iran: Wary Neutral

Eric Hooglund

Iran's official view of US policy in Iraq since 2002 has been characterized by considerable ambivalence. On the one hand, lingering mistrust of Saddam Hussein (as a result of the 1980–1988 war with Iraq) both created and reinforced an attitude that accepted the US containment of Iraq as being in Iran's interest. On the other hand, the United States since 1993 had proclaimed the containment of Iran to be of equal importance to that of Iraq, and therefore Iranian leaders felt encircled by the arrival of thousands of US troops in Iraq together with those in Afghanistan since the end of 2001. Indeed, Bush's 2002 inclusion of Iran in his "axis of evil" meant a US military presence in Iraq could constitute an existential threat for the government of the Islamic Republic. As circumstances in Iraq evolved from early 2003 to mid-2005, Iranian policymakers faced the challenge of crafting strategies to take advantage of new opportunities while simultaneously remaining out of the crosshairs of a triumphal and hostile United States.[1]

The Ministry of Foreign Affairs, which has steered Iran's policy, is perceived by the political cognoscenti in Tehran as having been relatively successful in devising short-term strategies to deal with the changing situation in Iraq; it has also managed to avoid becoming entangled in factional conflicts by incorporating advice from a plurality of viewpoints.[2] As regards the actual war, Iran refrained from taking a high-profile view in the international debate that preceded it and largely remained neutral. However, when it comes to devising longer-term strategies to address the implications of the US occupation of Iraq for Iran's future security, there is no consensus among Iranian policymakers on the dangers or appropriate policies. Indeed, a review of the rival ideas of different factions relevant to the foreign policy process provides insights on the complexity of Iran's perspectives with respect to the "Iraq issue," an issue that has become intertwined with the "American issue."

■ Prewar Iranian Policy

Prior to the US war against Iraq, the latter country was seen as Iran's principal security threat, even more so than the US military presence in the Persian Gulf since 1990 and in Afghanistan since December 2001. Theoretically, Iran and Iraq were neighbors maintaining polite, albeit not cordial, diplomatic relations. However, in an intellectual and psychological sense, Iranians neither had forgotten nor forgiven Saddam Hussein for what officially they called the "imposed war," the eight-year conflict that began in September 1980 when Iraqi forces invaded Iran. That war, especially in its initial phase (September 1980 to May 1982), was looked upon as a real existential threat to Iran as a country and the Islamic Republic as a government. Few Iranians regarded as a victory their country's acceptance in July 1988 of the UN Security Council cease-fire resolution that ended the fighting; rather, there was a genuine sense of relief that the country—and among the political elite also that the regime—had survived a devastating and costly war. Some fourteen years later, on the eve of the US war against Iraq, Iran still had not signed a peace treaty with its former enemy, although both countries had continued to observe the cease-fire and operated embassies in each other's capitals.

At the beginning of 2003, many of the leading political figures in both Iran and Iraq were the same people who had served in their respective governments during the Iran-Iraq War. Iranian leaders retained a deep distrust of Saddam specifically, and of the Baath Party that he headed more generally. Other than the unresolved issues from the war, their most serious political grievance was that his government provided both sanctuary and financial support for the Mujahidin-e Khalq, an Iranian opposition group that had the declared aim of overthrowing the Islamic Republic by armed force, had assassinated key Iranian leaders in the 1980s, had used its bases in Iraq to carry out several militarily insignificant but psychologically irritating attacks inside Iran in the 1990s, and had waged a sustained propaganda campaign against the Islamic Republic that caused public relations headaches for Iran's diplomacy over many years. By the early 2000s, however, the Mujahidin's international effectiveness had diminished substantially, and even Saddam's government recognized that it lacked a popular support base inside Iran. Nevertheless, Iraq continued to support the Mujahidin as a counter to Iran's backing for Iraqi opposition groups that maintained exile bases in Iran.

Indeed, Tehran provided very public support for the anti-Saddam Supreme Council for the Islamic Revolution in Iraq (SCIRI), which had been founded in Iran by Iraqi Shia exiles during the Iran-Iraq War and reinvigorated by an influx of new members when thousands of Iraqi Shias fled to Iran following the suppression of an uprising in several major towns of southern Iraq in March 1991. Iran's view of SCIRI as a Muslim resistance group seeking freedom from the persecution and oppression of an antireligious regime contributed to a generally unsympathetic attitude toward the fate of Saddam's regime in any confrontation with the United States. In fact, the Ministry of Foreign Affairs at the beginning of 2003 gave visas to prominent Iraqi opposition leaders living in exile in Europe and North America so that they could attend a SCIRI-organized meeting in Tehran on the future of a post-Saddam Iraq; attendees included some men who at the time were working closely with the US government, including Ahmad Chalabi and Kenan Makiya.[3]

Nevertheless, as mentioned above, Iran's leaders were uncertain what the political consequences of a US war might be. The Gulf War (1990–1991) convinced some of them that the US aim was not regime change, as it had been in Afghanistan, but rather the punishment and disarmament of Iraq—which would be to Iran's advantage, since its leaders shared the belief of the Bush administration that Saddam did have weapons of mass destruction (WMDs). The war on Afghanistan persuaded other Iranian leaders that Washington really might be determined to overthrow Saddam, although few, if any, who shared this view believed that the United States would commit large numbers of its own troops for a sustained occupation of Iraq.

As the US government failed to convince most of its major allies of the Iraqi threat, as well as the Arab states that had joined it in the Gulf War, Iranians perceived an international consensus for resolving the issue short of war—that is, through UN inspections of Iraq's allegedly concealed WMD stockpiles, a course they thought might constrain the United States. Under these circumstances, neutrality and support for a UN-sponsored disarmament of Iraq seemed to be the prudent policy for Iran to follow. If, for example, Saddam's regime were to survive the crisis with the United States, then it would have no cause to find fault with Iran. But if the United States were to act unilaterally and even to succeed in overthrowing the Baath, then no successor government would be able to accuse Iran of having supported Saddam.

■ Postwar Perspectives on US Intentions Toward Iran

Once the United States initiated war in March 2003, the situation developed in ways that Iran had not anticipated. The complete collapse of the Baath regime and the prospect of Iraq's long-term occupation by 150,000 US troops were a new reality for which few Iranians had been prepared. By June, officials in Tehran were listening with concern as various US officials boasted about plans for the rest of the Middle East, including the possibility of regime change in Tehran as a follow-up to its "success" in Iraq.[4] Although the United States had been perceived as hostile toward the Islamic Republic ever since 1979, it previously had not been considered a direct threat. The situation now had changed dramatically, and it required a carefully thought out strategy. The territory of Iraq still was a source of threat for Iran, but now it was under the control of a superpower that had demonstrated it was not the paper tiger depicted in the Islamic Republic's rhetoric for over two decades.[5] By late 2003, three general patterns of views had emerged among Iran's national security elite with respect to dealing with the US presence in Iraq. These do not represent monolithic factions, as numerous nuances in perspectives are present within each pattern of views and each continually is influenced by the evolving situation in Iraq.

Undermining US Arrogance

The first pattern of views sees the United States as the major threat to Iran. It tends to be expressed by those who had espoused an ideological opposition to the United States for many years.[6] They are convinced that the United States never has accepted the Islamic revolution, and they see regional developments, from the Iran-Iraq War to the US war against Iraq, as Washington-initiated or Washington-abetted strategies aimed directly or indirectly at overthrowing the Islamic Republic. The attribution of motives ranges from US opposition to Islam to a US perception of Iran as challenging its hegemony in the oil-rich Persian Gulf and Caspian Sea regions.[7] Because their views tend to mirror those of the US neoconservatives and because many, albeit not all, of them are associated with the conservative political faction in Iran, we can call those holding this pattern of viewpoints "Iranian neoconservatives." They believe in the unremitting hostility of the United States but have a realistic appreciation of US military power and the devastation that can result from its unrestrained use (such as in Iraq in 1991 and again in 2003); they are not intimidated by it and advocate proactive policies to deter an attack on Iran. Some senior military officers as well as civilian ideologues even boast periodically of Iran's readiness to take on US forces should they attempt an invasion. The general view, however, is more restrained with respect to confrontation and is similar to the assessment that one political adviser provided: "The Achilles heel of America's power is its arrogance. I mean the American government cannot accept any other country, but especially Asians and Muslims, as equal. You can see that in this occupation government [Coalition Provisional Authority (CPA)] in Iraq. Its policies have caused resistance to rise up, and I predict this resistance will gather more strength in the near future."[8]

Some Iranian neoconservatives have advocated undermining US influence in Iraq primarily through support for different Iraqi groups that are friendly toward Iran; but it is not possible to state whether those in relevant decisionmaking positions have approved of any clandestine military assistance to specific groups in Iraq, since such support officially is denied. The general attitude is that the resistance in Iraq is a "natural response" to a foreign invasion and occupation. There is, however, obvious discomfit about some resistance activities, especially those associated with Al-Qaida, which are seen as being as much directed against Iraqi Shias as against Americans. Nevertheless, at least one private organization, the Setad-e Pasdasht-e Shohada-ye Jonbesh-e Islami Jahan (Military Headquarters for Commemorating Martyrs of the International Islamic Movement), seems to embrace all resistance indiscriminately and began in June 2004 openly to recruit volunteers for suicide missions in Iraq; five months later, it claimed that 30,000 men and women had registered for training.[9] Setad seems to enjoy the "protection" and perhaps even financial support of at least a few influential political leaders.

More significant than any ideological support for Iraqi resistance in general are the long-standing political ties between SCIRI and members of Iran's political establishment. Indeed, the chief of the judiciary, Mahmud Hashemi-Shahrudi, who was born in Iraq and was among those Iraqis of Iranian ancestry expelled from Iraq in the 1970s, is one of the founders of SCIRI. However, SCIRI is not an Iranian organization, and since its members returned to Iraq in 2003, it has pursued an agenda of tacit cooperation with US forces in the expectation that participation in elections would enable Iraqi Shia Muslims to exercise political influence—long denied—commensurate with their numbers (estimated to be 60 percent of the total Iraqi population). Significantly, the Iranian neoconservatives, although they would like to see a US departure from Iraq sooner rather later, have not opposed SCIRI's strategy, which included participating in the coalition, the United Iraqi Alliance, that endorsed a list of over 200 candidates for the January 2005 elections, supported a new transitional government in April, and took an active role in negotiations for a new Iraqi constitution. Iranian neoconservatives tend to characterize SCIRI's approach as an effective and rational course, given the power imbalance within Iraq in favor of US military forces. They argue that an Iraqi government in which Shias have an influential voice would demand that the United States withdraw its forces and be a long-term natural ally of Iran.[10]

More problematic for Iran's neoconservatives is devising an effective policy toward Iraqi Kurds, whom they see as determined to maintain their de facto autonomous status and who they believe have an ultimate objective of an independent state. Iranian neoconservatives generally accept, or perhaps tolerate, the principle of autonomy for the Iraqi Kurds within an independent Iraq, arguing that this scenario would preclude supporters of Baathist ideology, if they ever should regain political influence, from being able to reestablish Iraq as a regional military threat. However, they oppose an independent Kurdish state out of concern about the potential impact of such a state on Iran's own Kurdish minority. The current situation of de facto autonomy is seen as fraught with possible security risks for Iran because, in their assessment, the autonomous Kurdish region of northern Iraq effectively is divided between two rival political factions, the Kurdistan Democratic Party (KDP) and the Patriotic Union of Kurdistan (PUK). The latter group has continued its long-standing ties to Tehran, but relations with the KDP often have been tense. In fact, many Iranian neoconservatives believe that the KDP provides clandestine support for the Iranian KDP and another Iranian Kurdish party, the Komala, both of which fought a guerrilla campaign against the Islamic Republic between 1979 and 1983 and presently maintain offices in territory under Iraqi KDP control.

More worrisome for holders of this perspective has been the emergence in 2004 of a new Iranian Kurdish organization, Pejak, which has proclaimed its commitment to armed struggle against the government of Iran until the latter grants "autonomy" to Iran's Kurds. Pejak operates independently of the other Iranian Kurdish groups, which have foresworn armed struggle, and it has ties to—and may be a wing of—the Kurdish group in Turkey known as the Kurdistan Workers Party (PKK). Significantly, after the PKK announced in June 2004 that it was abandoning the unilateral cease-fire with Turkish security forces that it had observed since 1999, Pejak began military raids into the Kurdish-populated districts of Iran's West Azerbaijan province, which borders both Iraq and Turkey. Since then, numerous and often deadly skirmishes have taken place between Iranian security forces and Pejak guerrillas in this mountainous border region of Iran, and up through the end of August 2005, Iranian officials said that as many as 120 Iranian police and other personnel had been killed.[11] In view of the close relations between the Iraqi Kurds, especially the Iraqi KDP militia, and US forces, it perhaps is not surprising that Iran's neoconservatives believe that the United States is supporting these "terrorist" incursions into their country. In fact, Revolutionary Guard commander General Yahya Rahim Safavi charged as early as November 2004 that Washington actually was funding Iranian Kurdish groups as part of a concerted effort to destabilize Iran.[12]

Don't Tempt an Angry Giant

A second perspective shares many of the Iranian neoconservatives positions on Iraq, but it holds a much more alarmist view of US intentions vis-à-vis Iran, and, accordingly, is preoccupied with devising policies to avoid becoming a US target. Those who share this perspective may be called realists, because they insist that they have a "realistic appreciation" of US power. The realists' fundamental belief is that the United States not only is hostile to the Islamic Republic but also wants to overthrow it. On those occasions when the United States has cooperated with Iran, such as in its war against the Taliban in Afghanistan, then such cooperation has been minor and only for immediate US tactical interests. The basic US hostility toward the Islamic Republic and desire for regime change in Iran has not been altered as a result of any cooperation, as is evidenced by the way Washington has responded *after* securing what it wanted from Iran. For example, realists cite the successful efforts that Tehran made in 1991 and 1992 to persuade Lebanese groups holding Western hostages in Beirut to free them to a United Nations mediator. They argue that Iran had received oral assurances that the United States would respond to its efforts favorably, but it reneged. Instead, US officials "defamed" and "demeaned" Iran and soon declared the Islamic Republic to be the object of a dual containment policy aimed at both Iraq and Iran. Similarly, after Iran had cooperated to help the United States in the removal of the Taliban, President George W. Bush castigated it as a member of an "axis of evil."[13]

The lesson that realists have "learned" from Iraq is that Washington is prepared to use Iranian exiles living in the United States to carry out regime change in Iran. They cite the score of Iranian expatriate satellite television stations that began operating in California in 2001 and broadcast anti–Islamic Republic programs into Iran as evidence of US intentions. Indeed, in early summer 2003, some of these Iranians watched in anger and horror as Iranian exiles on these satellite shows called on their compatriots in Iran to rise up and overthrow the government. Much can—and did—change in two years, and by June 2005, realists recognized that the situation in Iraq had not developed according to US expectations. They interpret this new reality as having created among some US decisionmakers misgivings about and even opposition to tackling a similar regime change strategy in Iran.[14] But is it possible to take advantage of this new situation in a way that lessens the danger to Iran's security?

For realists, the United States is capable of inflicting severe devastation on Iran and is too great a threat for Iran to contain in the absence of any major power ally; hence the priority must be averting an attack by abstaining from initiatives that might invite US ire or retaliation. Polices that amount to deliberate confrontation, as advocated by some Iranian neoconservatives, are regarded as unnecessarily provocative, because they ultimately may endanger Iran. However, this does not mean that Iran should be trying to find areas of cooperation, because the United States repeatedly has proven its bad intentions vis-à-vis Iran. Nevertheless, Iran cannot ignore the United States, as it not only is right next door in Iraq, but also literally surrounds Iran: it has troops in Afghanistan and operational military bases in Central Asia, Pakistan, and on the Arab side of the Persian Gulf; in addition, Turkey is part of the US-led NATO military alliance. These geopolitical realities best can be neutralized by cultivating diverse diplomatic and economic relations with neighbors, most of which do not share the "irrational"

US hostility toward the Islamic Republic. The same also is applicable to European allies of the United States and US rivals, such as China and Russia. The assumption is that these other countries can act as a moderating force on the United States, especially after it has been "burned" in Iraq.

Realists generally agree with Iran's neoconservatives about US arrogance, which they see as inciting opposition to its policies, notably the resistance in Iraq. They also are convinced that Washington does not fully understand why such opposition arises, and that this is why it tends to blame Iran for problems caused directly or indirectly by its own actions. This combination of superpower arrogance and ignorance is fraught with dangers but also offers long-term possibilities for outmaneuvering the United States. Iran, realists believe, should wait patiently, since the United States is creating the conditions that will force its exit from Iraq.

Searching for Agreement

A third perspective, which may be termed "pragmatic," sees Iran and the United States as sharing similar objectives with respect to stability in Iraq as well as elsewhere, such as Afghanistan. Those holding this view generally argue for quiet (i.e., nonpublicized) cooperation with the United States on matters of common interests, even though they recognize that Iranian and US perspectives differ on other issues, such as the continuing Israeli occupation of Palestinian territories. They accept that the United States is a superpower that often behaves in ways that may harm other countries and that some of its specific policies may defy reason and even may be contrary to its own national interests—notably US policies toward Iran in the post-Soviet era. Many of them tend to have a relatively sophisticated knowledge about the debate over these policies among different constituents of the US foreign policy establishment and believe that Iran could work with "rational elements" within it. The pragmatic perspective is not identical to that of the political faction known as reformists, although many reformists, as well as some conservatives, share a pragmatic view on Iraq.[15]

For pragmatists, the case of Afghanistan provides a precedent for a situation where it has been possible for Iran and the United States to work together, however tenuously, on specific issues of mutual concern. For example, pragmatists who were or currently are in positions to know about details of Iran's policies in Afghanistan insist that they encouraged the Northern Alliance—the Afghan resistance forces fighting against the Taliban government—to cooperate with the United States beginning in October 2001. Furthermore, they say that de facto cooperation has continued, even though the politicians in both Iran and the United States are loath to admit this. According to a high-ranking Iranian army officer, "[Afghan President Hamid] Karzai could be a more effective leader, but he has brought some stability to the country, and neither we [Iranians] nor the

Americans have any interest in [seeing a return of] the situation that prevailed under the Taliban."[16]

The foremost area of common interests is Iraq. Indeed, pragmatists do not hesitate to say that the removal of Saddam Hussein's regime was a positive development for Iran. In the immediate aftermath of that government's collapse, however, they acknowledged that the establishment of the US occupation regime (the CPA) was an unexpected development that impacted negatively on Iran. But by the end of 2003, Washington "realized it could not maintain a puppet regime in Baghdad except by a level of permanent military force [that it] was unwilling to keep there."[17] As evidence for Washington's grasp of the reality in Iraq, pragmatists cite the termination of the CPA, its replacement by an interim government, the authorization of elections in January 2005, and the subsequent installation of a transitional Iraqi government in April, all developments that they believe Washington accepted reluctantly.

According to this perspective, Washington's objective in Iraq increasingly has become stability, an aim that Tehran also shares. Significantly, US officials came to realize that stability could not be achieved unless Iraqi Shias were allowed to have a meaningful political role in their country's future, another point of common agreement. Pragmatists also tend to be less concerned than Iran's neoconservatives about the autonomous government that the Kurds have been developing in northern Iraq. According to one deputy minister, "The Americans are using the Kurds and really do not want them to have an independent state. But the situation could get beyond the control of the Americans . . . and even if the Kurds somehow succeed in keeping an independent status, they are landlocked and their eternal enemies are the Turks and the Arabs. . . . But Kurds and Iranians are the same peoples, brothers, you know, like the Turks in Istanbul and Baku and Tashkent are alike in their language, etc. . . . Sure, we [Iran] don't like the idea of an independent Kurdish state there [in northern Iraq], but we could live with it and be its natural ally."[18]

The perception that Iran and the United States share similar strategic interests with respect to Iraq does encounter the reality of frequent US official rhetoric that Iran is trying to undermine US forces in Iraq. US secretary of defense Donald Rumsfeld, for instance, charged in August 2005 that the governments of both Iran and Syria were not interdicting arms to Iraqi insurgents that were being shipped from their countries.[19] How do pragmatists square such US charges with their belief in the mutuality of interests? On this question, they tend to compare the processes of formulating foreign policy in Iran and the United States. For example, they view the neoconservatives in Washington as a "group of Christian, Jewish, and secular fundamentalists" who are similar to Iran's fundamentalists (their term for Iranian neoconservatives) in the sense of having a xenophobic worldview that stresses national security and is incapable of empathy with others.[20] They contend that the US neoconservatives pushed the United States into the war with Iraq as one element in a broader strategy that was focused on promoting the overall interests of Israel. However, because their promised "liberation" of Iraq was not realized, and because, instead, the United States found itself fighting an ever-spreading resistance movement, the US neoconservatives have lost their influence. Of course, they still can "invent" crises, such as trying to scare the world into believing that Iran is developing nuclear weapons.[21] However, those Americans who understand that Iran and the United States share a number of common strategic interests have reasserted influence in the policymaking process.[22]

Underestimating US Ideologues

The realists' views may encompass a more "realistic" appraisal of US power than do those of Iran's neoconservatives or pragmatists. However, none of the three perspectives seem to have a realistic appraisal of US intentions.[23] On the one hand, it is easy to find among Iranian analysts genuine fascination about the views of influential Americans who have expressed doubts about the US official policy of not engaging with Iran on many contentious issues. On the other hand, it is difficult to find any Iranians who understand the worldview of US neoconservatives and how Iran fits into this thinking. Perhaps one of the best-known articulators of that worldview is Robert Kagan, who argues that the law of the jungle dominates international politics, and that it is the mission of the United States, as the world's sole superpower, to intervene, unilaterally if necessary, to prevent international outlaws from disrupting peace and stability.[24] Iran is one of the international outlaws for US neoconservatives. And they have used a succession of colorful "diplomatic" code terms—from "state sponsor of terrorism," to "rogue state," to "axis of evil," to, most recently, "outpost of tyranny"—to describe Iran. One of their objectives, dating back at least to the early 1990s, is "regime change" in Iran. There are, of course, many articulate critiques of the US neoconservative vision. And even some members of the US foreign policy establishment seem to agree with Chalmers Johnson's argument that the unintended consequences for the United States of its foreign interventions already are being manifested in "blowback" from Iraq.[25] But for the neoconservative mind-set, if the US project in Iraq is not proceeding as they had predicted, then the problem is not the policy objective but the interference in Iraq of outlaw forces, such as Al-Qaida and Iran. This perception, rather than acting as a deterrent to the neoconservative agenda, has increased their desire for regime change in Iran. Nevertheless, the US neoconservatives have experienced at least a temporary setback in terms of their political influence in Washington due to a general view that the Iraq adventure is not going well for the United States. Indeed, it is noteworthy that since March 2005, US official rhetoric directed against Iran briefly became somewhat milder; Secretary of State Condoleezza Rice, for example, described US policy as trying to "mitigate the downsides of Iranian behavior," rather than regime change.[26]

However, while it is reasonable to conclude that US neoconservatives have failed to use Iraq to influence US policy toward Iran, it would be a mistake to assume they will be unsuccessful in persuading the US foreign policy establishment of the necessity for regime change in Iran *if* there is no resolution—acceptable to Washington—of the controversy over Iran's nuclear energy program. Neoconservative pundits long have argued that Iran's nuclear energy plans are a cover for a secret nuclear weapons program, and there has been a concerted stoking up of the nuclear issue since it was revealed in 2002 that Iran's nuclear development program was more extensive than it previously had acknowledged to the International Atomic Energy Agency. In fact, the circle of US officials and policy analysts who mistrust Iran's statements that it has no covert weapons program extends far beyond the neoconservatives. Curiously, inside Iran, among those involved with the formulation of foreign and national security, and irrespective of which perspective they may hold, there is a palpable underestimation of the determination in Washington to prevent Iran from acquiring nuclear weapons. This view even prevails among those Americans who advocate constructive dialogue with Tehran and accept the likelihood of Iraq in the future having closer relations with Iran than with the United States.

■ Notes

1. The analysis in this chapter has benefited from the suggestions of several colleagues who read the initial drafts. I am grateful to the following scholars for taking the time to comment on my ideas: Hamid Abdollahyan, Ervand Abrahamian, Arshin Adib-Moghaddam, Hamid Ahmadi, Jabbar Bagheri, Kaveh Ehsani, Saban Kardas, Afshin Matin-asgari, Ali Rezaei, Seyed Mohammad Moussavi-Rizvi, Jalil Roshandel, and Alexander Winder.

2. For a succinct overview of how factional political views are accommodated in the formulation of Iran's foreign policy, see Jalil Roshandel, "Evolution of the Decision-Making Process in Iranian Policy," in Eric Hooglund, ed., *Twenty Years of Islamic Revolution,* pp. 123–142. See also Anoushiravan Ehteshami, "Iran's International Posture in the Wake of the Iraq War," pp. 182–84.

3. See further the independent, bilingual English-Persian weekly *Iran Times* (Washington, DC), 31 January 2003.

4. For a summary of the debates within the Bush administration over regime change strategies for Iran, see *Iran Times,* 6 June 2003.

5. The change in attitudes with respect to US power can be seen in a series of public letters signed by many parliamentary deputies and other prominent persons calling on all officials to tone down anti-US rhetoric and to try to accommodate some US interests in the region in order to avert the possibility of a US invasion of

Iran from Iraq; the authorities would not allow the media to print these letters, but they circulated widely via the Internet and fax machines and were debated in various private gatherings. For excerpts from these letters, see *Iran Times,* 30 May 2003.

6. Such views have been expressed consistently in the editorials and opinion essays of the Tehran daily newspapers *Jomhuri-ye Islami* and *Kayhan;* see, for example, various issues of these papers for 2004 and 2005.

7. This same argument is made by some scholars in Europe and the United States, including Michael Klare, whose book *Resources Wars* was translated into Persian in 2004–2005.

8. Author interview with senior official who works in the office of the *faqih* (Ali Khamenehi), Tehran, January 2004.

9. *Iran Times,* 3 December 2004.

10. The relations between the Iraqi Shia party, Al-Dawa, and the government of Iran, at least since the early 1990s, have not been as close as those between SCIRI and Iran. According to Juan Cole (personal communication, April 9, 2005), Ibrahim al-Jafaari, the Al-Dawa leader appointed prime minister of the new government formed on 7 April 2005, lived in exile in Iran from 1980 to 1989 but may have left and moved to London in a dispute with fellow Al-Dawa members over keeping the party independent of Iran. See further http://www.juancole.com.

11. For more details on the security situation in Iran's Kurdish areas, see *Iran Times,* 9 September 2005.

12. *Iran Daily,* 25 November 2004.

13. The views of realists can be found in various issues of *Iran Times,* as well as in papers associated with the reformists, such as *Mardomsalari* and *Sharq,* January 2004 through August 2005.

14. Based on interviews with several realists in Tehran, 12–14 June and 25 June 2005.

15. The career officials of Iran's Ministry of Foreign Affairs, which tries, usually successfully, to keep foreign policy issues separate from the partisan political struggles over domestic issues, has been a bastion of the pragmatic perspective. Former foreign minister Kamal Kharrazi (1997–2005) actually called for cooperation between Iran and the United States over Iraq in a speech at the United Nations in September 2003 and in a subsequent interview with a major US newspaper; see his interview in the *Washington Post,* 25 September 2003. For his views on Iraq, see Kamal Kharrazi, "The View from Tehran," pp. 26–27.

16 Author interview, Fars province, Iran, 25 December 2003.

17. Ibid.

18. Author interview, Tehran, January 2004.

19. See further *Iran Times,* 19 August 2005.

20. This analysis is based on conversations with several Iranian scholars and analysts in Tehran, January 2004; in Ankara and Istanbul, Turkey, July 2004; and in Salmanshahr, Tehran and Shiraz, Iran, June 2005.

21. On the US debate over Iran's nuclear development program, see Kaveh Ehsani and Chris Toensing, "Neo-Conservatives, Hardliner Clerics, and the Bomb," *Middle East Report* no. 233 (Winter 2004), pp. 10–15.

22. According to these Iranians, the Council on Foreign Relations, publisher of the quarterly *Foreign Affairs,* is an "influential" organization that advocates "dialogue" with Iran over mutual interests. Significantly, several Iranian colleagues who subscribe to this view called or e-mailed me during summer 2004 to express their favorable reaction to a newly released council study paper *Iran: Time for a New Approach* (New York: Council on Foreign Relations, July 2004). Several prominent

former US officials also are cited as sharing this position, including Zbigniew Brzezinski and Brent Scowcroft.

23. For a fascinating analysis of foreign policy perspectives among Iran's elite as being shaped by a general "utopian romanticism" with a Muslim inflection, see Arshin Adib-Moghaddam, "Islamic Utopian Romanticism and the Foreign Policy Culture of Iran," *Critique* 14, no. 3 (Fall 2005), pp. 265–292.

24. See further Robert Kagan, *Of Paradise and Power.*

25. See further Chalmers Johnson, *Blowback.* For a similar view about the consequences of US intervention from inside the US government, see Michael Scheuer, *Imperial Hubris.*

26. For an analysis of and the excerpts pertaining to Iran from Rice, regarding her 15 September 2005 interview with the editors of *NBC News,* see *Iran Times,* 23 September 2005. On Rice's testimony to the US Senate that the US position vis-à-vis Iranian policy in Iraq was one of trying to have discussions in Baghdad between the US and Iranian ambassadors, see *Iran Times,* 28 October 2005.

15

Israel: Major Beneficiary

Clive Jones

F ew in Israel lamented the demise of the Baathist regime in Iraq. Israel had been in a state of war with Iraq since its establishment in 1948. The immediate outcome of the Iraq War, in which Tel Aviv did not participate militarily, was the final removal of any potential threat to Israel from what had once been the main Arab power. Israeli reaction to the Iraq War was shaped by its favorable impact on Israel's ability to deal with its own main security threat, the ongoing Al-Aqsa intifada.[1] Hopes that the US presence in Iraq would help establish a regional order more open to the Jewish state have yet to be realized; but with the United States now a Middle Eastern power in its own right, Israel's regional interests, perhaps for the first time in the history of the state, are now more usefully served by following carefully (though never submissively) in Washington's regional wake.

■ Israeli Interests and the Road to the Iraq War

Israel, of course, welcomed the prospect of the removal of Saddam Hussein's regime. Few Israelis evinced much sympathy for the mass public demonstrations against the war seen across the globe. Shimon Peres captured the national mood when he declared, "There is no greater killer in our time than Saddam Hussein. I'm not impressed by the demonstrators. When Saddam gassed 100,000 innocent Kurds nobody demonstrated. When he attacked Iran and a million people lost their lives, nobody demonstrated. . . . Where was public opinion during all the massacres, all the dictatorships, all the killings, all the terror."[2]

At any other time, the buildup to war in Iraq would have dominated political and public debate in Israel. The duration and ferocity of its own "war on terror," however, in essence an internecine conflict that by spring 2003 had claimed the lives of some 800 Israelis and over 2,000 Palestinians, meant that

187

events elsewhere were, if not remote, certainly removed from the immediate strategic horizon of most Israelis. The spate of suicide or "homicide" bombings was regarded as Israel's main strategic threat, even a denial of the Jewish people as a nation with a right to live in their own sovereign space.

While the home command of the Israeli Defense Forces (IDF) issued advice to the public at large on securing homes from the effects of a biological or chemical attack, and Israelis were urged to ensure that their gas masks met the required standard, the IDF general staff remained confident that the ability of Saddam Hussein to repeat his technical success of the Gulf War (1990–1991), in which thirty-nine Scud missiles hit Israel, had been reduced substantially. Even so, Israel made it clear to George W. Bush that should Israel be subjected to attack by Iraqi weapons of mass destruction (WMDs), it reserved the right to strike back with overwhelming force. Israel heightened its state of readiness along its northern border with Lebanon lest its erstwhile nemesis, Hizbollah, chose this moment to demonstrate, however symbolically, its fidelity to the idea of Arab solidarity. Concurrently, Palestinian towns and villages in the West Bank, already suffering under draconian restrictions as a result of the Al-Aqsa intifada, were placed under curfew.[3]

Israel was prepared to offer any assistance it could to the United States. With the belief that its forces would be involved in urban combat operations, Pentagon officials were keen to draw on the experience of IDF officers involved in operations against the various Palestinian militia groupings in the towns and cities of the West Bank, including the use of real-time intelligence gleaned from the use of unmanned aerial vehicles and undercover operations. While Israeli officers briefed their US counterparts in the United States, not all US intelligence officials were happy with what one unnamed officer summarized as advice on how to set up "an assassination program."[4]

Premier Ariel Sharon was most concerned to thwart any pressure by Western powers to impose solutions to the Al-Aqsa intifada at Israel's expense in an attempt to appear, at least to the wider Arab world, "evenhanded." Sharon was indeed instructed by Washington not to use the outbreak of the conflict to remove Palestinian Authority chairman Yasir Arafat from the Muqata'a in Ramallah—either through physical expulsion or assassination—lest it inflame regional passions still further.[5] With memories still fresh in Israel over the diplomatic arm-twisting that forced a reluctant Yitzhak Shamir to Madrid in the aftermath of the Gulf War, Sharon invested considerable effort in negating British pressure upon Washington to engage more fully in an Israeli-Palestinian peace process.[6] While Israel has participated in a number of diplomatic initiatives, most notably the "Performance-Based Roadmap to a Permanent Two-State Solution to the Israeli-Palestinian Conflict," with the onus upon the Palestine Authority to first take demonstrable and effective steps to rein in Palestinian "terrorism," it has yet to be tested on its commitment to the map. Indeed, Sharon, unfettered by regional or international constraints, acquired increased latitude in imposing his own unilateral solution to the Al-Aqsa intifada. Under the protection of the US diplomatic umbrella, Israel has continued apace with the construction of its "security fence," a clear physical boundary that, once completed, will encompass most Jewish settlements in the occupied West Bank within the protective embrace of Israel proper, irrespective of the wishes or desires of the Palestinians.

The war itself was seen as a means by which the regional order could be recast to Israel's benefit. Shaul Mofaz, a former chief of staff and the incumbent of the defense portfolio on the eve of war, made it clear that Iran and Syria were just as great a threat to Israel as was Iraq. Thus, the removal of the Baathist regime in Baghdad would either allow the other "dominoes to tumble" or, at the very least, act to encourage "moderates and reformers" in Tehran, Damascus, and Ramallah to put pressure on their own governments to adopt policies more benign to Israel's interests. Given Iranian and Syrian rhetorical backing of, and in some cases, material support for Palestinian insurgent and terrorist organizations, it was clear that Israel's political leadership regarded the outcome of the Iraq War as a palliative to their own particular war on terror.[7]

■ Consequences of the War for Israel

Implications for Policymaking

Although masked somewhat by the public and political approbation that greeted the fall of Saddam Hussein, critical reflection on the exaggeration by Israel's intelligence assessments of Iraq's WMDs came under close scrutiny in the aftermath of the war. A report written by Shlomo Brom, a senior reserve officer and a former deputy commander of the IDF planning branch, regarded the war as an intelligence failure for Israel. The failure by Britain and the United States to find Iraqi WMDs or substantial evidence of attendant programs reflected adversely not only upon the relationship between intelligence and policymaking in London and Washington, which had partly relied on Israeli estimates, but also on the fixed conceptions Israel had of its nemesis in Baghdad. According to Brom:

> The [Israeli] intelligence agencies were taken over by a mono-dimensional view of Saddam that fundamentally described him as the embodiment of evil, a man in the grip of an obsession to develop weapons of mass destruction to harm Israel and others without any other considerations. . . . [T]here was absolute indifference to the complexity of considerations that a leader like Saddam must have.[8]

This had damaged confidence in Israeli intelligence assessments among the public, who could be immunized to threats that were more real than apparent, and among states that had, hitherto, placed considerable value on Israeli intelligence assessments. In future crises, Israel's ability to mobilize support in the wider international community behind its interests could be greatly diminished, since any information provided by Israel would be met, at best, by skepticism.[9] A commission of inquiry by the intelligence sub-committee of the Knesset Foreign Affairs and Defense Committee, chaired by Likud Knesset member Yuval Steinetz, recommended that responsibility for political-strategic intelligence analysis be removed from the military and vested in a civilian agency.[10]

Israel's Regional Outlook

The immediate outcome of the Iraq War produced the most benign strategic environment that Israel, perpetually in search of external security, has hitherto known in the Middle East. Few states in the region now have the capability, let alone the intent to challenge Tel Aviv's clear military superiority. Despite the vicissitudes of relations with Cairo and Amman, the peace treaties signed in 1979 and 1994 still hold firm and, periodic bouts of tension aside, the border with Lebanon has remained quiescent since Israel withdrew its troops from its self-declared security zone in May 2000. Even Libya, long suspected of developing a nonconventional weapons capability, has since renounced any such intention. Ironically, the fall of Saddam Hussein removed at a stroke the *strategic* rationale for continued occupation of the West Bank: the need to retain this territory as a buffer against any Iraqi incursion through Jordan aimed at the state of Israel.

Only Iran and Syria remained potential threats, but the latter's fear of Washington has been sufficient to prompt Syrian president Bashar al-Asad to advocate a renewal of negotiations with Israel over the future of the Golan Heights.[11] The claim made by General Moshe Ya'alon in August 2004 that the ability of the IDF to defend Israel would not be impaired should the Golan Heights be returned to full Syrian sovereignty, was seen as a positive response to Syria. Israeli commentators are under no illusions about the dynamic behind such overtures. As Eyal Zisser noted, "they stem from the distress Syria feels as a result of growing American pressure, particularly since the conquest of Iraq. . . . [T]he best way to ensure his [Bashar's] survival and extract Syria from its economic travails is to reconcile with the United States. And for Syria, the road to Washington passes through Jerusalem."[12] However, Bashar al-Asad's room for maneuver remains constrained, while the extent to which any government led by the Israeli Right would condone withdrawal from such a prized strategic asset must remain open to some doubt. Nor is there any pressure being placed by Washington on Israel to reengage in negotiations with Syria. For Israel, it is a win-win situation: heavy diplomatic pressure on Damascus but without any concomitant arm-twisting being applied on Tel Aviv to be more forthcoming over any future peace negotiations.

Israel also had reason to hope for benefits from relations with a new Iraq. In August 2004, newspaper reports in Israel claimed that talks had been ongoing between the Pentagon and the Israeli Ministry of Foreign Affairs over the possibility of pumping oil from Kirkuk in northern Iraq, to the oil refineries at the port of Haifa via Jordan. According to *Ha'aretz,* the prime minister's office regarded the proposed construction of such a pipeline as the "bonus" owing to Israel for its unqualified support for the British and US action in the Iraq War.[13] Practical steps to realize such a proposal have yet to materialize. Indeed, the refusal of the interim Iraqi prime minister, Iyad Allawi, to countenance any diplomatic ties with Israel until or unless Israel abides by UN Resolutions 242 and 338, places clear water between the hopes of Washington and Tel Aviv, and the reality of Arab politics being played out on the streets of Baghdad. With his fragile legitimacy dependent on US largesse—both military and financial—Allawi (and his successors) are in no position to court diplomatic entreaties from Israel, whatever the material benefits might be. After all, such moves would only confirm what many in the Arab and Muslim world already believe: that a main motive for the war was to strengthen Israel's military and political hegemony in the region still further.

The outcome of the war also served to focus debate on Israel's future strategic worth to the United States and the extent to which, in the emerging postconflict regional environment, Israel's regional aims remained coterminous with those of the United States. By its very physical presence in Iraq, the United States became a Middle Eastern power in its own right. Despite the undoubted esteem in which the administration of George W. Bush holds Israel, Tel Aviv remained concerned that as a newly constituted Middle Eastern power, Washington had its own agenda, an agenda in which Israel's role would be greatly diminished. As Aviad Kleinberg argued:

> [The] threat [from Iraq] has been removed, more or less. However, the invasion of Iraq dramatically lowers Israel's stock as a strategic asset. And not because Israel is not loyal to Uncle Sam; on the contrary, it is a most obedient and faithful vassal. It's just that Israel is not really needed. Israel's great strategic weight stemmed from its ability to act—or to constitute a potential threat—in a region in which the United States did not want to intervene directly. Israel was a regional mini-power through which it was possible to threaten the Soviet bloc and its satellites, or the Arab world. Israel preserved American interests. If American involvement becomes direct, there is no further need for mediators.[14]

Even before the conflict, Israeli commentators had openly expressed the belief that the removal of Saddam Hussein "and the installation of a moderate regime in Iraq and reinforcement of the moderate camp in the Arab world will be of great importance to Israel."[15] But the scope and durability of the insurgency that Washington and London have faced in Iraq since April 2003 have presented Israel's decisionmakers with more immediate concerns. One unnamed Israeli intelligence official claimed that it was precisely the threat that a stable, democratic government in Iraq would present to the rest of the Arab state system that explained the intensity of the insurgency. A policy of benign neglect exercised over their respective borders by Syria, Saudi Arabia, and Iran had allowed "international jihad organizations," operating inside Iraq, to have their ranks filled and replenished by volunteers from across the Arab world. With the aims of the war yet to be met in their totality in such an unstable environment, intelligence officials in Tel Aviv expressed the fear that Washington may be tempted to cut its losses and seek an exit strategy that would only embolden Israel's regional foes.[16] According to the veteran investigative journalist Seymour Hersh, by the end of 2003 the Israeli intelligence community had concluded that "the Bush Administration would not be able to bring stability or democracy to Iraq, and that Israel needed other options."[17] These other options, were, according to Hersh, being realized in closer ties with the Kurds in northern Iraq, ties that encompassed training for Kurdish commando units. In return, Hersh alleged that Israel had been able to run covert operations in the Kurdish areas of Syria and Iran that included the placing of sensitive equipment close to suspected Iranian nuclear facilities.[18]

The claims made by Hersh have been subject to critical scrutiny, not least by Israeli government officials and by veteran Kurdish leaders and independent politicians. Thus, Mahmoud Othman argued that Hersh had been unduly reliant on Turkish officials. Such rumors, he opined, were an attempt to alienate Kurds from the Arab world, thereby pushing the Kurdish people into a greater dependency upon Ankara.[19] The truth remains hard to discern, but past precedent, coupled with more immediate concerns in Israel surrounding Iran's burgeoning nuclear program, would suggest that Israel has made some efforts to engage with Kurdish leaders. Yet even though Tel Aviv remains deeply suspicious of perceived Iranian malevolence, from sponsorship of Hizbollah and political support for Hamas, to the development of the Shihab-3 missile and the continued development of a nuclear reactor, it has, for the time being, preferred to exert diplomatic pressure through third parties on Tehran—most notably through the International Atomic Energy Agency, the European Union, and of course Washington—rather than engage in open threats and clandestine activity in its attempt to deter Iran. Indeed, Lieutenant-General Moshe Ya'alon, citing the precedent of Libya's glasnost on WMDs, argued that political pressure from such a triumvirate could produce a similar result.[20] Moreover, the attendant risks to Israel's ties with the United States and Turkey in being seen to support

Kurdish irredentism would seem to be counter to Israel's broader, and more pressing, security concerns. Notably, from the mid-1990s onward, Tel Aviv had invested great effort in developing its military ties with Ankara, a relationship that, according to Neill Lochery, was as important a development for the Jewish state as the formal peace treaties Israel had signed with Jordan and Egypt.[21] Bilateral ties did suffer over Israel's policy of targeted killings in the Occupied Territories, and at the end of May 2004, Abdullah Gul, the Turkish foreign minister, recalled the ambassador to Tel Aviv "for urgent consultations on how to revive the peace process." Even so, the strength of Israel's strategic relationship with Turkey endures, the alliance acting as a natural force multiplier for Israel as it seeks to maintain its comparative military advantage over Damascus.

■ Conclusion

In an oft-cited quote, David Ben Gurion was once recorded as claiming that in foreign policy, it does not matter what the world says—what matters is what Israel does. This tendency toward unilateral action has been the hallmark of Tel Aviv's engagement with the Middle East. Lacking any firm regional ally in an environment perceived by Israelis as "nasty and brutish," the Jewish state looked to itself to defend and pursue its interests as it saw fit. The preemptive attack against the Osirak nuclear reactor outside Baghdad in June 1981 remains but one of many striking examples. But Israel's position in the aftermath of the US-led invasion of Iraq marks a point of departure: it now has a strong regional ally *in situ* whose interests—both militarily and politically—conflate with its own and that is willing to use force to safeguard those self-same interests. Diplomatically, Washington has shielded Tel Aviv from worldwide opprobrium as the construction of its security fence continues. At relatively little cost, Israel has reaped substantial strategic gain, at least in the short to medium term. How it converts such gains into political capital will depend in large part on the determination of Washington to "stay the course in Iraq." For the moment, however, Tel Aviv is more than happy to allow Washington to shoulder Israel's security burden throughout the Middle East.

■ Notes

1. Amos Elon, "No Exit," *New York Review of Books* 49, no. 9 (23 May 2002), p. 16.
2. Ben Russell, "Peres Claims Defeat of Saddam Will Be Welcomed by the Arab world," *The Independent,* 3 April 2003. Gush Shalom (Peace Block) did organize peace vigils in Tel Aviv, but these attracted little in the way of broad public support.

3. Alan Phillips, "States in the Cauldron: Israel," *Daily Telegraph Special Report,* 18 March 2003.

4. Pierre Prier, "Americans at the Israeli Urban Warfare School," *Le Figaro* (in French), 6 April 2003; Julian Borger, "Israel Trains US Assassination Squads in Iraq," *The Guardian,* 9 December 2003. It was reported in summer 2004 that with the insurgency in Iraq still ongoing, US troops were still being instructed in urban warfare tactics in Israel. See "US Troops Training for Iraq in Israel," *Jerusalem Post,* 18 August 2004.

5. Amos Harel, "Ya'alon: Killing Arafat Was Debated," *Ha'aretz* (in Hebrew), 23 June 2003.

6. See John Kampfner, *Blair's Wars,* p. 385; Aluf Benn, "No Anglo-American Front Against Sharon," *Ha'aretz Special Edition: War in Iraq,* http://www.haaretz.com/hasen/pages/shartwar.jhtml?itemno278172&contrassid; Robert Tait, "Israel Turns on Blair for His Support of Palestine," *The Times* (London), 7 April 2003.

7. James Bennet, "Israel Says War on Iraq Would Benefit the Region," *New York Times,* 27 February 2003.

8. Shlomo Brom, "The War in Iraq: An intelligence Failure?" *Strategic Assessment* (Jaffee Centre for Strategic Studies, Tel Aviv University) 6, no. 3 (November 2003), http://www.tau.ac.il/jcss/sa/v6n3p3bro.html.

9. The US Senate intelligence report in the run-up to the Iraq War argues that Washington relied too heavily on foreign sources for its intelligence assessments. This included implicit criticism of information passed on by Israel, which Tel Aviv had in turn received from other governments and which, in turn, Washington often fed to the self-same governments. The Steinetz Committee, commenting on this process, stated that this was a "vicious cycle of sorts in the form of reciprocal feedback which at times was more damaging than beneficial." See Ori Nir, "Senate Report on Iraq Intelligence Points to Role of Jerusalem," 23 July 2004, http://www1.columbia.edu/sec/bboard/gulf2000/gulf2000-25/msg01139.html.

10. For a detailed appraisal, see Shlomo Brom, "The Steinetz Report: Israeli Intelligence After Iraq," *Tel Aviv Notes* (Jaffee Centre for Strategic Studies, Tel Aviv University) no. 103 (4 April 2004).

11. Eyal Zisser, "What's Behind Bashar al-Assad's Peace Offensive?" *Tel Aviv Notes* no. 95 (11 January 2004).

12. See Mark Heller, "Powell in Damascus: Will Policy Change in Syria Follow Regime Change in Iraq?" *Tel Aviv Notes* no. 76 (5 May 2003); Zisser, "What's Behind Bashar al-Assad's Peace Offensive?"

13. Amiram Cohen, "US Checking Possibility of Pumping Oil from Northern Iraq to Haifa via Jordan," *Ha'aretz* (in Hebrew), 6 August 2004. Such discussions, it seems, had been ongoing from the moment Saddam Hussein had been removed. See Ed Vuillamy, "Israel Seeks Pipeline for Iraq Oil," *The Observer,* 20 April 2003.

14. Aviad Kleinberg, "The War's Implications for Israel," *Ha'aretz Special Edition: War in Iraq,* http://www.haaretz.com/hasen/pagesshartwar.jhtml?itemno=282891&contrassid=33&.

15. Ephraim Kam, "Saddam: The Morning After," *Strategic Assessment* 5, no. 4 (February 2003), http://www.tau.ac.il/jcss/sa/v5n4p3kam.html.

16. See Amos Harel, "Disquiet on the Eastern Front," *Ha'aretz* (in English), 20 August 2004.

17. Seymour M. Hersh, "Plan B: As June 30th Approaches Israel Looks to the Kurds," *New Yorker,* 28 June 2004, http://www.newyorker.com/fact/content/?040628fa_fact.

18. Ibid.

19. Kamran Karadgahi, "Iraq's Kurds Are Not Collaborating with Israel," *Daily Star,* 4 August 2004.

20. Reuters, "Ya'alon on Iranian Threat: Political Pressure Must Be Exhausted," 28 July 2004, http://www1.columbia.edu/sec/bboard/gulf2000/gulf2000-25/msg01141.html; Leslie Susser, "Dropping Low Profile, Israel Goes on Offensive Against Iranian Nukes," *Virtual Jerusalem,* 5 August 2004, http://www1.columbia.edu/sec/bboard/gulf2000/gulf2000-26/msg000724.html.

21. Neill Lochery, "Israel and Turkey," pp. 45–46.

16

Turkey: Recalcitrant Ally

Gareth Winrow

On 1 March 2003 the Turkish parliament failed narrowly to approve a government motion to permit the deployment in Turkey for six months of 62,000 US troops, 255 jet aircraft, and 65 helicopters.[1] This would have allowed the opening of a northern front in an increasingly likely US-led military operation against the regime of Saddam Hussein. The motion also called for an unspecified number of Turkish troops to be deployed in northern Iraq. The failure to pass the motion surprised many even though opposition in Turkey among the public and within the ranks of the governing Justice and Development Party (AKP) against a war in Iraq was considerable. Following a series of high-level US political and military delegations to Turkey and in line with the approval of the Turkish parliament in a vote on 6 February, US military personnel had been upgrading and modernizing bases and port facilities in Turkey. Ankara and Washington were also negotiating a substantial aid package to offset Turkey's expected losses resulting from the military operation.

After a clearly exasperated Bush administration abandoned the northern front option, on 20 March the Turkish parliament approved a motion granting the United States and Britain overflight rights and permitting more Turkish troops—reportedly 10,000—to enter northern Iraq.[2] Unlike the Gulf War (1990–1991), though, coalition forces could not use Turkish airbases to launch air sorties against Iraq. Unwilling to further antagonize the United States and upset European Union member states, the AKP government decided against unilaterally intervening militarily in northern Iraq. The Turkish military shelved plans to intervene in early April.[3] Nevertheless, relations between Turkey and the United States deteriorated until October 2003, when the parliament in Ankara agreed to send Turkish peacekeeping units to help the embattled US-led international force in Iraq.[4] Vehement opposition from the northern Iraqi Kurds blocked the deployment of the Turkish force. Turkish policymakers are determined to prevent the formation of an independent Kurdish state in northern Iraq, which they believe could destabilize Turkey and the region.

Explaining Turkish Policy

External Factors

After the Gulf War, protected by coalition aircraft patrolling from the Incirlik airbase in Turkey, the northern Iraqi Kurds had established governments separate from Baghdad in what became an autonomous Kurdish region. The Turkish authorities were concerned that the administrations formed by the Patriotic Union of Kurdistan (PUK) and the Kurdistan Democratic Party (KDP) might unite, declare independence, and then act as a model or magnet for the Kurdish population concentrated in southeastern Turkey.

Division and instability in northern Iraq enabled Turkey's Kurdish rebel grouping, the Kurdistan Workers Party (PKK), to operate across the Iraqi-Turkish border. In clashes with the Kurdish rebels in Turkey, approximately 35,000 were killed over a fifteen-year period until the capture and imprisonment in 1999 of Abdullah Ocalan, the PKK's leader. Fearful of the possible fragmentation of the Turkish state, officials in Ankara were reluctant to allow the Kurds in Turkey to express their cultural and ethnic identity. An EU-supported reform package finally adopted in 2003, permitting broadcasting in Kurdish and courses to learn Kurdish in Turkey, was eventually implemented in 2004.[5]

Since 1991 Turkish governments have attempted to influence developments in northern Iraq. Ankara allowed the delivery of humanitarian aid, engaged in barter trade to procure illicit diesel fuel from the KDP, periodically militarily intervened to support the KDP in clashes with the PKK, and helped to cement a cease-fire in 1996 between warring KDP and PUK factions.[6] By March 2003, about 2,000 Turkish troops remained in northern Iraq.

The coalition government led by Bulent Ecevit, in office between May 1999 and November 2002 and which included the right-wing Nationalist Movement Party (MHP), was more suspicious of the northern Iraqi Kurds and of US sympathy for their cause. Ecevit made it clear that the formation of an independent Kurdish state in northern Iraq, and the Kurdish occupation of the oil-rich territory of Kirkuk—at the time under Baghdad's jurisdiction—would lead to war with Turkey.[7] In September 2002 the KDP and PUK agreed to a draft constitution for a post-Saddam Iraq that would include a federal Kurdish region with Kirkuk as its capital. Ecevit fumed that the situation in Iraq had "got out of control" and that "a Kurdish state has been founded in northern Iraq," and accused the Bush administration of "steering" the Kurdish groups.[8]

Recent Turkish governments have sought to play the Iraqi Turkmen card in their attempts to influence developments in northern Iraq. Ethnically and linguistically related to the Turks, the Iraqi Turkmen had been largely ignored by Turkey until a group of predominantly Sunni Iraqi Turkmen were encouraged to form the then Ankara-based Iraqi Turkmen Front (ITF) in 1995. The Iraqi Turkmen assumed more prominence when three-quarters of the 400-man Peace Monitoring Force (PMF), established in 1996 to separate KDP and PUK combat units, consisted of Iraqi Turkmen who took orders from Turkish officers.[9] The PMF became, in effect, a training school in which up to 2,000 Iraqi Turkmen received military instruction.[10] The ITF repeatedly argued that Kirkuk and Mosul were traditionally Iraqi Turkmen and not Kurdish territories. Claims that the Iraqi Turkmen population in Iraq numbered up to 3 million were obvious exaggerations.[11] The draft constitution prepared in September 2002 for the Kurdish autonomous region in northern Iraq referred to the Iraqi Turkmen as a "national minority."[12] The official Turkish line was that the Iraqi Turkmen should be recognized as one of the three main constituents of Iraqi society, along with Arabs and Kurds.[13]

The Baghdad regime appeared to pose a continued security threat to Turkey after the Gulf War. In February 1999, Saddam Hussein had warned Ankara that it would face attack if it continued to allow US and British aircraft to launch air sorties against Iraq from Turkish territory.[14] In July 2002 the Bush administration urged the Turkish authorities to take the Iraqi missile threat seriously and pushed the Turks to deploy surface-to-air missile batteries.[15]

Given these concerns over the PKK, northern Iraq, and the Baghdad regime, it seemed inevitable that the parliament in Ankara on 1 March 2003 would approve the motion for Turkish and US joint participation in a war against Iraq. This would have enabled Turkey to work with the United States to shape the political future of a post-Saddam Iraq.

Washington clearly expected parliamentary approval. In December 2002, warmly receiving AKP leader Recep Tayyip Erdogan, President George W. Bush spoke of Turkey as a "strategic ally and friend of the US."[16] In the same month, during a second visit to Ankara in that year, US deputy defense secretary Paul Wolfowitz confidently declared that Turkish support was "assured" in any possible military operation against Iraq.[17] After two weeks of extensive discussions between US and Turkish diplomats, a memorandum of understanding was signed on 22 February 2003. The correspondent of the Turkish daily *Milliyet,* Fikret Bila, revealed the details of this memorandum after the war. The Turkish and US militaries had agreed to enter northern Iraq together. Turkish units could engage the PKK, while US forces would seize control of Mosul and Kirkuk. No heavy weaponry would be allocated to the KDP and PUK, and Kurdish *peshmerga* (fighters) would return all light weapons handed to them by coalition forces after the cessation of hostilities. Air operations over northern Iraq would be under Turkish control, and the United States would meet all the costs of the campaign.[18] With reports that 40,000 Turkish troops would participate in this combined operation, the memorandum has been referred to as the "deal of the decade."[19]

Prior to 1 March, Washington was also in talks with Ankara over the terms of an extensive aid package. The debt-ridden Turkish economy had just recovered from a severe financial crisis, with support from the International Monetary Fund. Turkish officials believed that Turkey had not been properly compensated for its support in the Gulf War and were thus determined to strike a hard bargain. It was reported that up to $92 billion in aid and loan guarantees was demanded from the United States.[20] The Bush administration was only prepared to offer a package of $4 billion in grants and $20 billion in loan guarantees.[21] After the outbreak of war this package was removed. Instead, in April 2003 the US Congress approved a $1 billion grant or $8.5 billion loan on the condition that Turkey would cooperate with the United States in Iraq—that is, Turkey should not intervene unilaterally in northern Iraq. An agreement fixing the terms of the loan was signed in Dubai in September 2003.[22] In practice, Turkish officials were unhappy at the restrictions placed on the grant/loan. In March 2005, citing recent economic growth, the Turkish treasury announced that it was no longer interested in the package.[23]

Some Turkish officials and businessmen had been eager to cultivate expanding commercial ties with the Saddam regime and were thus opposed to war with Iraq. In autumn 2002 a report released by the Turkey-Iraq Business Council noted that Turkey had lost $100 billion as a consequence of the Gulf War and UN economic sanctions against Baghdad. The report added that with another conflict Turkey could incur losses totaling up to $150 billion because of the impact on trade, tourism, and oil prices, and because of military costs and other expenses.[24] War could also lead to an indefinite closure of the Kirkuk-Yumurtalik pipeline network connecting Turkey and Iraq, thereby depriving Ankara of oil transit revenues.

Policymakers in Ankara had also been worried that a war could have negative repercussions for regional security, given that Iran and Syria also had sizable Kurdish populations. Abdullah Gul, the AKP prime minister at the time, visited Syria and Iran, and also Egypt, Jordan, and Saudi Arabia, in January 2003, and the foreign ministers of these states met in Istanbul on 23 January. The moderate Islamist AKP government was here also attempting to placate its domestic supporters by showing that Turkey was seeking a common front with key Muslim states on the Iraqi issue. However, the Istanbul meeting achieved little apart from a bland declaration that urged Baghdad to comply with UN Security Council resolutions while the territorial integrity and sovereignty of Iraq should be respected.[25]

Internal Factors

Domestic circumstances help explain why the Turkish parliament failed to approve the motion on 1 March. An inexperienced AKP government had assumed office in November 2002 and was distracted by other pressing issues, such as Cyprus and Turkey's bid for EU membership. Prime Minister Gul's hand was weakened because AKP leader Erdogan was waiting in the wings to take over the premiership. Constitutional amendments adopted in December 2002 meant that the previously convicted Erdogan could be elected to parliament and thereby become prime minister. Conveniently, a by-election would be held on 9 March 2003, because of previous election irregularities in the province of Siirt, enabling Erdogan then to be appointed prime minister on 14 March.[26] It was striking that Bush invited Erdogan rather than Gul to the White House in December 2002 to discuss Iraq.

Traditionally, Turkish foreign policy has been entrusted to professional diplomats at the Ministry of Foreign Affairs working closely with the foreign minister, prime minister, and military chiefs. Gul and Erdogan were also apparently influenced, though, by less experienced personal advisers, who believed that the United States could not launch a military campaign against Iraq without opening a northern front. Foreign Minister Yasar Yakis often played second fiddle to Erdogan on the latter's trips abroad. Unusual for a foreign minister, Yakis caused consternation within the ministry by issuing off-the-cuff remarks. Yakis was quickly forced to retract a statement made on 3 December 2002 in which he announced that Turkey would allow the United States to use its airbases in the event of a war against Iraq.[27] In early January 2003, Yakis alleged that Turkey was examining whether it had any historical and legal claims to Mosul and Kirkuk, both formerly part of the Ottoman Empire. Erdogan swiftly reacted by noting that these remarks only reflected the personal views of the foreign minister.[28]

Unwilling to alienate its domestic constituents, the AKP experienced serious divisions within its ranks over whether Turkey should participate in a US-led military operation against a predominantly Muslim country. Many newly elected AKP deputies had little knowledge or experience of international politics. However, according to Article 92 of the Turkish constitution, parliamentary approval was required for a declaration of war, the stationing of foreign troops in Turkey, and the dispatch of Turkish forces abroad "in cases where there is international legitimacy." Bulent Arinc, the Speaker of parliament, and a prominent member of the conservative wing of the AKP, argued that without a second UN Security Council resolution in addition to Resolution 1441, there would be no international legitimacy.[29] In a fractious AKP cabinet meeting on 24 February 2003, Construction Minister Zeki Ergezen echoed the views of much of the Turkish public when he voiced that he opposed the bombing of Muslims.[30]

Gul and Erdogan realized, though, that US-Turkish relations would come under tremendous strain if a motion permitting the deployment of US troops in Turkey for a military operation in northern Iraq were not quickly brought before parliament. The cabinet agreed to hold a free vote in parliament on the motion. Without the party whip, evidently Gul and Erdogan were resigned to losing thirty to forty votes from their party, but ninety-nine AKP deputies opposed the motion on 1 March. With a vote of 264 to 250 in favor, and with nineteen abstentions, the motion was not adopted, because three more votes were needed to secure the required majority of those present in parliament.[31] It seems that a number of AKP deputies representing districts in southeastern Turkey were keen not to upset their Kurdish and Arab constituents.

The opposition party, the Republican People's Party (CHP), opposed the motion. Although in favor of more Turkish units in northern Iraq, Deniz Baykal, the CHP leader, argued that the movement of US troops across Turkish territory smacked of aggression.[32] Encouraged by disagreements within the AKP and by mounting popular discontent, various nongovernmental organizations in Turkey orchestrated large-scale antiwar protests. In early December 2002 the results of a survey conducted in July and August by the Pew Research Center revealed that 83 percent of the Turkish public even opposed the use of Turkey's airbases by the United States for an operation against Iraq.[33] Clearly, this mounting popular opposition had an impact on the 1 March vote.

President Ahmet Necdet Sezer, a former Constitutional Court judge with little background in international diplomacy, also opposed a war because of the absence of "international legitimacy." Sezer played a key role when presiding over a meeting of Turkey's National Security Council (NSC) on 28 February 2003. Gul and Erdogan had been pressing for the NSC to recommend that parliament should approve the motion. However, Sezer personally intervened to cut short the NSC meeting by noting that the NSC had already decided at its previous session on 31 January that the government should seek parliamentary authorization.[34] Crucially, therefore, AKP leaders failed to secure support from the powerful NSC immediately before the 1 March vote.

One may have expected the influential military at the NSC meeting to prevail upon Sezer to recommend backing the motion given the terms of the memorandum of understanding that had just been concluded with US officials. But the Turkish armed forces were not keen to be seen to be openly backing the moderately Islamist AKP government. On 8 January, General Hilmi Ozkok, chief of general staff, had for the first time publicly accused the government of promoting Islamic activism in Turkey. This was after Prime Minister Gul in an unprecedented move had objected to the expulsion of officers from the armed forces on the grounds that they were Islamic agitators.[35] It appears that the military expected parliament to approve the motion without a recommendation from the NSC. Apparently, Ozkok was loath to press the government to adopt the motion, as the EU would have then probably complained about the military dominating Turkish politics. The Turkish armed forces also did not want to be seen to be openly backing a highly unpopular war.[36] Too little too late, on 5 March Ozkok declared that firm support for any US military deployment would be in Turkey's political and economic interests.[37]

Given the awareness of Washington's resolve to overthrow Saddam, there were no obvious divisions within the top echelons of the Turkish military concerning opening a northern front. Throughout the 1990s a close working relationship had developed between the Turkish and US militaries. Turkish generals had welcomed the use of Incirlik by coalition aircraft to enforce a no-fly zone over northern Iraq, as this had enabled the Turkish military to avoid international censure and operate relatively freely on the ground in northern Iraq.[38]

Interviewed in May 2003, Wolfowitz could not hide his disappointment at what he perceived to be the failure of the Turkish military to provide a leadership role.[39] Relations between the US and Turkish militaries further worsened in July when eleven of Turkey's special forces were apprehended by US units in Suleymaniyeh and detained for three days on the grounds that they were plotting to murder the Kurdish mayor of Kirkuk.[40] Ties only improved after the parliament in Ankara, in October, approved of the possible dispatch of Turkish peacekeepers to Iraq.

The impact of the Turkish media on foreign policy making and on public opinion is difficult to gauge. Newspapers and many private television and radio stations in Turkey articulate opinions across the political spectrum. In the print media, well-known and informed commentators have presented differing viewpoints on Iraq. However, by summer 2002 a substantial part of the Turkish public objected to a war with Iraq, and press coverage notwithstanding, this opposition continued in the following months. Significantly, though, more details about the negotiations between Turkish and US diplomats and friction within the AKP ranks in the buildup to the war would only be published by leading press analysts several months after the end of the military campaign.[41]

■ Impact of Turkish Foreign Policy

The assumption that decisionmaking in key areas of Turkish foreign policy is largely in the hands of the foreign ministry and the Turkish armed forces, which share certain mind-sets, has been seriously challenged with the failure of the Turkish parliament to approve the 1 March motion. Although equipped with only limited formal powers in foreign policy making,

President Sezer was able to exert his personal influence over a hesitant military. With Turkey continuing to democratize in its bid to secure membership of the EU, the impact of Turkish public opinion on foreign policy issues must also now be taken more into account.

Not participating in the war, Ankara lost a golden opportunity to have a major say in the political reconstruction of a post-Saddam Iraq. Since 1991 Turkish governments had pursued a policy that aimed to preserve the territorial integrity and unity of Iraq, forestall the emergence of an independent Kurdish state in northern Iraq, and crush PKK insurgents holed up in KDP- and PUK-controlled territory. The AKP government and the Turkish armed forces have made it clear that these remain Turkey's main priorities in Iraq. Nevertheless, Ankara will find it more difficult to press its case in Washington, given US sympathies for the Iraqi Kurds and bearing in mind the Pentagon's bitter disappointment at the failure of the Turks to open a northern front. The strategic partnership between Turkey and the United States had suffered a major setback. Some in Washington must have seriously questioned Turkey's geopolitical value after the United States was unable to use Turkish airbases and ports in a major military operation.

However, relations between Turkey and the United States improved when Erdogan met Bush in the White House in January 2004. With Incirlik being used as a staging post for the rotation of US troops to Iraq, Bush again referred to Turkey as "a friend and important ally."[42] US officials remain aware of Turkey's strategic location on a future east-west energy transportation corridor stretching from the Caspian Sea to western Europe—although throughout 2004 and the first half of 2005 the Kirkuk-Yumurtalik oil pipeline was repeatedly damaged by insurgents. At the NATO summit in Istanbul in June 2004, Bush referred to Turkey as a key state in the war on terrorism and an important model for a future democratic Middle East.[43] Relations between Washington and Ankara deteriorated again, though, when in November 2004 Mehmet Elkatmis, the chairman of the Turkish parliament's Human Rights Commission, condemned the United States for committing "genocide" against the Iraqis in the military operation against Fallujah.[44]

The diplomatic maneuvers immediately prior to the war enabled Turkey to improve ties with Iran and the Arab world. Previous governments in Ankara—with the exception of the 1996–1997 administration, led by the more radically Islamist Necmettin Erbakan—had focused little attention on their Muslim neighbors. Arab states had remained suspicious of their former colonial ruler. Although membership in the EU remains a priority for the Erdogan government, the conservative AKP is also naturally interested in the Muslim world. Significantly, in June 2004 a Turkish academic would be appointed secretary-general of the Organization of Islamic Conference.

■ Conclusion

Unilateral Turkish intervention in northern Iraq to prevent the formation of an independent Kurdish state is not impossible given that Ankara regards this as an issue of crucial importance for Turkey's own national security. Such action would have disastrous repercussions for Turkish-US relations. Turkish officials have become resigned to the possibility of a federal Iraq in which the Kurdish autonomous region would be an important component. However, Ankara remains opposed to the division of Iraq. In January 2004, receiving Abdul Aziz al-Hakim, the Shiite leader and a member of the then Iraqi Governing Council, Erdogan warned that moves toward the breakup of Iraq could prompt intervention from its neighbors.[45] Ankara has also lobbied for Kirkuk to be given a special status in which all resident ethnic groups would be involved in the city's administration.[46] Turkish policymakers are concerned that the possible inclusion of the oil-rich Kirkuk territory in an enlarged Kurdish autonomous region after the holding of a referendum by December 2007—as envisaged in the draft Iraqi constitution announced in August 2005—could encourage the northern Iraqi Kurds to push for independence.

The Turkish authorities have developed better contacts with the northern Iraqi Kurds. In postwar Iraq, Turkish construction companies established a significant presence in PUK-controlled territory. Turkish-Iraqi commercial relations, in general, had quickly recovered, so that by May 2005, Turkish state minister Kursat Tuzmen set a target to attain in the foreseeable future an annual business volume of $10 billion through cooperation in trade, investment, transportation, and contracting services.[47] Kurdish appreciation of the messages of condolence sent by Ankara after the two suicide bomb attacks in Erbil on 1 February 2004 helped improve ties between Turkey and the PUK and KDP. But the northern Iraqi Kurds' demands for the withdrawal of Turkish troops from their territory were not seriously considered by Ankara, given the continued presence of the PKK in northern Iraq.[48] Despite this rapprochement, officials in Ankara are not prepared to countenance the formation of an independent Kurdistan.

The Iraqi Turkmen have proven to be a major disappointment for Ankara. The ITF has failed to become an umbrella organization for all Iraqi Turkmen, and instead has become increasingly regarded as a mouthpiece of the Turkish authorities. This led to a formal split in April 2005 when the pro-Kurdish Erbil branch broke away from the Ankara-controlled ITF with its headquarters in Kirkuk.[49] Previously, Shiite Iraqi Turkmen, not affiliated with the predominantly Sunni-based ITF, had clashed with the northern Iraqi Kurds in August and December 2003. In January 2005 in the elections to the transitional Iraqi National Assembly, the ITF had only secured three seats.

Turkish officials would feel less apprehensive about developments in northern Iraq if the PKK were eliminated. In October 2003, Ankara and Washington agreed to a joint action plan to employ economic, political, and legal means to render the PKK redundant.[50] However, the Bush administration has been reluctant to use force in what would most probably be a costly military operation to eradicate the PKK, even though the Kurdish rebels ended their cease-fire and resumed hostilities in June 2004. Possible unilateral intervention by the Turkish military to attempt to uproot PKK units from their mountain strongholds could lead to a serious deterioration in US-Turkish relations.

Sharing concerns about the future of Iraq, Turkey is likely to continue its rapprochement with Iran and Syria, although not at the expense of US-Turkish ties. In March 2004 there were violent protests by Kurds in Syria demanding more rights. Bashar al-Asad had become the first Syrian president to visit Ankara in January 2004, and this was followed by visits to Damascus by Erdogan and Sezer in December 2004 and April 2005 respectively. Iran recognized the PKK as a terrorist organization when Erdogan was received in Tehran in July 2004.[51] By mid-2005 the Iranian security forces were clashing with supporters of the Kurdistan Independent Life Party (PJAK), an affiliate of the PKK.

Gul suggested at a meeting in Damascus in November 2003 of foreign ministers of states neighboring Iraq—such meetings having become regularized after the January 2003 gathering in Istanbul—that they should form a Contact Group at the UN to discuss the Iraqi issue.[52] The following month, UN Secretary-General Kofi Annan established an Iraqi Advisory Group that included the five permanent members of the Security Council as well as Egypt and Iraq's neighbors. In addition to its contacts with Washington, Ankara is seeking to use this group as a mechanism to influence future developments in northern Iraq. However, at the time of writing, there remained a possibility that the failure of Kurds, Shiites, and Sunnis to agree to a new Iraqi constitution could lead to the disintegration of Iraq and the eventual formation of an independent Kurdistan with Kirkuk as its capital.

■ **Notes**

1. *Turkish Probe,* 2 March 2003.
2. *Daily Telegraph,* 22 March 2003.
3. Kemal Kirisci, "The Kurdish Question and Turkish Foreign Policy," p. 310.
4. *Turkish Daily News,* 8 October 2003.
5. Coinciding with the introduction of Kurdish language broadcasting, and pending the conclusion of their retrial, in June 2004 Leyla Zana and three other for-

mer deputies of the Democracy Party were released. The four pro-Kurdish deputies had been sentenced in December 1994 because of their reported close links with the PKK. By summer 2005 Zana and her colleagues were establishing a new party—the Democratic Society Movement. One should note that after the war in Iraq in 2003 the nonviolent politically active members of Turkey's Kurdish population concentrated on securing political reforms in Turkey and were less interested with developments in Kurdish-controlled northern Iraq.

6. For background to developments in northern Iraq and Turkey's interests there in the 1990s, see Kemal Kirisci and Gareth M. Winrow, *The Kurdish Question and Turkey,* pp. 162–167; and Philip Robins, *Suits and Uniforms,* pp. 312–342.

7. Soner Cagaptay, "Enhancing the Turkish-American Alliance," p. 2.

8. Bulent Aliriza, "Turkey's Iraq Jitters," p. 1.

9. "War with Iraq—Iraq: Compliance, Sanctions, and US Policy," *Strategypage,* 27 November 2003, http://www.strategypage.com/iraqwar/americanpolicy/15.asp.

10. Soner Cagaptay, "Turkmens," p. 2. The Turkish Ministry of Foreign Affairs announced the ending of the PMF mission on 2 July 2004. See "Tan Says Mission of Peace Monitoring Force in Iraq Ended," *Anadolu Agency* (Ankara), 2 July 2004.

11. Carol Migdalovitz, "Iraq," pp. 3–4. According to Cagaptay, "Turkmens," p. 1, the Iraqi Turkmen population may total 1–1.5 million. Other commentators believe this figure could be as low as 300,000.

12. See Articles 4 and 49 of the *Draft Constitution of the Iraqi Kurdistan Region,* http://www.krg.org/docs/k_const.asp.

13. *Turkish Daily News,* 2 March 2004. For more details on the Iraqi Turkmen, see H. Tarik Oguzlu, "The 'Turkomans.'"

14. Kemal Kirisci, "Turkey and the Muslim Middle East," p. 45.

15. Sebnem Udum, "Missile Proliferation in the Middle East," p. 88.

16. "Remarks by the President in Meeting with the Chairman of Turkey's AK Party," transcript, White House, Office of the Press Secretary, 10 December 2002, http://www.whitehouse.gov/news/releases/2002/12/images/20021210-8.html.

17. *Turkish Daily News,* 5 December 2002.

18. See the series of four articles by Fikret Bila in *Milliyet,* 22–25 September 2003.

19. Philip Robins, "Confusion at Home," p. 564.

20. *Financial Times,* 19 February 2003.

21. *Financial Times,* 20 February 2003.

22. "United States–Turkey Financial Agreement: Joint Statement Following Signing of the Agreement, 22 September 2003, Dubai UAE," JS-747, Press Room, Office of Public Affairs, 22 September 2003, http://www.ustreas.gov/press/releases/js747.htm.

23. *Turkish Daily News,* 5 March 2005.

24. *Turkish Times,* 1 October 2002.

25. "Regional Initiative on Iraq—Joint Declaration," Istanbul, 23 January 2003, http://www.mfa.gov/tr/grupa/ad/add/irak.htm.

26. These distractions prevented the possible swift approval by parliament of a second motion similarly worded to that of 1 March. This was at a time when ships carrying tanks and heavy equipment for the US Fourth Infantry Division, planned to be deployed in northern Iraq, were still waiting off the Turkish Mediterranean coast.

27. *Turkish Daily News,* 5 December 2002.

28. *Milliyet,* 7 January 2003.

29. *Turkish Daily News,* 25 February 2003.

30. Sedat Ergin, "Tezkere AKP'yi Catlatti" [Memorandum Splits the AKP], *Hurriyet,* 24 September 2003.

31. Soner Cagaptay, "An Accident on the Road to US-Turkish Cooperation in Iraq," p. 1.

32. "Baykal: We Should Not Allow US Troops in Our Country," *Kurdistan Observer,* 4 February 2003, http://home.cogeco.ca/~observer/4–2-03-baykal-not-to-allow-us-troops.html.

33. "What the World Thinks in 2002," *Pew Research Center for the People and the Press: Survey Reports,* 4 December 2002, http://people-press.org/reports/display.php3?reportid=165.

34. Sedat Ergin, "Galiba o Tren Kacti" [I Suppose That Train Has Left] *Hurriyet,* 25 September 2003.

35. *Turkish Daily News,* 10 January 2003.

36. I am grateful to Gareth Jenkins for these observations.

37. *Turkish Daily News,* 6 March 2003.

38. Heinz Kramer, *A Changing Turkey,* p. 128.

39. *Turkish Daily News,* 7 May 2003.

40. Jeffrey Donovan, "Iraq: US Pressing Governing Council to Accept Turkish Troops," *Radio Free Europe/Radio Liberty* (Washington, DC), 9 October 2003.

41. Fikret Bila and Sedat Ergin produced a series of articles in the mass-circulation newspapers *Milliyet* and *Hurriyet* respectively in September 2003. In January 2004, Murat Yetkin prepared articles for the center-left newspaper *Radikal.*

42. *Financial Times,* 29 January 2004.

43. *Los Angeles Times,* 29 June 2004. Note that the terrorist attacks against synagogues and British targets in Istanbul in November 2003 were condemned by the Turkish public and government and did not spark a rise in anti-US or anti-British sentiment.

44. *Turkish Daily* News, 27 November 2004.

45. "Prime Minister Erdogan: 'Kurds Have Been Trying to Take Oil Reserve Areas in the North Under Their Influence,'" *Anadolu Agency* (Ankara), 14 January 2004.

46. *The Guardian,* 15 February 2005.

47. "Export to Iraq Increases: Target Is $2.5 billion," *Zaman,* 22 May 2005, http://www.zaman.com/?bl=economy&alt=&hn=19822.

48. *Turkish Daily News,* 10 February 2004; "Iraqi Kurd Tries to Reassure Turkey over Rebels," *Reuters* (Ankara), 10 February 2004.

49. Kathleen Ridolfo, "Iraq: Will the Turkoman Split Break Turkish Interference?" *Radio Free Europe/Radio Liberty* (Prague), 6 April 2005.

50. "Turkey, US Craft Plan to Defeat Kurdish Rebels Left in Iraq," *Bloomberg,* 2 October 2003.

51. *Turkish Daily News,* 30 July 2004.

52. "Foreign Minister Gul Says Suggestion of Annan About Iraq Shows Importance of Regional Initiative Which Turkey Has Started," *Anadolu Agency* (Naples), 29 November 2003.

Part 3

Context and Consequences

17

War and Resistance in Iraq: From Regime Change to Collapsed State

Toby Dodge

> People say to me, you [the Iraqis] are not the Vietnamese, you have no jungles and swamps to hide in. I reply let our cities be our swamps and buildings our jungles.
>
> Former deputy prime minister Tariq Aziz[1]

Why, despite the overwhelming military defeat of the Iraqi army, has the United States failed to secure its ostensible goal in Iraq, a stable pro-US regime? The removal of Saddam Hussein has proved to be the beginning, not the culmination, of a long and very uncertain process of occupation and state building. The lawlessness and looting that greeted the US force's seizure of Baghdad on 9 April 2003 have evolved into a self-sustaining dynamic that combines violence, instability, and profound uncertainty. US troops and the nascent Iraqi security services now face an insurgency that has managed to extend its geographic scope, while increasing the level of violence and the capacity for destruction and instability.

■ The Roots of Instability in Iraq

The chaos and violence that greeted regime change have their roots in the legacies that Saddam's government bequeathed to Iraq. Iraqi regimes, because of their perceived domestic and international vulnerability, have sought to maximize their autonomy from society. This process reached its apex under the Baathist regime, built by Hasan al-Bakr from 1968 and consolidated under Saddam after 1979. They built a powerful set of state institutions through the 1970s and 1980s that managed to reshape society, breaking organized resistance to their rule, effectively atomizing the population.[2] It was not possible to talk of a functioning civil society in Iraq before 2003. The regime had broken, co-opted, or reconstructed all intermediate institutions that would have shielded society from the force of the state.

However, the Iran-Iraq War, the Gulf War (1990–1991), and finally the imposition of draconian sanctions changed the Iraqi state and with it Saddam's strategy of rule. From their application in 1990 until 1997, when UN-supervised oil revenues began to arrive, sanctions on Iraq effectively curbed the government's access to large-scale funding, with deleterious consequences for state and society. From 1991 until 2003 the effects of government policy and the sanctions regime led to hyperinflation, widespread poverty, and malnutrition. The historically generous state welfare provision that had been central to the regime's governing strategy disappeared overnight. The large and well-educated middle class that had grown in the years of plenty to form the bedrock of Iraqi society was impoverished. The story of Iraq from 1991 until 2003 is of a country suffering a profound macroeconomic shock.[3]

As sanctions began to take effect after 1991, there was a rapid decline in the official and visible institutions of the state. The government in Baghdad was forced to cut back on the resources it could devote to the armed forces and police. Before 1990, the bureaucracy of the Iraqi state had been complex and all-pervasive. During the 1990s the effects of "self-financing" meant these institutions were hollowed out. Bribery was commonplace, as civil servants' official wages became at times almost valueless. The 1990s saw many professionals leaving the public service, to take their chances in the private sector or flee into exile.

It was the supposed power of Iraq's state institutions that the US forces assumed they would inherit once they reached Baghdad. To quote Condoleezza Rice, "The concept was that we would defeat the army, but the institutions would hold, everything from ministries to police forces."[4] However, these state institutions were by April 2003 on the verge of collapse. The third war in twenty years and three weeks of looting in its aftermath pushed them over the edge. Civil servants did not return to work after the cease-fire, instead opting to protect their families and property as best they could. Their offices across the country, but especially in Baghdad, were stripped by looters and burned.[5] The combination of war, sanctions fatigue, and rampant criminality led to a complete state breakdown. The subsequent extended exercise in state building has been far more costly and has required much greater expertise and resources than the Pentagon had anticipated. State institutions still remain to be built, and their relationship with society renegotiated. This will have to be done in the face of increasing resentment while meeting demands for Iraqi participation.

■ War and Invasion

The difficulties in establishing law and order in the aftermath of the war also have roots in the type of campaign that US planners thought they were going to fight and the type of resistance that the Baathist regime attempted to organize. There is strong evidence that those planning the invasion underestimated the resistance they would face, most importantly by sections of the mainstream army and irregular forces, notably the Fedayeen Saddam. In February 2003, in the run-up to war, US Army chief of staff Eric Shinseki in a Senate hearing called for "something in the order of several hundred thousand soldiers" to guarantee order. Other assessments concluded that occupying forces would need twenty security personnel, both police and troops, per thousand people to control the country. This compares to the forty-three per thousand that sustained Saddam in power.[6] This means coalition forces should have had between 400,000 and 500,000 soldiers to impose order on Iraq.[7] However, senior civilians at the Pentagon played a key role in limiting the number of troops available to US commanders on the ground in Iraq. They were working on the assumption that at the advent of the air war or in the immediate aftermath of the invasion, a coup would remove Saddam from power and leave governing structures largely in place.[8] President George W. Bush himself, in an eve-of-war speech, actively encouraged the Iraqi armed forces to move against their leaders.[9] If a coup failed to materialize, then the supposition was that Iraqi forces would implode or simply refuse to fight in a fashion similar to that in the Gulf War, with thousands surrendering to allied forces.[10] In addition, US secretary of defense Donald Rumsfeld, as part of his commitment to a "revolution in military affairs," put great emphasis on the use of precision bombing and technological advantage and encouraged General Tommy Franks, the man responsible for drawing up the plans for the invasion, to keep troop numbers as low as possible. The result was that in the middle of the invasion, the United States had 116,000 soldiers in Iraq with 310,000 personnel in the theater as a whole, compared with the 500,000 anticipated by the Pentagon's planners before Franks's revision of their plans.[11]

Faced with the overwhelming military superiority of the US Army and US Air Force, the Iraqi government had very few options when planning the defense of the country. With the reliability of the mainstream army in doubt, plans focused on the security services, Special and Republican Guards, and on 30,000 irregular forces, the Fedayeen Saddam and the Arab fighters who came to Iraq before the invasion to do battle with US forces. The regime also appears to have learned from the mistakes its military made in both the Iran-Iraq War and the Gulf War, when units had no ability to act on their own initiative.[12] In an attempt to counter this, Baghdad decentralized army command and control down to the lowest level possible. By giving local control to a senior military officer, resistance could continue after Baghdad was cut off from its hinterland while the large arms dumps spread around the country supplied the postwar insurgency.[13]

The reality of the war and its aftermath differed from the assumptions of US planners. The optimistic prognosis of Washington-based analysts that the Baathist government in Baghdad would be removed by a coup proved to be incorrect. Sections of the mainstream army fought more tenaciously than many had expected. The level of Iraqi resistance in the south of the country, especially around Umm Qasr and Nasiriya, surprised US Central Command.[14] In motivational terms, this resistance reflected a factor that continues to dominate Iraq: nationalism. There is no doubt that ordinary conscript soldiers, 80 percent of whom were Shia, hated Saddam Hussein, but there still exists in the country a militant Iraqi nationalism, born of three wars in the past two decades, and over a decade of punishing sanctions known to be engineered by the United States. This was rallied during the war to motivate troops fighting against US forces that were widely seen to be out to grab Iraq's oil, not to benefit its people.

■ Occupation and Insurgency

The Conditions of Insurgency

The US occupation itself has facilitated insurgency. Previous best practice from post–Cold War peacekeeping operations stresses that establishing law and order within the first six to twelve weeks of any occupation is crucial for the credibility and legitimacy of the occupiers.[15] For military occupation to be successful, the population has to be overawed by both the scale and the commitment of the occupiers. The speed with which US and coalition forces removed Saddam's regime certainly impressed the Iraqi population, and US military superiority initially appeared absolute. However, what began in April 2003 as a lawless celebration of the demise of Saddam's regime grew into three weeks of uncontrolled looting and violence. To Baghdad's residents, coalition forces appeared unable or unwilling to curtail the violence that swept across the city, encouraging the perception among would-be insurgents that the United States could not control the country.[16] At the same time, with the collapse of Saddam's regime, thousands of Iraqi troops simply merged back into their own communities while the stockpiling of weapons by the Baathist regime in numerous dumps across the country provided supplies of small arms and explosives for those who wanted to use them. Historically, there has been a high rate of private automatic-weapon ownership in Iraq, as the regime never tried to disarm the general population. The rapid collapse of the regime allowed munitions to become widely available at very low prices.

The security vacuum that came to dominate Iraq did a great deal to undermine the initial impression of US omnipotence and helped turn criminal violence and looting into an organized and politically motivated insurgency. The initial goodwill that greeted the liberation of Baghdad quickly turned into popular disenchantment with the occupation's failure to establish order, and into increased nationalist resentment of it. To this extent the insurgency has fed off the mistakes of the occupation, utilizing the anger and alienation felt among sections of society.

Finally, in this vacuum, it was easy to resurrect the long tradition of Iraqi political discourse, which historically was strongly shaped by the ideological influences of Islam, Arab nationalism, and the increasingly Iraqi specific nationalism.[17] Those fighting are mobilized by these influences to see their mission as ridding their country of a foreign invader and its collaborators.

The Forces of Insurgency

The evolving insurgency, involving diverse tactics and different targets, springs from several separate sources and a multitude of causes. The first identifiable group of insurgents are the "industrial-scale" criminal gangs operating in the urban centers of Basra, Baghdad, and Mosul. It is organized crime that constitutes 80 percent of violence in Iraq and makes the lives of the population miserable.[18] The organized criminal groups predate regime change, having come to prominence in the mid-1990s at the peak of the social and economic suffering and state weakening caused by sanctions. These groups have been revitalized by the lawlessness of present-day Iraq, capitalizing on readily available weapons, the lack of an efficient police force, and the US occupation's paucity of intelligence. They terrorize the remnants of middle-class Iraq, car-jacking, house-breaking, and kidnapping, largely with impunity. It is groups like these that make the roads leading from Baghdad so dangerous, regularly kidnapping and killing foreign workers and Iraqis alike. In many cases these gangs are better armed and organized than the Iraqi police trying to stop them. Their continued capacity to operate is the most visible sign of state weakness.

A second group involved in violence comprises the remnants of the Baath regime's security services, party loyalists, and Saddam's clientage network. This group is estimated to be responsible for up to 60 percent of the politically motivated violence.[19] Sensing both the vulnerability and the incoherence of the occupation, they began launching hit-and-run attacks on US troops in May 2003 and have increased the frequency, skill, and geographic scope of their operations. The speed with which Saddam Hussein's government collapsed in the face of invasion and the chaos that caused meant that the beginning of the insurgency was reactive and highly localized. Interviews that I conducted with various levels of former regime loyalists in Baghdad in spring and summer 2003 paint a picture of a fractured and spontaneous rebellion against the United States.[20] However, the dissolution of the army and de-Baathification in May 2003 put an estimated 750,000 people out of work and available for the insurgency.[21] Against this background it was a small step for the Baath Party, an organization with a long history of covert operations, to move from reactively organizing for self-defense to proactively moving to offensive action. By November 2003 the Baathist arm of the resistance had begun to cohere. Documents seized by the US military when it took Saddam into custody in December 2003 indicated that he had been in regular contact with those organizing the resistance. By 2004 a new politburo at the head of the Iraqi Baath Party had been formed, with representation of both the civilian and military wings of the party, and with personnel resident in the country and outside.[22]

Another source of violence is certainly the most worrying for the new Iraqi government and the hardest to deal with. This can be usefully characterized as Iraqi Islamism, with both Sunni and Shia variations. After the Gulf War and the imposition of sanctions, Saddam infused the Baath Party's long-established, secular, broadly socialist rhetoric with an Islamism that reflected the Iraqi population's return to religion in the face of economic collapse and social dislocation.[23] The strong nationalist and Islamic currents running through the Iraqi polity have combined to create a political ideology that preaches the defense of the *Watan,* the Iraqi homeland, against foreign and non-Muslim invaders. The battalions of the 1920 revolution are a good example of this dynamic. Formed in the suburban hinterland of Baghdad, they have, as their name suggests, merged an Iraqi nationalism with an Islamic radicalism. This potent combination meant that in 2004, groups like this were the fastest-growing wing of the insurgency, responsible for up to 20 percent of the violence against the US military and Iraqi security forces. This ideological aspect to the resistance movement is not going to disappear.

An early indication of the cause and effect behind the mobilization of political violence in Iraq can be seen in the case of Fallujah, a market city of some 300,000 people, thirty-five miles west of Baghdad. Notwithstanding Paul Wolfowitz's incorrect assertions, far from being a "hotbed of Ba'thist activity,"[24] Fallujah was known in Iraq as the "Medinat al-Masajid," the City of Mosques, highlighting its deeply conservative reputation, famed for its adherence to Sunni Islam and,[25] along with Ramadi, as a city where the secular government's influence was at its weakest, and where the state found it difficult to impose law and order.

It was two weeks after the fall of Baghdad before US troops entered Fallujah. In the interim, Iraqi troops and Baath Party leaders left the town. Imams from the local mosques stepped into the sociopolitical vacuum, bringing an end to the looting, even managing to return some of the stolen property.[26] Fallujah became a center of violent opposition to US occupation so soon after liberation because of a series of heavy-handed missions by US troops searching for leading members of the old regime.[27] Resentment escalated when two local imams were arrested. Events reached a climax when US troops broke up a demonstration with gunfire, resulting in seventeen

Iraq fatalities and seventy wounded. This caused a spiral of violence and revenge that has destabilized the area and overshadowed the US military's attempts to impose order on the whole northwestern region of Iraq. The result was the killing of four private security guards at the end of March 2004 and a bloody retaking of the city by US Marines.

The political organizations that emerged from Fallujan society to control the town and negotiate an end to the siege, the Mujahideen Shura (Resistance Council) and the Hayat al-Ulama al-Muslimin (Muslim Scholars Council), are indicative of the diversity of ideological trends within the opposition. Members of both groups claim to represent the variety of Islamic trends found in the northwestern region of Iraq. These include the Sufi tradition, which is influential in Fallujah, but also the much more austere and radical Salafi approach to Islam.[28]

Muqtada al-Sadr has been the political figure who has successfully rallied the nationalist and radical Islamic trends among Shia sections of the population. Sadr's support originates in the poorest and most disadvantaged sections of the Shia population. Capitalizing on a large charitable network set up by his late father, Sadr has used radical anti-US rhetoric to rally the disaffected to his organization. As the occupation failed to deliver significant improvements to people's lives, Sadr's popularity began to increase. In the run-up to the handover of power on 28 June 2004, Sadr's rhetoric and actions became more extreme in an attempt to convince the Coalition Provisional Authority (CPA) that he could not be excluded from the postoccupation political settlement, as the CPA intended. Sadr deployed his own militia, the Mahdi Army, to increase his power in the large Shia slum of Baghdad, Al-Tharwa (renamed "Sadr City" following the war, after his dead father), and across the south of the country.

This game of cat and mouse, with Sadr upping his rhetorical radicalism while highlighting his military capacity, meant that strategically the CPA could not ignore him. But it proved ill-judged to confront his organization at the same time that US Marines were trying to contain the Fallujan uprising. The CPA, by closing down Sadr's newspaper and arresting Sheikh Mustafa al-Yacoubi, one of Sadr's key deputies in Najaf, drew him into open conflict. The resulting revolts in key towns across the south of Iraq—Basra, Amara, Kut, Nasiriya, Najaf, Kufa, and Karbala—as well as in Baghdad itself, highlighted two things. First, Sadr's organization had been preparing for just such a confrontation since the invasion at least, organizing the Mahdi Army with this in mind. Second, even with this lead time, the geographic scale of the southern uprising indicated a bandwagoning effect; other smaller militias and local armed groups used the cover of Sadr's confrontation to launch their own preemptive strikes against coalitions forces.

In twice confronting the superior military forces of the occupation, Sadr's Mahdi Army clearly overreached itself. The full force of US air power used against the rebellion in Sadr City and Najaf broke it. However, the constituency that Sadr aspires to represent, the economically disadvantaged and politically alienated, will not disappear. The widespread casualties resulting from the suppression of the revolt, particularly in Baghdad, have created a wellspring of resentment that will take years to diffuse. Sadr or politicians like him will have continued access to a constituency large enough to fuel radical political mobilization.

The final contributing factor to the insurgency is the most controversial and difficult to judge: the role played by Arab fighters from neighboring countries, and behind them the organizing capacity of Al-Qaida in Iraq. The US occupation has presented the actions of Abu Musab al-Zarqawi, a Jordanian-born Islamist, as evidence of a sustained Al-Qaida presence in Iraq. There is clear evidence of foreign fighters playing a role in the insurgency and the suicide bombings that have plagued the country. Mobilized through diffuse and informal networks across the Middle East, they have been making their way to Iraq in an uncoordinated fashion. However, their numbers appear to be comparatively low, estimated by the US Army to be between 500 and 2,000. In March 2004 less than 150 of the 10,000 security prisoners held by the US military in Iraq were non-Iraqi Arabs.[29] Although it may be politically expedient for US and Iraqi politicians to stress the non-Iraqi aspects of the insurgency, the revolt is very much a homegrown phenomenon.

The Course of Insurgency

The insurgency is diffuse in command and control, in personnel and in strategy. Clearly, US troops initially formed the main target. In a classic case of asymmetrical warfare, small bands of highly mobile assailants, making use of their local knowledge, inflicted increasing fatalities on US troops. With its genesis in late May 2003, by July the insurgents were beginning to show signs of greater professionalism, deploying organized reconnaissance to perfect a modus operandi that used small groups of ten to fifteen fighters to attack with maximum efficiency and minimum loss of life.[30] Capitalizing on the lack of US armored transportation, the insurgents used rocket-propelled grenades and improvised roadside bombs to great effect. By early summer 2003, road travel for US convoys had become very dangerous. By the autumn, US forces recognized the increased geographical spread of the insurgency, the improved coordination between the different groups, but also their use of a wider range of arms, including mortars and mines.[31] The downing of several US Army helicopters with heavy loss of life, in the first two weeks of November 2003, further indicated the vulnerability of US forces on the move. This gave rise to a negative dynamic in which increasing US casualties gave the impression that the insurgents could strike with impunity. In addition, the increasing violence spread a deep sense of insecurity across the population of Iraq, in turn increasing resentment of the occupation.

As US troops have increasingly been redeployed to more secure bases outside urban areas, to reduce their vulnerability and political visibility, the insurgents have sought out more accessible targets. A small minority of those perpetrating the violence have deliberately targeted international institutions, specifically foreign embassies, the United Nations and the Red Cross, signaling that they would try to make any multilateralization of the occupation both costly and unworkable. Second, they began to target the nascent institutions and personnel of the new Iraqi state. This change in tactics was heralded by the attack on three police stations in Baghdad on the same day in October 2003. Since then, this method has broadened in its geographical scope and ferocity, with the use of car bombs to target police stations and army recruiting centers across the country. These attacks are designed not only to discourage Iraqis from working for the new state but also to stop the growth of its institutions. They undermine attempts to deliver to the Iraqi population what they have been demanding since the fall of the Baath regime: law and order.

The final tactic adopted by radical Sunni jihadis was to target high-profile Shia and Kurdish political figures in an attempt to fracture and destabilize the Iraqi polity. This has the potential to be most damaging to Iraq's long-term stability. The first indication of this was in August 2003, when a massive explosion outside the Imam Ali Mosque in Najaf (one of the holiest shrines of Shia Islam) not only cost the lives of a hundred innocent civilians but also killed Ayatollah Mohammed Baqir al-Hakim, the leader of the Supreme Council for the Islamic Revolution in Iraq, a group that the UK and US governments had been assiduously courting to form the cornerstone of a new political order in post-Saddam Iraq. This bombing not only signaled the high cost of becoming involved in the governance of Iraq but also hinted at the increasingly sectarian nature of targeting. In February 2004, the tactic was extended to the Kurdish areas of Iraq when two suicide bombers killed 101 people in Arbil at the offices of the main Kurdish parties, the Kurdish Democratic Party and the Patriotic Union of Kurdistan. In a series of attacks on 2 March, by targeting the large crowds who gathered to commemorate the Shia festival of Ashura in Baghdad and Karbala, the perpetrators were clearly attempting to trigger a civil war between Iraq's different communities. This assumption was strengthened by the discovery in Baghdad of a letter allegedly written by a senior Islamist figure, the Jordanian Abu Musab al-Zarqawi, who argued that the only way to "prolong the duration of the fight between the infidels and us" is by "dragging them into a sectarian war, this will awaken the sleepy Sunnis who are fearful of destruction and death at the hands of the Shia."[32] US officials and Iraqi politicians have been keen to blame the use of suicide bombers and the rise in sectarian violence on outside forces,[33] but the speed, number, and efficiency of these attacks point to a large amount of Iraqi involvement and direction. Such jihadis seek to create a new brand of radical sectarianism and mobilize Sunni fears of Shia and Kurdish domination. Although the use of indiscriminate violence has alienated the majority of Iraqi public opinion across all sections of society, the carnage it has produced has been a major setback for state building and stability. Those deploying this form of violence believe that the resulting chaos will further delegitimize the Iraqi government and hasten the departure of US troops. These groups hope that they would be best placed to exploit and eventually control the resulting political and security vacuum.

■ The Creation of Postwar Political Structures

US planners anticipated a limited exercise in regime change and easily managed state reform in the aftermath of the war. However, once the institutions of government had collapsed, the task facing the occupation became complex and potentially contradictory: the building of a new political order that would be stable and legitimate yet also in broad agreement with US foreign policy aims.

Toward this end, the role of former Baathists in the government had to be minimized, but other political forces that might destabilize a pro-US agenda also had to be identified and marginalized, not least in order to create a space within which a new, pro-US ruling elite could be nurtured. However, this policy objective clashed with the needs and demands of the Iraqi population. De-Baathification, the dissolution of the army and expulsion of 40,000 former administrators from the civil service, greatly hindered the restoration of government services and law and order. And the United States faced a highly mobilized society vocally expressing its newfound political freedom. Legitimizing a new government both internationally and even more importantly, domestically, had to involve, at some stage, handing power over to an Iraqi governing elite that was either popularly elected or could at least mobilize a significant section of Iraqi popular opinion to support its rule. Reactive US policy measures to meet these contradictory demands and interests were largely short-term, paying little attention to the medium- to long-term consequences of each new initiative.

Apart from the collapse of the state itself, the central problem that hampered the occupation was an acute lack of knowledge about the country. The occupation authorities took up residence in the old seat of government, the Republican Palace, at the heart of the secure "green zone" in the center of Baghdad. It was dependent upon a small group of Iraqi exiles, long absent from the country. They returned with the invaders to act as a conduit between US forces and the Iraqi population, helping them to understand an unfamiliar society. Most important, it was hoped that these exiles would become the basis of Iraq's new governing class.

However, this reliance created distinct problems. The main organization formed in exile, Iraqi National Congress and its allies, brought back to the country a view of Iraqi society as irrevocably divided between sectarian groupings and mobilized by deep communal antipathy, a view that bore little resemblance to the real state of Iraqi society in 2003–2004.[34] This "primordialization" of Iraq clearly influenced the way the Iraqi Governing Council (ICG) was formed in July 2003, after negotiations between the US authorities and seven exiled parties. The United States promoted the IGC as "the most representative body in Iraq's history," but this could not come from the undemocratic method of its formation; instead it reflected the supposed religio-ethnic divisions in the country: thirteen Shias, five Sunnis, five Kurds, a Turkman, and a Christian. The forced and rather bizarre nature of this arrangement was highlighted by the inclusion of Hamid Majid Mousa, the Iraqi Communist Party's representative in the "Shia block" of thirteen. Such sectarian mathematics was also used to expand the number of cabinet portfolios to twenty-five, so that the spoils of office could be divided up in a similar fashion. The manner of the IGC selection caused a great deal of consternation across Iraqi opinion. Criticism focused on the fostering of an overt sectarianism that had previously not been central to Iraqi political discourse,[35] and on the damage that selection on the basis of sectarian or religious affiliations, rather than competence, would do to the restoration of government. Indeed, senior US officials themselves became rapidly disillusioned with its ability to deliver either leadership or legitimacy, noting that "at least half the council is out of the country at any given time and that at some meetings, only four or five members show up." A new governing structure was needed to cope with the rising insurgency but, as a senior occupation official said at the time, "it is unlikely that we will want to make a provisional government out of a council that has been feckless."[36]

Faced with increasing pressure from the UN Security Council for real sovereign power to be delegated to an Iraq governing body, the increasing alienation of the Iraq population, and a rising tide of political violence, the Bush administration set 30 June 2004 as the deadline for transferring sovereignty to Iraq. But it was the intervention of the most senior religious figure in the country, Grand Ayatollah Ali al-Sistani, that forced the democratization of this hasty process. Sistani has continually pressed for early elections as the only way to reduce violence, guarantee Iraq's progress to democracy, and lessen the influence of the United States in running the country. His ability to influence events was highlighted by the hundred thousand people who demonstrated in Baghdad in January 2004 in support of his demands for nationwide elections. The transitional law finally agreed to by the Iraqi

Governing Council in March 2004 reflected this demand and set a clear timetable for progress toward democracy, stating that national elections must be held no later than 30 January 2005. Ayatollah Sistani then encouraged the formation of a "Shia list" to fight the elections, a disparate group of 228 candidates and parties brought together and vetted by Sistani's advisers.

The voting of 8.5 million Iraqis in the 30 January 2005 elections was certainly a historic moment. Despite nine suicide bombings in Baghdad and 260 attacks across the whole of the country, 58 percent of those eligible to vote did so. The elections, held under US occupation, were certainly not flawless; however, it would be churlish not to recognize the bravery and hope that propelled the majority of the Iraqi electorate to the ballot box. The Shia list, the United Iraqi Alliance, won 48 percent of the vote and 140 seats in the 275-member assembly. The Kurdish Alliance, formed by the two main Kurdish parties, won 75 seats, with the list of US-appointed interim prime minister Ayad Allawi winning 13 percent.

Elections, by themselves, however, leave unresolved broader issues of political reconstruction. Iraq at the time of the elections was a country still lacking effective institutions, military, administrative, or political. The two political parties at the core of the victorious United Iraqi Alliance, the Al-Dawa Party and the Supreme Council for the Islamic Revolution in Iraq, were swept to power not by their own organization, canvassing, or legitimacy, but by their association with Grand Ayatollah Ali al-Sistani. The danger is that they will not solidify the societal mobilization of the election by building mass party organizations and will instead lose the political momentum they have achieved and revert to a neopatrimonial strategy of using state resources to buy political loyalty. The Iraqi population would then come to experience politics not as citizens but as subjects, whose votes and political participation would become meaningless, causing them to revert to the cynicism and mistrust that has dominated postwar Iraqi politics.

■ Conclusion

Since its creation in 1920, Iraq has never had a stable functioning democracy. The legacies that Saddam Hussein has left the country will make building a sustainable democracy extremely difficult. With ruthless efficiency the Baath Party co-opted or broke civil society through violence and patronage, forcing people to interact with the institutions of the state on an individual basis. For the Iraqi population, additionally traumatized by three wars in twenty years and the lawlessness and violence that have come to typify regime change, the legitimate expression of overt political opinion has only just begun. Most of the political parties now being used as the cornerstone of the new Iraqi government were imported into the country after regime change and have had a short period of time to gain the attention of the population, much less win their trust or allegiance. Attempting to build organized, institutionalized party politics in Iraq is certainly possible, but it will take both time and effort. Those who run the state may feel they have neither the resources nor the support to take this route.

■ Notes

1. Author interview carried out in the cabinet complex, Baghdad, 11 September 2002, in the run-up to regime change.
2. See Isam al-Khafaji, "The Myth of Iraqi Exceptionalism," p. 68.
3. See Peter Boone, Haris Gazdar, and Athar Hussain, "Sanctions Against Iraq: Costs of Failure," paper presented at the conference "Frustrated Development: The Iraqi Economy in War and in Peace," University of Exeter Centre for Gulf Studies, in collaboration with the Iraqi Economic Forum, 9–11 July 1997.
4. Quoted in Michael Gordon, "'Catastrophic Success': The Strategy to Secure Iraq Did Not Foresee a 2nd War," *New York Times,* 19 October 2004.
5. "So massive was the looting that, just three days after the US secured the capital, computers were selling for as little as $35 in the thieves market." Mark Fineman, Robin Wright, and Doyle McManus, "Washington's Battle Plans: Preparing for War, Stumbling to Peace," *Los Angeles Times,* 18 July 2003.
6. See Faleh A. Jabar, "Postconflict Iraq," p. 6.
7. See James Dobbins et. al., *America's Role in Nation-Building.*
8. See Lawrence Freedman's comments in Alan George, Raymond Whitaker, and Andy McSmith, "Revealed: The Meeting That Could Have Changed the History of Iraq," *The Independent of Sunday,* 17 October 2004.
9. "Its not too late for the Iraqi military to act with honor and protect their country." George W. Bush, address to the American people, 19 March 2003.
10. See Lawrence Freedman and Efraim Karsh, *The Gulf Conflict,* p. 307.
11. See Bob Woodward, *Plan of Attack,* pp. 8, 36, 406.
12. Author interview with Tariq Aziz, deputy prime minister, Baghdad, 11 September 2002.
13. "In Nasiriyah Iraqi paramilitaries and elements of the 11th Regular Army division waged a week-long urban battle against the Marine Corps' Task Force Tarawa, a reinforced three-battalion regimental-scale formation. In Samawah, Iraqi paramilitaries fought for a week against the Army's 3–7 Cavalry, the 3rd Brigade of the 3rd Infantry Division, and the 2nd Brigade of the 82nd Airborne Division in turn. In Najaf, urban warfare in and around the city center continued for more than a week, tying down in series multiple brigades of American infantry." Stephen Biddle et al., *Toppling Saddam,* p. 9.
14. See Biddle et al., *Toppling Saddam,* pp. 6, 9, 10.
15. See Simon Chesterman, *You, the People,* pp. 100, 112.
16. US secretary of defense Donald Rumsfeld was quoted at the time as saying, "Freedom's untidy. Free people are free to make mistakes and commit crimes and do bad things."
17. See Isam al-Khafaji, "War as a Vehicle for the Rise and Decline of a State-Controlled Society."
18. The US military's own figures estimate that 80 percent of all violence in

Iraq is "criminal in nature." See Eric Schmitt and Thom Shanker, "US Says Resistance in Iraq Up to 20,000," *The Guardian,* 23 October 2004.

19. Estimates taken from author interviews with Iraqis politically active in the antioccupation movement in spring 2005.

20. Author interviews. This conclusion is supported by other work on the insurgency. See, for example, Ahmed S. Hashim, "The Sunni Insurgency," p. 3.

21. See the CPA's own estimates, cited in Phillis Bennis et al., *A Failed "Transition,"* p. 37. On the influence of de-Baathification on the intensity of the insurgency, see Jon Lee Anderson, "Out on the Street. The United States' de-Ba'thification program fuelled the insurgency. Is it too late for Bush to change course?" *New Yorker,* 15 November 2004.

22. This section is based on extensive author interviews in winter 2004 and spring 2005.

23. Based on interviews carried out with senior Baath Party officials charged with supervising the Islamic education of party cadres.

24. See Paul Wolfowitz, deputy secretary of defense, testimony before the Senate Foreign Relations Committee, 22 May 2003.

25. Author interviews in Baghdad, May 2003.

26. See Jonathan Steele, *The Guardian,* 6 May 2003.

27. Based on author interviews in Baghdad, 2003.

28. See Nicolas Pelham, "'Political Arm' of Falluja Militants Claims Key Role," *Financial Times,* 26 April 2004.

29. See James Drummond, "A Year After the Invasion the Specter of Murderous Civil War Still Hangs over Iraq," *Financial Times,* 20 March 2004.

30. See Hashim, "The Sunni Insurgency," p. 10.

31. See, for example, military spokesman Lieutenant Colonel George Krivo, quoted in Patrick E. Tyler and Ian Fisher, "Occupiers, Villagers, and an Ambush's Rubble," *International Herald Tribune,* 1 October 2003.

32. For analysis of the text and its authenticity, see Dexter Filkins, "Memo Urges Qaeda to Wage War in Iraq," *International Herald Tribune,* 10 February 2004; Justin Huggler, "Is This Man the Mastermind of the Massacres?" *Independent on Sunday,* 7 March 2004.

33. See, for example, Abel Abdul Mehdi, an Iraq Governing Council spokesman quoted in Rod Nordland, "Thousands Attend the Funeral of Dozens Killed in the Karbala Explosions on March 2," *Newsweek,* 7 March 2004.

34. See Isam al-Khafaji, "A Few Days After."

35. See Rend Rahim Francke, "On the Situation in Iraq," pp. 8–9.

36. Daniel Williams, "Iraqi Warns of Delay on Constitution Vote," *Washington Post,* 10 November 2003.

18

From Sanctions to Occupation: The US Impact on Iraq

John Gee

The US government's policies have had a profound effect on Iraq, from its insistence on the maintenance of a punishing sanctions regime to its invasion and occupation of the country. Their damaging impact has obstructed Washington's ability to achieve its ostensible goal in Iraq, a stable but pro-US regime.

■ Iraq Under Sanctions

Whatever ambitions Saddam Hussein had earlier entertained, following the catastrophic defeat of 1991 his first imperative was the survival of his regime. With good reason, their enemies portrayed Saddam and his Baathist colleagues as a group who would stop at nothing to retain power, but few took this to its logical conclusion. To survive, the regime habitually reacted with brutality toward those suspected of disloyalty, but survival also meant being ready to bow to superior force even at the expense of abandoning supposedly fundamental principles. This meant that sanctions could be effective in securing their declared aim of stripping Iraq of the weaponry with which it might pose a threat to other states in the region, but they were a blunt instrument in Washington's campaign for regime change, since the regime could adapt to the conditions they created, while inflicting the costs on the general population.[1]

Saddam had never relied purely on force to retain power. Those employed in the institutional pillars of the regime, notably the secret police forces, the elite Republican Guard and other special forces, as well as the administrative elite, were well paid. Large-scale planned investment had raised Iraq's standards of literacy and health and its level of overall economic development to a place among the region's best by the time of the 1990–1991 Gulf War: almost all children attended school, affordable health-care was available to the whole population, and in 1987 Iraq's human development index rating was third in the Arab world after Kuwait and the United Arab Emirates (though it should be added that this status was already threatened by a halving of oil revenues since 1979, and the costly 1980–1988 war with Iran). For Iraqis prepared to cooperate with the regime, there were rewards, including well-paid jobs. Young people were courted and coerced through the education system: none were able to go to university without at least appearing to support the regime and, among those who were sent abroad, a high proportion were government supporters who were prepared to inform on their fellow students if they stepped out of line to the slightest degree.

Two wars and over a decade of sanctions had a devastating impact upon Iraq, but the suffering and burdens they imposed were distributed very unevenly among the country's population. There were some changes in the way patronage operated; it became a less centrally managed operation. Some people became party to smuggling operations to circumvent sanctions. But patronage continued to reward those considered reliable and loyal, mostly a minority from the Sunni Muslim community[2] who were shielded from most of the worst consequences of sanctions, partly by the employment and spending policies of the regime. Tribal identity had become relatively unimportant to Iraqis in modern times, particularly in the urban areas, but with the partial breakdown of the state under the impact of sanctions the regime began co-opting influential tribal leaders to fill the authority vacuum, giving them an enhanced status as arbitrators in disputes involving members of their tribe and others, as well as land rights or the promotion of relatives to rewarding posts in the more favored cases. This "retribalization"[3] was a retrograde step judged by the standard of the Baathists' proclaimed nationalist principles, but it reinforced a crumbling power base.

It was the people whose loyalty had been seen as at best suspect or who were deemed unimportant to conciliate who suffered most under sanctions. Though they included some Sunni Muslim Arabs, the Shiite Muslim majority of southern and central Iraq suffered the most. Encouraged by George H. W. Bush, they had revolted against Saddam's rule in 1991 and expected to receive US support. Instead, they were left to their fate when Saddam rallied his loyal troops and drowned the rebellion in blood. It was widely believed that the United States, alarmed at rebels whose political leaders called for an Islamic republic and who were considered close to Iran, regarded its former ally, Saddam, as a lesser evil. Sanctions rubbed salt into their wounds; a vindictive regime that controlled whatever was imported into most of Iraq saw to that.[4] The experience of Iraq's Kurds, some 20 percent of Iraq's population, was very different. Backed by the imposition of the northern no-fly zone and a stronger foreign reaction to Saddam's attempt to crush their revolt in 1991, they succeeded in establishing an autonomous region under its own elected parliament, which was not subjected to as rigorous an application of the sanctions regime as was the rest of Iraq after 1991, and also, under the oil-for-food program, received a 13 percent share of the proceeds of Iraqi oil sales.

The oil-for-food program, which was agreed in 1996 and subsequently modified, allowed Iraq to sell more oil internationally and to pay for permitted imports after a 30 percent cut of the takings had been allocated mainly for reparations payments to Kuwait. As its critics claimed, the program was manipulated by the regime, which ensured that its supporters received the greatest benefits, but it did check the decline in standards of living and the child mortality rate fell. To what extent Iraqis blamed Saddam for the sanctions varied according to their relationship to the regime, but many who loathed it and longed for its downfall also regarded the United States and the United Nations as responsible for their suffering in the repression of the 1991 uprisings and under sanctions.

■ Weapons of Mass Destruction and the US Drive for War

Following the attacks of 11 September 2001, the George W. Bush administration resolved to embark on regime change in Iraq (former treasury secretary Paul O'Neill claims that planning for an invasion began earlier, within days of Bush taking office in January 2001). The administration used the weapons of mass destruction (WMD) issue to justify and secure support for war on Iraq, but war was never necessary to disarm Iraq.

Hussein Kamil, Saddam Hussein's son-in-law, told Western intelligence agencies after his defection from the regime in 1995 that Iraq's WMDs had been secretly destroyed following the earlier war.[5] He was well placed to know the truth, having headed Iraq's biological weapons program, but in 2002–2003 the hawks in the West chose to sweep this inconvenient testimony under the carpet. The weapons had been destroyed because the United States and United Nations had demanded it, and Saddam's regime did not believe that it was possible to conceal them. Their destruction was undertaken secretly, it appears, lest the regime lose face before the peoples of Iraq and the rest of the region.

There was a similar outcome in the case of Iraq's medium-range ballistic missiles. The Samoud-2 was not a formidable weapon. When armed with its payload, the Iraqi government maintained, its range would conform to the tight UN-declared restrictions upon Iraqi armaments. Neither the United States nor a UN Security Council that was seeking to placate it agreed: without a warhead, the missile had a range that exceeded the prescribed limit of 150 kilometers, and all stocks had to be eliminated. So it was that in the final days before their country was attacked, Iraqi soldiers were obliged to cooperate in the destruction of a weapon that would have allowed their army to hit the bases in Kuwait where the US and allied invasion forces had gathered to attack them. This was a telling indication both of the weakness and of the priorities of Saddam Hussein's regime. With war all but inevitable, it sought to avert it by yielding to external pressures that reduced its military capabilities. Neither this, Iraq's cooperation with the UN inspectors, nor their failure to find weapons of mass destruction could deter Washington from the war it had already determined upon.

■ Iraq Under Occupation

The immediate impact of the US invasion on Iraq's economic and social life was relatively limited. Civilian casualties were fewer than most humanitarian agencies had expected, and the nightmare predictions of millions of refugees fleeing the tide of war did not come true. The worst damage came later, inflicted by the application of a blinkered ideological approach.

The triumph of the US forces in Iraq was symbolized by the episode of the felling of Saddam's statue in Baghdad's Paradise Square on 9 April 2003, although not in the way intended when it was offered up as a spectacle for a cooperative media by an army psychological operations team. A US marine colonel had decided to pull the statue down, but loudspeakers were used to call upon Iraqis to come, so that it would appear as if the liberated masses were spontaneously venting their hatred upon Saddam. US troops initially placed a US flag over the statue but removed it when they realized it would symbolize conquest rather than liberation. The smallish crowd of Iraqis proved incapable of pulling down the statue and the sun was sinking fast, threatening to ruin the photo opportunity of the statue's fall, so the marines used one of their vehicles to tug it from its plinth. The mighty statue was a hollow shell.[6]

In the first months of its rule, Washington acted as if Iraq was its property, to do with as it wished, although all would take place in the name of freedom and Iraqis would be found to give it a veneer of legitimacy. Paul Bremer, a conservative career diplomat who had earlier served as ambassador at large for counterterrorism, was appointed head of the occupation administration, dubbed the Coalition Provisional Authority (CPA), and a team of twenty-five Iraqi political leaders who were prepared to cooperate with it were appointed to a body dubbed the Iraqi Governing Council. A portion of central Baghdad around one of Saddam's former palaces was fortified against attack, and this became the CPA's base of operations. When the provisional Iraqi government was set up under Iyad Allawi, a former

Baathist and leader of the US-backed Iraqi National Accord, in 2004, the CPA morphed into one of the largest US embassy establishments in the world, headed by John Negroponte, whose illustrious career had included service as US ambassador to Honduras during Ronald Reagan's campaign to bring down the Sandinista government in neighboring Nicaragua. Iyad Allawi became prime minister. Despite the symbolism of the handover of sovereignty, the United States remained in charge: the provisional government's scope for decisionmaking was limited and it certainly had no power to veto or interfere in the conduct of military operations by US or allied forces.

It is now widely considered by supporters of the US invasion that Bremer's dissolution of the Iraqi army—making some 400,000 armed and trained men unemployed—was a serious mistake. The move was justified at the time as part of a process of de-Baathification—the removal of all vestiges of the regime of Saddam Hussein from Iraqi life. It has included purges of the state bureaucracy and academia that have added another 100,000 to the ranks of the unemployed and discontented. This was a case of ideology prevailing over reason.

The Iraqi army was founded following World War I, not after the Baathist coup in 1968. Its command levels were staffed by men regarded by Saddam as regime loyalists, but (except for the Republican Guard) its rank and file were not politicized supporters of the government; many soldiers were alienated from it because of Saddam's repression of their communities, the severity with which they were treated by their officers, and late payment of wages. This national institution needed a weeding out of the cruel and corrupt, not abolition. The US-created police and armed forces lack credibility as Iraqi institutions: they are widely regarded as mere tools of the occupier. It is unemployment and poverty that drive men to join them, not belief, although this wins them no sympathy from the resistance groups, which attack recruits pitilessly. Their primary goal is to survive from one day to the next. As a result, people complain of a law-and-order situation that is much worse than it was under Saddam's regime. Theft and burglary are common; the kidnapping of individuals by criminal gangs for ransom by their families, practically unknown before the US invasion, is now a common occurrence; all middle-class families have either experienced it for themselves or have friends who have. The streets have become no-go areas at night for women in Baghdad and the other central Iraqi cities.

The purge of Baathists from the state bureaucracy, professions, and academia revealed its instigators' refusal to let their ideological zeal be tempered by mere practical considerations. Saddam Hussein's regime had tried to co-opt highly skilled and talented people. They were offered social prominence and promotion in their professions in exchange for proclaiming their support for the regime, while many also acted as monitors of any opposition to the regime among their colleagues. Anecdotal evidence suggests that the initial post-Saddam purge of these people was conducted with insufficient consideration for how much harm each individual had really done and for the probable consequences for society of the sudden removal of experienced policemen, administrators, and academics. The negative impact of the partial implementation of this policy has been exacerbated as tens of thousands of members of the middle class and intelligentsia have fled the violence and hardships of what some insist upon calling, in defiance of reality, "postwar Iraq."

Economic reconstruction has been disastrously mishandled. Iraq's infrastructure had decayed since the late 1980s as a consequence of war and sanctions. During the US-led invasion and its aftermath, bombing and the movement of heavy tanks along streets fractured water and sewage pipes, already in a state of poor maintenance: water supplies remain unreliable in many areas. Electricity is often available for twelve hours or less a day in Baghdad, and most of the country receives a supply of under three hours. Insurgent attacks and the deterioration under Saddam of the supply system, which now necessitates large-scale repair programs, were blamed, but this is no consolation to most Iraqis. They contrast the present state of the repair effort unfavorably with what happened in 1991, when the old regime restored electricity supplies to pre–Gulf War levels in a matter of weeks. In the ten months before the US invasion, Baghdad had electricity almost round the clock. The unreliability of the electricity supply has worsened the problem of fuel distribution. Power outages stop pumps from working, leading to lengthening queues of frustrated motorists at gas stations. In the country with the second largest oil reserves in the world, they may wait five hours to fill up their cars—unless they can afford to go to a hawker, who will sell them gasoline for up to fifty times its official pump price. Those who can afford to have bought private generators that they can use whenever the electricity supply fails, but this has increased demand for gasoline, which would be better used earning export revenues.

The infant mortality rate is nearly twice its preinvasion level, according to a survey conducted by the Iraqi Ministry of Health in cooperation with the UN Development Programme and the Norwegian Institute for Applied International Studies. The report, published in November 2004, revealed that a rate of acute malnutrition among children under five that peaked at 11 percent in 1996 under the sanctions regime, fell with the oil-for-food program to 4 percent in 2002, but in 2004 had shot up to 7.7 percent—about 400,000 children. This is despite the continuation of the distribution of the food rations. In September 2004 the World Food Programme concluded, following a survey, that 6.5 million Iraqis—one in four of the population—remained highly dependent on food rations. Some 2.6 million were so poor that they had to resell part of their rations to pay for necessities such as medicines and clothing. It is not yet known what the overall loss of life among Iraqis from all war-related causes is, as the occupying powers have deliberately refrained from collating this information, but an assessment published by the prestigious British medical journal *The Lancet* in October 2004 estimated it at 98,000 people.[7] US and British government sources disputed this figure, but are unable or unwilling to provide a "realistic" count of their own.

Had the warriors in Washington and London given serious thought to postwar reconstruction before their attack, they might have been ready with a practical economic program that would have served both to repair damage speedily and to provide employment and income to desperate people. Iraq has a large middle class and no shortage of skilled workers for most trades; those who lived there were better equipped than anyone else to understand how its infrastructure worked, who needed to be approached to tackle specific problems, and how to lay hands on necessary supplies. They might have been contracted to handle reconstruction at a fraction of what foreign businesses would demand, and the money they were paid would then have been diffused into the wider economy, stimulating supply industries and the retail sector. Instead, the Bush administration bestowed its largesse on the likes of Halliburton, chiefly for rehabilitation of the oil industry and provision of services to the military. Much is made of the $18 billion that the United States has committed to Iraq for reconstruction, but only around $2 billion of that has so far been spent. Of the money passing through the hands of the ministries set up since the occupation began, huge amounts have gone missing. In a report issued on 30 January 2005, Stuart Bowen, special inspector-general for the reconstruction of Iraq, concluded that the Coalition Provisional Authority had failed to keep track of almost $9 billion that it had transferred to Iraqi ministries. The money derived from sales of Iraqi oil and from seized assets of the previous regime.[8]

It wasn't that the occupiers were without ideas about what to do with the Iraqi economy; they were just the wrong ones. There was a large state sector, which included the oil industry: What could be better than to throw it open to the bracing winds of the market? That would shake out a lot of inefficiency in the system, and short-term pain would translate into long-term gain. And wasn't a well-functioning free enterprise system a cornerstone of democracy? In this case, the neoconservative ideological approach hit a wall of Iraqi opposition that included most of those who were cooperating with the United States. They recognized that throwing even more Iraqis out of work while their country was in a state of turmoil was not a good idea. They saw that a privatization of the Iraqi oil industry that could lead to its wholesale takeover by foreign companies would provoke a strong reaction from the entire population of their country, as well as confirming many in their view that the United States invaded their country in order to seize its oil. The would-be privatizers were not encouraged by the reaction of the international business community. Much as sectors of the Iraqi economy might have seemed like an appealing investment, many companies doubted that security could be guaranteed, and recognized that the proposed sell-off could be invalidated as contrary to international law: an occupying power's rights to make changes in the laws or economic system of an occupied state are strictly limited under Articles 53, 55, and 56 of the 1907 Hague Regulations Respecting the Laws and Customs of War on Land. A commonsense approach eventually prevailed; the oil industry remains Iraq's property and the demolition of the state sector has been frozen, but the anger, outrage, and fear that the mooted reforms provoked have done their harm. There is no deep-rooted opposition to the privatization of most of the bloated state sector in Iraq, but it has to take place on Iraqi terms, not Washington's.

■ The Struggle over Iraq's Political Future

The Bush administration's economic and social policies after the invasion, thus, did nothing to conciliate most Iraqis. Many say that they are worse off now than they were under Saddam Hussein, and some have reacted with armed resistance to the occupation of their country by a foreign invader. Those who responded most forcefully came from the communities who had most to lose by the imposition of a new order in Iraq, the Sunni Arab minority, who see their traditionally dominant position slipping away, to the benefit of the Shiite majority.

While the United States hoped to consolidate a pliant Iraqi leadership, the foremost Shiite cleric, Ayatollah Ali al-Sistani, insisted on an elected parliament that would write a new constitution and the United States had to accede. It was the Shiite religious leadership who were chiefly responsible for keeping most predominantly Shiite areas out of the violent struggle against the occupation. While their community as a whole was deeply hostile to the invaders, the leadership saw an opportunity to assert their rights in Iraq after decades of living under regimes that privileged the Sunni Arab minority. That required making temporary tactical compromises with the occupier; it also required calling for patience and restraint from Shiite Iraqis in the face of a series of sectarian suicide bombings. This approach finally paid off when the United Iraq Alliance (UIA), the political grouping backed by the Shiite religious leadership, won a majority of the seats in the January 2005 elections.

Although Sunni Muslim Arab Iraqis had answered resistance calls to boycott the elections, and although the elections were held under conditions of war and occupation, they were not simply a sham. They are likely to be recognized in the future as marking a decisive moment in the reordering of Iraq's power structure. The coalition headed by US favorite Iyad Allawi came in a distant third, after the UIA and the Kurdish alliance. The preferred course of the Shiite leadership will be to seek to unify Iraqis around agreed political goals and an acceptable power-sharing structure. If the process of establishing a national consensus is not derailed by deliberate sectarian attacks by elements of the resistance, it could result in a broad-based agreement on a constitution, the restoration of a functioning Iraqi government, and a firm deadline by which the foreign occupation forces must leave every inch of Iraqi soil or face far stronger opposition than they have yet encountered. This is not the outcome of which the architects of the invasion dreamed.

■ Conclusion: The United States in Iraq

When Bush stood for reelection in 2004, he told Americans that their army was fighting the terrorists in Iraq so that it wouldn't have to fight them in the United States. However, it would never have had to fight against at least nineteen out of twenty of the people shooting at and blowing up US soldiers in Iraq if it had not invaded their country. When the history of "what went wrong in Iraq" comes to be written, there will be a school of thought that insists upon seeing the US intervention as a noble enterprise that was derailed by a combination of the misguided policies followed later and an insurgency of unanticipated strength, fed by those policies. Put simply, those who argue this view will claim that a different set of postoccupation policies, particularly toward economic reconstruction, could have resulted in success. They will be wrong. The basic problem is the occupation itself—but insensitivity to Iraqi opinions, failure to meet desperate social and economic needs, and ill-considered policy initiatives that play well in neoconservative think tanks in Washington but not in the real world, only made things worse. Iraq is not US property to be partitioned, privatized, or remolded, and its people really do want freedom.

■ Notes

1. Charles Tripp, *A History of Iraq,* pp. 259–271, provides a good overall summary of the sanctions regime and why Saddam's regime proved resilient despite their ruinous impact on Iraq's people.

2. On US policy toward Iraq with particular stress on the sanctions issue, see Phyllis Bennis, "And They Call It Peace," pp. 4–7. On the overall impact of sanctions, see Sarah Graham-Brown, "Sanctioning Iraq," pp. 8–13; Sarah Graham-Brown, *Sanctioning Saddam.*

3. Faleh A. Jabar, "Shaykhs and Ideologues."

4. Faleh A. Jabar, *The Shi'ite Movement in Iraq,* is an invaluable account of modern Iraqi Shiism, and particularly of its political movements.

5. Nicholas D. Kristof, "Missing in Action: The Truth About Iraqi Arms," *New York Times,* 5 July 2003.

6. A US army study of the event was reported by the *Los Angeles Times,* reprinted in the *Sunday Times* (Singapore), 4 July 2004.

7. Les Roberts, Riyadh Lafta, Richard Garfield, Jamal Khudhairi, and Gilbert Burnham, "Mortality Before and After the 2003 Invasion of Iraq." *The Lancet* released the paper on its website on 29 October 2004, ahead of its print appearance in November. The survey was based on interviews conducted with thirty-three clusters of thirty households. The estimate of 98,000 is for the excess number of deaths over what would have been expected to occur during a comparable period of time before the war. Most deaths by violence were ascribed to air strikes by the allied coalition, which habitually plays down the impact of air attacks and stresses the death toll inflicted upon Iraqis by insurgent attacks. Other estimates of the number of Iraqi dead include the running total compiled by Iraq Body Count, based solely on news reports. As of 2 September 2005, this stood at a minimum of 24,495 and a maximum of 27,705: the lower total provides for possible double counting based upon different reports of the same incidents. "A Dossier on Civilian Casualties in Iraq 2003–2005," published by Iraq Body Count in association with the Oxford Research Group, offered a breakdown of 24,865 deaths in the first two years of the war that agrees with the *Lancet* study in ascribing the largest proportion of deaths to coalition action: 37 percent of civilian victims are estimated to have been killed by US-led forces, 9 percent by "anti-occupation forces/insurgents," and 36 percent by criminal violence. The proportion of deaths inflicted by insurgent action upon Iraqi civilians has undoubtedly increased as the conflict has dragged on. In June 2005, Interior Minister Bayan Jabr told reporters that insurgents had killed about 12,000 Iraqis since the start of the occupation. The Ministry of Interior later told the *New York Times* that 8,175 Iraqis were killed by insurgents in the ten months that ended on 31 May 2005. It did not provide a breakdown between civilians and police, but it did exclude Iraqi soldiers. Sabrina Tavernise, "Iraqi Death Toll Exceeded 800 a Month, Data Shows," *New York Times,* 15 July 2005.

8. Yochi J. Dreazen, "Former Bush Aide Turns Critic As Iraq Inspector," *Wall Street Journal,* 26 July 2005. Bowen conducted audits of spending in Iraq and reported his findings to the Defense and State Departments. They have exposed incompetence, embezzlement, and fraud on the part of US personnel in Iraq, as well as corruption in the new Iraqi ministries. It was Bowen who, in November 2004, called upon the US Army to withhold close to $90 million from Halliburton because it could not justify what it had charged. The Iraqi Board of Supreme Audit has concluded that at least half of the $1.27 million supposedly spent on military procurement by the Iraqi defense ministry in the eight months following the "transfer of sovereignty" on 28 June 2004 has disappeared. It has been paid to middlemen who have disappeared, given it away as kickbacks, or spent it on useless equipment. Ed Vulliamy and Richard Norton Taylor, "Millions Embezzled at Iraqi Ministry," *The Guardian,* 22 August 2005.

19

Islamic Militancy

Henry Munson

George W. Bush has portrayed the overthrow of Saddam Hussein as a great victory in the "war on terror." The reality is that the US-led invasion strengthened the very groups it was supposed to weaken. During the Cold War, the United States tended to ignore the nationalistic and social grievances that fueled communist movements and attributed them to Russian or Chinese machinations; similarly, the United States now tends to ignore the nationalistic and social grievances that often fuel militant Islamic movements while attributing all terrorism in the Islamic world to the machinations of Al-Qaida. Militant Islamists articulate widespread resentment of foreign domination *as well as* a xenophobic and intolerant conception of Islam.[1] The US-led invasion of Iraq increased this resentment and thus facilitated recruitment by militant Sunni Islamists with views similar to those of Osama bin Laden.

To use a metaphor favored by Donald Rumsfeld, to defeat terrorism one must drain the swamp in which it thrives. But instead of draining the swamp, the US-led occupation of Iraq flooded it. That is, rather than dilute the humiliation and the rage that fuel Islamic militancy, the United States and its subordinate allies exacerbated it by occupying yet another Muslim country. In response to US preparations for the invasion of Iraq, the Egyptian singer Shaaban Abd al-Rahim recorded a song titled "The Attack on Iraq," which became a great success in the Arab world in 2003. Among the lyrics were:

> Enough!
> Chechnya! Afghanistan! Palestine! Southern Lebanon! The Golan Heights!
> And now Iraq too? And now Iraq too?
> It's too much for people! Shame on you!
> Enough! Enough! Enough![2]

Where the officials of the Bush administration saw a decisive blow in the war on terror, most Muslims saw yet another attack on their fellow Muslims. And this was grist for bin Laden's mill.

■ US Troops in Saudi Arabia and the Emergence of Al-Qaida

In an address to a joint session of Congress on 20 September 2001, nine days after the attacks of 11 September, President Bush explained the hostility of Islamic extremists to the United States as follows: "They hate our freedoms—our freedom of religion, our freedom of speech, our freedom to vote and assemble and disagree with each other."[3] It is true that militant Islamists like bin Laden hate US conceptions of religious and sexual freedom, but if we examine bin Laden's writings and broadcast statements, we find that they stress opposition to US policies rather than US freedoms.[4]

Before invading Iraq on the basis of unsubstantiated assumptions about Saddam Hussein's weapons of mass destruction and links to Al-Qaida, the Bush administration should have borne in mind the fact that Osama bin Laden turned to violence as a result of his rejection of the occupation of a Muslim country by an infidel army, not as a result of his hatred of Western values. From 1979 to 1989, he actively supported the resistance to the Soviet occupation of Afghanistan, which he inevitably saw as a jihad, or holy war.

The next phase in bin Laden's jihad was triggered by what he has portrayed as the US occupation of Saudi Arabia in the Gulf War (1990–1991). When Saddam Hussein invaded Kuwait in August 1990, bin Laden offered to raise an international Muslim army, composed largely of veterans of the Afghan war, to defend Saudi Arabia. Instead, King Fahd invited US troops, among others, to come to the kingdom and defend it against a possible Iraqi invasion. General Norman Schwarzkopf and Secretary of Defense Richard Cheney convinced him that such an invasion was likely.[5] The Saudis allowed 425,000 US troops, 25,000 British troops, and 15,200 French troops, as well as troops from various Muslim countries, to attack Iraq from bases in Saudi Arabia. This, and not hatred of US values, is what led to bin Laden's holy war against the United States.[6] Bin Laden's condemnation of what he portrayed as the US occupation of "the land of the two holy places" became a major theme in most of his writings and statements of the 1990s, although it became less central as he became more famous in the late 1990s.

In a video broadcast on 7 October 2001, when the United States began bombing Afghanistan, bin Laden portrayed the attacks of 11 September as a response to what he saw as the US oppression of Muslims: "What America is tasting now is insignificant compared to what we have been tasting for decades. For over eighty years our Islamic world has been tasting this humiliation and this degradation. Its sons are killed, its blood is shed, its holy places are violated, and it is being killed by other than that which God has revealed. Yet no one hears. No one responds." Praising the perpetrators of the 9/11 attacks, bin Laden said:

> When they responded on behalf of their oppressed sons, and on behalf of their brothers and sisters in Palestine and in many of the lands of Islam, the entire world screamed. The infidels screamed as did their followers the hypocrites [i.e., pro-Western Muslims]. A million innocent children are being killed right up to this moment I am speaking [because of sanctions on Iraq]. They are being killed in Iraq yet they have done nothing wrong. Yet we hear no condemnation, no fatwa from the rulers' religious judges (hukkam al-salatin). And these days, Israeli tanks ravage Palestine, in Jenin, Ramallah, Rafah, Beit Jalah and elsewhere in the land of Islam and yet no one speaks, no one moves.

Bin Laden concluded by declaring: "I swear by God Almighty who raised the heavens without support that America and those who live in America will not dream in peace and security before we really live in peace and security in Palestine and before all the infidel troops have left the land of Muhammad, God's blessings and peace be upon him."[7]

Bin Laden's speech in this video broadcast on 7 October 2001 clearly focused on US policies rather than US values. For many Muslims, even Muslims who condemn the 9/11 attacks and have no sympathy for bin Laden's Islamist agenda, he articulates some of their deepest grievances, notably with respect to the Palestinians and Iraq. In fall 2001, Gilles Kepel found that even Arab girls in tight jeans saw bin Laden as an anti-imperialist hero.[8] A young Iraqi woman and her Palestinian friends told Kepel, in fall 2001, "He stood up to defend us. He is the only one."[9]

Bin Laden articulates the sense of impotence and the rage that pervade much of the Islamic world. The US-led invasion of Iraq intensified this sense of impotence and this rage, and thus intensified support for bin Laden.

■ The "War on Terror" as Seen in the Islamic World

On 3 June 2003, the Pew Research Center for the People and the Press released a report titled *Views of a Changing World,* only weeks after the fall of Saddam Hussein.[10] The study found a dramatic increase in Muslim hostility toward the United States from 2002 to 2003, even in countries traditionally allied to the United States. In summer 2002, 61 percent of Indonesians had a favorable view of the United States. By May 2003, only 15 percent did. In Turkey, the decline during the same period was from 30 percent to 15 percent. In Jordan, it was from 25 percent to 1 percent.[11]

Already in 2002, most Muslims felt considerable hostility toward the United States, but the Iraq War has clearly intensified this hostility.

The Bush administration's approach to the war on terror has been a major reason for the increased hostility toward the United States. The Pew Center's 2003 survey found that few Muslims supported this war as waged by the Bush administration. Only 23 percent of Indonesians did so in May 2003, down from 31 percent in summer 2002. In Turkey over the same period, support dropped from 30 percent to 22 percent. In Pakistan, the drop was from 30 percent to 16 percent. In Jordan, it was from 13 percent to 2 percent.[12] These decreases reflected the overwhelming Muslim opposition to the war in Iraq, which most Muslims saw as an imperial act involving Westerners once again subjugating and humiliating Muslims.

A Zogby International poll of 3,020 people in Egypt, Morocco, Saudi Arabia, Lebanon, Jordan, and the United Arab Emirates conducted between 19 February and 11 March 2003 found that most Arabs believed that the United States attacked Iraq to gain control of Iraqi oil and to help Israel.[13] Most Arabs clearly did not believe that the United States overthrew Saddam out of humanitarian motives. Even in Iraq itself, where there was considerable support for the overthrow of Saddam, primarily among Shiites and Kurds, a Gallup poll undertaken in Baghdad from 28 August to 4 September 2003 found that only 5 percent of the 1,178 Iraqis polled believed that the United States invaded Iraq to help the Iraqi people.[14]

While the prevailing perception of the US-led invasion of Iraq in 2003 throughout the Islamic world was that it was an imperialist act designed to gain control of Iraqi oil and protect Israel, there were significant regional, sectarian, and ethnic differences in attitudes. Kuwaitis and Iranians may have been as suspicious of US motives as most other Muslims, but many of them welcomed the invasion as a way of eliminating a ruler who had caused tremendous suffering in both Kuwait and Iran.

■ Occupation as the Root of Islamic Resistance

In Iraq itself, most Shiites and Kurds welcomed the invasion as a means of eliminating a tyrant who had slaughtered or tortured hundreds of thousands of their own ethnic groups.[15] To a lesser degree, some Iraqi Sunnis also welcomed Saddam's overthrow, although many of them saw Saddam Hussein as a defender of the Sunni Arabs of Iraq.

But, and this is crucial, support for a foreign invasion that promises to end an oppressive situation does not entail prolonged support for occupation by a foreign army. The Catholics of Northern Ireland initially welcomed British troops in 1969 in the hope that they would protect them from Protestant militias.[16] The Shiites of southern Lebanon initially welcomed the Israeli invasion of 1982 because they had suffered at the hands of the Palestine Liberation Organization (PLO) in Lebanon. But as the Israeli occupation dragged on and Israeli troops searched Shiite homes and rounded up Shiite men indiscriminately, the initial welcome turned into hostility. The Israeli occupation played a crucial catalytic role in the emergence of the Lebanese Shiite movement Hizbollah, which was soon causing far more Israeli deaths than had PLO forces in the years before the invasion.[17] The Israeli occupation of southern Lebanon created a far more serious problem than the problem it was supposed to solve. The US-led occupation of Iraq did the same thing. It led to the emergence of militant Islamist-cum-nationalist movements among both Sunni and Shiite Iraqis. (Muqtada al-Sadr's Shiite Mahdi Army did not exist before the US-led occupation.) The Sunni movements in particular killed over 2,000 Americans during the first two and a half years of the US-led occupation.[18]

Both the Sunni and the Shiite Islamist movements that emerged in Iraq to resist the US-led occupation had a strongly nationalistic dimension. One of the many Sunni groups that emerged in 2002 called itself the Iraqi Islamic Patriotic Resistance (Al-Muqawama al-Islamiyya al-Wataniyya al-Iraqiyya).[19] DVDs sold in Iraqi markets in 2004 praised the people of Falluja "who didn't submit to humiliation by the Americans."[20] In 2003, US soldiers interrogated the imam of a Sunni mosque in Ramadi for eight hours because of his critical Friday sermons. The imam, who had been imprisoned for three years by Saddam Hussein, asked his interrogators "whether they would not resist if Germans or Fidel Castro occupied Washington."[21]

In July 2003, CBS reporter David Hawkins interviewed three Iraqis involved in attacks on US forces in Iraq:

> "Why do you fight? Why do you attack American soldiers?" Hawkins asked. "This is occupation, so we fight against the occupation," said a fighter. "You're very upset that the Americans are here," asked Hawkins, "but are you glad Saddam is gone?" "We feel happy now because we can speak freely, but at the same time we don't want Saddam . . . or America. We just want the American soldiers to leave our country," reported the translator.[22]

In December 2003, the leader of a small group of insurgents in Baghdad declared, "We could not accept that our country that has such a great history could be occupied by an illegitimate foreign army."[23] In August 2004, Ahmed Manajid, a member of the remarkable Iraqi Olympic soccer team from Falluja, declared, "If a stranger invades America and the people resist, does that mean they are terrorists?" Manajid said that the occupation forces had killed his cousin and several of his friends. He also said that if he were not playing soccer at the Athens Olympics, he would "for sure" be fighting the US troops in Iraq.[24]

While the Ayatollah Ali al-Sistani, Shiite groups like the Supreme Council for the Islamic Revolution in Iraq (SCIRI), and the various factions of Al-Dawa cooperated with the United States and its subordinate allies, Muqtada al-Sadr's Mahdi Army and some other Shiites repeatedly clashed with the occupying forces in 2004 and 2005.[25] Already in March 2003, Sadr asserted that "the Iraqi will not accept subjugation, humiliation, subordination, and occupation."[26] During the US siege of Najaf's Imam Ali Mosque in August 2004, Sadr boasted that "Najaf has triumphed over imperialism and imperial hubris."[27] Also during this siege, a member of Sadr's Mahdi Army who had twenty-seven relatives killed by Saddam Hussein's regime told a reporter for the *Washington Post:*

> "It's not true that the Americans came to get rid of Saddam. It was only a trick to occupy the country. We all know that Bush announced twice that this is a crusade. So we know they are targeting a certain group" (the Shiites), he said. "We know the strategic importance of Iraq in the region and the wealth of our country. They want to control it. They want to control our oil, our wealth and the world." "There is something called patriotism," he added. "I like my country, and I saw the U.S. forces did not come to protect us. So I wanted to follow the leader who can demand my rights and defeat the occupation. The U.S. forces are occupiers, so we have to resist them."[28]

A thirteen-year-old member of Sadr's Mahdi Army proclaimed his willingness to die for God and country during the siege of Najaf in August of 2004, saying, "Iraq belongs to us and we have to fight to protect it and our religion. We're not scared of the Americans."[29] A Shiite merchant of Najaf who was critical of Sadr's tactics observed, "Everyone here wants the occupier to leave. We only differ on the method to be employed. And if we were united, the United States would experience a second Vietnam in Iraq."[30]

The point of all of these quotations is not to deny that the Iraqi Islamists fighting the United States (and its allies) are Islamists. It is rather to demonstrate that these movements have a nationalist dimension and that the US-led occupation spawned them. Just as the United States failed to recognize that the Vietnamese communists were also Vietnamese nationalists, so too has the government of the United States failed to recognize that the Iraqi Islamists opposed to the US-led occupation of their country are also Iraqi nationalists.

A US-led occupation of an Arab country was in fact bound to spawn resistance, as well as outrage throughout the Arab and Muslim worlds. George H. W. Bush realized this and therefore deliberately avoided "marching on Baghdad" in 1991.[31] The fact that much of the Iraqi resistance to occupation has had an Islamist dimension should not come as a surprise, given the extent to which religion still suffuses national identity in the

Islamic world, and given the failure of the secular nationalism and socialism once espoused by Saddam Hussein.

■ The Sunni-Shiite, Kurd-Arab Divides

Nevertheless, the divided communal identities of Iraqis do shape differential reactions to the war and occupation. Kurds and Shiite Muslims *did* see the overthrow of Saddam Hussein as a form of liberation. The Kurds probably include less than 2 percent of the world's 1.2 billion Muslims, and the Shiites somewhere between 10 and 15 percent. In Iraq, it is generally assumed that Kurds constitute about 20 percent and Shiites about 60 percent of the population. Kurdish Islamists are politically insignificant, but Shiite Islamists are another matter.[32]

With respect to the linkage between religious and national identity, several points should be noted. Kurdish nationalism-cum-separatism in Iraq has generally lacked an Islamist dimension, even though Kurds generally assume that to be a Kurd is to be a Muslim. Moreover, Arab Iraqis, Sunnis, and Shiites, including Islamists, do not have the same conception of Iraqi national identity. For the Shiites, the overthrow of Saddam meant the end of subjugation and oppression by the Sunnis and the emergence of a new Iraq largely controlled by Shiites. For most Sunnis, this was an unacceptable scenario. They generally assumed that they had the right to govern Iraq, much as white Anglo-Saxon Protestants once assumed that they had the right to govern the United States. Iraqi Sunnis generally see Shiism as a primitive, heretical, and Persian form of Islam.[33] A Sunni tribal leader told a journalist from the *New York Times* that the Shiites "cannot rule Iraq properly, they cannot take charge of Iraqis in the same manner as the Sunnis" because "they are barbarians, savages, they do not know the true religion, theirs is twisted, it is not the true religion of Muhammad."[34]

The idea that Arab Shiites are in fact more Persian than Arab has existed for centuries, perhaps ever since Shiism became the official religion of Persia (Iran) in the sixteenth century. Fouad Ajami describes his reaction when the Iranian-born cleric Musa al-Sadr visited his school in Beirut in 1963:

> As I was a Shia assimilé, from a background in the rural south, anxious to pass in the modern [i.e., Sunni and Christian] world of Beirut, I showed no interest in the cleric. My school then was devoutly pan-Arabist, the Egyptian Gamal Abdul Nasser its hero. My great-grandfather had come from Iran to Lebanon in the mid–nineteenth century. This was part of some buried past, unexplored. It was given away in my last name, Ajami, which in Arabic meant "the Persian." The Arab-Ajam divide was very deep. And a Shia mullah wearing the black turban of a sayyid (a descendant of the Prophet) and speaking Persianized Arabic was a threat to something unresolved in my identity.[35]

These lines could have been written by a Shiite student in Baghdad in the 1960s. Ostensibly a secular ideology, Arab nationalism has always had a Sunni Muslim coloration, much as Irish nationalism has always had a Catholic coloration, Charles Parnell and W. B. Yeats notwithstanding. Iraqi intellectuals, including some of the exiles who convinced the Bush administration that occupying Iraq would be a "cakewalk," condemn popular stereotypes about Sunnis, Shiites, and Kurds. And intermarriage, until recently, was common, especially among more educated Iraqis. But the stereotypes remain powerful in the popular imagination, and they have been reinforced by the rage, the yearning for revenge, and the fear bequeathed by Saddam's oppression of the Shiites and the Kurds.

The invasion of Iraq strengthened Shiite Islamists in both Iraq and Iran, and potentially elsewhere as well. After the Iraqi elections of January 2005, the Shiite Islamist groups Al-Dawa and the Supreme Council for the Islamic Revolution in Iraq became the dominant political forces of Iraq, along with the Kurds, who really wanted (and in practice had) their own state.[36] Al-Dawa and SCIRI had close ties with Iran's Islamic Republic, which thus benefited from the invasion of Iraq in ways the Bush administration had not foreseen.[37] All of this forced Lebanon's Hizbollah, which was closely tied to Iraq's Al-Dawa Party in particular, to take an ultimately ambivalent position on the invasion and occupation of Iraq. Like most Sunni Islamist groups, it never stopped condemning the war as an imperial act of aggression, but it could not ignore the fact that the war was a blessing from the point of view of Iraqi Shiites and Iran.[38] The invasion freed Iraqi Shiites from an oppressive despot and enabled Shiite Islamists with worldviews similar to Hizbollah's to gain control of the Iraqi state. Moreover, the slaughter of Iraqi Shiites by Sunni militants like Abu Musab al-Zarqawi made it impossible for any Shiite organization, even militant groups like Hizbollah in Lebanon and Muqtada al-Sadr's Mahdi Army in Iraq, to join Sunni Islamists in supporting the Iraqi insurgency. While that insurgency had an anti-imperial dimension, it also had an anti-Shiite dimension. Sunni Islamists could ignore this, Shiite Islamists could not. Thus one consequence of the invasion of Iraq was a sharpening of the line between Sunni and Shiite Islamists. But the invasion's most obvious consequence, insofar as Islamic militancy is concerned, was to increase support for, and facilitate recruitment by, militant Sunni groups that shared the worldview of Al-Qaida.

The Iraq War and Al-Qaida

While George Bush and Tony Blair continue to portray the Iraq War as a great victory in the war on terror, most intelligence analysts and academics have acknowledged that it actually increased Sunni Muslim hostility toward the United States and support for militant Islamic movements like Al-Qaida. Richard Clarke served as a national security official under Ronald Reagan and George H. W. Bush. He was national coordinator for security, infrastructure protection, and counterterrorism under Bill Clinton's administration and during the first year of George W. Bush's presidency. He has criticized the Iraq War as follows:

> Rather than seeking to work with the majority in the Islamic world to mold Muslim opinion against the radicals' values, we did exactly what al-Qaida said we would do. We invaded and occupied an oil-rich Arab country that posed no threat to us, while paying scant time and attention to the Israeli-Palestinian problem. We delivered to al-Qaida the greatest recruitment propaganda imaginable and made it difficult for friendly Islamic governments to be seen working closely with us.[39]

Michael Scheuer, a twenty-year veteran of the CIA who was in charge of the bin Laden "station" in the CIA's Counterterrorism Center from 1996 to 1999,[40] has written two valuable books under the pseudonym "Anonymous." In his book *Imperial Hubris,* Scheuer writes that by invading and occupying Afghanistan and Iraq, the United States was "completing the radicalization of the Islamic world, something Osama bin Laden has been trying to do with substantial but incomplete success since the early 1990s."[41] Scheuer contends that "there is nothing Bin Laden could have hoped for more than the American invasion and occupation of Iraq."[42]

In October 2003, the International Institute for Strategic Studies (IISS) published the 2003–2004 edition of *The Military Balance,* which stated that the "war in Iraq has probably inflamed radical passions among Muslims and thus increased al-Qaida's recruiting power and morale and, at least marginally, its operating capability." The report went on to say that "the immediate effect of the war may have been to isolate further al-Qaida from any potential state supporters while also swelling its ranks and galvanizing its will."[43] In May 2005, another report by the IISS declared: "From al-Qaida's point of view, Bush's Iraq policies have arguably produced a confluence of propitious circumstances: a strategically bogged down America, hated by much of the Islamic world, and regarded warily even by its allies." This report also noted that Iraq "could serve as a valuable proving ground for 'blooding' foreign jihadists, and could conceivably form the basis of a second generation of capable al-Qaida leaders . . . and middle-management players."[44] Many other prominent specialists in the study of Islamic militancy and national security have made the same basic points more emphatically, namely that the invasion of Iraq strengthened rather than weakened militant Islamist groups in Iraq and in the Islamic world generally.[45]

■ Conclusion

If the prewar claims of the Bush and Blair administrations regarding weapons of mass destruction or ties between Saddam Hussein and Al-Qaida had been accurate, one could argue that eliminating the danger posed by these weapons and ties outweighed the resentment generated by the occupation of Iraq. But those claims were not accurate and there was considerable evidence suggesting that this was the case long before the war began.[46]

On 7 September 2003, President Bush declared that "Iraq is now the central front in the War on Terror."[47] The key word in this sentence is "now." Iraq only became a central front in the war on terror *after* it was occupied by US and British forces. The US-led occupation of Iraq did, of course, deliver the Iraqi people from an evil tyrant. But George Bush and Tony Blair argued that overthrowing Saddam Hussein would constitute a major victory in the war on terror. In fact, the war ended up strengthening the very terrorists it was supposed to weaken.

■ Notes

1. Henry Munson, "Islam, Nationalism, and Resentment of Foreign Domination"; Robert Anthony Pape, *Dying to Win.*

2. Anthony Shadid, *Night Draws Near,* p. 16.

3. George W. Bush, "Address to a Joint Session of Congress and the American People," 20 September 2001, http://www.whitehouse.gov/news/releases/2001/09/20010920-8.es.html.

4. See Michael Scheuer, *Imperial Hubris;* Bruce B. Lawrence, *Messages to the World;* Robert O. Marlin, ed., *What Does Al-Qaeda Want;* translations of bin Laden's statements in Barry Rubin and Judith Rubin, *Anti-American Terrorism.*

5. H. Norman Schwarzkopf and Peter Petre, *It Doesn't Take a Hero,* pp. 304–306. Saddam Hussein did not in fact intend to invade Saudi Arabia immediately after invading Kuwait, and one would assume that he would have known that the United States would not allow him to do so. However, some CIA analysts, notably Kenneth Pollack, did believe that an Iraqi invasion of Saudi Arabia was at least possible in the days following the occupation of Kuwait. See Kenneth M. Pollack, *Threatening Storm,* pp. 37–38.

6. Peter L. Bergen, *Holy War,* p. 80. Jason Burke contends that "years later, Bin Laden said that it was the [Saudi] government's imprisonment of al-Hawali and Salman al-'Awda . . . that turned him against the royal family as much as their rejection of his proposal for an armed international of Islamic militants." Jason Burke, *Al-Qaeda,* p. 126. But the Saudis imprisoned al-Hawali and al-Awda in large part because of their criticism of the government's decision to allow US troops on Saudi soil to fight Saddam Hussein.

7. My translation, from the Arabic original available at http://www.elaph.com:9090/elaph/arabic/frontendprocess.jsp?screenid=article&command=fe.article&fepageparm=1002493570416644600. The BBC translation is in Rubin and Rubin, *Anti-American Terrorism,* pp. 249–251.

8. José Garçon and Véronique Soulé, "La Quête du Martyre s'Est Propagée," *Libération,* 19 November 2001.

9. Giles Kepel, *Chronique d'une Guerre d'Orient,* p. 66.

10. The Pew Research Center for the People and the Press, *Views of a Changing World, June 2003,* http://people-press.org/reports/pdf/185.pdf. This study was based in part on a survey of nearly 16,000 people in twenty-one countries (including the Palestinian Authority) from 28 April to 15 May 2003. The results of this survey were supplemented by data from earlier polls, especially a survey of 38,000 people in forty-four countries in 2002.

11. Pew Research Center for the People and the Press, *Views of a Changing World, June 2003,* p. 19.

12. Ibid., p. 28.

13. See *Arab Public Opinion Survey,* by Shibley Telhami, Anwar Sadat chair for peace and development at the University of Maryland, in cooperation with Zogby International, 19 February–11 March 2003, http://www.bsos.umd.edu/sadat/mesurvey.htm.

14. Walter Pincus, "Skepticism About U.S. Deep, Iraq Poll Shows," *Washington Post,* 12 November 2003.

15. Human Rights Watch has estimated that the Iraqi government was responsible for the "disappearances" (mostly deaths) of about 290,000 Iraqis from the late 1970s through December 2002. See "Justice for Iraq: A Human Rights Watch Policy Paper," December 2002, http://www.hrw.org/backgrounder/mena/iraq1217bg.htm.

16. Chris Ryder, "Joe Cahill," *The Guardian,* 26 July 2004, http://www.guardian.co.uk/obituaries/story/0,3604,1268933,00.html.

17. Ze'ev Schiff, "The Blunders of Lebanon," *Ha'aretz,* 7 June 2002; Augustus R. Norton, *Amal and the Shi'a,* pp. 107–109.

18. As of September 20, 2005, 1,906 US soldiers and marines and at least 103 US "contractors" had been killed. See http://icasualties.org/oif. This same source lists 96 British troops and 30 British contractors as having been killed by September 20, 2005, along with smaller numbers of dead from the other countries involved in the US-led occupation. Far greater numbers of Iraqis died as a result of the invasion and occupation. See http://www.iraqbodycount.net; Les Roberts et al., "Mortality Before and After the 2003 Invasion." All casualty counts in an ongoing conflict are of course obsolete within days if not minutes.

19. "Hujum 'ala al-Quwat al-Amrikiyya fi Baghdad," *Al-Jazeera,* 10 July 2003.

20. Melinda Liu, "War of Perceptions," *Newsweek,* 29 April 2004.

21. Jonathan Steele and Michael Howard, "US Confused by Iraq's Quiet War," *The Guardian,* 18 July 2003.

22. See http://www.cbsnews.com/stories/2003/07/21/eveningnews/main564357.shtml.

23. Thierry Oberlé, "Voyage à l'Intérieur de la Guérilla Irakienne," *Le Figaro,* 27 December 2003.

24. "Unwilling Participants: Iraqi Soccer Players Angered by Bush Campaign Ads," *Sports Illustrated,* 23 August 2004, http://sportsillustrated.cnn.com/2004/olympics/2004/writers/08/19/iraq/index.html.

25. Mark Etherington, *Revolt on the Tigris;* "Al Sistani Yu'akkid da'm La'iha al-Hakim wa al-Sadr Yuwadhdhif Azmat al-Wuqud Intikhabian," *Al-Hayat,* 17 January 2005; Sabrina Tavernise, "British Army Storms Basra Jail to Free 2 Soldiers from Arrest," *New York Times,* 20 September 2005.

26. "Al-Sadr Yutalibu bil-Rahil Amrika . . . ," *Al-Quds al-'Arabi,* 26 July 2003.

27. Pepe Escobar, "A Unifying Factor Across Iraq," *Asia Times,* 17 August 2004.

28. Saad Sarhan and Doug Struck, "To Mahdi Militiaman, Firing on Americans Is Act of 'Patriotism,'" *Washington Post,* 15 August 2004.

29. Orly Halpern, "A New Iraqi Army Takes Aim at U.S.-led Coalition," *Globe and Mail,* 11 August 2003.

30. Didier François, "Si Nous Étions Unis, ce Serait un Second Vietnam en Irak," *Libération,* 12 August 2004.

31. George Bush and Brent Scowcroft, *A World Transformed,* p. 489.

32. Before the invasion in March 2003, the Bush administration stressed the alleged links between the Kurdish group Ansar al-Islam and Saddam Hussein on the one hand, and Al-Qaida on the other. This group was never important. See "Radical Islam in Iraqi Kurdistan: The Mouse That Roared?" International Crisis Group briefing, 7 February 2003, http://www.crisisgroup.org/home/index.cfm?id=1823&l=1; "Ansar al-Islam in Iraqi Kurdistan," Human Rights Watch briefing, 5 February 2003, http://www.hrw.org/backgrounder/mena/ansarbk020503.htm.

33. This assertion is based in part on statements made by an Iraqi Sunni living in the United States in 2003.

34. Neil MacFarquhar, "Iraq's Anxious Sunnis Seek Security in the New Order," *New York Times,* 10 August 2003.

35. Fouad Ajami, *The Vanished Imam,* p. 11.

36. Juan Cole, "The Shiite Earthquake," 1 February 2005. http://www.salon.com/news/feature/2005/02/01/future/print.html. Juan Cole also discussed the election results in greater detail on his blog, http://www.juancole.com, on 22 February 2005.

37. Richard A. Clarke, "Is a State Sponsor of Terrorism Winning?" *New York Times* magazine, 27 March 2005; Juan Cole, "The Iraq War Is Over, and the Winner Is . . . Iran," http://www.salon.com/news/feature/2005/07/21/iran/print.html.

38. Christophe Ayad, "La Chaînes des Martyrs Palestiniens," *Libération,* 14 December 2004.

39. Richard A. Clarke, *Against All Enemies,* pp. 263–264.

40. Douglas Jehl, "Book by C.I.A. Officer Says U.S. Is Losing Fight Against Terror," *New York Times,* 23 June 2004.

41. Scheuer, *Imperial Hubris,* p. xv.

42. Ibid., p. 212.

43. "Iraq War Swells Al Qaeda's Ranks, Report Says," *Reuters,* 15 October 2003, http://www.iiss.org/confpress-more.php?confid=434.

44. Richard Norton-Taylor and Michael Howard, "Five More Years?" 25 May 2005, http://www.salon.com/news/feature/2005/05/25/peace_in_iraq/index.html.

45. Don Van Atta Jr. and Desmond Butler, "Anger on Iraq Seen As New Qaeda Recruiting Tool," *New York Times,* 16 March 2003; Jessica Stern, "How America Created a Terrorist Haven," *New York Times,* 20 August 2003; Peter Bergen, "Backdraft: How the War in Iraq Has Fueled Al Qaeda and Ignited Its Dream of Global Jihad," *Mother Jones,* July–August 2004, pp. 40–45; Andrew J. Bacevich, "We've Done All We Can Do in Iraq," *Washington Post,* 21 August 2005.

46. See Joseph Cirincione, Jessica Mathews, and George Perkovich, *WMD in Iraq,* http://www.ceip.org/files/pdf/iraq3fulltext.pdf.

47. See http://www.whitehouse.gov/news/releases/2003/09/20030909.html.

20

Oil and the Global Economy

Atif Kubursi

If an epoch is to be identified by its most essential material, ours will have to be called the "Oil Age." Oil has become the major fuel and probably the most indispensable raw material of contemporary industrial civilization. It is now the largest single component of international trade, with over $250 billion in exports; it supplies 40 percent of the world's primary consumption of commercial energy and constitutes the mainstay of industry, the lifeblood of transport, and the sinews of war. Oil has perhaps become the major determinant of today's global military-political-economic balance.[1]

While oil is versatile and its uses are pervasive, its consumption and production are concentrated in few areas and hands. On the demand side are the large industrial economies of the West, together with Japan, China, and India as primarily oil-consuming nations. On the supply side is a small group of developing countries, predominately Arab, that produce and export almost all their production. Production, exploration, and particularly refining and distribution are dominated, even in the oil-exporting countries, by a handful of large, fully integrated multinational corporations flying the flags of primarily two countries (five of these corporations are US and two are European) that only too recently colonized or monopolized the production of oil.

Oil production, distribution, pricing, and exploration involve complex issues of economics, but they are by no means wholly determined by the market. Natural resources mainly belong to governments. Decisions concerning the pace of exploration and development and rates of extraction are now assumed by governments in the producing states. Regulation and taxation of the oil industry is a matter of political policy in the consumer states. And a wide margin of fluctuation in the price of oil is brought about principally by political instability and the periodic crisis situations that involved either the threat or actual disruption of supply. The list of these crises is long but familiar: Musaddeq in 1951, Suez in 1956, the Arab-Israeli wars of

1967 and 1973, the Iranian revolution in 1979, the Iran-Iraq War of 1980–1988, the Iraqi invasion of Kuwait in 1990, and more recently the US invasion of Iraq.[2] Hence, matters of oil are by no means purely economic questions, and to view them in terms only of theoretical and practical economics is to adopt a distorting and misleading perspective; the analysis of oil is more properly a matter of political economy.

■ How Important Is Arab Oil?

Middle Eastern oil is an inventory, exhaustible and nonrenewable. It is nonetheless a huge inventory (the largest in the world). In the early 1950s the Middle East held almost 49 percent of the world's proven reserves and almost 16 percent of global output.[3] Since then both the level of reserves and the output have expanded rapidly. In 1990, Middle Eastern oil accounted for almost two-thirds of world reserves, and by 2002 this share had declined only slightly, to 63.5 percent (see Tables 20.1–20.3). Middle Eastern oil production, which was as low as 5.5 percent of total world production in 1938, climbed rapidly to 16 percent in 1950 and kept its steady increase until 1975, when it peaked at 35.6 percent. While it fell to 19 percent in 1985, by 1990 the region's share had climbed to 27 percent; this percentage share has since increased to more than 31 percent and is expected to rise as other non-Arab producers limit their production and exports.[4] Moreover, if export shares are taken into consideration, the Middle East accounted for 41 percent of total world exports in 2002, which is substantially higher than its share in total oil production. Middle Eastern oil is also produced at very low costs (the lowest in the world). In the early days of oil production following World War II, the cost per barrel was less that $0.16, when Nigerian oil cost $0.50 and US oil $1.75 a barrel. This low cost has remained a feature of Arab oil production.[5] Even today this cost is put between $0.5 and $2.5, when comparable costs in Europe and the United States exceed $13.75. Middle Eastern oil is thus a source of enormous profit for those who control it. Finally, the region has been the major potential source of incremental supplies and will increasingly play this role as other regions wind down their supplies and as those that assumed this role, such as Mexico and the North Sea, in the past, are exhausted. Thus the dependence of the consuming world on Middle Eastern oil is heavy and increasing.

■ The Pivotal Role of Oil in US Policy

It is axiomatic that oil is the linchpin of US policy toward the Middle East, as it has been since World War II. As early as August 1, 1945, James

Table 20.1   Proven Oil Reserves in the Middle East

	Barrels (billions)	Share of World Total (percentage)
1951	48.0	48.8
1970	340.0	54.8
1975	368.0	55.5
1980	362.0	55.3
1985	390.0	54.2
1990	660.0	65.2
2000	726.8	63.5

Sources: Presidential Materials Commission, *Resources for Freedom,* Washington, DC, June 1952; *BP Statistical Review of World Energy,* 1975 and 2004, www.bp.com/statisticalreview; "World Crude Oil and Natural Gas Reserves, January 1, 2000," *Annual Energy Review 2000,* Energy Information Administration, http://tonto.eia.doe.gov/FTPROOT/multifuel/038400.pdf.

Table 20.2   Middle East and World Production of Oil (million barrels per day)

	Middle East	World	Middle East Share of World (percentage)
1938	0.3	5.5	5.5
1950	1.7	10.4	16.3
1955	3.2	15.5	20.6
1960	5.2	21.1	24.6
1965	8.3	31.3	26.5
1970	13.8	47.3	29.0
1975	19.5	54.7	35.6
1980	18.5	61.6	30.0
1985	10.7	56.1	19.0
1990	17.9	66.7	26.8
2002	23.7	74.7	31.7

Sources: Sam H. Schurr and Paul T. Homan, with Joel Darmstadter, *Middle Eastern Oil and the Western World,* New York: American Elsevier, 1971; *BP Statistical Review of World Energy,* 1975 and 2004, www.bp.com/statisticalreview.

Forrestal, secretary of the US Navy, wrote to James Byrnes, secretary of state: "Because of my firm conviction that within the next twenty-five years the United States is going to be faced with very sharply declining oil reserves and because oil and all of its by-products are the foundation of the ability to fight a modern war, I consider this to be one of the most important problems of the government."[6] As Daniel Yergin points out, while actual US reserves increased from 21 billion barrels in 1948 to 38 billion barrels by

Table 20.3   Reserve Production Ratios, 2002

	Proven Reserves (billion barrels)	Reserves/Production (years)
North America	65.5	12.8
Latin and Central America	100.5	39.6
Europe and Eurasia	1,004.3	17.6
Norway	9.0	7.4
United Kingdom	4.5	5.0
Middle East	726.8	95.2
Africa	101.7	35.0
Total Asia Pacific	47.5	16.4
Total world	1,146.3	42.4

Source: BP Statistical Review of World Energy, 2004, www.bp.com/statisticalreview.

1972, the US share of world reserves had shrunk from 34 percent to a mere 7 percent.[7]

Oil, as Yergin has chronicled its history, is the prize sought by the great powers, and control of the Middle East region has been critical for the relative position of the great powers among themselves. US policy designed to make the United States the hegemonic power in the Persian Gulf region succeeded without any requirement for a massive military operation. Britain was squeezed out of the area after Suez, and US hegemony came to be contested only by regional forces, at first Arab nationalism and later, after 1979, by the appeal of Islam. US control of oil gave it hegemony over its allies, for as Europe recovered from the ruins of World War II her dependence on Middle Eastern oil grew proportionately. The United States made consistent attempts to increase the dependence of European economies on resource sectors in which it possessed controlling influence, above all oil; thus, for example, the European economies were traditionally reliant on rail transportation systems, but the European request for freight cars under the Marshall Plan was reduced by the United States from 47,000 to 20,000 while it insisted instead on allocating 65,000 trucks under the program, although none were requested. At the same time, the United States used various crises to marginalize the role of European powers in the control of Middle Eastern oil fields.

Similarly, the politics of the Middle East cannot be separated from the politics of oil. The toppling of the Mossadeq government in 1953 in Iran, and the reinstallation of the Shah by the CIA, indicated how slight is the tolerance of the Western powers of any attempts by the oil-producing countries in the Middle East to control their resources for the development of their own societies. The Suez crisis of 1956 was also about oil, the canal being the jugular artery of oil supply from the Gulf to Europe and North America.

The Suez crisis clarified the interest and purpose of the United States in the Middle East. Responding to his adviser, Dillon Anderson, President Dwight Eisenhower noted in July 1957, "I think you have, in the analysis presented in the letter, proved that should a crisis arise threatening to cut the Western world off from the Mid East oil, we would *have* to use force."[8] Twenty-two years later, in the wake of the Soviet invasion of Afghanistan in December 1979 and the fall of the Shah's regime in Iran earlier in that year to the Islamic revolution, Jimmy Carter restated Eisenhower's view as the central plank of US policy toward the Middle East. It is abundantly clear that the hegemonic control of Middle Eastern oil resources was and remains an essential element in guaranteeing the status of the United States as a superpower. For US political and business elites this is self-evident; its consequences are for others to work out.

The real moment of truth for US policy toward the Middle East came with the decision by the Organization of Petroleum Exporting Countries (OPEC) to quadruple oil prices following the 1973 Arab-Israeli war. This was the moment when the logic of US policy would have dictated the use of force. There were some threats made and voices raised advocating the use of force against the OPEC monopoly.[9] Henry Kissinger explained, however, that force was only appropriate "where there's some actual strangulation of the industrialized world" and not in a dispute over price.[10] Disputes over price, as it would be illustrated in subsequent years, neither threatened US control of the region nor adversely affected its interests. The United States, as the records show, actually began to make background noises and plant suggestions for higher oil prices well before the events of 1973–1974. The US oil multinationals, which together supported Richard Nixon's bid for reelection in 1972, constructed scenarios for higher prices. The US National Petroleum Council, an organization constituted of senior government officials and industry representatives, published a study prepared at the request of the White House that recommended higher oil prices, to double by 1985 in constant prices, as an incentive for discovery of new oil.[11] William Simon, at the time treasury undersecretary and chief of the White House Committee on Oil Policy, floated the suggestion that increased revenues of OPEC members from higher oil prices would not pose a problem, as these were "recycled" through US banks and other financial institutions.[12] The oil policy of the Nixon administration after 1971 was based on three objectives, which underscored these considerations: (1) to develop new energy sources based on higher crude prices of Middle Eastern oil; (2) to undermine European and Japanese competition, since both these economies were greatly dependent on imported oil; and (3) to raise OPEC revenues as a tax on consumers to stimulate US exports to the oil-producing countries. For political reasons, both domestic and foreign, higher oil prices could only be levied on consumers by suppliers (and not via gasoline taxes), and if blame were to be assigned, OPEC would be held responsible.

This must be put in the context of the early 1970s, when the situation among the capitalist-industrial powers had dramatically changed. Western Europe and Japan had emerged as economic competitors to the United States, and the latter's growing current account deficit, owing to the Vietnam War, was shifting the balance of financial power to their advantage. However, the oil price boom actually provided the United States with the chance to recover the massive funds (the trillion eurodollars) it had lost, and the Europeans and Japanese had amassed, during the war. In the early 1950s, Arabian oil cost less than $0.16 a barrel to produce; thus the markup of over 3,000 percent after the 1974 price boom represented the price extracted by the producers from the consumers. This differential proved to be a decisive element in transferring the eurodollar surpluses from Japan and Germany via the Gulf to US banks and the US Treasury.

The US quarrel with the Arabs, as Kissinger's diplomacy toward the Middle East revealed, was thus not with OPEC's quadrupling of the oil price; it was pointedly with the *idea* that the Arabs, with their newfound diplomatic weapon, could change the political status quo in the region—that it could form the basis of Arab power against the West and Israel. Absolutely crucial in mitigating this threat was the strategic alliance formed with Saudi Arabia, which opened a wedge between Saudi Arabia and other producers within the oil cartel. It is believed that an agreement was reached on a "special relationship" between Riyadh and Washington based on the understanding that the Saudis would place their immense assets at the disposal of the United States. The kingdom would use its position as the swing producer within OPEC to ensure "moderate" prices and a constant supply of oil to the industrial world. The Saudis also promised the United States that the kingdom would use its economic influence to moderate Arab politics. In return, the United States undertook to guarantee the security of the kingdom and to assist in its techno-industrial development.[13]

■ Oil and War in the Post–Cold War Era

Throughout the Cold War years the enormous strength and global deployment of the US military masked the gradual relative decline of the country in economic terms. In 1945 the United States had stood far ahead of any potential or real rival in both military and economic terms; but by 1990 its relative position was no longer unassailable by its immediate industrial and financial rivals.[14] The United States became caught in the dilemma of "imperial overstretch," a condition defined as one wherein the global interests of an imperial power exceed its capacity to defend them simultaneously without damaging its economic base; one indicator of imperial overstretch was the quadrupling of the federal debt during the 1980s. The global hegemony of the United States had come to rest precariously on one pillar, the military.[15]

The end of the Cold war, however, brought an opportunity to restore unchallenged US hegemony. The disintegration of the Soviet Union and the massive escalation in defense spending under Reagan made the United States an unmatched military superpower, while US Cold War military deployments, organized around specified commands designated to police US interests in every region of the world, remained intact. If during the Cold War years the projection of US power worldwide had to be somewhat cautiously conducted to avoid direct confrontation with the Soviet Union, this was no longer necessary. Thus the end of the Cold War presented the United States with a rare opening to reimpose its conception of a *liberal* world order, a Pax Americana, based on the ideology of democracy bolstered by free markets. It was an opportunity to advance what would be called the Project for the New American Century.

In spring 1992, one year after Operation Desert Storm, a Pentagon document under discussion within the George H. W. Bush administration titled "Defense Planning Guidance for the Fiscal Years 1994–1999" was leaked to the press.[16] The central thrust of this document, prepared under the supervision of Paul Wolfowitz, policy undersecretary for the Department of Defense, was to make the case for positioning the United States as the only hegemonic power in the world and for convincing "potential competitors that they need not aspire to a greater role or pursue a more aggressive posture to protect their legitimate interests." Wolfowitz's document, in its identification of new threats and its advocacy of a new buildup of US military power, was analogous to the National Security Council's Memorandum 68 of April 1950, the defining document of the Cold War. And just as the Korean War, coming at an opportune moment, made the task of selling the memorandum to a skeptical public easier for Harry Truman, so the war against Iraq made relatively easier the task of the Pentagon in selling the arguments for continued defense expenditure, at about the same level prior to the disintegration of the Soviet Union, in the post–Cold War period. The Wolfowitz document also focused on two pressing necessities. One was "the integration of Germany and Japan into a U.S.-led system of collective security" to replace the defunct anti-Soviet alliance. As to the second, referring to the Middle East and Southwest Asia, the Pentagon document states: "our overall objective is to remain the predominant outside power in the region and preserve U.S. and Western access to the region's oil."

The context of the new doctrine was shaped not just by great power rivalry, but also by the struggle between the core and periphery of the world system. George Kennan, in a policy planning study prepared for the State Department in February 1948, had long ago articulated what would become the fixed defining proposition of US foreign policy in an unequal world: "We have about 50% of the world's wealth, but only 6.3% of its population. . . . In this situation, we cannot fail to be the object of envy and resentment. Our real task in the coming period is to devise a pattern of relationships which will permit us to maintain this position of disparity without positive detriment to our national security."[17]

In the post–Cold War period, with the triumph of neoliberal ideology over its socialist rival, the spread of neoliberalism to the less developed countries, and the widening of the wealth disparity between North and South, the global class struggle between rich and poor has intensified. In this context, the centers of international capitalism, with their respective satellites—the United States within the Americas, Germany within Europe, and Japan within the Pacific Basin—are at once allies against the population of the South and rivals for markets and resources among themselves. The military superiority of the United States provides it with the strategic leverage to police the neoliberal world order against third world challengers, bargain for advantage against its capitalist-industrial competitors, and ensure the unchallenged access to world resources, above all oil, that underpins its unchallenged supremacy.

In a unipolar world of US global military hegemony there is no further need for restraint when a third world country like Iraq appears to threaten US interests. Operation Desert Storm was a demonstration of US willingness to unleash military might whenever such an occasion arises. The Gulf War also showed the extent to which oil can give leverage to extract compensation for US military expenses from US industrial competitors and client Arab oil producers. The Gulf War was the first war waged by the United States that not only was fully paid for by other countries, but also turned a tidy profit for the US military establishment.[18] The leverage reinforced in the war would ensure for economic rivals a continued dependency on the United States for secure access to oil.

■ 9/11, Oil, and the Iraq War

11 September 2001 may not have changed the world, but it certainly gave the US neoconservatives the pretext for pushing their agenda. The catastrophic events provided the impetus to mobilize domestic and world public opinion behind a new assertion of US military domination of the world political order, to demonstrate its resolve to resort to lethal power to deal with any real or perceived threat, and to restore its unchallenged hegemony over Middle Eastern oil. Two factors had reinforced Washington's concern for its oil hegemony and provide the material context for the Iraq War.

First was the recent increase in US oil imports from the Middle East. Imports (from all areas) in 1990 accounted for about half of US oil consumption, compared to 35 percent as late as 1985. Virtually all the additional imports came from the Gulf. In 1985 the share from the Gulf was less than 8 percent of total US oil imports, but by 2003 had risen to 21 percent. According to the Centre for Global Energy Studies, US dependence on Middle Eastern (Gulf) oil was expected to increase to 43 percent of total oil imports in the early 2000s if US production remained unchanged. However, if US oil production continued to decline at the rates observed during the period 1985–2000 (an almost 5 percent annual reduction), it was anticipated that US dependence on Middle Eastern oil could reach as high as 57 percent.[19]

Yet at the same time, the Saudi alliance on which US oil hegemony had hitherto depended was now in doubt. Saudi Arabia was the major birthplace of the 9/11 hijackers and the bin Laden movement; this posed a formidable challenge to the five-decade-old policy of dependence on the kingdom's oil and political influence to support US policy objectives and oil access. The stationing of US troops in the land of the Islamic holy places was resented by Muslims all over the world and was proving to be a major battle-rallying call for Al-Qaida.

In this context, the twin occupations of Afghanistan and Iraq simultaneously provided US neoconservative planners with a replacement for Saudi Arabia, control of the entire Gulf, a wedge between Syria and Iran, bases in and around Central Asia (where new energy sources are emerging), and the elimination of any potential threat to Israel. All has not, of course, gone totally according to plan. The neoconservatives had expected to exploit Iraqi divisions to gain a welcome from the Shia and Kurds, but their overriding preoccupation with seizure and control of Iraqi oil drove a cleavage between them and Iraqis. They squandered quickly any goodwill the Iraqi population might have had for them as they protected the oil ministry and turned their back on the museums and overall security of the people. It was apparent, too, that US force configurations were not designed for the stabilization of Iraq; this would have required a larger and more labor-intensive policing presence. The smaller, more capital-intensive force (high-tech and high-firepower weaponry, air power), however, is designed to make it impossible for the United States to be militarily dislodged from Iraq and to subordinate and make dependent any Iraqi government, thereby ensuring control of Iraq's oil.

■ Notes

1. Atif Kubursi and Salim Mansur, "From Sykes Picot Through Bandung to Oslo."

2. Robert Mabro, *Political Dimensions of the Gulf Crisis.*

3. Atif Kubursi. "Oil, Influence, and Development."

4. Atif Kubursi and Salim Mansur, "The Political Economy of Middle Eastern Oil."

5. George W. Stocking, *Middle East Oil.*

6. Cited in J. H. Noyes, *The Clouded Lens,* p. 44.

7. Daniel Yergin, *The Prize,* p. 500.

8. Anderson to Eisenhower, 24 July 1957; Eisenhower to Anderson, 30 July 1957; *italics* given (Dwight D. Eisenhower Library, Abilene, Kansas). Letter cited in Burton I. Kaufman, "Mideast Multinational Oil, U.S. Foreign Policy, and Antitrust."

9. See A. Sampson, *The Seven Sisters,* p. 323; Robert W. Tucker, "Oil," pp. 21–31.

10. Quoted in P. Terzian, *OPEC,* p. 198.

11. Ibid., p. 191.

12. Ibid., pp. 192–193.

13. Ibid., p. 236.

14. See Lester C. Thurow, *The Zero-Sum Society,* especially chap. 1.

15. Paul Kennedy, *The Rise and Fall of the Great Powers,* p. 515.

16. See P. E. Tyler, "U.S. Strategy Plan Calls for Insuring No Rivals Develop," *New York Times,* 8 March 1992; also see the excerpts from the leaked Pentagon document in the same edition of the *New York Times.*

17. Quoted in Noam Chomsky, *On Power and Ideology,* p. 15.

18. According to the Arab Economic Report (see *New York Times,* 8 September 1992), the Gulf War cost Arabs an estimated $620 billion, of which the infrastructural damage to Iraq and Kuwait amounted to $190 billion and $160 billion. Saudi Arabia, Kuwait, and the United Arab Emirates paid $84 billion to the United States, Britain, and France for military expenses, while direct logistical support to US and coalition forces cost $51 billion to Saudi Arabia and Kuwait.

19. Fadhil J. al-Chalabi, "Comment," *Energy Studies Review* 4, no. 1 (1992), pp. 40–44.

21

The Role of
the United Nations

Ian Williams

According to critical observers disillusioned for quite different reasons with the United Nations, the organization is a failure because it did not support the US invasion of Iraq—or because it failed to prevent it. Certainly, ideologically motivated commentators in the United States cited the failure of the UN to endorse the attack on Iraq as evidence of the organization's uselessness, and in the aftermath of the invasion, neoconservative Richard Perle exulted that "the UN was dead—Thank God!"[1] However, a more nuanced view of the organization would be that its failure to support the invasion maintained at least the principles, if not the practice, of international law, and that the US return to the organization to assist in the aftermath was recognition, albeit grudging, of what Kofi Annan has called the "unique legitimacy" that only the United Nations can provide.

■ The Prewar Struggle in the Security Council

During 2002 it became increasingly clear that the United States was bent on war against Iraq, the only question being whether it would act unilaterally or take a multilateral route through the United Nations. The advice of former US president George H. W. Bush, US secretary of state Colin Powell, and British prime minister Tony Blair constituted the compelling factors behind President George W. Bush's speech to the UN General Assembly on 12 September 2002. Set in the context of decades of perennial US conservative abuse of the United Nations, the president's speech was a relatively skillful attempt to woo the UN and its member states to join in his attempt to deal with Saddam Hussein. Invoking the ineffectuality of the League of Nations and its consequent fate, he pointed out that the UN was supposed to be different. Praising the organization for its part in liberating Kuwait, he cataloged Iraqi defiance of the UN, which was at the time undeniable: he referred to Iraqi breaches of resolutions on weapons inspectors, refusal to hand over prisoners, and Saddam's continuing repression of his own people.

Giving notice of the administration's impending demands on the UN, Bush declared, "Our partnership of nations can meet the test before us by making clear what we now expect of the Iraqi regime." He demanded that Iraq abide by all outstanding resolutions. However, without being irremediably offensive, the speech gave warning that Washington would only stay on the UN highway as long it went swiftly and smoothly in the direction the president wanted. "If Iraq's regime defies us again, the world must move deliberately, decisively, to hold Iraq to account. We will work with the UN Security Council for the necessary resolutions, but the purposes of the United States should not be doubted. The Security Council resolutions will be enforced, the just demands of peace and security will be met, or action will be unavoidable, and a regime that has lost its legitimacy will also lose its power." Iraqi intransigence over admitting inspectors had in fact left the regime with few friends in the UN, while making the strictly legal case against it incontrovertible.

However, when the US draft resolution on Iraq finally arrived at the Security Council, it included provisions that had no chance of being accepted by other Council members, but that were there to please the hawks in the Pentagon and around Vice President Dick Cheney's office. The draft, which was originally only shared with the five permanent members of the Security Council, recalled the original resolutions authorizing the use of force by members, and found Iraq "in material breach" of the cease-fire resolutions. It demanded entry for UN weapons inspectors and mandated armed UN security forces to be deployed to protect them; it also would allow the five permanent members of the Security Council the right to recommend sites to be inspected and individuals to be questioned, and request permission to have their representatives join the inspections. Of course, only two of the five, the United States and United Kingdom, were likely to exercise such rights, or provide forces.

The inspectors would have the right to declare no-fly/no-drive zones, exclusion zones, and/or ground and air transit corridors. Iraq would have to provide the Security Council, before inspections, but within thirty days from the date of the resolution, "a complete list of its programs to develop chemical, biological and nuclear weapons, ballistic missiles, and unmanned aerial vehicles as well as all other chemical, biological and nuclear weapons production or material."

Iraq would have to provide a list of personnel involved in the programs, whom the inspectors would have the right to interview in or outside Iraq. Any false statements or omissions in the list of programs or personnel submitted by Iraq and or its failure "at any time to comply and cooperate fully in accordance with the provisions laid out in this resolution, shall constitute

a further material breach of Iraq's obligations, and that such breach authorizes member states to use all necessary means to restore international peace
and security in the area."

Seeing the writing on the wall, the Iraqis agreed to talk to Hans Blix of
the UN Monitoring, Verification, and Inspection Commission (UNMOVIC)
and Mohamed El-Baradei of the International Atomic Energy Agency
(IAEA), and following their discussions seemingly announced that the
inspections could resume, but the letters they sent presenting their version
of what had been agreed were so hedged with qualifications that they bolstered the US case for war.

Even when the issue of UN access to Iraq was cleared up, Blix and El-
Baradei then refused to send in inspectors until the US draft resolution was
dealt with, since they did not want to send staff into a war zone. The draft
was frozen, not least because the only version ten elected members of the
Council had seen was in the newspapers, which did not dispose them favorably to the process. In any case, neither they, nor the inspectors, liked what
they had read of it.

A principal issue in negotiation over the draft was whether member
states (meaning the United States and Britain) could act on their own
authority against Iraq if they deemed it to be in noncompliance. US secretary of state Powell pledged an additional meeting of the Council before the
United States acted on the trigger clauses in the draft resolution, but this
was not enough for most members, since it would still give Washington a
free hand to determine when to mete out the threatened "severe consequences" and what form they would take.

The steady stream of belligerent leaks from civilians at the Pentagon
did not help, since they brought the hidden agenda—war at any cost—out in
the open. Sergei Lavrov, Russian ambassador to the UN, articulated the suspicions during the debate. "If we're talking, not about the deployment of
inspectors, but about an attempt to use the Security Council to create a legal
basis for the use of force, or even for a regime change of a UN member
state, and this goal has been constantly alluded to by several officials publicly, then we see no way how the Security Council could give its consent to
that."

Even Powell, the most urbane member of the US administration, did
not reassure others when he said that "any resolution that emerges from this
will be a resolution that preserves the authority and the right of the president of the United States to act in self-defense . . . in concert with the international community or with like-minded nations rather than through the UN
should it not wish to act."

When the resolution was finally brought back to the permanent five on
21 October 2002, there were still not enough concessions to win over the
doubters. It still included the key language that members feared would give

the White House the excuses it wanted: seven days for the Iraqis to comply, a declaration that Baghdad was already in "material breach" of UN resolutions, and a warning of consequences.

While the hawks dictated the initial US positions, the White House in the end opted to go with the more diplomatically feasible route of UNMOVIC and IAEA inspections backed by a strong resolution. Bush and Cheney's meetings with Blix and El-Baradei were in part a reassuring signal to the waverers on the Security Council that after the president's initial diplomatically disastrous fit of pique when Iraq had first accepted inspections, the White House was now backing them.

Based on previous experience of Iraqi intransigence, the other members of the Security Council almost all conceded that when the inspectors went into Iraq, they should be backed by the threat of force and the implication was that if Baghdad resisted, then the Council would back military action. In private the Russians, Chinese, and French all admitted that this was Iraq's last chance, not so much because they wanted it that way, but because they saw no percentage in resisting Washington to cover for Iraqi irrationality.

In the end, most members were also prepared to accommodate US whims, even fairly lethal ones, to preserve the appearance of legality, since they tacitly bought into the US administration's argument of the irrelevance of the UN if it failed to enforce its resolutions. If the alternative was the world's most important nation ripping up the UN Charter, it was best to go along with it and try to keep what Blair called a hand on the steering wheel. As it was to turn out, it was a runaway train, with no steering wheel, and little in the way of brakes.

With the final unanimous acceptance of UN Security Council Resolution 1441 on 8 November 2002, just after the US elections, the United States had certainly triumphed in its major point. Despite the dubiety of every other nation except Israel, Iraq was now elevated to the top of the global security agenda. However, the United States had now made its plans for an invasion of Iraq legally and diplomatically contingent on the regime's noncooperation with the inspectors, or at least on their discovery of undeclared weapons of mass destruction. The much amended resolution seemed to offer Iraq a genuine opportunity to avoid war by cooperation with UNMOVIC and the IAEA.

The resolution also avoided giving the United States the automatic right to attack that the hawks had originally insisted on, and Blix had successfully secured the removal of the provisions allowing the permanent five members to foist staff onto the inspection teams. He was less successful with his argument that the thirty days for "full and frank" disclosure by the Iraqis was not enough.

The United States had made assumptions in depth that its casus belli was on the way. Washington assumed that Iraq would not cooperate, that it either would not deliver the disclosure in time or, if it did, would provably lie. Fanned to fever heat by Washington leaks, the next few months were to see a succession of alleged make-or-break dates. First, would Iraq accept the resolution, and second, would Baghdad deliver the "full and frank" disclosure that was demanded?

In the end, the Iraq regime belatedly offered unprecedented cooperation to the UN inspectors, who began their rounds in Baghdad. Frustrated, the Washington hawks tried to talk up Iraqi potshots at US planes patrolling the no-fly zone into a material breach of the resolution meriting the "serious consequences" that they so seriously wanted to mete out. However, the rest of the world, from Kofi Annan to every other member of the Security Council, pointed out that this had been specifically excluded when the terms of the resolution were negotiated, since no one else accepted that the allied overflights were sanctioned by UN resolutions.

Similarly, nagging press spin from Washington about the weakness, or suspected collusion, of inspectors seemed designed to preemptively devalue any report that did not match the expectations of the US hawks. As the 12,000 pages of definitely full, and possibly frank, hard copy dropped with a depleted-uranium-like thump on their desks, the disappointed hawks realized that this casus belli was not going to fly—or at least not very soon. By the volume, and even the Arabic medium, of much of the declaration, the Iraqis ensured that the inspectors could not produce a reliable assessment of fullness or frankness until the end of January 2003.

Since the disclosure could not be proven to be other than full and frank, and had indeed landed on time, the hawks in the US administration now had to fall back on finding actual weaponry that the Iraqi documents had not declared. As the new year began, the pressure on Washington to return to the UN for a second resolution before military action built up, both inside and outside the Council, as key allies like the Turks and Saudis, from whose territories the invasion was planned, demanded a UN mandate before cooperating. Most of the world wanted solid evidence of Iraqi defiance of Resolution 1441, and was not prepared to accept that Washington could unilaterally determine when and how to apply previous UN resolutions. Even London preferred a second resolution, but chose not to regard its absence as an absolute prohibition on military reaction if the Council "unreasonably" withheld its support—for example, if there were a veto in the face of clear evidence of Iraqi "flagrant breaches."

UNMOVIC chief Hans Blix had started the inspections with the assumption that Saddam's previous declarations of disarmament were untrue, and was frustrated that despite unprecedented cooperation from the Iraqis, there was no sign of the suspected weaponry. It was a task that UNMOVIC complained was being carried out with minimal assistance from the much vaunted resources of US intelligence, which Blix reportedly compared with a librarian who would not lend books.[2]

By then, however, the unprecedented Iraqi cooperation with the inspectors was beginning to raise doubts in Blix's mind about the existence of undeclared weapons of mass destruction, and inspection after inspection following US leads was showing no results.[3] There were no such doubts in Washington. On 5 February, Colin Powell made his famous presentation on Iraqi weapons. It was professional, well illustrated, slick, yet sadly unconvincing and, as he himself now admits, totally insubstantial.

On 14 February 2003, the battle lines were really drawn. In their reports to the Security Council, Blix and El-Baradei implicitly contradicted many of the specifics of what Powell had presented, and the tone of their reports and the comments of most other delegates dashed any hopes that Bush and Blair may have had to use the weapons issue as an excuse to let slip the dogs of war within the next two weeks.

When French foreign minister Dominique de Villepin spoke, the diplomats, press, and staff clustered behind the actual delegates burst into applause, the first time this had happened in the Security Council since Nelson Mandela had spoken there. They were applauding the clear Cartesian logic of Villepin's speech: "the option of inspections has not been taken to the end and . . . it can provide an effective response to the imperative of disarming Iraq. The second is that the use of force would be so fraught with risks for people, for the region and for international stability that it should only be envisioned as a last resort."

Before they voted for Resolution 1441, other members, particularly France, had successfully extracted US agreement that there should be another meeting of the Council to consider the weapons inspectors' reports on whether or not Iraq had culpably failed to cooperate and that there had to be a second resolution to authorize force. Tony Blair won his case with George W. Bush that the two allies should go for a second resolution to secure Security Council support for the war, but he did not win an absolute guarantee.

Bush insisted that the invasion would not be delayed past March 2003, with or without a resolution. Washington pled the climate, but no one has yet provided a truly convincing or rational explanation for the obduracy about the launch date. The Anglo-American draft of the "second" resolution, which Blair called a "last push for peace," noted that "Iraq has submitted a declaration pursuant to its resolution 1441 (2002) containing false statements and omissions and has failed to comply with, and cooperate fully in the implementation of, that resolution," and concluded that the Security Council "acting under Chapter VII of the charter of the United Nations, decides that Iraq has failed to take the final opportunity afforded to it in resolution 1441." The difficulty with this resolution was that the actual inspectors were still reporting increasing cooperation from Iraq—and had found no evidence of serious evasion, so the core of the resolution was simply untrue as far as most of the Council was concerned.

The draft's allusive and elusive wording also derived from Washington's insistence that it already had war powers from the cease-fire aspects of Resolution 687 and that anyway, in matters of "national interest," the United States claimed the right to do whatever it likes regardless of the UN. The United States did not, indeed, seek an explicit authorization of the use of force in the draft, because to do so would have been to concede that it did not have that right to act unilaterally.

It was clear that the resolution was dead in the water. Most of the Council members, despite visible oscillation, were increasingly inclining toward a nay vote or abstention, meaning that the resolution would not even get the basic nine votes needed to pass under Council rules regardless of any vetoes. Determined to go to war against a majority of the Council, the United States and United Kingdom tried to fudge the matter by ensuring that the votes were never counted, and to blame France for its veto as if that were all that stood against the resolution's adoption. Cannily, Sir Jeremy Greenstock, the British ambassador, left the resolution on the table. It could then be argued that the Council was still "seized of the matter," and that, since the Council was technically not deadlocked, arguably the resolution could not be taken to the General Assembly under the "uniting for peace" procedure, which applied when a resolution had been vetoed. The invasion went ahead.

It is significant that despite the opinion repeated by so many nations and by Kofi Annan himself that the invasion was a breach of the UN Charter, not one resolution was moved to say so, either in the Council or in the General Assembly. The United States exerted huge diplomatic pressure behind the scenes, warning member states that it would be considered an extremely unfriendly act if any of them supported convening a special General Assembly, which could consider any matter on which the Council was deadlocked and which could have asked the International Court of Justice for an advisory ruling: the president of the General Assembly, Jan Kavan, former Czech dissident and foreign minister, who would have acted on any such request to convene a meeting, waited in vain.[4] In the end, the UN could not impose sanctions on the United States and Britain, partly because they could and would veto any resolution, but more importantly in concession to the realities of world power.

To be fair, the member states scrupulously refrained from retrospectively legitimizing the deed—as had implicitly happened, for example, with Kosovo. Scrutiny of the Security Council resolutions will show that at no point did they legitimize the invasion itself, even as they sought to deal with its consequences. No UN body ever considered the invasion, let alone passed a resolution that legally condoned it, but neither did any UN body legally condemn it.

■ The Role of the Secretary-General

Even as President Bush outlined his plans for Iraq on September 2002, Kofi Annan responded to the war drums, which could already be heard thudding in the US administration. He put his cards on the table in his speech, just before Bush's: "Any State, if attacked, retains the inherent right of self-defense under Article 51 of the Charter. But beyond that, when States decide to use force to deal with broader threats to international peace and security, there is no substitute for the unique legitimacy provided by the United Nations."

He was to repeat that formulation often, strengthening it as the contingency against which he was warning came to pass. A year later, the debate that had bubbled under the surface for a year was summarized again by Annan, who repeated this advice to the 2003 General Assembly, but in his most explicit consideration—and rejection—of the US and British positions, added that

> now, some say this understanding is no longer tenable, since an "armed attack" with weapons of mass destruction could be launched at any time, without warning, or by a clandestine group.
> Rather than wait for that to happen, they argued that states had the right and obligation to use force pre-emptively, unilaterally and even on the territory of other States, even while weapons systems that might be used to attack them are still being developed, and are not obliged to wait until there is agreement in the Security Council.

However, he countered: "This logic represents a fundamental challenge to the principles on which, however imperfectly, world peace and stability have rested for the last fifty-eight years. . . . If it were to be adopted, it could set precedents that resulted in a proliferation of the unilateral and lawless use of force, with or without justification."

Somewhat provocatively, he had also suggested that the UN "needs to consider how it will deal with the possibility that individual States may use force 'preemptively' against perceived threats." The formulation usually used by Annan was that the war was "outside the UN Charter," but in September 2004 one particularly relentless BBC reporter stayed on the offensive long enough to wrest from him an admission that this meant that it was "illegal."

At the end of October 2004, as the United States launched the offensive that flattened Fallujah, Annan sent a private letter to the US, UK, and Iraqi administrations suggesting caution, thereby missing an opportunity to go on record publicly as the conscience of the international community. The letter was leaked from Washington, and added to the ire of die-hard conservative opponents of the UN who used inflated or invented allegations of corruption in the oil-for-food program to attack the organization, and Annan personally. Annan may have originally been the candidate favored by the United States for Secretary-General, but Washington found, to its dismay, that holders of the office tend to take their role as keeper of international law and world peace quite seriously.

■ The UN's Vital Role in the Aftermath

In the aftermath of the invasion, both the UN Secretariat and like-minded countries were keen to bring about a UN role in the postwar administration and relief of Iraq. Resolution 1472, unanimously passed on 28 March, decided that "to the fullest extent of the means available to it, the occupying Power has the duty of ensuring the food and medical supplies of the population" and that under the fourth Geneva Convention, "those causing the war should meet the humanitarian needs of the civilian population." In diplomatic language this was a fairly clear message that the war had not been part of any UN operation. The resolution allowed the UN officials of the continuing oil-for-food program to act as a surrogate for the disbanded Iraqi government and was essentially about helping the Iraqi people—a cause that even opponents of the war could and did support.

The United States was forced to come back to the UN yet again in May 2003, because it could not sell Iraqi oil without the clear title that only a UN resolution could give, and because even many alleged coalition countries wanted a UN resolution before they would join in the occupation. Although the UN and the international community had considerable leverage, the United States secured key concessions.

First, under UN Resolution 1483 of 22 May 2003, it secured the right to sell Iraqi oil and use the revenues. The surplus from the oil-for-food program was to be handed over, along with any Iraqi funds across the globe, to the "Iraqi Development Fund," to help fund the occupiers' responsibilities, and though the fund was to be monitored by an independent board, with representatives from the UN, US noncooperation made that a dead letter. The board has never been able to find out exactly what happened to this money, which was eventually to total over $10 billion. The US courts in the "Custer Battles" case decided that if there was no money from the US Treasury involved, then it was not even possible to prosecute companies that looted the development fund.

Resolution 1483 also welcomed the "willingness" of other states to provide troops, thus giving a UN fig leaf to the many hitherto nominal coalition members who would want to ingratiate themselves further with the White House by sending troops, without themselves having the obloquy and legal obligations of occupying powers. Given the reality of US power and its fait accompli, the Security Council substantially gave Washington what it wanted. In effect, the UN provided a legal framework for the functioning of an occupation that resulted from an invasion that most of its members considered illegal.

As part of these developments, the UN did, however, secure a foothold in Iraq. Kofi Annan appointed UN Commissioner for Human Rights Sergio Vieira de Mello as UN representative in Iraq. He was able to speak to factions in Iraq that would not talk to the Americans, and used his influence to ensure that the US-appointed interim governing council was representative of more than just the Iraqi exiles whom the Americans brought with them. However, in retrospect, most UN officials, including Kofi Annan, felt that the price of close involvement with the United States was too high. There is no way of telling if the terrorists who blew up the UN headquarters in Baghdad on 19 August 2003 were really interested in the nuances of UN resolutions, but the explosion and the death of de Mello certainly reinforced the fairly general feeling in the Secretariat staff that the organization had allowed itself to be too closely identified with the occupation. Annan withdrew the UN international staff, and effectively kept them outside the country as the security situation grew progressively worse.

But by then, the White House was itself perturbed that events were not following the script written by the war's promoters. It began to see a genuinely vital role of the UN: getting the United States out of the hole it had dug for itself. In view of the failure of the previous resolutions to entice more troop contributions, the United States wanted a resolution that would be more successful in doing so, and in coaxing more contributions and cash for reconstruction from reluctant governments. It wanted the return of UN civilian staff to Iraq and for the UN to legitimize the occupation in the face of the resistance. The key issue for which Russia, France, and Germany had been holding out was a timetable for a constitution, elections, and independence. Resolution 1511 of 16 October 2003 provided for that. It amounted to a timetable for a timetable: the Iraqi Governing Council was to present a timetable for a constitution and elections by 15 December; it also laid out the steps for a handover of authority. The former occupying army became a multinational force present at the request of the government it had installed.

The resolution also "requested" the Secretary-General to send civilian personnel back to Iraq "as circumstances permit" in order to help with rebuilding and the electoral process. Annan promised to do his utmost, "bearing in mind the constraints on building up the required capacity, and my obligation to care for the safety and security of United Nations staff."

But even a year later, at the beginning of 2005, most of the UN civilian staff were still outside the country. The UN position became one of not returning to Iraq until security had been restored. No more than the other resolutions did 1511 secure additional troop contributions. Indeed, as attacks on those present increased, more and more countries withdrew their token forces.

In 2004, as Bush faced reelection amid continuing resistance in Iraq, the United States, wanting to give the appearance of a transfer of sovereignty to Iraq and playing with the idea of Iraqi elections, became aware of the usefulness of a UN role, especially as the Iraqis were keen for "the unique legitimacy" that the UN could confer on a postoccupation regime. The United States wanted the UN to send a technical mission to Iraq to advise on the feasibility of elections. By the time the debate began in May 2004 over what would become Resolution 1546, the balance of power had shifted against Washington, given doubts as to whether Bush would be reelected, the torture pictures and stories from US prisons in Iraq, and the failure to find weapons of mass destruction.

The resolution held that US troops were to lose their mandate as soon as the constitutional process was finished, and that their presence could be "reviewed" even earlier—as soon as the Iraqi government wanted and in any case within twelve months. Those sunset clauses were insurance against Bush and his administration changing their minds were the president to be reelected. One of the main fudges in the resolution was over the extent to which the Iraqi administration had effective direction, if not direct command and control, of the so-called multinational force (the occupation forces). Powell's compromise pledge—in an exchange of letters—endorsed by the resolution but not in the text itself, was that "the commander of the [multinational force] will work in partnership with the sovereign Government of Iraq in helping to provide security while recognizing and respecting its sovereignty." This bows to the Pentagon by not giving the Iraqis an explicit veto, and to the Security Council and the Iraqis by reemphasizing the latter's sovereignty. Hastily contrived, verbose, fudged, and filled with diplomatic ambiguity as it is, Security Council Resolution 1546 was an epitaph to the wilder dreams entertained by the more extreme unilateralists in the US administration, since for all its failings, it was the UN that was to provide legitimacy and certify the sovereignty of the new Iraqi administration.

The appointment of Lakhdar Brahimi as the Special Representative of the Secretary-General was indispensable for reaching any type of agreement on a new interim government or on elections among the Iraqi factions. Without his role, it would not have been possible to form the interim government on 30 June 2004. Brahimi brokered the timetable and modalities of the elections, but Annan resisted US demands for a substantial UN presence in monitoring the elections, given the lack of security on the ground. Still, the insistence of the United States on a UN presence was an oblique testimony that only the United Nations could declare a handover to be legitimate and genuine. There was a price. The press furor over the alleged "oil-for-food scandal" was originally fomented by figures who objected to Brahimi's exclusion from a central role in the interim government of Ahmed Chalabi and other Iraqi exiles originally favored by the Pentagon, and who also disliked Annan's lack of support for the US enterprise in Iraq. Although Annan was eventually cleared of any criminal or unethical behavior, his negotiating power was certainly weakened by the long scandal and the inquiry that he was forced to convene.

■ Conclusion

The failure of the United States and United Kingdom to be bound by the UN has had damaging consequences for world order; for example, it has tended to discredit the notion of "humanitarian intervention," reinforcing third world suspicions that the invasion of Iraq was only a ploy to cover Western hegemony. Quite apart from the issues of national sovereignty, and the rights or wrongs of enforced regime change, it is difficult to avoid the conclusion, too, that Iraq would be in better shape, and the world a safer place, if the United States had not been prevented by its ideologues from involving the United Nations in a more realistic and meaningful way right from the beginning. On the other hand, the invaders had to concede eventually that they needed the UN's "unique legitimacy" to cope with diplomatic, legal, and indeed economic outcomes of their unilateral actions.

■ Notes

1. Richard Perle, *The Guardian,* March 21 2003.
2. Hans Blix, *Disarming Iraq;* personal interviews.
3. Ibid.
4. Personal interview.

22

The Role of
International Law and Ethics

Anthony F. Lang Jr.

C an normative analysis contribute anything to our understanding of why
the United States went to war with Iraq? An increasing number of
scholars and political analysts are turning to normative analyses to further
our understanding of international affairs and the use of force more specifically.[1] Yet while there is an increased interest in this form of analysis, many
political analysts believe that a focus on ethics or even international law
ignores the material concerns that actually motivate foreign policy, a position described by Stephen Krasner:

> Outcomes in the international system are determined by rulers whose vio-
> lation of, or adherence to, international principles or rules is based on cal-
> culations of material and ideational interests, not taken-for-granted prac-
> tices derived from some overarching institutional structures or deeply
> embedded generative grammars. Organized hypocrisy is the normal state
> of affairs.[2]

Such a dismissal is unsustainable if an analyst is interested in understanding
the practices of international relations. For normative factors have an
important impact that recent work in both the social sciences and more
humanist modes of analysis have identified. This "constructivist" turn in
international relations theory points to not only the importance of ideas but
specifically normative ideas in the structure of international affairs.[3]

Focusing on norms is particularly useful in understanding the war in Iraq,
for moral discourse and legal interpretations actually may have played a role
in causing the war. This does not mean that the war can be justified morally or
legally; rather, the point of this chapter is to demonstrate that the "moralism"
so characteristic of US foreign policy came out with stunning certainty in the
Bush administration's policy toward Iraq. Even international law, toward
which many critics of the war turned, reflecting as it does the interests of the
most powerful, perhaps contributed to the outbreak of the war.

Yet ethics and law can also serve as restraints on action. By focusing on the concept of justice, particularly in interpretations of Security Council resolutions and the just war tradition, there are grounds for disputing the Bush administration's claim that the war was moral and legal. When seen through the lens of justice, the war can be seen as a clear violation of the norms that the United States and United Kingdom were supposedly seeking to advance.

■ Norms as Causes

The initiation of hostilities between the United States and Iraq in spring 2003 can be explained by numerous variables but the norms specific to US political culture may be one of them. A norm can be defined as the "collective expectations about the proper behavior of actors with a given identity" with both constitutive and regulative effects on agents.[4] Three norms articulated by US elites seem most important in motivating or justifying to the public the decision to launch the war with Iraq:

1. The promotion of particular liberal ideals benefits not only the United States but also all nations by increasing the sphere of freedom and peace.[5]
2. The United States alone is the guardian of the international system against dangers such as terrorism and nuclear proliferation.
3. States that defy the United States on these issues should be considered "rogues" that can be sanctioned in various ways, including the most extreme sanction of complete regime change through military force.

These norms, importantly, are not unique to the Bush administration. Rather, they result from historically grounded assumptions of US foreign policy, post–Cold War debates about US foreign policy, and particular ideas of the neoconservative movement with which the Bush administration is closely identified.

The first norm, that the United States is responsible for promoting its particular form of liberalism around the world, has been part of US foreign policy since the country's founding, manifest in the Puritan belief in the creation of the "city on a hill,"[6] the nineteenth-century concept of "manifest destiny,"[7] and the ideas of Woodrow Wilson.[8] When the Cold War ended, US policymakers drew even more heavily on this tradition of exporting US ideals, notably the Clinton administration's policy of "engagement and enlargement" of democratic, capitalist states around the world.[9]

How did this norm inform the decision to launch the war with Iraq? In one interview, Bush made clear his commitment to the export of US notions of freedom: "I believe that the United States is the beacon for freedom in the world. And I believe we have a responsibility to promote freedom that is as solemn as the responsibility is to protecting the American people, because the two go hand in hand . . . it's very important you understand that about my presidency."[10] Others in the administration argued that the example of freedom in Iraq would lead to freedom throughout the Middle East.[11] Paul Wolfowitz, the deputy secretary of defense and a leading neoconservative intellectual in the administration, took the teachings of Leo Strauss and Allan Bloom to mean that the United States could transform the world along the lines of freedom and democracy.[12]

The second norm, that the United States alone has a responsibility to protect the international system from various dangers, was encouraged by the belief that, with the end of the Cold War, the United States could act unilaterally rather than rely on the multilateral institutions. While the Clinton administration came to office proclaiming a policy of multilateralism, in practice it soon edged toward unilateralism.[13] The Bush administration further embraced this norm. For the neoconservatives, the United States must lead the world, and according to a clear moral compass that makes distinctions between right and wrong.[14] Vice President Dick Cheney and Wolfowitz made this case most forcefully in their authorship of the defense policy guidance document written at the end of the first Bush administration, which argued that the United States should be the sole leader of the international community for the indefinite future, and, to ensure this, should prevent any other power from rising to challenge it. Based not only on power politics, this paper is infused with a moral claim that the United States has a responsibility to ensure international order. The same thinking appeared in the Project for the New American Century with which many of the current Bush administration officials are associated.[15]

In the case of the war with Iraq, this norm manifested itself in the Bush administration's rhetoric that the United States was only seeking to enforce UN resolutions concerning Iraq. Rather than pursuing its own interests, the United States was working to give the UN real "teeth."[16] In a speech to the UN General Assembly, George W. Bush made clear his belief that the United States needed to challenge the UN to live up to its mandates, when he asked, "Are Security Council resolutions to be honored and enforced, or cast aside without consequence? Will the United Nations serve the purpose of its founding, or will it be irrelevant?"[17]

The final norm, punishment of "rogue states," was reflected in the Bush administration's case that Iraq was in "material breach" of its obligations under Security Council resolutions. The idea that the Iraqi regime should be punished for its violations of international law, particularly the UN resolutions, was an important justification for the British in their support for US actions.[18]

Constructivist international relations theory would suggest that these norms could be seen as causes of the war, although not the only causes. They were used to mobilize support for a war that carried heavy risks for US national interests,[19] and they served as a counternorm to overcome the standard international law and Security Council procedures upheld by most other states, including some traditional allies of the United States, that might have restrained US action. But the US leadership did not rely solely on these ideals; rather, it sought to construct a legal argument for the war as well.

■ Law and Justice

The legal justification of the war with Iraq draws upon two primary rationales: preemptive self-defense and the failure of Iraq to comply with its obligations under various UN Security Council resolutions. The first legal argument suggests how interpretations of principles designed to limit war can, occasionally, be used to promote war. Self-defense is one of the two conditions under which the use of force is allowed in international law. Article 51 of the UN Charter states quite clearly that despite its overall spirit of promoting peaceful settlement of disputes, "nothing in the present Charter shall impair the inherent right of individual or collective self-defense." At the same time, this provision is qualified by the phrase "if an armed attack occurs." In other words, the Charter would appear to prohibit the use of force by any state until after it has been attacked.

Prior to the charter there existed general prohibitions on the use of force that nevertheless accepted the possibility of "anticipatory self-defense" or preemption.[20] The right to preemptive self-defense was articulated but also sharply circumscribed by Daniel Webster in the celebrated "Caroline" case, in which US sailors were attacked by Canadian soldiers in 1837 on the grounds that they were a threat; Webster argued that such a preemptive threat was only justified if "the necessity of that self-defense is instant, overwhelming and leaving no choice for means, and no moment for deliberation."[21] The Bush administration suggested that it might undertake such preemptive military actions in its national security strategy statement of September 2002. In that document, the administration argued that the law governing the use of force must take into account new technologies and new radical groups that could attack the United States without any prior warning.[22] The regime of Saddam Hussein was said to fulfill the criteria of an adversary that was prepared to and capable of attacking the United States. As the US Department of State's legal adviser concluded:

> A central consideration, at least from the U.S. point of view, was the risk embodied in allowing the Iraqi regime to defy the international community by pursuing weapons of mass destruction. . . . Both the United States and the international community had a firm basis for using pre-emptive force in the face of the past actions by Iraq and the threat that it posed, as seen over a protracted period of time.[23]

In spite of this argument, what the Bush administration proposed was not preemptive military action, but preventive or anticipatory self-defense. Iraq did not pose an immediate threat to the US homeland at the moment of the war. The administration could not make a clear claim for why this particular moment justified waging war.[24] Instead, this was a war for preventing future possible attacks by the regime of Saddam Hussein. Such actions are clearly illegal. They violate the spirit of the twentieth century that sought to outlaw anticipatory military actions. Indeed, the launch of World War I can be seen as one large preventive war, undertaken by various sides linked by alliances. The way in which the current international legal structure arose from that war suggests that it was designed to prevent such actions. The assumption against preventive war does imply some form of collective security that only very imperfectly exists, but, as Chris Brown notes, it is still prudent to avoid preventive wars for they threaten the world system with utter chaos.[25] Richard Betts also argues, "Preventive war is almost always a bad choice, strategically as well as morally."[26] Preventive war, then, is both legally and prudentially wrong. It not only undermines the international law on use of force, but could also potentially encourage a destabilizing outbreak of further wars. The US use of this argument (it was much less a part of the UK argument) demonstrates how legal principles can be abused by the most powerful, even when they fly in the face of almost all evidence.[27]

The other legal potential justification for the war with Iraq, while plausible at one level, fails upon closer examination. Both the US and British governments argued that the launching of war on 20 March 2003 was triggered by the Iraqi regime's failure to comply with Security Resolution 1441, passed unanimously on 8 November 2002. This resolution made the case that Iraq was in "material breach" of its obligations under previous Security Council resolutions, specifically 678 of November 1990 and 687 of April 1991, which required Iraq to disarm and produce clear and compelling evidence that it had destroyed all its weapons of mass destruction (WMDs), along with any missiles or missile technology capable of firing over 150 kilometers.

Stating that Iraq was in material breach of these obligations as of the date of passage of Resolution 1441, the resolution goes on to state that the Council will give Iraq one more chance. Beginning from 8 November, the Iraqis had exactly thirty days to comply with the provisions of the previous resolutions, that is, to provide "a currently accurate, full and complete declaration of all aspects of its programmes related to weapons of mass destruction." Furthermore, any "false statements or omissions" would mean Iraq was in further material breach of the previous resolutions. If Iraq failed to comply, the resolution stated that it would face "serious consequences"— the strongest language the drafters of the resolution were able to generate.

The organization responsible for ensuring that Iraq was disarming was the UN Monitoring, Verification, and Inspections Commission (UNMOVIC). This UN body was responsible for issuing reports to the Security Council on the process of Iraq's disarmament. The report following the November 2002 resolution was delivered on 28 February 2003 by Hans Blix, the executive chairman. In that report, Blix distinguished between cooperation in "process"—or enabling UNMOVIC inspectors to continue their work in Iraq unimpeded—and in "substance"—or providing actual evidence of disarmament. While noting that Iraq was cooperating in terms of process, the report notes that Iraq in its recent statement to the commission did not provide any new evidence. Moreover, during the time covered by the report, "Iraq could have made greater efforts to find any remaining proscribed items or provide credible evidence showing the absence of such items."[28]

On 6 March 2003, UNMOVIC issued a larger report to the Council titled "Unresolved Disarmament Issues: Iraq's Proscribed Weapons Program." This report, referred to as the Cluster Report because it clustered together various unresolved issues, distinguished between the 1991–1998 period and the post-1998 period, when UN inspectors had been removed from the country. The report suggests that while Iraq claims it had not engaged in any "proscribed" activities during the 1998–2003 period, "such a declaration needs to be supported by evidence," evidence that the report indicates was not forthcoming from Iraqi authorities.[29]

UNMOVIC never declared Iraq in material breach of its obligations, nor was this its responsibility. Rather, the evidence provided by UNMOVIC, and reinforced by presentations before the Security Council by US officials, was selectively used to suggest that Iraq was not being completely up-front about its WMD programs. To make this point is not to agree that these provisions were just or to suggest that all the claims made by the US—such as that Iraq was cooperating with terrorists—were true. Rather, on the limited legal grounds of failing to live up to its obligations under various UN Security Council resolutions, particularly 687 and 1441, it could be construed that Iraq was in violation of the law, which is exactly what the United States did.

Yet claiming that Iraq was in violation of these particular resolutions does not equate to Iraq being in violation of larger principles of international order or morality. Rather, one could argue that the resolutions put a completely intolerable burden upon the regime, that is, the regime had to demonstrate it did not have something, a confession that can always be called into question. This suggests that the Security Council, essentially an arena in which the most powerful states make rules from which they benefit, may not be the best system for generating just international outcomes.

The consequences of Iraq's purported failure to conform to those resolutions were not clear. Many argued that the United Kingdom and United States were required to return to the Security Council for a resolution agreeing that the claimed Iraq breaches authorized the use of force after 1441. In response to this point, the British attorney general, Lord Goldsmith, argued that the Security Council's wording that it would "decide" what the proper response was rather than "consider" gave the United States and United Kingdom the right to decide unilaterally on the use of military force.[30] The other permanent members of the Council—France, Russia, and China—raised strong objections to this logic. Pragmatically, they also argued that the Council should let the inspections process continue and that UNMOVIC had yet to find any serious violations but was still in the process of collecting information. The fact that the United States and United Kingdom refused the demand of the other members of the Security Council that the Council as a whole had to determine whether Iraq was in breach of its obligations implies that the will of the international community was not respected. It would seem, then, that according to the legal arguments of both self-defense and violation of UN resolutions, the war against Iraq was illegal.

If this interpretation is correct—that the law promulgated by the Security Council resolutions and interpreted by its leading great power can result in injustice—we need to think more clearly about the relationship of justice to war. Such thinking can be found in the just war tradition. With its criteria of *jus ad bellum*—the justice of initiating a war—and *jus in bello*—the justice of how to wage war—the just war tradition provides guidelines on how to evaluate particular instances of the use of force. Its *jus ad bellum* standards—just cause, right authority, right intention, last resort, and probability of success—are often used to determine the justice of particular wars.

Rather than mechanistically applying these criteria to evaluate the war with Iraq,[31] it is more useful to examine the war through two overarching debates among those engaged in utilizing the tradition: (1) Should the tradition assume a "presumption" against war or against injustice? (2) Is the tradition a list of principles to be applied or a body of thought for aid in reflecting on particular situations? For these debates help identify some of the contested issues in evaluations of the war with Iraq from within the tradition. Indeed, there is not one agreed-upon determination about the war, with supporters and dissenters both employing the tradition to support their evaluation.

This debate has its origins in one of the first debates within the tradition, pitting early pacifist Christian thought based in the presumption against war against the ideas of the fifth-century bishop Augustine of Hippo, who argued that war could be used to pursue justice.[32] James Turner Johnson, a historian of the latter tradition, argued, "The use of armed force is not itself a moral issue, but whether the use of force does or does not serve the cause of a just human order and the goal of peace."[33] Those who have made a case that a war with Iraq is justified according to the just war tradition—such as Johnson[34] and George Weigel[35]—have argued that the dangers faced by the United States from terrorists and rogue states demand military action. Their arguments do not rely on avoiding war at all costs, but rather in ensuring a *tranquillitas ordinis,* to use Weigel's phrase; that is, a just and peaceful order that can only be created through occasional uses of force.

Those who employ the tradition to argue against the war, on the other hand, tend to support the idea that the tradition has a presumption against the use of force except under sharply limited conditions. A number of Christian churches, including the Vatican and the Catholic Church in the United States, drawing upon both the just war tradition and international law, came out against the war. The Vatican argued: "The concept of 'preventive war' is not found in the moral principles of just-war theory—not even if it is authorized by a vote of the United Nations."[36] Bishop Wilton Gregory, president of the US Conference of Catholic Bishops, sent a letter to George W. Bush on 13 September 2002 in which he stated that Catholic bishops in the United States "fear that resort to force [in Iraq] would not meet the strict conditions in Catholic teaching for overriding the strong presumption against the use of military force."[37] The conference mirrored Gregory's statement, reviewing the just war criteria, namely that war had to be declared by the proper authority—that it be waged in self-defense, that peaceful means be exhausted, that the amount of force not be excessive and innocents spared; there had to be proportionality between the ends and means—and concluding that the war with Iraq was not justified according to the tradition.

Along with the Catholic Church, the Anglican Church in the United States and United Kingdom opposed the war with Iraq. The current Archbishop of Canterbury, Rowan Williams, argues that the tradition is based upon a presumption against war.[38] The House of Bishops of the Anglican Church issued a statement to Parliament on 9 October 2002 in which it concluded that "a preventive war against Iraq at this juncture would be to lower the threshold for war unacceptably."[39] The Episcopal Church of the United States stated in a letter to members of the US Congress that the use of force would not accord with the just war tradition.[40]

It is important to note that the arguments made by the Roman Catholic and Anglican churches focus primarily on the failure of the war to live up to the just cause of self-defense, a point that some scholars argue is not the only legitimate criterion.[41] More important, however, those who argue that the war was undertaken to support justice fail to provide a coherent definition of what justice would result from the war with Iraq. It might be the case that removing a single dictator from power would be just for those in that country. But the failure to plan for the aftermath of the war suggests that the Bush administration was not acting in support of justice for those in Iraq.

Moreover, the war certainly did not create justice on a wider scale in the international community. The point here is not to suggest that the tradition has a presumption in favor of peace; rather, it is to suggest that those who argue it has a presumption in favor of justice fail to articulate what that justice is and how it manifested itself in Iraq. Moreover, one of the most important theorists of the just war tradition, Michael Walzer—who clearly believes that tradition should be about pursuing justice—found the war unjust.[42] But in making that case, Walzer did not simply condemn the United States and Great Britain. Rather, he offered up a challenge and a set of alternatives. He challenged the international community to develop better ways to disarm Iraq (which he saw as a legitimate and worthy goal and that contributed to a just world order) and to bring the other great powers, such as France, Germany, and Russia, to play a greater role in the diplomatic and military efforts needed to disarm the regime. For Walzer, evaluating the war is not a moment to list criteria and check off how they were fulfilled or not in this case. Rather, the war is an opportunity to reflect upon the challenges facing the international system and to suggest ways to reorient the international community toward greater attention to justice and peace. Specifically, in my view, it is worth examining the issue of whether UN Security Council resolutions are likely to produce just outcomes.

■ Conclusion

This chapter has not provided a single critique of the war with Iraq but has reviewed a few different forms of evaluation to suggest how ethics remains relevant to our understandings of international affairs. At the same time, it has suggested that ethical argument and rhetoric, when yoked to powerful interests, can actually lead to conflict rather than constrain it. And while international law remains paramount for both understanding and evaluation, its principles arise from a somewhat unjust order (i.e., a Security Council dominated by great powers). By drawing on the concept of justice, especially as it is articulated in the just war tradition, the morality of US ethical and legal discourse can be critically assessed, providing limits on the pursuit of power rather than enabling it.

In conclusion, it is appropriate to quote another US president who was also prone to employing moralistic language, but for different purposes. In the days leading up to the launch of the war against Iraq, former president Jimmy Carter published an opinion piece in the *New York Times* titled "Just War—or a Just War?" He ended his article with the following:

> The heartfelt sympathy and friendship offered to America after the 9/11 attacks, even from formerly antagonistic regimes, has been largely dissipated; increasingly unilateral and domineering policies have brought international trust in our country to its lowest level in memory. American stature will surely decline further if we launch a war in clear defiance of the United Nations. But to use the presence and threat of our military power to force Iraq's compliance with all United Nations resolutions—with war as a final option—will enhance our status as a champion of peace and justice.[43]

Carter's appeal suggests that if the United States wishes to live up to the norms that supposedly inform its foreign policy, it will need to remember that moral and legal principles are not simply for enabling military action, but should serve to constrain it as well.

▪ Notes

1. See Anthony Lang Jr., Albert C. Pierce, and Joel H. Rosenthal, eds., *Ethics and the Future of Conflict,* for a sample of both scholarly and policy oriented articles in this general vein.
2. Stephen Krasner, *Sovereignty,* p. 9.
3. "Constructivist" is a term with a wide range of interpretations, stretching from the postpositivist to more social scientific modes. For analyses from the former category, see Hakan Seckinelgin and Hideaki Shinoda, eds., *Ethics and International Relations,* and from the latter, see Peter Katzenstein, ed., *The Culture of National Security.*
4. See introduction to Katzenstein, *Culture of National Security,* p. 5.
5. Liberal ideals here can include democracy, individual freedom, capitalist economics, or various versions of human rights. These are not exactly the same in each era, but they all coalesce around certain assumptions in the US political tradition.
6. For the "city on a hill," see Jonathan Winthrop's sermon reprinted in Thomas Paterson and Dennis Merrill, eds., *Major Problems in American Foreign Relations,* vol. 1, pp. 29–30.
7. Walter Russell Mead, *Special Providence.*
8. Frank A. Ninkovich, *The Wilsonian Century.*
9. US Government, *A National Security Strategy of Engagement and Enlargement* (Washington, DC: US Government Printing Office, 1994), pp. 18–19.
10. Bob Woodward, *Plan of Attack,* p. 88.
11. It is important to clarify here that the motives behind the attack are most certainly much wider than the normative ones I identify here. That is, Bush himself

and members of his administration may have had a number of motives (personal gain, belief in primacy of the United States) that prompted the attack. Materialist explanations of foreign policy tend to discount any ethical motives by assuming that what drives all actors is personal gain or concern about security; see, for example, Bruce Bueno de Mesquita et al., *The Logic of Political Survival,* for such an argument. In fact, however, no one can really know motives; all we can do as analysts is seek to provide explanations based on certain assumptions about politics, actions, and outcomes.

12. Some have argued that Wolfowitz and others in the neoconservative movement are animated more by a Zionist preoccupation with protecting Israel in their Middle East policies. But Wolfowitz served as assistant secretary of state for Asian affairs during the Reagan administration, where he played an important role in the toppling of the Philippine dictator Ferdinand Marcos. The lessons he drew from that episode seem to have powerfully influenced his views on the importance of US support for democracy. See James Mann, *Rise of the Vulcans,* for a fuller explanation of Wolfowitz's views and the translation of those views into his policies on Iraq.

13. Robert Luttwak, *Rogue States and U.S. Foreign Policy,* pp. 39–40.

14. Mann, *Rise of the Vulcans,* pp. 72–73.

15. Ibid., pp. 209–215. See also Robert Kagan and Gary Schmitt, *Rebuilding America's Defenses: Strategy, Forces, and Resources for a New Century* (Project for the New American Century, 2000), http://www.newamericancentury.org/rebuildingamericasdefenses.pdf.

16. Woodward, *Plan of Attack,* pp. 180–185.

17. George W. Bush, "President's Remarks at the United Nations General Assembly, September 12, 2002," obtained from Cian O'Driscoll, "A Charge to Keep, a Law to Serve, a War to Wage: How the Language of Punishment Figured in Bush and Blair's Justifications for the Invasion of Iraq," paper delivered to the British International Studies Association meeting, University of Warwick, December 2004, p. 16.

18. O'Driscoll, "A Charge to Keep," p. 19.

19. See John Mearsheimer and Stephen Walt, "An Unnecessary War.".

20. Louis Henkin, *International Law,* p. 927, quoting Oscar Schacter.

21. Quoted in ibid., p. 872.

22. US National Security Council, *The National Security Strategy of the United States of America,* p. 15.

23. William H. Taft IV and Todd F. Buchwald, "Preemption, Iraq, and International Law," p. 563.

24. See Ruth Wedgewood, "The Fall of Saddam Hussein," p. 581.

25. Chris Brown, "Self-Defence in an Imperfect World," p. 4.

26. Richard Betts, "Striking First," p. 18.

27. The point being made here is not that the revelation that there were no weapons of mass destruction undermines the legal argument. Rather, the point is that even if weapons of mass destruction existed, a preventive military action was not justified. A preemptive war might be justifiable, but such wars must be launched at a moment much closer to when an attack could be made.

28. United Nations, *Twelfth Quarterly Report of the Executive Chairman of the UN Monitoring, Verification, and Inspection Commission (UNMOVIC),* UN Doc. S/2002/232, February 28, 2003, http://www.un.org/depts/unmovic/new/documents/quarterly_reports/s-2003-232.pdf.

29. UN Monitoring, Verification, and Inspections Commission (UNMOVIC), *Unresolved Disarmament Issues: Iraq's Proscribed Weapons Programmes,* March 6,

2003, http://www.un.org/depts/unmovic/new/documents/cluster_document.pdf, p. 4.

30. United Kingdom, *Iraq: Legal Position Concerning the Use of Force,* March 17, 2003, http://www.fco.gov.uk/files/kfile/iraq%20-%20use%20of%20force. pdf, pp. 4–5.

31. See Nicholas Rengger, "On the Just War Tradition in the Twenty-First Century," for an argument as to why viewing the tradition as a "checklist" ignores its deeper insights into justice and war.

32. See Augustine of Hippo, *Political Writings.*

33. James Turner Johnson, "Can Force Be Used Justly? Questions of Retributive and Restorative Justice," 2001 Kuyper Lecture, delivered at Gordon College, Wenham, Massachusetts, 1 November 2001, p. 7.

34. Johnson, James Turner, "Using Force Against the Saddam Hussein Regime: The Moral Issues," lecture delivered at the Foreign Policy Research Institute, 4 December 2002, http://www.fpri.org/enotes/americawar.20021204. johnson.militaryagainsthusseinmoralissues.html.

35. Rowan Williams and George Weigel, "War and Statecraft."

36. Joaquin Navarro-Valls, Vatican spokesperson, interview with *Catholic News Service,* March 5, 2003, http://www.usccb.org/sdwp/peace/quotes.htm.

37. Bishop Wilton D. Gregory, "Letter to President Bush on Iraq," September 12, 2002, http://www.usccb.org/sdwp/international/bush902.htm.

38. Williams and Weigel, "War and Statecraft."

39. Church of England, House of Bishops, "Evaluating the Threat of Military Action against Iraq: A Submission by the House of Bishops to the House of Commons Foreign Affairs Select Committee's Ongoing Inquiry into the War Against Terrorism," http://www.cofe.anglican.org/info/socialpublic/iraq_-_submission_to_ the_foreign_affairs_selection_committee_-_house_of_bishops.doc.

40. Episcopal Church of the United States, "A Letter from the House of Bishops of the Episcopal Church," October 2, 2002, http://www.episcopalchurch. org/1866_6738_eng_print.html.

41. See O'Driscoll, "A Charge to Keep."

42. Michael Walzer, *Arguing About War,* pp. 143–170.

43. Jimmy Carter, "Just War—or a Just War?" *New York Times,* 9 March 2003.

Part 4

Theoretical Implications

23

Hegemonic Stability Theory Reconsidered: Implications of the Iraq War

Raymond Hinnebusch

The Iraq War was less about some putative threat from a debilitated Iraq than it was about the US determination to "play the world hegemon."[1] The war sharply underlined the fact and consequences of US hegemony in world politics. The tradition that has most consistently addressed the role of US global leadership is one of the centerpieces of the international relations (IR) and international political economy (IPE) disciplines, namely hegemonic stability theory (HST). The Iraq War is arguably a watershed in America's global role that calls for a major reconsideration of this body of literature.

■ The Role of Hegemony in the Literature

The idea of a hegemon, appearing as it does in all of the three traditional rival schools of IR/IPE,[2] has clearly captured a central reality of world politics. The consensus is that the hegemon is qualitatively different from other states, its function global. For liberals, a hegemon is needed to establish international regimes that permit an open economy and to provide "public goods" such as a common currency. World systems theorists argue that a hegemon is needed to promote the globalization of capitalism against the fragmentation of the states system (i.e., to provide the predictable environment and enforceable property rights needed for global capital accumulation) and, having the largest, most competitive economy, the hegemon has the biggest stake in this process.[3] While HST began as an explanation for the maintenance of free trade, realists like Gilpin argued that the anarchic world system was vulnerable to disorder without the security provided by a hegemon.[4] All agree that, while the hegemon has predominant military power and economic resources, hegemony, being something less than coercive empire, cannot persist without legitimacy: it is accepted by many states as long as the hegemon defends a world order that benefits more actors than itself.

However, if there is agreement that hegemony is based on a combination of power and consent, there is disagreement on the mix, on how benign, self-interested, or even predatory the hegemon may be, on how indispensable it is to the founding and persistence of international regimes and to global cooperation, and over how equitable the regimes it establishes are likely to be. The weakness of all versions of HST, exposed by the Iraq War, is their failure to appreciate that a "hegemon" may be a source of global *disorder.*

The Debates over Hegemonic Stability Theory

Is Hegemony Benign?

The liberal version of HST, in particular, sees the US hegemon as benign. It abstracts from post–World War II experience, when liberals saw the United States as providing indispensable public goods—security against the USSR and the benefits of free trade—for other states whose free-riding eroded the hegemon's relative position. Thus the United States provided world liquidity by running a balance of payments deficit that undermined confidence in the dollar, exported investment that undermined its own competitiveness, and kept its markets open even when its allies did not.[5]

This benign version of HST, however, has been under sustained attack. The idea of an altruistic hegemon defies the core traditions of realist and Marxist thought, which expect large asymmetries of power to produce large maldistributions of benefits. Classical realism, of course, sees a *balance* of power—seemingly the opposite of hegemony—as the key to avoiding the twin evils of domination and war. For Isabelle Grunberg, liberal HST reflects an ethnocentric myth that the United States is so uniquely virtuous that it uses its power differently than ordinary states.[6] For many critics, liberal HST overly generalized from and gave an excessively benign interpretation to a particular post–World War II episode of US leadership. Thus it ignored the fact that the United States extracted a quid quo pro: the opening of Europe and of dismantled European empires to US capital. Moreover, US leadership soon gave way to self-interested behavior: Susan Strange argued that, once the costs of hegemony rose, the United States tended to become predatory, and David Calleo showed that the disruptions in the Bretton Woods system in the 1970s were caused, not by the free-riding of others, but by the exploitative policy choices of the United States.[7] Jan Pieterse and others observed a creeping militarization and aggressive unilateralism (such as demands for market access) in post–Cold War US foreign policy, and especially under George W. Bush, a celebration of hard over soft power and a disparagement of allies and of the very rule-based system US hegemony had previously helped construct.[8]

By contrast to liberalism, realist versions of HST always acknowledged that the hegemon pursues its own interest. Thus it structures the world trading system to its own advantage and, while other competitive states will also benefit from free trade, the hegemon is able to "tax" the beneficiaries for its services.[9] A. F. K. Organski's version of realist HST assumes that the hegemonic order almost by definition excludes as well as includes and that there will be dissatisfied states that had no say in the order's creation and get few benefits from it; this is particularly so of the "periphery" states of the third world. He also argues that a strong, dissatisfied, perhaps number-two power will naturally challenge the hegemon for control of the international system by mobilizing the deprived periphery states.[10] This has the advantage of bringing in the role of the Soviet Union under bipolarity, the curiously missing actor in most HST. Arguably, it was the Soviet challenge, seen to threaten the open economy on which US prosperity depended, that was the main incentive for the hegemon to provide benefits—"public goods"—to its own allies and clients. It may be that the condition for benign hegemony is, after all, a sufficient *balance of power* to constrain the hegemon such as existed under bipolarity; but if we are in a "unipolar moment" when the United States no longer feels the need for willing allies or to accept constraints on its actions, there is little to prevent it from becoming predatory.

Is Hegemony Sufficient?

HST was preoccupied by the unrealistic fear that free-riding by other states would lead to the decline of the hegemon and hence to world disorder. To be sure, there was a relative decline in US power after the 1960s, but Samuel Huntington attributed it not to free-riding by others but overconsumption and undertaxation at home, and Paul Kennedy to "imperial overreach"— concerns that the policy of the Bush Jr. administration has revived.[11] Marxists, free of realism's state-centrism, were better equipped to dispute the extent of hegemonic decline, observing that, while the economic power of the US state, per se, appeared to decline relative to Europe and Japan once they recovered from World War II, US hegemony was sustained by its *structural power:* the power to make the rules and to structure the situation owing to the penetration of the economies of other states by US transnational corporations, their need for the massive US market, their reliance on the dollar as the international currency, the ideological hegemony deriving from US media corporations, and so forth—all of which made other states vulnerable to the hegemon. Marxists' disaggregation of the state into classes also allowed them to see that the costs of hegemony need not undermine its durability, since they are disproportionately paid by ordinary taxpayers while the ruling classes—the military industrial complex and multinational corporations—reap enormous profits and have therefore an incentive to sustain hegemony.[12] Generally, not only was the concern in mainstream HST that *insufficient* hegemonic power would lead to world disorder misplaced, but also, arguably, it led HST to neglect the equally real problem, namely, the possibly malign effects of *excessive* hegemonic power.

Is Hegemony Needed?

HST, particularly its realist version, is also problematic because of its insistence that a hegemon is essential to international cooperation. Realist HST argues that even if many states would gain from cooperation, most of them, fearing rivals would gain more and pose an enhanced security threat, eschew it; the hegemon, however, is so superior that it can take the risk of providing the public goods that facilitate cooperation. However, liberals have effectively demonstrated that states under conditions of complex interdependence will seek to reap absolute gains by cooperation through international regimes.[13] Marxists argue, moreover, that the collective action problem preoccupying realists has been overcome by the emergence of a trans-state capitalist class that bridges the remaining conflicts of interests between the national capitals of the core states (e.g., over markets) while the core exercises collective hegemony over the periphery, notably through international economic institutions.[14] This is consistent with non-Marxist arguments that the core states constitute a collective hegemon, which has replaced the sole US hegemon.[15] However, this view seems to underrate the possibility that aggressive US unilateralism might disrupt the core's collective hegemony. Indeed, as the hegemon now bypasses and weakens the UN and obstructs or refuses to sign up to the international regimes agreed by other states to resolve global problems—whether global warming, international financial regulation, or human rights abuses—many analysts would agree with Pieterse that "the world leader turns out to be a global bottleneck."[16] Thus realist HST not only exaggerates the need for hegemonic power to facilitate cooperation, but also ignores the possibility that it may *obstruct* it.

In summary, the central claims of HST that hegemony is both relatively benign and necessary to global order appear to be greatly overstated. Moreover, preoccupied with the supposed deleterious consequences of *insufficient* hegemonic power, HST neglects structural power and the opposing potential problem, the abuse of *excessive* power. Indeed, the theory must make greater allowance for the possibility of *malign* hegemony and be able to distinguish the conditions of benign and malign hegemony. As Duncan Snidel argued, "the common presumption that [hegemony] is widely beneficial rests on such special assumptions that it should be rejected"; the main issue is what factors determine whether "hegemony will be exploitative" or "will be constrained to operate in the more general inter-est."[17] I argue in this chapter that the US hegemon is turning malign, that the single most important driver of this is its policy toward the Middle East, and that the apotheosis of this policy, the war on Iraq, signals a turn toward coercive empire in place of hegemonic leadership by consent. This water-shed event confirms and extends accumulated doubts about mainstream HST.

■ Historical Context: US Hegemony, Oil, and Israel

A key pillar of US post–World War II hegemony, as Simon Bromley shows, has been the domination of the "world" oil resources concentrated in the Middle East by US companies, as well as the US role in containing any threats from either the USSR or local nationalism to the (usually) cheap energy needed by the capitalist world economy.[18] Moreover, US oil companies initially, and thereafter the US alliance with Saudi Arabia, were pivotal to oil price stability, which was crucial to global economic prosper-ity: cheap oil fueled post–World War II recovery while subsequent price shocks precipitated global recessions. However, whether this can be seen as the provision of a global "public good" is called into question by the increasing exercise of US hegemonic "responsibility" in ways that have stimulated challenges to it, and by periodic Middle Eastern conflicts that put energy security at risk.

The periodic challenges to US oil hegemony, far from being fortuitous, are rooted in the basic contradiction in US policy identified by Sherle Schwenninger: "For more than three decades, American policy has been driven by two at times incompatible goals: the support of Israel and (indi-rect) control over the world's oil markets. Managing the tensions between these two goals has been one of the most important and difficult policy challenges of every president since Lyndon Johnson." Moreover, the increasing breakdown in the US effort to manage this contradiction derives from the fact that, as Schwenninger argues, "US policy-makers have not in practice been able to distinguish between the legitimate defense of Israel and tacit support for its illegal occupation of the West Bank and Gaza Strip and its overly aggressive military policy."[19]

It is Washington's indiscriminate support of Israel that politicizes what would otherwise be a normal economic relation between Western oil con-sumers and the Arab oil producers and that obliges the United States to peri-odically confront crises that threaten Middle Eastern and global stability. The single most important key to depoliticizing oil is therefore a resolution of the Arab-Israeli conflict; this is what the international community expects of the hegemon, and there is an internationally accepted formula for doing so—UN Security Council Resolution 242, the land-for-peace solution, which the United States cosponsored and was formally committed to. As part of an effort to balance between Israel and its Arab clients, the United States has made periodic attempts to arrive at partial solutions, but its leadership of the peace process has been consistently compromised by the pro-Israeli lobby, and the more this lobby has achieved dominance in the policy process of the United States toward the Middle East, the more the United States has moved away from the evenhanded role expected of a global hegemon and toward becoming itself a party to the conflict. The result, Oystein Noreng observes, is that Washington is in a state of permanent hostility with many of the key Middle Eastern oil producers as well as regional public opinion, depriving its hegemony of legitimacy in the region and inviting periodic challenges that spill over into world crises.[20] According to Richard Betts, the United States failed to resolve the Arab-Israeli conflict precisely because its hegemonic power allowed its leaders to pay the international costs (from periodic crisis) rather than the domestic costs of confronting the Zionist lobby.[21] But in fact the United States, far from paying the costs of the politicization of oil, has managed to use Middle Eastern crises to reinforce its hegemony while off-loading their main costs onto others.[22]

A brief review of the historical record illustrates both how US policy precipitates oil crises and how it uses them to sustain hegemony at the expense of others. The first challenge to US oil hegemony was stimulated by Washington's rebuff of Egyptian efforts at a diplomatic settlement of the Arab-Israel conflict prior to the 1973 Arab-Israeli war and the arms deliveries to Israel in this war that prevented the Arab states from recovering territories occupied by Israel in the previous 1967 war. The oil embargo that this precipitated initially seemed to Keohane to mark a decline of US hegemony, as control of oil appeared forfeited to the Organization of Petroleum Exporting Countries (OPEC) at a time when US oil self-sufficiency was declining.[23]

But the United States managed to turn the oil crisis to its advantage by striking a close alliance with Saudi Arabia in which it provided security in return for the Saudis' use of their position as "swing producer" to moderate oil prices. Given the privileged position of the dollar as the international currency in which oil is sold, the new wealth of the oil producers was disproportionately "recycled" through US banks and via US arms purchases and investments in the United States. The hegemony of the United States is based on the dollar as much as its military; during the oil price boom of the 1970s, oil hegemony reinforced US dollar hegemony, because all states needed dollars to buy oil and needed access to the US market to get them. Michael Hudson and others argue that dollar seignurage allowed the United States to levy a tax on the world's economy to finance massive US military spending and imperial overreach, and to impose economic measures that hurt its competitors.[24] After the oil price boom, the competitive position of Europe and Japan declined as the price of their energy increased, ushering in the stagflation of the 1970s, followed by the Thatcherist attack on the European welfare state. The more limited damage of the boom on the United States was very disproportionately distributed: if consumers suffered, Texas oil barons got higher oil prices and power shifted to the military/oil industries concentrated in the Sunbelt, crucial in the rise of Ronald Reagan and the Republican right.[25] In the longer term, the US-Saudi alliance had, by the early 1980s, secured the stabilization of oil prices, which was followed thereafter by a precipitous price decline.

The next episode, the Gulf War (1990–1991), was the result of a long chain of events, mixing, to one degree or another, US policy toward the Middle East and oil, but it was unimaginable in a Middle East in which the Arab-Israeli conflict had been resolved; for one thing, it was only the stalemate in the peace process that led Saddam Hussein to think the time was right to seize pan-Arab leadership against Israel and to miscalculate that his invasion would spark an Arab nationalist arousal forcing the Arab states to accept his annexation of Kuwait. The subsequent US war on Iraq headed off a potent challenge to US oil hegemony: were Iraq to have retained Kuwaiti oil fields and remained in a position to intimidate Saudi Arabia, thereby acquiring "control" of over 40 percent of world oil reserves, it might have had the power to shape the oil market in ways inimical to US interests. While the conservative Gulf monarchies, by virtue of their security dependence on the United States and their Western investments, had a shared interest with the West in ensuring stable unpoliticized access to oil at moderate prices, Iraq had no such stake. Iraq was of course in dire need of revenues and had to sell its oil at prices consumers would pay; but Saddam's threat to make the terms of oil sales conditional on a favorable Western policy in the Arab-Israeli conflict caught US politicians between two powerful contradictory domestic demands—cheap gasoline and the advancement of Israel's interests. What was at stake, therefore, was not access to oil but access on *Washington's terms.*[26]

In the end, the war actually enabled Washington to *reinforce* its oil hegemony. The United States used the war to demonstrate its continuing indispensability to protecting the world capitalist core's control of oil against third world challenges; at the same time, in making Gulf clients of the United States, above all Saudi Arabia, more dependent on the United States for their security, the conflict enhanced the US protectorate over global oil resources. The war boosted the relative economic standing of the United States, for while Japanese and European capitalism had become more energy efficient, US capitalism, protected by the special benefits of hegemony, had built its competitiveness on low oil prices; the war ensured that prices would stay low and that Gulf petrodollars would be disproportionately recycled through US banks and firms. In addition, the United

States actually managed to make its imperial policing profitable by inducing its economic competitors (Germany, Japan) and clients (Saudi Arabia, Kuwait) to pay for the war.[27] There followed a decade in which US economic growth, outpacing that of its rivals, reestablished Washington's hitherto declining hegemonic position.

The downside, however, was that the Gulf War was merely a piece with the thrust of a US policy that had locked the world hegemon into a pattern of repeated interventions in the Middle East that, being sharply biased against Arab/Muslim actors, tended to further inflame regional hostility. This, especially when combined with the "blowback" resulting when regional surrogates fostered by the United States were either overthrown or later turned by its biased policies against their patron, repeatedly generated dangerous crises.[28] Thus the CIA overthrow of Iran's Mossadeq government ultimately produced Khomeni's Islamic revolution; Saddam Hussein was then built up by the United States and the West as a counter to Iran, and his oversized army posed a fateful temptation to seize Kuwait. But the most egregious case of blowback, 9/11, illustrates the intimate connection of oil, Israel, and regional violence. Al-Qaida, initially partly sponsored by the United States against the threat that the Soviets in Afghanistan allegedly posed to the Middle Eastern oil fields, was turned against its US patron by US policies growing out of the Gulf War: a heavy postwar US presence in Saudi Arabia, the heartland of Islam and of the region's oil; continued siege of (and semigenocidal sanctions imposed on) a defeated Iraq; and the blatant double standards by which the United States exempted Israel from the kinds of UN resolutions it claimed to be enforcing against Iraq.[29] In Slavoj Zizek's words, "it is as if some invisible hand of destiny repeatedly ensures that U.S. intervention only makes more likely the outcomes the United States sought most to avoid."[30] The result has been that every five to ten years, a Middle Eastern crisis, rooted in the linked struggles over oil and Israel, spills out of the region: 1956, 1967, 1973, 1979, 1982, 1990, 2001, 2003. Moreover, with each crisis, animosity toward the United States has steadily widened from the Arab heartland, to Iran, then Afghanistan, and now to the wider Islamic world, including the Muslim diaspora in the West itself. While Washington's response to these crises *could* have been to pursue more limited goals that accommodated the interests of Middle Eastern peoples, its actual response under George W. Bush was to use its rapidly increasing military power to try to impose its will on them.

■ Coercive Hegemony in Action: Explaining Bush's War on Iraq

The George W. Bush administration marks a qualitative escalation in the coercive character of US foreign policy in the Middle East. The administration saw the region as both the key to and the main threat to its global project to sustain and extend US global hegemony. The Bush government's ambitions were spelled out by the Project for the New American Century and in the Bush Doctrine's assertion of America's exceptionalism and unilateralism, its reach for "full spectrum dominance," and its right to impose a liberal world order—the only model seen as compatible with US security and from which no nation was to be exempted by the claims of sovereignty. The doctrine also invoked the right to deal with the resistance that hegemony inevitably provokes, not simply through traditional containment, but also via "preventive wars."[31] Preventive war on Iraq, advocated by hard-liners within the administration even *before* 9/11, was seen as the key to the hegemonic project.[32]

While the ideology—"war on terrorism," "liberal empire"—used to legitimate the Bush administration's project tends to take on a life of its own (as explicated in Chapter 22), it is incumbent on the analyst to uncover the interests it expresses and disguises and to understand why the project has taken a specific form, war in the Middle East and particularly war on *Iraq*. Indeed, an analysis of the Iraq War is pivotal to exposing the objective factors behind this new episode in US hegemony. We are in no position to get inside the heads of the policymakers or trace the intricacies of the policy process in order to know exactly what combination of interests and motives produced the decision for a war on Iraq; that must be left to future and ongoing research. But sufficient evidence has already emerged from the words and actions of the actors, uncovered by their critics or available in the public record, to make informed guesses.

First, it is clear that the Bush administration saw 9/11 as an *opportunity* to mobilize support for a "war on terrorism" that could realize their project.[33] But in order to turn the "war on terrorism" against Iraq, Bush had to claim that Saddam Hussein was linked to Al-Qaida and was actively developing weapons of mass destruction (WMDs), and hence represented an imminent threat to the United States. Not only have these claims been discredited, but additionally there is mounting, almost conclusive, evidence that the war party deliberated exaggerated unreliable claims and knew that its depiction of Iraq as a threat to the United States was false.[34] The unwillingness of the Bush administration to listen to the experts who discounted alarmist claims, or to welcome the return of UN weapons inspectors to Iraq, indicates that the war was no mistake deriving from an intelligence failure: as deputy Pentagon chief Paul Wolfowitz later admitted, WMDs were merely the issue the war party believed would raise the most support—for what it wanted to do on other grounds.[35]

What, then, were the real reasons for the war, and why was Iraq targeted when it represented no particular threat to the United States? The main alternative explanation is oil—energy security, the control of oil supplies, and the stability of the oil price market.[36] As Wolfowitz famously explained when asked why Iraq and not North Korea was targeted, Iraq was "swimming in oil."[37] Vice President Dick Cheney warned of Saddam's ambition to control world energy supplies: "If Saddam Hussein were ever to control the Persian Gulf oil resources, his past record suggests that he would be willing to cut or even halt oil exports altogether whenever it suited him, in order to force concessions."[38] While, in reality, Saddam posed no such threat, it is clear that oil was on the minds of the oil-men in the administration; indeed, Cheney authored the US national energy policy report (the "Cheney Report"). US oil production was in decline and, with the US economy and lifestyle as energy-wasteful as ever, US import dependence was rising in an ever-tighter oil market; in 2002, just prior to the Iraq War, the United States imported 53 percent of its oil consumption, with a rising proportion of that coming from the Gulf (20 percent in 2004). Moreover, US vulnerability was predicted to increase, especially as exports of the non–Middle Eastern oil producers on which it had hitherto relied were declining, forcing the United States to seek access to other reserves—hence its drive to penetrate Central Asia.[39] Even if the United States were to reduce its dependence on Gulf supplies, any disruption of oil supplies from there would inevitably precipitate an oil shock within the United States, since it was part of a "single, seamless oil market driven by supply and demand."[40] Crucially, oil shocks were associated with global recessions and rises in the cheap gasoline prices Americans expect; presidents whose tenure coincided with such shocks have historically lost reelection (Gerald Ford in 1976, Jimmy Carter in 1980, and George H. W. Bush in 1992). The United States was well aware that almost all available global oil production capacity was being utilized, and that, indeed, this production was possibly peaking, raising the chances of an oil-supply crisis with grave consequences.[41]

Historically, of course, Saudi Arabia had been the key to oil security and price stability, traditionally playing an effective "swing" role in moderating oil prices at the behest of the United States. But although Saudi Arabia remains the only state with substantial surplus production capability, the United States evidently feared that strong growth in global energy demand was eroding this capacity, especially the ability to smooth out disruptions in oil exports.[42] Growing tensions within Saudi Arabia, provoked in part by the US presence there, raised the specter that Saudi instability could put oil market stability at risk; a US diplomatic source told an interviewer that "a rehabilitated Iraq is the only sound long-term strategic alternative to Saudi Arabia."[43]

Yet given that the single most important determinant of oil shocks has been conflict in the Middle East, the Bush administration should have known that a war could jeopardize oil price stability. To be sure, the neoconservatives and Iraqi exiles downplayed the risks and exaggerated the prospects that Iraqi oil would rapidly start pumping after a quick war (while also advocating oil privitization);[44] but the administration was certainly warned, and the fact that it nevertheless chose such a high-risk policy suggests that oil price stability was only one consideration and not necessarily the most important one.[45]

Indeed, the war makes little sense unless its aim was to sustain and extend the control of "world oil," on which Washington's hegemony partly rests. Iraq had the potential to be one of the world's largest oil exporters, with enormous, substantially untapped reserves and very low production costs, making it very attractive to international oil companies. It was the only country with the potential to add millions of barrels per day of increased oil production. Yet the US determination to maintain sanctions on Iraq as long as Saddam was in power, and Saddam's record of using oil for political purposes, meant that this potential could not be tapped to the benefit of the United States or US oil companies, and meant keeping Iraq's oil production levels well below capacity at a time of growing supply constraints.[46] Worse, Iraq was selling oil concessions to other countries, notably Russia, China, and France—which US-backed Iraqi exiles promised to cancel if they came to power. The conquest of Iraq, which would give the United States control of the world's second largest oil reserve, would enhance US structural power over Europe, Japan, and the new Asian industrializers, notably India and the main putative global rival to the United States, China; it would also cut out Russia and France (whose quest for a position in Iraq was a constant from the 1920s). As oil-geopolitics expert Michael Klare put it: "Whoever gains possession of [Iraq's] fields will exercise enormous influence over the global energy markets of the twenty-first century."[47] Removing Saddam would also remove any residual threat he might pose to the oil fields of his neighbors, allow Iraqi oil production to be rapidly increased, and, as a former energy secretary said, "make Iraq [America's] new strategic oil reserve."[48]

However, the targeting of Iraq must also be seen in the context of the *threats* to US oil hegemony. This hegemony rested on the Pax Americana that Washington had tried to establish in the region after the Gulf War (1990–1991), based on the peace process, the Saudi alliance, and the "dual containment" of Iran and Iraq, but all of these were unraveling. First, Iraq and Iran were gradually escaping from the isolation that Washington had sought to impose on them, for while US sanctions kept its own companies out of their oil fields and markets, its rivals were poised to enter. Iran, in particular, had rebuilt ties with Europe and its Gulf neighbors. The sanctions on Iraq had increasingly been discredited for the humanitarian damage they did and were opposed by France and Russia, while Saudi Arabia and other Arab states were seeking the normalization of Iraq's position in the region. US hawks claimed that enervation of the sanctions regime would allow Saddam to recover his military power.[49] Of no minor significance was the fact that Iran and Iraq were demanding payment for oil in euros, thereby threatening the dollarization of the oil market that so favors Washington.[50]

Second, the breakdown of the peace process amid continued Israeli settlement activity in the Palestinian territories, which had sparked the outbreak of the second intifadah, the unleashing of Islamic terrorism, and the rise of the hard-line Sharon government, drove an increasing wedge between the United States and the Arabs who had been promised a peace settlement in reward for their support of the United States in the Gulf War. Worse, George W. Bush's ever more overt support for Sharon's annexation plans and massive anti-Palestinian violence in the Occupied Territories made US and Israeli policies indistinguishable in Arab and Muslim eyes.

Third, there was a growing feeling that Saudi Arabia could no longer be relied upon. Dependence on it placed constraints on US policy toward the Middle East;[51] Saudi Arabia had put restrictions on the use of US forces based there in the "containment" of Iraq and in the US-Afghan war, and hostility to the presence of those forces within Saudi Arabia was making them politically unsustainable.[52] The participation of Saudi citizens in the 9/11 attacks and in funding Al-Qaida gave the neoconservatives the opportunity to demonize the Saudis in US public opinion.[53] For its part, Saudi Arabia, feeling that the United States had ignored its interests—notably in a resolution of the Arab-Israel conflict—began looking for alternative security solutions to ease its total US dependence, by conciliating Iran and Iraq as well as domestic opinion, which required that it decline to moderate rises in oil prices to suit Washington.[54] The oil hegemony of the United States rested on its unique ability to balance special relationships with *both* Israel and Saudi Arabia, but this balance was being destabilized. In conquering Iraq, the United States, in the words of one pundit, "would acquire a [new] compliant swing producer in one blow."[55]

Yet the threat to US hegemony was merely potential, not immediate; there were less risky ways to address it, and the traditional mechanisms of control over the Gulf were largely intact. Rising oil demand, far from putting US oil hegemony at risk, made its unrivaled political and military position in the Gulf more pivotal. Nor did a debilitated Iraq really pose any threat to US dominance in the region; on the contrary, the residual threat Saddam posed to the Gulf states only increased their dependence on US protection.

It is therefore probably less useful to seek an explanation of the war in an analysis of US *national* interests (assuming hegemony to be one of them) than in the *particular* interests of the very distinctive ruling coalition in George W. Bush's Washington. First, Bush represented a power shift from the Treasury, Commerce, Wall Street, and mainstream corporate power, to a much narrower military-oil complex of interests.[56] Second, it embodied a convergence of the Zionist (neoconservative) and the arms/oil lobbies—or more precisely, their extremist/militarist wings—that were traditionally opposed over Middle East policy. The result was that the latter dropped its traditional concern to appease the Arab regimes and embraced the Zionist agenda.

What drove this convergence? Their shared interests in arms spending date back to their collaboration in driving the Reagan administration's arms race against the Soviet Union, and they continued to share an advocacy of increased military spending, which was threatened by the major cutbacks at the end of the Cold War. They came together in the 1990s in the Project for the New American Century, whose main platform was global US hegemony; military supremacy; "full support to Israel," whose "fight against terrorism is our fight"; and—the centerpiece of their project—regime change in Iraq, "even if evidence does not link Iraq directly to the [9/11] attack."[57]

However, it is not self-evident why the oil-men in the administration would consider a war on Iraq in their interest. Some in the US oil industry saw the chance to restore the direct ownership of oil curtailed by the rise of OPEC (and the increased profits this would allow) through privatization of Iraqi oil.[58] As Pieterse points out, energy companies are the most territorial and geo-political of all corporations.[59] Another consideration may have been awareness of the association of conflict in the Middle East with high oil prices—especially needed for high-cost Texas producers—and high oil company profits. Shimshon Bichler and Jonathan Nitzan show that relative performance of oil companies is associated with high oil prices; that every Middle Eastern crisis of the past fifty years has been followed by periods in which the oil majors outperform the Fortune 500 average; that during the oil price boom of the early 1980s, oil company profits reached nearly 19 percent of total corporate profits, only to fall back to 3 percent in the late 1990s as oil prices fell.[60] A boom for armaments firms paralleled the oil boom, only to suffer decline with the oil price slump experienced by Middle Eastern purchasers. War in the Middle East was expected to—and in fact did—drive up oil prices, oil company shares of relative corporate profits, and renewed arms spending.

Yet given the risks to the overall economy of an oil shock, this scenario implies an extremely reckless sacrifice of broader capitalist class interests to the narrow interests of one, albeit pivotal, fraction of capital; moreover, it leaves unexplained the lack of any broad opposition to the war from the wider business community, which presumably needed moderate stable oil prices. As Pieterse observes, not only is there no "capitalist necessity" in preventive war, but corporations cannot afford to be risk-takers on this scale and deterritorialized high-tech capitalism does not have the same need for territorial control that is typical of energy companies.[61] However, Bichler and Nitzan argue that the interest of the arms/oil coalition coincided with the wider need of "dominant capital." The US boom of the 1990s, which had been driven by mergers, acquisitions, and the globalization of investment, was exhausted by 2000, and US capital faced a crisis of overproduction and deflation. To get out of this, an alternative strategy of inflation, which historically leads to a redistribution of wealth from labor to capital and small to larger firms enjoying price power, was on the agenda; the main driver of inflation is booming oil prices, and the single most important driver of oil prices is Middle Eastern conflict. What the George W. Bush administration may have wanted was oil prices at a level that would suit their particular oil/arms interests and would induce an inflationary burst serving the interests of the overall ruling class without jeopardizing the national economy or Bush's political electability.

The other essential ingredient of war, however, was the exceptional influence of the neoconservatives that enabled them to put forward *their* favored solution to the US conundrum of reconciling oil hegemony with the interests of Israel—resulting in what has been called the "Israelization of American foreign policy."[62] Their solution cannot be understood apart from the priority they gave to the protection of Israel's regional hegemony and the consolidation of its expansion into the Palestinian-populated territories. Closely associated with the Israeli Likud Party, the neoconservatives conflated a US interest in global hegemony with the project of "Greater Israel" and had long worked systematically to harness US power to Israeli interests.[63] Their nightmare was that the United States would subordinate Israeli ambitions to appeasement of the Arab oil producers, especially Saudi Arabia (as George H. W. Bush had done);[64] it was this that explains neoconservative pundits' use of 9/11 to demonize Riyadh, a move that appears foolish from the viewpoint of US interests. Since Israeli expansion was incompatible with resumed US brokerage of a peaceful resolution of the Arab-Israeli conflict, essential to appeasing Arab opinion, the neoconservatives needed an alternative solution: the seizure of Iraq would allow the US to secure access to Arab oil without Arab alliances and consent. Control of Iraq could be used to drive down oil prices, break OPEC, and destabilize Arab oil producers unfriendly to the pro-Israeli policy of the United States.[65] While this project risked stimulating further anti-US terrorism, dominance in Iraq would position the United States to directly threaten the two main nationalist states that had hitherto provided some safe haven for militant groups and that stood in the way of a peace settlement on Israeli terms, Syria and Iran. No one doubts that the Sharon government was also keen for a US war on Iraq and used its influence in Washington to promote one (there are allegations that Israeli intelligence misled the US and British governments about Saddam's WMD, and that Israeli spooks were closely linked with the special intelligence bureau set up by neoconservatives in the Pentagon that tailored intelligence to promote the war).[66]

What was crucial, however, is that the oil/arms faction led by Dick

Cheney and Donald Rumsfeld accepted the neoconservative solution; we can only surmise that they saw no other way to solve the contradiction between promoting Israel's ambitions and protecting US oil hegemony in the Middle East. More than that, the war on Iraq was expected to decisively *advance* this hegemony. In Noam Chomsky's view, the Bush administration sought to establish a new norm, the US right to attack countries it deemed threats, and Iraq, being both weak and easily demonized, was an exemplary case to establish the precedent.[67] Smashing Saddam Hussein, who had famously defied US power, would send the message that the limits of US global power had been overcome and finish the job left undone in 1991; it would also, in intimidating the Muslim world, burst the "bubble of terrorism." Marc Lynch observes that the Arab/Muslim worlds were the main centers of rejection of US hegemony, and that an easy victory in Iraq followed by images of Iraqis welcoming US troops as liberators would demoralize US opponents.[68] The United States had long sought permanent bases in the Gulf, and conquering Iraq would allow their establishment.[69] As Patrick Seale put it, Iraq was a "strategic stronghold at the heart of the Middle East and astride its oil fields." Invading Iraq would allow the imposition of liberalism there and, in a domino effect, spread it in the rest of the Middle East.[70]

Finally, the private interests of both wings of the ruling coalition stood to gain from a war. Bush's main political adviser, Karl Rove, evidently saw war as a way of winning elections; indeed, each time Bush's poll ratings started to fall, they were rescued by the invocation of some new external threat.[71] The representatives of the international oil, construction, security, and armaments industries expected to (and did) reap huge profits from noncompetitive contracts after the conquest of Iraq, but the neoconservatives were also positioned to profit. Thus, on the eve of the invasion, neoconservatives in the Pentagon were already collaborating with Bush and Cheney to funnel reconstruction contracts to firms in which they both had stakes. The evidence is strong that the ruling group anticipated—and got—lucrative pickings in Iraq. And, of course, Bush was indeed reelected as a war president.[72]

In summary, the Middle East is the center of the world's most strategic resource, oil, on which US global hegemony greatly depends; the Middle Eastern oil and arms trades have long been the sources of private superprofit for the right-wing of the US establishment; but the Middle East is, at the same time, the center of the main ideological resistance to US hegemony—Arab nationalism and especially Islam—and the location of the main irritant in Western-Islamic relations, Israel, which stimulates this resistance. The conquest of Iraq was seen as the key to cutting through these conundrums and vanquishing resistance to US dominance over the region. As neoconservative guru William Kristol put it, toppling Saddam Hussein aimed at changing the dynamics in the Middle East and reconstructing a new Pax-Americana in place of the old one.

■ The Neoconization of US Foreign Policy

Translating this project into reality, however, required harnessing the whole US political system, against its built-in checks and balances, for a war that, up to this point, had been merely the pet project of a faction of extreme right-wingers by no means representative of US establishment opinion. The election of Bush and Cheney and the appointment of Rumsfeld to the Pentagon were of course decisive. Bush, a man convinced of his divinely appointed mission but woefully ignorant of international affairs, was uniquely vulnerable to the advice of the hawks, particularly Paul Wolfowitz, the most consistent advocate of war, whom Bush appears to have found especially persuasive.[73] Also central, however, was the capture of the wider executive branch by the alliance of the "corporate militarists" (Cheney and Rumsfeld) and the neoconservatives, the ideological core of the Bush administration and the main lobby group for war. The neoconservatives acted as a solidarity movement, getting their members systematically appointed across the national security bureaucracy; there they worked to impose their agenda against the opposition of the career civil servants, senior military officers, diplomats, and intelligence analysts who were unconvinced Saddam was a major threat. Believing that they alone had the truth, they viewed deception (and force) as legitimate means to their ends[74] and, as one insider put it, "behaved as though they had seized control of the government in a silent coup."[75] They set up a "shadow government," with the neoconservatives staffing ad hoc "special offices" that bypassed normal bureaucratic procedures meant to ensure objectivity and balance, and were pivotal in promoting the case for war.[76]

Crucial to winning the struggle for war outside the executive branch was the alliance between the neoconservatives, the wider Zionist lobby, and the right-wing "Christian Zionists," a mass movement whose literal reading of the Bible convinced them that Christ would reappear only after the Jews repossessed the whole promised land and who viewed Islam as "a very wicked and evil religion."[77] Congress, under the influence of these lobbies and a flawed national intelligence estimate that no congressperson questioned, was brought to abdicate its war-deciding responsibilities.[78] Additionally, public opinion was systematically softened up by a concerted propaganda campaign led by administration officials, right-wing think tanks,[79] advertising agencies,[80] and media pundits, largely uncontested by a critical or even an objective press.[81] The "politics of fear" was institutionalized: according to Zbigniew Brzezinski, the government propagated "a fear that periodically verges on blind panic . . . fueled by a demagogy that emphasize[d] worst-case scenarios [and] induce[d] a dichotomous view of world reality."[82] The public was misled to believe that Saddam had a hand in 9/11 and had WMDs, that the invasion would be welcomed by Iraqis, that Iraqi oil would pay the costs of war, that US troops would be quickly in and out, and that Iraq would be readily transformed into a democracy.[83] According to Pieterse, US public opinion was peculiarly vulnerable to propaganda because of the US culture of exceptionalism: Americans' collective narcissism, ignorance of world affairs, glorification of the military, and lack of any (common ethnic) identity save that of a supposedly uniquely virtuous "American way" that must be exported to save the world.[84]

The convergence of these factors upset the system of checks and balances that normally restrains US foreign policy behavior. In a wider sense, Louis Fisher argues that the war resulted from *institutional failures;* indeed, the ease with which the political establishment was harnessed by what George Soros called an "extremist cabal"[85] suggests that the system has profound built-in flaws: the vulnerability of the fragmented policy process to moneyed single-issue interests; the politicization of the senior ranks of the bureaucracy; the foreign policy subordination of Congress to an imperial presidency; the enervation of the electoral system by campaign financing abuses, sound-bite political debate, mass absenteeism, and voting irregularities; and the ready manipulation of an ill-informed public by a corporate-controlled partisan media—all spell a "decayed condition of American democracy."

■ Consequences of the Iraq War for US Hegemony

Will the Iraq War advance or set back the US reach for muscular hegemony? This will depend on whether the war demonstrates the utility of "preventive war" and sustains or undermines the global legitimacy of US leadership.

The Utility of "Preventive War"

The Iraq War is a test case of the doctrine of preventive war and of the neoconservatives' belief that overwhelming military superiority can be translated into unchallenged hegemony in the Middle East, but the play has not gone according to script.

First, the exposure of intelligence failures and its manipulation for political ends undermined the credibility of the doctrine of preemption. Thus, even David Kay, Bush's weapons inspector in Iraq, said of the failure to find Iraqi WMDs after the war: "If you cannot rely on good, accurate intelligence, that is credible to the American people and others abroad, you can't have a policy of pre-emption."[86]

The neoconservatives argued that military force against Saddam Hussein would be welcomed by Iraqis and a pro-US "democracy" readily imposed. But this was never likely, since Iraqis combined national pride with a profound mistrust of the United States and Britain rooted in the colonial experience, the near-total support of the United States for Israel, and the near-genocidal sanctions the United States had imposed on Iraq.[87] But the breakdown of security, infrastructure, and public health; the mass unemployment inflicted by the dissolution of the army, purge of the bureaucracy, and public sector layoffs;[88] the death of perhaps 100,000 people, mostly civilians, in the first year of war and occupation;[89] the halving of gross national product per capita compared to 2001; the imposition of a puppet government of mostly exiles without popular bases in Iraq;[90] the flooding of the country with foreign mercenaries and contractors; the open avowal of the intention to occupy Iraq for at least three years and to acquire permanent basing rights; and the attempt, in violation of the Geneva Conventions, to privatize and sell off Iraq's oil assets to Western buyers[91]—all ensured that Iraqis would view the foreign armies as occupiers, not liberators. And the self-defeating conduct of the United States in Iraq, far from being a mere "mistake," owes everything to the influence of Rumsfeld's Pentagon and the neoconservatives.[92]

The United States responded to the growing resistance it encountered with tactics pioneered by Israel in occupied Palestine: bombing and firing on densely populated urban areas, demolishing homes, collective punishment of villages, herding of thousands into detention camps,[93] and food blockades of suspected insurgent areas,[94] not to mention the "daily humiliations and occasional brutalities that come with the presence of an occupying army."[95] Western polls in the year after the invasion showed that 82 percent of Iraqis opposed the occupation and 57 percent wanted foreign troops to leave immediately; US troops were widely seen as "lacking in respect for the country's people, religion and traditions" and "indiscriminate in their use of force when civilians are nearby." Five percent or fewer of Iraqis believed the United States invaded "to assist the Iraqi people," destroy WMDs, or establish democracy, while 43 percent said the aim was "to rob Iraq's oil." More than 50 percent said attacks on US troops were "justified" or "sometimes justified."[96] A US commander infamously declared: "With a heavy dose of fear and violence, and a lot of money for projects, I think we can convince these people that we are here to help them."[97] However, this approach only inflamed resistance, which mushroomed from about "5,000 Hussein loyalists using leftover Iraqi army equipment, into a disparate yet potent force of up to 20,000 equipped with explosives capable of knocking out even heavily armored military vehicles."[98] The inability of the United States to pacify the country shattered its aura of military invincibility, showing that asymmetric warfare can delay and possibly checkmate the strongest military power in the world.[99] Over two years of occupation, Iraqi opinion only hardened against the occupation.[100]

But the United States has no intention of giving up its prize, and seeks to use techniques borrowed from the earlier British occupation to ensconce itself in permanent military bases and an enormous fortified embassy—comparable to the former British High Commission—from which the occupier hopes to pull the strings of any future Iraqi government from behind the scenes. These techniques include exploitation, hence exacerbation of Iraq's built-in communal cleavages, notably in the reliance on the Kurds against the Arabs; the near-imposition under US pressure of a constitution that locks in provisions guaranteeing US privileges in the country and institutionalizes the sectarian divisions among Iraqis;[101] the holding of elections, at least partly manipulated, in which the main issues, above all the occupation and the measures it imposes by fiat, are off the agenda; the use of such elections to co-opt a pliant leadership that has some legitimacy but that, being caught between the occupier and the populace, is likely to become increasingly dependent on the former against the latter; and the reconstruction of a security force prepared to back the occupier and its clients against the populace. Finally, the deconstruction of the Iraqi state into a loose confederation deprives Iraq of collective purpose or identity, ensuring that it cannot be resurrected as a champion of Arab nationalism.[102]

However, it is uncertain whether this strategy will work. Constructing a reliable Iraqi army willing and able to suppress the insurgency has proved elusive, although the United States has been more effective in arming (or allowing the arming of) Kurdish and Shia militias that use violence to counter that of Sunni insurgents.[103] It could also have unintended consequences, for were post-Saddam Iraq actually to be democratized, popular anti-US sentiment would find more outlets and the country would be more open to Iranian influence. Alternatively, permanent sectarian instability, even the civil war and the breakup of the country, may already be entrained (an outcome by no means incompatible with neoconservative aims of debilitating a potential Arab power but fraught with risks for regional stability).[104] As Edward Rhodes argues, a liberal order cannot be imposed at gunpoint, since it depends on consent and the internalization of liberal values. The outcome has, so far, validated Robert Jervis's warning that while the United States has the military power to overthrow weak regimes, sustaining replacement client states is likely to prove costly and enmesh it in continuing intervention.[105]

It remained to be seen whether the Iraq War was the beginning of "imperial overreach." The neoconservatives promised that the cost of the war would be carried by Iraq itself, but Iraqi oil exports came nowhere near doing so.[106] Rather, the war cost the US Treasury an estimated $160 billion in fiscal year 2003–2004, and reached $204.4 billion by 2005, with only $2 billion of that going for reconstruction of the country as late as 2005.[107] Bush's combination of tax cuts and military adventures turned the $127 billion budget surplus he inherited in 2001 into a $374 billion deficit in 2003.

By 2005, over 2,000 US troops had been killed and total casualties (including injured) numbered over 17,000.[108] Half of US units in Iraq suffered low morale and the military was badly overstretched. Revelations of the deception practiced by the neoconservatives in their drive to war threw into doubt the triumphalist discourse on US empire encouraged by the initial military victory. Moreover, Americans increasingly agreed with influential members of the national security elite who were claiming that the war on Iraq, far from making Americans more secure, was a new generator of terrorism.[109] The fear that empire abroad was incompatible with liberal democracy at home was reinforced by the erosion of civil liberties, the most egregious of which was the government's claim that it could keep a US citizen designated an "enemy combatant" imprisoned indefinitely without charges.[110] The media, which had almost uniformly propagandized in favor of war, began to criticize it as the costs mounted. Americans, Jervis argues, have no record of willingness to sacrifice significantly for the sake of imperium.[111] Indeed, as the costs rose and the administration's deceptions were exposed, public opinion turned against Bush's war.[112] The US expectation that it would direct the remaking of the Middle East while Europe, Asia, and the Gulf Arab states would pay for it, no doubt encouraged by the Gulf War, proved hollow.[113] Pieterse argues that the United States is a "deficit empire" that, instead of exporting capital, drains the world of resources on a massive scale, with its current account deficit needing an annual inflow of $500 billion to keep it going.[114] While seignurage arguably allows the United States to evade the full immediate costs of military hegemony, the combination of excessive military spending with high domestic consumption and low taxes may still bring the Bush juggernaut to a halt.

Soft Power at Risk?

Has the Iraq War put the soft power, the legitimacy on which US hegemony has rested, at risk? Iraq was a test case both of Bush's strategy of constructing ad hoc "coalitions of the willing" that would unquestioningly follow US leadership, and of whether his declared right of "preventive war" would be accepted by allies and rivals alike.

There is normally a powerful incentive to bandwagon with rather than balance against the hegemon. But the United States had to expend considerable political capital in its effort to legitimize the war. Iraq is extraordinary in that even core allies, France and Germany, resisted, while Washington was unable to get the UN Security Council votes of even weak states like Guinea and Cameroon and otherwise friendly neighbors like Mexico. On 18 February 2003, when the Council allowed member states to speak on the impending war, *all* of sixty-four speakers over three days opposed war.[115] Even many of those states that bandwagoned with the United States in Iraq did so less out of belief in the rightness of the invasion than for reasons of self-interest, inducement, intimidation, or attempts to minimize the damage that a unilateralist hegemon could inflict on the wider global order. Jervis argues that certain European countries supported the United States because "the dominance they fear most is not American, but Franco-German or Russian."[116] According to one insider analysis, Blair took Britain into war for fear that, if left alone, the paranoid hyperpower would prove dangerous and destabilizing, and in the vain hope that, in return, the United States would revive the Arab-Israeli peace process and thus address the main source of regional instability.[117] Japan may have encouraged the United States in Iraq to divert it from stirring up trouble with North Korea.[118] In the Middle Eastern region, weak states, enjoying little legitimacy at home, could not afford to balance against their protector (the Gulf states) or paymaster (Jordan, Egypt) and, despite fearing that it would destabilize the region, accommodated themselves to the invasion (with the exception of Syria, which alone expressed widespread regional opinion in its opposition).

Washington's use of the expression "coalition of the willing" conveys the illusion that the war was an international venture; but the vast majority of states in this "coalition" provided only token support and many actually sought aid packages in return for it. Moreover, US-aligned governments were opposed by large majorities of their own populations, among whom support for a war carried out "unilaterally by America and its allies" and widely seen to be about oil, did not rise above 11 percent in any European country, including in Eastern Europe.[119] Even if, in the short term, bandwagoning leaders defied home opinion, their alignment with Washington was based on calculations that are likely to be reversible, rather than a societal-rooted belief in the legitimacy of US leadership; in Spain, Prime Minister José María Aznar defied 90 percent of his public and paid the electoral price for what most Spaniards considered an illegitimate occupation of another county in violation of international law.[120]

The war was a test of how far overwhelming military power can impose fait accomplis that reshape international norms. The United States succeeded in getting post facto partial UN legitimation of the occupation and it had some success in inducing other states to assume small parts of its burdens. The main reason was that few states believed it to be in their interest that Iraq become an epicenter of instability in the Gulf; hence, through its fait accompli, the United States coerced Security Council members into postwar acquiescence in policies they opposed. Still, other states proved quite unwilling to contribute significant funding or troops to rescue the US project as long as Washington refused to turn over its authority to the UN.[121]

The longer-term costs of the war for US hegemony appear to be significant. Others states are beginning to perceive a hegemon that declares it will not be constrained by international institutions or the opinions of allies to be a threat to, rather than a guarantor, of global stability. Arguably, Bush has seriously eroded the alliance system upon which the hegemonic leadership of the United States rests. Europe's main security fear was no longer, as in the Cold War, that Washington would abandon it, but that Washington would destabilize the Middle East and stir up Western-Islamic tensions. Complained one European official: "many of us who will be deeply affected [by US policy in the Middle East] have no opportunity even to make our voice heard, let alone to influence anything."[122] Europe is also acutely aware that the Iraq War has considerably worsened the threat of terrorism.[123] According to Brzezinski, trust, an essential ingredient of power, had been sacrificed by the neoconservatives' preoccupation with "reshaping the Middle East at the expense of maintaining America's ability to lead globally."[124] As for US rivals, Bush weakened what was after 9/11 a budding cordial relationship with Russia, based partly on a perception of a shared interest in countering the Islamist threat; thereafter a Russian leader spoke for many in declaring that, "if someone tries to wage war on their own account . . . without an international mandate, it means all the world is . . . a wild jungle."[125] Evidence that in 2005 China, Russia, and India were banding together to block sanctions against Iran over its nuclear program, while China and South Korea were trying to restrain US actions against North Korea, were indicative that the world no longer trusted the hegemon to deliver stability, and feared the opposite.

Another major cost of the war has been the loss of respect suffered by Washington in global public opinion. Arthur Schlesinger wrote that "the global wave of sympathy that engulfed the US after 9/11 has given way to a global wave of hatred of American arrogance and militarism" and the belief that Bush was "a greater threat to peace than Saddam Hussein";[126] the proportion of people around the world who had a favorable view of the United States dropped precipitously as a result of the war.[127] In a *Time* magazine poll just before the war, 84 percent of Europeans identified the United States as the main threat to world peace.[128] In the Arab and Muslim worlds, the United States was even more widely disliked, and what is most striking is how Bush had managed to alienate the publics of allied states in which the United States had invested over decades: Turkey, Egypt, and Saudi Arabia.[129] The Iraq War undermined the authority of the hegemon to lay down the law to other countries in the name of universal standards.[130] For Jurgen Habermas, "the moral authority of the United States lies in ruins."[131] As the Japanese daily *Asahi Shinbun* observed, Bush's policies were highly divisive: dividing publics that are against its wars from governments that support it, setting the Western alliance at odds and dividing the West from Islam.[132]

US soft power had hitherto substantially been exercised *through, not against,* international law and institutions, but "at no time in the last 50 years," David Hendrickson argues, "has the US stood in such antagonism to both the primary norms and the central institutions of international society," namely sovereignty and the presumptive judgment against the first use of force, a norm established because of "disastrous experience with the contrary practice."[133] The war, which the UN Secretary-General declared illegal,[134] was launched in defiance of the UN, while the Geneva Conventions and the laws of war were disregarded in the treatment of prisoners and the occupation of Iraq.[135] The message from Washington was that it was exempt from the rules that applied to others. The root of the problem was arguably, as Samuel Huntington has observed, the failure of Washington to adjust to a world in which "the rest" must take their equal places; as Huntington put it: "The widespread parochial conceit that the . . . civilization of the West is now the universal civilization of the world" and the US attempt to impose a single model, rife with "hypocrisy and double standards," are "probably the single most important source of instability and potential global conflict."[136] The very rationale of a hegemon, of course, is to deliver *stability.*

▪ Implications of the Iraq War for Hegemonic Stability Theory

The Iraq War exposes major weaknesses in all forms of HST. Liberal claims of a benign hegemon appear most in need of revision, but the realist view of the hegemon as a unitary rational actor pursuing the national interest also seems wide of the mark. The big weakness shared by all versions of HST is that they do not convincingly explain why the hegemon should use its preponderant power in a *stabilizing* way, whether this be interpreted as serving global, national, or ruling-class interests. The Iraq case provides new evidence on these issues.

Malign or Benign Hegemony?

For John Ikenberry, US hegemony is benign because US power is not threatening, since the United States is content to be an "off-shore balancer" and eschews territorial aggrandizement; because, being democratic, its policy is predictable and self-restraining, not arbitrary; and because it is exercised through multinational institutions where its power is constrained by mutually agreed rules.[137] The Iraq War suggests that predictability, self-restraint, and multilateralism no longer hold. The war denotes, too, that in the Middle East the United States has become a partisan player, not a balancer, and that it does seek some territorial control, even if indirect. Ikenberry claims that US hegemony provides security and economic benefits, but coercive hegemony has made the Middle East the cockpit of global instability, putting global energy security at risk, encouraging terrorism, and inflicting many of the costs on the global and regional allies of the United States. Arguably, also, the Iraq War shattered the assumption in HST that because the hegemon created and benefits most from the status quo, it has a natural interest in stabilizing it; in fact, the hegemon may be basically satisfied with the configuration of world power, yet so dissatisfied with certain aspects of it that it is prepared to risk global stability to get its way.[138]

The Conditions of Benign Hegemony

The Iraq case suggests that at least two conditions must be met if the hegemon is to be benign. One is systemic, that is, as A. F. K. Organski points out,[139] the existence of a challenger state that could check or make unilateral power projection by the hegemon risky. Without such a state, Washington had little incentive to maximize its coalition at the cost of restraining its ambitions, relying instead on ad hoc "coalitions of the willing." According to Robert Jervis, "it is the exception rather than the rule for states to stay on the path of moderation when others do not force them to do so."[140] Without actually acknowledging it, HST *assumes* the countervailing power of a bi- or multipolar world, but Iraq suggests that under *unipolarity* the problem of hegemony is not the traditional fear that the hegemon lacks *enough* power to lead but that *excessive* power may make it malign.[141] As Kenneth Waltz observed, "unchecked power is a threat, no matter who wields it."[142]

A second condition is the realist assumption that the hegemon can be treated as a unitary actor defending the national interest that it presumably possesses in a stable world order or alternatively, as Marxist versions see it, the similar interests of world capitalism. This is perhaps compatible with the dominance of US foreign policy by an experienced mainstream globalist establishment. But, as Stephen Krasner recognized, the US policy process appears particularly vulnerable to colonization by narrow special interests.[143] Such interests, as Marxists would anticipate, may take the form of the oil/arms fraction of US capital; certainly the latter have benefited handsomely from the Iraq War, while ordinary taxpayers/consumers and soldiers have carried the burdens. However, as no version of HST would have expected and as Iraq exposes, special interests may take the form of religious-based identity movements—fundamentalist Christianity, Likudist Zionism—with trans-state reach and messianic agendas that may threaten both national and ruling-class interests in stability.

The World Order and Hegemonic Stability

What does the war tell us about the hegemonic capacity of the United States and its importance for world order? Kenneth Waltz believes that, eventually, hegemons overextend themselves, and their misuse of power provokes *bal-*

ancing against them,[144] while Birthe Hansen sees *bandwagoning* (and free-riding) with the hegemon as the natural behavior under unipolarity.[145] What the war precipitated from other states was, in fact, differentiated and ambivalent behavior, with various mixes of semicooperation and semiresistance to the hegemon.

Bandwagoning was quite limited (especially by comparison with the Gulf War); in only a few cases did states seem to cooperate with the hegemon because they thought the war legitimate or likely to deliver "public goods." As Stephen Walt argues, even Washington's close allies are now looking for ways to tame US might, while the many other countries that fear it have devised numerous strategies to manage and limit it.[146] Yet despite the widespread fear of the potential threat to world order from US unilateralism, and although some powers, perhaps France, China, and Russia, thought the hegemon was seeking "relative gains" at their expense, there was remarkably little anti-US balancing either. William Wohlforth argued that US state-to-state power was so immense that no countervailing coalition was possible.[147] Nor, perhaps, were the vital interests of other great powers sufficiently threatened to provoke such power-balancing. But the relative lack of balancing against the hegemon cannot be fully understood without appreciation of the structural (economic) power the United States enjoys over other states in the world capitalist market, and—especially in the core capitalist states—the reluctance of elites to damage the trans-state capitalist networks that tie their dominant groups to those in the United States.

Despite this, Thomas Volgy and Alison Bailin show convincingly that the United States lacks sufficient structural and state power for global rule except *through* the collective hegemony of the core powers, and that this, in turn, depends on the legitimacy of US leadership.[148] Nor can the US fight the "war on terrorism" without international cooperation, as the US security elite has started to realize.[149] Yet, far from facilitating cooperation, US unilateralism in Iraq, at the expense of the UN and the cohesion of the core's collective hegemony, is of a piece with its increasing obstruction of global cooperation; its insistence on unilateral control over Iraq and rebuff of UN authority there obstructs a multilateral solution to the conflict and, indeed, makes the country—and the region—a generator of terrorism. Jan Pieterse argues that Iraq produced hegemony-in-reverse: "Never has so much soft power been squandered in so short a time."[150]

Whether US authority can be restored depends on whether there is wide acceptance of the US claim that new threats—pariah states, terrorism, Islam itself—make US military hegemony indispensable to world order or whether other states will come to fear that Washington is itself part of the problem in helping to construct a "clash of civilizations" that threatens this order.[151] This, in turn, will depend, in part, on the outcome in Iraq. The case already highlights the difficulty and the high costs of translating even unprecedented military power into political victory over deep-rooted societal resistance. It seems likely that, far from resolving the problem, US intervention is only intensifying the reaction from the Islamic world, which, as it is neutered by US power at the state level, increasingly takes trans- and sub-state forms (Al-Qaida) amid the chaos unleashed by Washington's policy of "regime change."

▓ Notes

1. The expression is from Michael Hudson, "To Play the Hegemon."
2. Namely realism, liberalism, and structuralism.
3. Immanuel Wallerstein, *The Politics of the World Economy.*
4. Robert Gilpin, *War and Change in World Politics.*
5. Charles Kindleberger, "Dominance and Leadership in the International Economy," pp. 242–254; Robert Keohane, "The Theory of Hegemonic Stability and Changes in International Economic Regimes," pp. 131–162.
6. Isabelle Grunberg, "Exploring the 'Myth' of Hegemonic Stability," pp. 431–477.
7. Susan Strange, *States and Markets;* David P. Calleo, *Beyond American Hegemony,* pp. 82–108, 138.
8. Jan Nederveen Pieterse, *Globalization or Empire?* pp. 17–29, 33, 43.
9. Gilpin, *War and Change in World Politics,* pp. 153–156, 217–219; Stephen Krasner, "State Power and the Structure of International Trade."
10. A. F. K. Organski, *World Politics.*
11. Samuel Huntington, "The US," pp. 76–96; Paul Kennedy, *The Rise and Fall of the Great Powers.*
12. Stephen Gill, *Power and Resistance in the New World Order,* pp. 41–65, 73–115.
13. Robert Keohane, *After Hegemony;* Duncan Snidal argues that states will cooperate if they stand to gain, since the danger of cheating by others, at least in the capitalist core states, is seldom high enough to nullify such benefits. Duncan Snidal, "The Limits of Hegemonic Stability Theory."
14. Kees van der Pijl, *Transnational Classes and International Relations;* William I. Robinson, "Capitalist Globalization and the Transnationalization of the State."
15. Thomas J. Volgy and Alison Bailin, *International Politics and State Strength.*
16. Pieterse, *Globalization or Empire?* p. 122.
17. Snidel, "Limits of Hegemonic Stability Theory," pp. 613–614.
18. Simon Bromley, *American Hegemony and World Oil;* Atif Kubursi and Salim Mansur, "Oil and the Gulf War."
19. Sherle R. Schwenninger, "Revamping American Grand Strategy."
20. Oystein Noreng, *Crude Power,* p. 51.
21. Richard Betts, "The Soft Underbelly of American Primacy," p. 23.
22. For more detailed argument, see Chapter 20.
23. Keohane, *After Hegemony,* pp. 139–141, 190–194.
24. Michael Hudson, *Super Imperialism,* argues, for example, that US dollar

hegemony allowed it to impose the Plaza and Lourve accords that made Japan artificially lower its interest rates and triggered the bubble economy that broke the "Japanese challenge" to the United States.

25. Bromley, *American Hegemony and World Oil,* pp. 205–244. See also Kubursi's argument in Chapter 20.

26. Raymond Hinnebusch, *The International Politics of the Middle East,* pp. 214–218.

27. Kubursi and Mansur, "Oil and the Gulf War"; Paul Aarts, "The New Oil Order"; Cyrus Bina, "The Rhetoric of Oil and the Dilemma of War and American Hegemony."

28. Chalmers Johnson, "Blowback," *The Nation,* 15 October 2001.

29. Julie Kosterlitz, "America's Track Record in the Persian Gulf and Afghanistan Suggests that Today's Solutions Can Lead to Tomorrow's Problems," *National Journal,* March 2003.

30. Slavoj Zizek, "Iraq's False Promises," *Foreign Policy* (January–February 2004), http://www.foreignpolicy.com. Similarly Zbigniew Brzezinski, critiquing Bush's attempt to deflect blame for Muslim animosity toward the United States, writes: "It is as if terrorism is suspended in outer space as an abstract phenomenon, with ruthless terrorists acting under some Satanic inspiration unrelated to any specific motivation. American involvement in the Middle East is clearly the main impulse of the hatred that has been directed at America. They do not simply hate freedom, [they hate specific policies of the US]." Zbigniew Brzezinski, "Confronting Anti-American Grievances," *New York Times,* 9 January 2002.

31. Robert Jervis, "Understanding the Bush Doctrine"; Edward Rhodes, "The Imperial Logic of Bush's Liberal Agenda."

32. Cabinet-level insiders, notably Treasury Secretary Paul O'Neil and terrorism adviser Richard Clarke, revealed that an attack on Iraq was broached at the first National Security Council meeting of the Bush administration and that, in the immediate aftermath of 9/11, Rumsfeld advocated an attack on Iraq. Bush sought to hold Iraq responsible in defiance of the advice of senior intelligence aides that it was not involved. Ron Suskind, *The Price of Loyalty;* Richard Clarke, *Against All Enemies; Sunday Herald,* 11 January 2004; *The Independent,* 22 March 2004; *New York Times Review of Books* 50, no. 19.

33. After 9/11 Bush gushed, "this is a great opportunity," while Rumsfeld told the *New York Times* that it was a great opportunity to refashion the world. Bob Woodward, *Bush at War,* pp. 32–37.

34. The report of the Carnegie Endowment for International Peace, *WMD in Iraq* (by Joseph Cirincione, Jessica Mathews, and George Perkovich) concluded that Iraqi WMD capabilities were not a threat, since Iraq's nuclear program had been suspended for many years and large-scale chemical weapon production capabilities destroyed or dismantled. International constraints, sanctions, and weapons inspections had been effective. On 6 October 2004, the Duelfer report by the special adviser to the CIA on fifteen months of work by 1,200 CIA inspectors concluded that Iraq had destroyed its WMDs right after the 1991 war, the last factory capable of producing them in 1996, and that it was not working to restart its programs. Dilip Hiro, *Secrets and Lies,* p. 507. Moreover, the Carnegie report affirmed that there was no solid evidence of a cooperative relationship between Saddam's government and Al-Qaida. As John S. Duffield, "Oil and the Iraq War," noted, Saddam would hardly have supplied WMDs to Al-Qaida, since, if used, they might well have been traced back to their source, prompting devastating retaliation—even if no direct link could have been found. The Kean report of the National Commission on Terrorist Attacks

also reported no evidence of collaboration of Iraq and Al-Qaida. Hiro, *Secrets and Lies,* p. 505.

Evidence that the Bush administration knew its claims were false or misleading is copious. The Carnegie report concluded that the absence of any imminent nuclear or chemical threat was knowable before the war, that the CIA's national intelligence estimates had been deliberately misrepresented by administration officials, and that none of Secretary of State Colin Powell's claims at the UN stood up to verification. Weapons inspector Scott Ritter observed that plenty of experts and former Iraq weapons inspectors had discounted the threat before the war. *International Herald Tribune,* 6 February 2004, http://www.iht.com. CIA director George Tenet testified before Congress in February 2001 that Iraq posed no immediate threat to the United States or to other countries in the Middle East and that the CIA had no evidence Iraq was stockpiling WMDs or developing nuclear weapons; yet in October 2002 the CIA changed its stand with a national intelligence estimate that was decisive in the congressional vote to authorize Bush to go to war. Jason Leopold, "CIA Intelligence Reports Seven Months Before 9/11 Said Iraq Posed No Threat to U.S.," *Countercurrents.org,* 21 September 2005. In July 2004 the US Senate Intelligence Committee concluded that unqualified claims that Saddam was reconstituting nuclear weapons should not have been included in the intelligence estimate. Hiro, *Secrets and Lies,* p. 504. US Special Forces units had been sent into Iraq before the start of the war to investigate sites suspected of being missile or chemical and biological weapon storage depots and came up with nothing; similarly, the UN inspectors were finding nothing. According to Sheldon Rampton and John Stauber, *Weapons of Mass Deception,* pp. 79–99, specific deceptions by the Bush administration included the claim that Iraqi aluminum tubes were for uranium enrichment, that Iraq had drones able to reach the United States, and that it tried to buy uranium from Niger. The claim that 9/11 hijacker Atta had met Iraqi agents in Prague (when he was actually in the United States) continued to be repeated by the neoconservatives even after it was discredited. Bush cited a report by the International Atomic Energy Agency, which did not exist, that Saddam could go nuclear in six months. Tenant implied that the Anthrax scare of 17 October 2002 was attributable to Iraq, while the most likely suspect was a disaffected US expert on germ warfare. Hiro, *Secrets and Lies,* pp. 13–15, 426–427. Congressman Henry Waxman compiled a list of 237 misleading prewar statements by top administration officials from the president on down. Compelling evidence that the administration was deliberately misleading Americans about WMDs, Iraq, and Al-Qaida can be found in the following: David Sarota and Christy Harvey, "They Knew," *In These Times,* 4 August 2004; Colonel Karen Kwiatkowski, "The New Pentagon Papers," http://www.salon.com/opinion/feature/2004/03/10; David Corn, "Willful Ignorance," *TomPaine.com;* Robert Dreyfuss and Jason Vest, "The Lie Factory," *Mother Jones,* January–February 2004; John B. Judis and Spencer Ackerman, "The Selling of the Iraq War," *New Republic,* 30 June 2003; Seymour Hersh, "Who Lied to Whom?" *New Yorker,* 31 March 2003; Seymour Hersh, "Selective Intelligence," *New Yorker,* 12 May 2003; Julian Borger, "The Spies Who Pushed for War," *The Guardian,* 17 July 2003; Jason Leopold, "CIA Probe Finds Secret Pentagon Group Manipulated Intelligence on Iraqi Threat," http://www.antiwar.com, 25 July 2003; Peter Canellos and Bryan Bender, "Questions Grow over Iraq Links to Al-Qaida," *Boston Globe,* 3 August 2003; Robert Dreyfuss, "More Missing Intelligence," *The Nation,* 7 July 2003; Scott Ritter, *Iraq Confidential.*

    35. *The Guardian,* 4 June 2003.

    36. Duffield, "Oil And The Iraq War"; Mark Almond, "It's All About Control,

Not the Price of Petrol," *New Statesman,* 7 April 2003; Linda Diebel, "Oil War: 23 Years in the Making," *Toronto Star,* 9 March 2003; Michael T. Klare, "For Oil and Empire?" Dave Lindorff, "Crude History Lesson: Is the War All About Oil After All?" *In These Times,* 27 March 2003, http://www.inthesetimes.com/site/main/article/crude_history_lesson; Arundhati Roy, "The New American Century," *The Nation,* 9 February 2004; *Foreign Policy in Focus,* 26 May 2004; *The Guardian,* 2 December 2003.

    37. *The Guardian,* 4 June 2003.

    38. Eric Schmitt, "Cheney Lashes Out," *New York Times,* 11 October 2003; see also Cheney's 2002 speech, at http://www.whitehouse.gov/news/releases/2002/08/20020826.html.

    39. The US Energy Information Agency predicted net oil imports by the United States nearly doubling to 19.8 million barrels per day by 2025, and that the share of all oil exports coming from the Persian Gulf would exceed 67 percent by 2020. Energy Information Administration, *Annual Energy Outlook 2002* (Washington, DC: US Department of Energy, December 2001), pp. 59–60; Energy Information Administration, *United States Country Analysis Brief,* January 2005, http://www.eia.doe.gov; Joe Barnes, Amy Jaffe, and Edward L. Morse, "The New Geopolitics of Oil," http://www.nationalinterest.org.

    40. Shibley Telhami et al., "Does Saudi Arabia Still Matter?"

    41. "Strategic Energy Policy Challenges for the 21st Century," report of an independent task force sponsored by the James A. Baker III Institute for Public Policy of Rice University and the Council on Foreign Relations, 2001, p. 4. See also Colin Campbell, *The Coming Oil Crisis.*

    42. Jeff Gerth, "Forecast of Rising Oil Demand Challenges Tired Saudi Fields," *New York Times,* 24 February 2004; Jeff Gerth, "Saudis Debate Expert in U.S. on Outlook for Their Oil," *New York Times,* 25 February 2004.

    43. Trevor Royle, "The World's Petrol Station: Iraq's Past Is Steeped in Oil . . . and Blood," *Sunday Herald,* 6 October 2002, http://www.sundayherald.com/print28226).

    44. Before the war began, Deputy Defense Secretary Paul Wolfowitz estimated that Iraqi oil revenues could bring in between $50 and $100 billion over the next two to three years. Gal Luft, "Iraq's Oil Sector One Year After Liberation," *Saban Center Middle East Memo* no. 4 (17 June 2004). Marie Cocco, *Washington Post,* August 9, 2005, concluded that "the rash predictions about Iraqi oil paying for the American conquest of Iraq were always suspicious, part of the marketing campaign that sold the war."

    45. Neela Banerjee, "Stable World Oil Prices Are Likely to Become a War Casualty, Experts Say," *New York Times,* 2 October 2002.

    46. Duffield, "Oil and the Iraq War"; "Guiding Principles for U.S. Post-Conflict Policy in Iraq," report of an independent working group cosponsored by the Council on Foreign Relations and the James A. Baker III Institute for Public Policy of Rice University, December 2002, p. 18, http://www.cfr.org/pdf/post-war_iraq.pdf.

    47. Michael T. Klare, "Oiling the Wheels of War," *The Nation,* 7 October 2002; Michael T. Klare, "Washington's Oilpolitik," *Salon.com,* 18 July 2002.

    48. *Los Angeles Times,* 23 March 2003.

    49. Duffield, "Oil and the Iraq War," pp. 10–13; Kenneth M. Pollack, *The Threatening Storm,* p. 167.

    50. See the review and critique of this argument in Robert Looney, "Petrodollars: A Threat to US Interests in the Gulf?" *Middle East Policy* 9, no. 1 (Spring 2004).

51. Michael Dobbs, "Oil Reserve Is 'First Line of Defense' for U.S.," *Washington Post,* 18 February 2003, wrote: "The Bush administration does not want to be held hostage by an Arab country rife with anti-Americanism that has previously used oil as a weapon against the United States."

52. Gregory Gause, "The Approaching Turning Point: The Future of U.S. Relations with the Gulf States," Brookings Project on U.S. Policy Towards the Islamic World, Analysis Paper no. 2, May 2003, p. 2.

53. A controversial July 2002 briefing by a neoconservative analyst for Richard Perle's Defense Advisory Board described Saudi Arabia as the "kernel of evil" in the Middle East and concluded that a pro-Western Iraq could reduce US dependence on Saudi energy exports and enable the United States to force the monarchy to crack down on financing and support for terrorism within its boundaries. Dan Morgan and David B. Ottaway, "War-Wary Saudis Move to Increase Oil Market Clout," *Washington Post,* 30 November 2002.

54. Noreng, *Crude Power,* pp. 3–5, 50–53, 70–82, 94–102.

55. Jay R. Mandle, "A War for Oil."

56. Pieterse, *Globalization or Empire?* pp. 22–25.

57. Jim Lobe, "Uncertain Anniversary for Iraq War Champions," September 2005, http://www.lewrockwell.com/ips/lobe243.html.

58. Roger Burbach and Jim Tarbell, *Imperial Overstretch,* pp. 155–157.

59. Pieterse, *Globalization or Empire?* p. 20.

60. Shimshon Bichler and Jonathan Nitzan, "Dominant Capital and the New Wars."

61. Pieterse, *Globalization or Empire?* p. 27.

62. The expression is cited in Pieterse, *Globalization or Empire?* p. 23. Only a sampling of the mountain of evidence accumulating on the role of the neoconservative-Likud association in the Iraq War can be indicated here. Their close association was suggesting by Thomas Neuman of the Jewish Institute for National Security Affairs, who exalted at the rise of the neoconservatives: "The Likudniks are really in charge now." Laurence A. Toenjes, "US Policy Toward Iraq: Unraveling the Web," June 2003, http://www.opednews.com. Neoconservatives famously authored a report to the Likudist Netanyahu government advocating a policy of aggressive confrontation with Israel's neighbors, advice even the Israeli prime minister rejected as too risky and extreme; many of the same neoconservatives later followed up in sponsoring a famous letter to President Bill Clinton urging the removal of Saddam Hussein. In his magisterial account, George Packer, *The Assassin's Gate,* concludes that the one thing the neoconservatives had in common was "an obsession with Israel" and a belief that the removal of Saddam Hussein would be very good for Israel and enable it to annex the Palestinian territories. A neoconservative reaction to 9/11 was to exclaim, "We are all Israelis now," implying an identity of interests between the United States and Israel in confronting the Arab-Islamic world. According to Joe Klein, *Time,* 5 February 2003: "Israel is very much embedded in the rationale for war with Iraq. It is part of the argument that dare not speak its name, a fantasy quietly cherished by the neo-conservative faction in the Bush administration and by many leaders of the American Jewish Community." According to General Anthony Zinni, a former commander of US forces in the Middle East, the neoconservatives' role in pushing the war on Israel's behalf was "the worst-kept secret in Washington." Ori Nir and Ami Eden, "Zinni Charges Neocons Pushed Iraq War to Benefit Israel," *Forward,* 28 May 2004. According to Philip Zelikow, a neoconservative member of the President's Foreign Intelligence Advisory Board at the time of the attack on Iraq, the "real threat" of Saddam's WMDs was not to the United States: "I'll tell you what

I think the real threat (is) and actually has been since 1990—it's the threat against Israel." *The Guardian,* 30 November 2003; *Daily Star,* 10 April 2004. For exhaustive documentation of the neoconservative role, see James Bamford, *Pretext for War.* The fact that several of the key players most aggressively pushing the Iraq War had originally proposed it for the benefit of another country (Israel) raises, Bamford observes, "the most troubling conflict of interest questions." Uri Avnery argues that "the small group that initiated this war—an alliance of Christian fundamentalists and Jewish neo-conservatives . . . constitutes a danger to the world, and especially to the Middle East, the Arab peoples and the future of Israel. . . . It does not dream only about an American empire, . . . but also of an Israeli mini-empire, under the control of the extreme right and the settlers. It wants to change the regimes in all Arab countries. It will cause permanent chaos in the region, the consequences of which it is impossible to foresee." "Israeli Journalist Uri Avnery Exposes Israel's Role in 'The Night After,'" http://www.counterpunch.org/avnery04102003.htm. See also Burback and Tarbell, *Imperial Overstretch,* pp. 96–100; Michael Lind, "The Israeli Lobby"; Joel Beinin, "Pro-Israeli Hawks and the Second Gulf War."

63. According to Stephen Green, Wolfowitz was blocked from transferring technology to Israel while several neoconservatives were investigated for or suspected of passing secrets to Israel covertly. Stephen Green, "Serving Two Flags: Neo-Cons, Israel and the Bush Administration," *Counterpunch,* 28–29 February 2004. Richard Perle, a leading figure in the Jewish Institute of National Security, which led the team that produced the report to Netanyahu advising a belligerent policy toward the Arabs, was investigated by the *New York Times* over allegations that he received a commission for recommending purchase of an Israel weapon. Hiro, *Secrets and Lies,* pp. 17–20.

64. Noreng, *Crude Power,* pp. 3–4; Seymour Hersh, "The Iraq Hawks: Can Their War Plan Work?" *New Yorker,* 24 December 2001.

65. Joe Barnes, Amy Jaffe, and Edward L. Morse, "The New Geopolitics of Oil."

66. See Chapter 15, on Israel. See also *Daily Star,* 10 April 2004.

67. Noam Chomsky, "Preventive War: 'The Supreme Crime,'" *Z Net Interactive,* 11 August 2003, http://www.zmag.org. Thus, neoconservative Michael Ledeen famously declared: "Every 10 years or so, the US needs to pick up some small crappy little country and throw it against the wall, just to show the world we mean business." Burbach and Tarbell, *Imperial Overstretch,* p. 149.

68. Marc Lynch, "Taking Arabs Seriously."

69. Joseph Cirincione, "Origins of Regime Change in Iraq."

70. Quoted in James Chase, "Quixotic America."

71. Frank Rich, "Karl and Scooter's Excellent Adventure," 23 October 2005, http://select.nytimes.com/2005/10/23/opinion.

72. Pieterse, *Globalization or Empire?* pp. 47–54, observes that companies linked to the ruling group cashed in on Iraq: the Carlyle Group, Halliburton, Dyna Corp International, and Bechtel in particular, which operated in Iraq under a no-risk government guarantee against losses and immunity for any wrongdoing. US and UK firms received the lion's share of contracts and Iraqis a mere 2 percent. There are an estimated 20,000 foreign security contractors currently in Iraq, with some being paid more than $1,000 a day, while funds for reconstruction are scarce.

Ellen Pringle has most thoroughly exposed what she considers the war-profiteering engaged in by top administration officials. She examines Richard Perle's Defense Policy Board, a group of thirty people, for the most part chosen by Rumsfeld and Feith, who are literally making a fortune off a war that they had been promoting for years. Other administrative officials and Republican lobbyists have also been assiduous in seeking to cash in on the war by brokering contracts in Iraq or from their stake in companies getting contracts. Halliburton, the firm formerly headed by Vice President Cheney (and from which he received "deferred pay" while in office) was awarded controversial no-bid contracts in Iraq by the Pentagon on the eve of the invasion and has earned more than $9 billion. According to Pringle and a June 2004 article in *Time* magazine ("The Paper Trail: Did Cheney Okay a Deal?"), Douglas Feith, whose dubious intelligence data was used to create a sense of threat from Iraq, approved the no-bid contract for Halliburton. Also, Feith was a partner in a law firm that teamed up with Ahmad Chalabi's nephew to facilitate business in Iraq by investors and contractors. Former CIA chief James Woolsey, a founding member of the Committee for the Liberation of Iraq who accused Iraq of aiding Al-Qaida's 9/11 attack, worked for or was a partner in private companies doing security business in Iraq after the invasion and was a featured speaker at a May 2003 conference for corporate executives on business opportunities in Iraq. There was, in Pringle's words, "a web-like profiteering network, that was specifically set up to funnel tax dollars through Iraq and back into the pockets of the Bush gang." She details the reports by government auditors and inspectors of the circumvention of federal contracting procedures and shabby accounting practices that opened the door to monumental fraud and waste as the US occupation authorities failed to account for the disposal of Iraqi money and US tax dollars. Pentagon audits showed $1.03 billion in "questioned" costs and $422 million in "unsupported" costs claimed by Halliburton. See http://news.yahoo.com/s/nm/20050910. A United Nations sanctioned audit concluded that about half of the $5 billion in Iraq reconstruction funds could not be accounted for. See Evelyn Pringle, "Top War Profiteer Douglas Feith Retires Wealthy," http://www.sierratimes.com/05/09/07/24; Evelyn Pringle, "Iraqis to Bush—Where Did All Our Money Go?" *Media Monitors Network,* 12 September 2005; Chris Floyd, "How the WMD Scam Put Money in the Bush Family's Pockets," *Counterpunch,* 5 March 2004. Bunnatine Greenhouse, the highest-ranked civilian employee in the Army Corps of Engineers, responsible for signing off on Iraq contracts, testified that her superiors forced her to sign no-bid contracts for Halliburton on the eve of the invasion of Iraq—"the most blatant and improper contract abuse I have witnessed during the course of my professional career." In retaliation, she was demoted. *Boston Globe,* 15 July 2005.

73. "I glance at the headlines but rarely read the stories," Bush admitted, in acknowledging his heavy dependence on advisers for his information. Hiro, *Secrets and Lies,* p. 417. Wolfowitz, whom Hiro says can rightly be considered the author of the war, impressed Bush with the idea that overthrowing Saddam would bring peace and democracy to the Middle East and allow abundant oil to flow to the US. Hiro, *Secrets and Lies,* pp. 385.

74. Shadia B. Drury, *Leo Strauss and the American Right,* the definitive history of the neoconservatives, points to their Machiavellianism and cabal-like organization. See also Jim Lobe, "The Strong Must Rule the Weak: A Philosopher for an Empire," *Foreign Policy in Focus,* 12 May 2003; A. Atlas, "A Classicist's Legacy: New Empire Builders," *New York Times,* 4 May 2003; Gregory Bruce Smith, "Leo Strauss and the Straussians: An Anti-democratic Cult?" *PS: Political Science & Politics* 30, no. 2 (June 1997).

75. W. Patrick Lang, "Drinking the Cool-Aid," *Middle East Policy* 11, no. 2 (Summer 2004), pp. 42–46. Joseph Cirincione, director of the Non-Proliferation Project at the Carnegie Endowment for International Peace, observed that the neoconservatives are "a textbook case of how a small, organized group can determine

policy in a large nation, even when the majority of officials and experts originally scorned their views." Secretary of State Colin Powell and the Joint Chiefs of Staff opposed them. "Powell's view was that Wolfowitz was fixated on Iraq, that they were looking for any excuse to bring Iraq into this [9/11]." Cirincione, "Origins of Regime Change in Iraq." See also http://news.ft.com/cms/s/afdb7b0c-40f3-11da-b3f9-00000e2511c8.html for the charge of General Colin Powell's chief of staff, Colonel Lawrence Wilkerson, that a "Cheney 'cabal' hijacked US foreign policy."

76. Douglas Feith's Office of Special Plans (OSP) was specifically created by Rumsfeld and Wolfowitz to bypass the usual bureaucratic channels in charge of analysis and collation. It used raw intelligence and disinformation, often from a single source, combining the most inflammatory claims, taken out of context, to promote the war. Cheney made a series of highly unorthodox visits to CIA headquarters in which he is said to have badgered low-level analysts to come up with information to substantiate claims of an Iraqi threat. Greg Thielman, director of the State Department's Bureau of Intelligence and Research until September 2002, testified: "This [the Bush] administration has had a faith-based attitude. . . . 'We know the answers—give us the intelligence to support those answers.'" The Carnegie Endowment report *WMD in Iraq* concluded that the intelligence community, being unduly influenced by policymakers' views, overestimated the threat while the latter misrepresented it to the public. For further documentation on the abuse of the policy process by the neoconservatives, see the exposé by former CIA counterterrorism analyst Michael Scheuer, *Imperial Hubris;* James Bamford, *Pretext for War;* Chapter 2 in this volume.

77. The words are those of Reverend Franklin Graham, chosen by George Bush to deliver the prayers at his presidential inauguration. *The Guardian,* 10 November 2003. On the Christian Zionists, see Norman Madarasz, "A Christian Fundamentalist and Rational Secularist United Front," *Counterpunch,* 12 January 2004; Godfrey Hodgson, "From Frontiersman to Neo-Con," *openDemocracy.net,* 24 April 2003.

78. Louis Fisher, "Deciding on War Against Iraq."

79. The role in selling the war of right-wing-funded advocacy think tanks, which masquerade as objective research groups but which actually exist to promote a policy line in government and the media, is documented in Burbach and Tarbell, *Imperial Overstretch,* pp. 76–124, 149–171.

80. For example, the Rendon Group public relations firm (responsible for inventing the fantasy of Iraqi soldiers ripping Kuwaiti babies out of their incubators that was pivotal in legitimizing the Gulf War) was literally responsible for the *invention* of the Iraqi National Congress, which lobbied for the Iraq War. "Saving Private Lynch" was another Rendon product. See Pieterse, *Globalization or Empire?* p. 51.

81. Sheldon Rampton and John Stauber document the abuse of and failures of the media in *Weapons of Mass Deception,* pp. 176–188. They expose why Americans were so ill informed: 70 percent got their information about the war from the likes of Rupert Murdock's Fox Network, which, together with his 140 sensationalist tabloids, peddled a common jingoism in the English speaking world. Fox won the ratings war with belligerent hyperpatriotism, which its competitors then tried to imitate. Clear Channel Communications, owning 1,200 radio stations, also propagandized for war. All the news media reported on Iraq under the government's label: "Operation Iraqi Freedom." "Embedded" reporters openly identified with the military while any critical reporting evoked an orchestrated avalanche of protest mail. This promoted pervasive media self-censorship: the *Donahue* show was axed by NBC for the perceived antiwar stance of many guests, antiwar rallies were given lit-

tle press coverage, peace groups were refused the right to buy air time by the major networks, CIA testimony to Congress on the low probability of Iraq using WMDs was hardly reported, and Americans received a sanitized version of the war's violence. A study at the University of Massachusetts showed that the more television people watched, the less they knew about Iraq, while greater knowledge was correlated with opposition to the war. That the major media are corporate owned and that oil companies, in particular, have major stakes in the media giants goes a long way toward explaining the lack of major dissenting views.

82. Zbigniew Brzezinski, "Another American Casualty: Credibility," *Washington Post,* 9 November 2003, p. B01.

83. By the start of the war, 66 percent of Americans thought Saddam Hussein was behind 9/11 and 79 percent thought he was close to having a nuclear weapon. Polling data released in October 2004 by the University of Maryland's Program on International Policy Attitudes (PIPA) (http://www.csmonitor.com/2004/0203) showed that "even after the final report of Charles Duelfer to Congress saying that Iraq did not have a significant WMD program, 72% of Bush supporters continue to believe that Iraq had actual WMD (47%) or a major program for developing them (25%)." Similarly, 75 percent of Bush supporters continued to believe that Iraq was providing substantial support to Al-Qaida. Asked whether the United States should have gone to war with Iraq if US intelligence had concluded that Iraq was not making WMDs or providing support to Al-Qaida, 58 percent of Bush supporters said the United States should not have, and 61 percent assumed that in this case the president would not have. PIPA, 21 October 2004.

84. Pieterse, "Hyperpower Exceptionalism" in *Globalization or Empire?* pp. 121–141; see also Andrew Bacevich, *The New American Militarism: How Americans Are Seduced by War.*

85. Fisher, "Deciding on War Against Iraq." According to George Soros, US foreign policy was in the hands of a "group of extremists" under whom "the abnormal, the radical, and the extreme have been redefined as normal." "The Bubble of American Supremacy," *Atlantic Monthly,* December 2003. For Michael Lind, *Made in Texas,* Bush II marks a takeover by an extreme right-wing cabal. Similarly, Seymour Hersh of the *New Yorker* mused in a speech on 8 October 2004 at the University of California, Berkeley: "How could eight or nine neo-conservatives come and take charge of this government? . . . They overran the bureaucracy, they overran the Congress, they overran the press, and they overran the military! So you say to yourself—How fragile is this democracy?" Quoted in Patrick Seale, "George W. Bush and the 'Politics of Fear,'" *Mafhoum,* 30 October 2004. Former ambassador Chas Freeman lamented that checks on the war party failed because patriotism was confused with silent acquiescence by those who knew better in policies that led the country into disaster. "The opposition party does not only not oppose, it does not propose alternatives. . . . This is . . . a systemic breakdown in the American democracy." Speech to the fourteenth annual Policymakers Conference of the National Council on US-Arab Relations, September 2005, http://weekly.ahram.org.eg/2005/762/op8.htm. See also the analysis of the policy process that led to war by Michael C. Hudson, "The United States in the Middle East," especially pp. 295–303.

86. See http://www.csmonitor.com/2004/0203.

87. Anthony Shadid, *Night Draws Near.*

88. "Continuing Collateral Damage: The Health and Environmental Costs of War on Iraq—Iraq Faces Severe Health Crisis," http://news.bbc.co.uk, 11 November 2003; http://news.independent.co.uk, 20 January 2004.

89. The British medical journal *Lancet* of October 2004 reported a Johns

Hopkins Medical School estimate, based on projections from household surveys, of 100,000 Iraqi deaths. Iraq Body Count's public database, based on actual reported deaths compiled by the Geneva-based Graduate Institute of International Studies, counted 39,000 Iraqis killed as a direct result of combat or armed violence since March 2003. An Iraqi humanitarian organization, *Iraqiyuun,* reported 128,000 Iraqis killed since the US invasion began in March 2003 based on data from relatives and families of the deceased and from Iraqi hospitals. Fifty-five percent of those killed were women and children. Since deaths are usually undercounted in war situations, the 100,000 figure seems plausible. *World Peace Herald,* 7 December 2005; http://news.bbc.co.uk, 11 November 2003; http://news.independent.co.uk, 8 February 2004.

90. The *Philadelphia Inquirer*'s 13 November 2003 report on a top-secret CIA report from Iraq.

91. Anthony Cordesman, *Iraq's Evolving Insurgency.* Falah Aljibury contends that it was the plan to sell off Iraq's oil that ultimately led to the insurgency and attacks on US occupying forces. "We saw an increase in the bombing of oil facilities, pipelines, built on the premise that privatization is coming," he reported. See Evelyn Pringle, "Iraqis to Bush—Where Did All Our Money Go?" *Media Monitors Network,* 12 September 2005; Tariq Ali, "The Same Old Racket in Iraq: To the Victors, the Spoils," *Counterpunch,* 13–14 December 2003; Phyllis Bennis, "Bush on Middle East 'Democracy' and also 'Ending Occupation in Iraq,'" *Foreign Policy in Focus,* 21 November 2003, 7 June 2004, http://www.fpif.org; Naomi Klein, "Bring Halliburton Home," *The Nation,* 24 November 2003.

92. According to Anthony Cordesman, the most prominent expert on Gulf security, US decisions were so flawed because they bypassed the interagency process and ignored the experts in favor of neoconservative ideologues and exile groups and because of Rumsfeld's pressure on the military to underman the invasion and the Pentagon's failure to plan for nation building. Cordesman, *Iraq's Evolving Insurgency.* George Packer, in *Assassins Gate,* reveals that the war party eschewed postwar planning because, in exposing the difficulties the United States would face, such planning might have obstructed the drive to war. He writes: "The arrogance phase [of the US war] was going in undermanned, under-resourced, [expecting to] skim off the top layer of leadership, take control of a functioning state, and be out by six weeks and get the oil funds to pay for it." See http://www.washingtonpost.com/wp-dyn/content/article/2005/10/06. One could also argue that for the neoconservatives, chaos in Iraq was perhaps no bad thing in that it would keep a potential major Arab power debilitated; they speak approvingly of unleashing "creative destruction" to remake the Middle East on Israel's behalf. Moreover, as long as the chaos in Iraq persists, the Iraqi government will need a US presence, a key Washington goal. Mark LeVine, "Where Chaos Is King," http://tomdispatch.com/index.mhtml?pid=30881.

93. Tony Karon, "Learning the Art of Occupation from Israel," *Time* magazine, 8 December 2003; "Israel Trains US Assassination Squads in Iraq," *Time* magazine, 9 December 2003; Julian Borger, *The Guardian,* 12 September 2003; *Christian Science Monitor,* 11 December 2003.

94. See http://news.bbc.co.uk/2/hi/middle_east/4344136.stm.

95. Mark Danner, "Delusions in Baghdad," *New York Review of Books* 50, no. 20 (18 December 2003).

96. *Washington Post,* 13 May 2004; *Christian Science Monitor,* 29 April 2004; Thomas Melia and Brian Katulis, "Iraqis Discuss Their Country's Future: Post-War Perspectives from the Iraqi Street," National Democratic Institute, 28 July 2003,

http://www.ndi.org; "Most Iraqis Mistrustful of US-Led Coalition, Poll Finds," *Agence-France Presse,* 12 January 2003, http://www.middle-east-online.com.

97. *Christian Science Monitor,* 11 December 2003.

98. *Los Angeles Times,* 7 October 2005.

99. Anthony Cordesman, *The Eroding US Position on Iraq.*

100. In 2004 polls, only 7–10 percent of Iraqi Arabs had a positive view of the United States; 92 percent saw the United States as an occupier and 2 percent as a liberator, while 55 percent would feel safer if the United States left compared to 29 percent less safe. Hiro, *Secrets and Lies,* pp. 486–488. A secret 2005 poll, undertaken for the UK Ministry of Defence, showed that up to 45 percent of Iraqi citizens supported attacks on the US/UK occupation forces, fewer than 1 percent thought allied military involvement was helping to improve security in the country, 82 percent were "strongly opposed" to the presence of occupation troops, and 67 percent of Iraqis felt less secure because of the occupation; 71 percent of people rarely got safe, clean water and 47 percent never had enough electricity. See http://telegraph. co.uk/news/main.jhtml;jsessionid=ehktkxoylvoovqfiqmfcnagavcbqyjvc?xml=/news/ 2005/10/23.

101. The occupation authorities attempted to lock in what *The Economist* described as "the wish-list of international investors." "Let's All Go to the Yard Sale: Iraq's Economic Liberalization," *The Economist,* 27 September 2003. US decrees gave foreign investors equal rights with Iraqis; permitted the full repatriation of profits; abolished tariffs; and authorized the sale of state-owned companies, reductions in food and fuel subsidies, and privatization of social services. By contrast, under an original draft of the constitution drawn up by Iraqi representatives, all of Iraq's natural resources would be owned collectively by the Iraqi people and the state would be legally bound to provide employment opportunities to everyone. However, all these provisions disappeared as US officials constantly intervened in the writing of the permanent constitution. US ambassador to Iraq Zalmay Khalilzad, a member of the Project for the New American Century who had called for invading Iraq, was described by *Reuters* as being a "ubiquitous presence" in the process and by the *Financial Times* as playing a "big role in the negotiations" over the constitution. Complained one Kurdish member of the constitutional committee: "The Americans say they don't intervene, but they have intervened deep. They gave us a detailed proposal, almost a full version of a constitution." Notably, the provision affirming the Iraqi people's collective ownership of Iraq's oil was replaced by a provision that Herbert Docena believes lays the legal ground for selling off Iraq's oil. He argues that the Shia and Kurdish parties seem to have accepted the neoliberal economic provisions in the constitution in return for US acquiescence in their plans to balkanize the country—against the wishes of most Iraqis. According to a July 2005 survey conducted by the International Republican Institute, 69 percent of Iraqis wanted the constitution to establish "a strong central government" and only 22 percent wanted to give "significant powers to regional governments." Even in Shia-majority areas in the south, only 25 percent wanted federalism while 66 percent rejected it. Jonathan Finer and Omar Fekeiki, "U.S. Steps Up Role in Iraq Charter Talks," *Washington Post,* 13 August 2005; Michael Georgy, "Iraq Parliament May Back Charter, Sunnis Opposed," *Reuters,* 28 August 2005; Steve Negus and Dhiya Rasan, "Iraqi Parliament Delays Constitution Vote," *Financial Times,* 23 August 2005; Herbert Docena, "Iraq's Neoliberal Constitution," *Foreign Policy in Focus,* 2 September 2005, http://www.fpif.org; International Crisis Group, "Unmaking Iraq: A Constitutional Process Gone Awry," *Middle East Briefing* no. 19 (26 September 2005).

102. Pieterse, *Globalization or Empire?* p. 55.

103. General John Abizaid of Central Command told Congress in early October 2005 that the Iraqi army had only one fully independent battalion—about 500 men. In the vacuum, the insurgents—numbering perhaps 20,000—and sectarian militias, proliferated. *Newsweek,* 10 October 2005. One reason the Iraqi army is so ill equipped in the face of well-armed insurgents is because its procurement budget of over $1 billion had been siphoned out of the country; weapons either were never supplied or were discovered to be useless on delivery. The Iraqi government was expected to issue a warrant for the arrest of Hazem al-Shaalan, the former defense minister and formerly a London businessman, in connection with the disappearance of more than $1 billion. Patrick Cockburn, *Independent on Line,* 20 September 2005, http://news.independent.co.uk.

104. According to *Newsweek,* 10 October 2005, there is an undeclared civil war in Iraq, with rival Sunni, Shiite, and Kurdish militias and death squads precipitating ethnic cleansing. A UN report called the new constitution a formula for territorial breakup, with the Kurds and Shia creating mini-states, the latter linked to Iran. This is precisely the scenario about which Arab leaders repeatedly warned Washington before the war.

105. Rhodes, "Imperial Logic," p. 142; Jervis, "Understanding the Bush Doctrine."

106. Owing to the dilapidated oil infrastructure and sabotage by insurgents, oil export revenues totaled only $5 billion in 2003 and just over $17 billion in 2004, while a sabotage campaign created an inhospitable investment climate for foreign oil companies.

107. See http://news.independent.co.uk, 20 January 2004; Erik Leaver, "The Costs of Quagmire," *Foreign Policy in Focus,* 14 September 2005, http://www.ips-dc.org/iraq/quagmire.

108. *Reuters,* 13 November 2003.

109. The book *Imperial Hubris,* by Michael Scheuer, formerly the top CIA official responsible for the fight against Al-Qaida, accuses Bush of diverting energies from the real security threat by invading Iraq. Lieutenant-General William Odom, director of the National Security Agency under Ronald Reagan, declared Bush's invasion of Iraq to be the "greatest strategic disaster in United States history." Paul Craig Roberts, "The Greatest Strategic Disaster in US History," http://counterpunch.com/roberts10032005.html.

110. *New York Times,* 8 May 2004. According to Paul Craig Roberts, a former assistant secretary of the Treasury in the Reagan administration: "In the US today nothing stands in the way of the arbitrary exercise of power by government. Federal courts have acquiesced in unconstitutional detention policies. There is no opposition party, and there is no media, merely huge conglomerates or collections of federal broadcasting licenses, the owners of which are afraid to displease the government." Paul Craig Roberts, "Government by Star Chamber," *Counterpunch,* 16 September 2005.

111. Jervis, "Understanding the Bush Doctrine."

112. In March 2004, 65 percent of Americans supported the decision to wage war in Iraq. A year later, support had sagged to 44 percent, with 53 percent thinking the war a mistake and 57 percent of Americans believing that they were "less safe" than before the war. Only 40 percent of Americans approved of and 59 percent disapproved of Bush's handling of Iraq. *Reuters,* 16 August 2005.

113. Schwenninger, "Revamping American Grand Strategy."

114. Pieterse, *Globalization or Empire?* p. 44.

115. Hiro, *Secrets and Lies,* p. 150.

116. Jervis, "Understanding the Bush Doctrine."

117. David Marquand, "Why Blair Dressed Up War Realpolitik in Dodgy Moralistic Rhetoric," *The Guardian,* 21 February 2004.

118. See Chapter 8.

119. According to a Pew Research Center poll conducted shortly before the war began, a majority of respondents in France (75 percent), Germany (54 percent), and Russia (76 percent) agreed with the statement that "the United States wanted to control Iraqi oil." But opposition to the war in states nominally supporting the United States ran at least as high: 73 percent in Italy, 79 percent in Denmark, 67 percent in the Czech Republic, 82 percent in Hungary, and 63 percent in Poland. *Reuters,* 30 January 2003; Noam Chomsky, "Invasion as Marketing Problem: The Iraq War and Contempt for Democracy," *Counterpunch,* 14 November 2003; Anatol Lieven, "The Hinge to Europe: Don't Make Britain Choose Between the U.S. and the E.U.," Carnegie Endowment for International Peace, policy brief, 25 August 2003.

120. See http://www.telegraph.co.uk//2004/03/15.

121. Countries assembled at a conference to aid the reconstruction of Iraq pledged $8 billion, against an overall estimate of $55 billion in reconstruction needs between 2004 and 2007, and actually paid out much less. Duffield, "Oil and the Iraq War."

122. Clyde Prestowitz, "America the Arrogant: Why Don't We Listen Anymore?" *WashingtonPost.com,* 7 July 2002, p. B01.

123. The director of intelligence coordination for the German government, Ernst Uhrlau, declared that the Iraq War had become the single most important motivating factor for terrorist activities in contemporary Europe. European security agencies were bracing themselves for the possible return from Iraq of Arab fighters to western Europe and worried about the growing radicalization of the diaspora Muslims in Europe. See http://www.theaustralian.news.com.au/common/story_page/0,5744,16608035%255e2703,00.html. The National Intelligence Council, a CIA think tank, reported in January 2005 that Iraq was providing a training and recruitment ground for a new generation of Islamic militants, just as Afghanistan had done for Al-Qaida. Hiro, *Secrets and Lies,* p. 523. Dilip Hiro notes that the flypaper theory that terrorists are attracted to Iraq, where they can be killed so they don't harm the United States itself, assumes there is a finite number of them; but the pool of possible disaffected dramatically grew because of the war. Even 1 percent of the world's 1.3 billion Muslims is 1.3 million people. Hiro, *Secrets and Lies,* p. 387.

124. Zbigniew Brzezinski, "Another American Casualty: Credibility," *WashingtonPost.com,* 9 November 2003, p. B01.

125. Gabriel Kolko, "The Coming Elections and the Future of American Global Power," *Counterpunch,* 12–14 March 2004.

126. Arthur Schlesinger, *Los Angeles Times,* 23 March 2003.

127. Those with a favorable view of the United States decreased in France from 63 to 31 percent, in Italy from 70 to 34 percent, in Russia from 61 to 28 percent, in the UK from 75 to 48 percent. Rampton and Stauber, *Weapons of Mass Deception,* p. 6.

128. Cited in *International Herald Tribune,* 1–2 February 2003.

129. A congressionally mandated advisory panel warned that "America's image and reputation abroad could hardly be worse." A fact-finding mission to the Middle East had found that "there is deep and abiding anger toward U.S. policies

and actions." Large majorities in Egypt, Morocco, and Saudi Arabia "view George W. Bush as a greater threat to the world order than Osama bin Laden" and the United States is viewed as "less a beacon of hope than a dangerous force to be countered." See http://www.washingtonpost.com/wp-dyn/content/article/2005/09/23. Only 7 percent of Saudis, 15 percent of Turks, and 6 percent of Egyptians had a favorable view of the United States. See http://www.nytimes.com/2004/02/05. One percent of Jordanians and Palestinians, 17 percent of Indonesians, and 19 percent of Pakistanis had a favorable view of the United States in summer 2002. Hiro, *Secrets and Lies,* pp. 352–353. More remarkably, in Kuwait, a country the United States had recently liberated from Iraq, only 28 percent had a favorable view. Rampton and Stauber, *Weapons of Mass Deception,* pp. 30, 34.

130. According to Alain Gresh, the scandals of Guantanamo Bay and Abu Ghraib and the erosion of civil liberties in the United States undermined Washington's claims that it alone was capable of defining universal values of human rights and democracy and had the sole authority to decide whether regimes were acceptable or not. Alain Gresh, "Just Saying No," http://mondediplo.com/2005/09/01.

131. Quoted in Pieterse, *Globalization or Empire?* p. 29.

132. *Asahi Shinbun,* 18 February 2003.

133. David Hendrickson, "Toward Universal Empire."

134. In September 2003, Kofi Annan said that "if this doctrine [of preventive war] were to be adopted, it could set precedents that resulted in a proliferation of the unilateral and lawless use of force, with or without credible justification. This logic represents a fundamental challenge to the principles on which, however imperfectly, world peace and stability have rested." *New York Times,* 24 September 2003. Eight out of ten international lawyers would agree, said the dean of Princeton School of International Affairs. Robert Black, Edinburgh University professor of law, said the real legal test of US justifications for the war would be whether the International Court of Justice would accept the argument, the odds against which were, he thought, ten to one. Hiro, *Secrets and Lies,* p. 167.

135. Kenneth Roth. "The Law of War in the War on Terror."

136. Quoted in Glenn Perry, "Huntington and His Critics."

137. John Ikenberry, "American Power and the Empire of Capitalist Democracy."

138. Thus, Anatol Lieven observed that while the United States should have acted like a satisfied power, it was behaving as a revisionist one, "kicking to pieces the hill of which it is king." "The Empire Strikes Back," *The Nation,* 7 July 2003.

139. Organski, *World Politics.*

140. Jervis, "Understanding the Bush Doctrine," p. 380.

141. As Kenneth Waltz argues, "The vice to which great powers easily succumb in a multipolar world is inattention; in a bi-polar world, overreaction, in a unipolar world, overextension." Kenneth Waltz, "Structural Realism After the Cold War," p. 12.

142. Waltz, "Structural Realism After the Cold War," pp. 12, 27.

143. Stephen Krasner, *Defending the National Interest.*

144. Waltz, "Structural Realism After the Cold War," pp. 12, 27.

145. Birthe Hansen, *Unipolarity and the Middle East.* Actually Hansen uses the term "flocking" to denote deference to the hegemon, rather than "bandwagoning"; certainly it is true that for most states, following the hegemon is not usually the traditional form of bandwagoning in which a state heads off an attack on itself by *joining* (rather than balancing against) a threatening state. Rather, as she points out,

most states are threatened by regional rivals, not the distant hegemon, and seek the latter's support against the former. But this may be changing as the United States goes beyond offshore balancing.

146. Stephen Walt, "Taming American Power: The Global Response to U.S. Primacy," *Foreign Affairs* (September–October 2005).

147. William Wohlforth, "The Stability of a Unipolar World."

148. Volgy and Bailin, *International Politics and State Strength.*

149. The New America Foundation, a grouping of foreign policy and security elites, argues (in an oblique criticism of the Bush government) that the war on terrorism requires "strong partnerships with allies based on mutual respect" and "living up to traditional U.S. principles, such as the rule of law, in conducting the war, at home as well as overseas." Jim Lobe, "Four Years After 9/11, Anti-Terror Strategy in Doubt," 9 September 2005, http://www.antiwar.com/lobe/?articleid=7207.

150. Pieterse, *Globalization or Empire?* pp. 26, 29.

151. Symptomatic of this, Control Risk, a UK security consultancy, identifies aggressive US unilateralism as the most important single factor driving up global risk. *Financial Times,* 11 November 2003.

24

Lessons of the Iraq War

Raymond Hinnebusch and Rick Fawn

W hat are the lessons of the Iraq War for our understanding of foreign policy making and international relations? Does the war revalidate the once dominant paradigm, realism, which since the end of the Cold War has been under increasing attack by liberal, constructivist, and international society alternatives? Does it revalidate Marxist theories of imperialism after Marxism's post–Cold War decline?

■ The Iraq War and Theories of Foreign Policy Making

The Iraq case reveals some interesting anomalies in the foreign policy process, at least in the US and UK cases. In both cases, war was driven from the top by an ideological-minded leader. What is more remarkable, however, is how much of the permanent bureaucracy, believed by the bureaucratic politics approaches to shape outcomes, was systematically ignored, bypassed, or pressured by politicians or political appointees to support a policy that did not enjoy much support among foreign policy "experts." Another remarkable phenomenon that some analysts believe was exposed by the war was the intimate links between the US neoconservatives and the Israeli Likud Party, suggesting a role of transnational networks in the policy process. While Robert Keohane and Joseph Nye see a role for such networks under conditions of complex interdependence,[1] it is specifically thought to be characteristic of low politics—material interests subject to compromise; in this case, however, such networks were operating within the domain of peace and war and involved identity movements with messianic agendas. The importance of the neoconservative-Likud connection is, of course, highly contested and might best be taken as a hypothesis deserving of further research. Finally, however, certain stereotypic aspects of bureaucratic-politics behavior were in evidence, such as the accusations of intelligence agencies keeping information from one another, and of the exclusion of State Department specialists on the Middle East from Pentagon-run actions on-ground in Iraq. Does the Iraq experience undermine the realist view of the state as a unitary rational actor, or reaffirm it in that top elites were able to overcome opposition in their own foreign policy establishments to pursue their own views of the national interest?

In this respect, constructivism's view that there are no objective interests and that, rather, identity shapes conceptions of interest and threat, seems validated.[2] Washington's particular conceptions of the US interest seemed to have been radically altered with the rise of Bush's particular coalition to power, marginalizing the "realist" establishment that had seen interests and threats in a quite different way. Moreover, the systematic and successful effort of the Bush administration to "construct" an imminent Iraqi threat by invoking the widespread sense of fear and insecurity created by 9/11, even though no such threat materially existed, supports the notion, long familiar from the writings of scholars such as Robert Jervis and John Stoessinger,[3] that threats—and the wars they drive—do not objectively matter apart from perceptions and misperceptions of them.

Iraq is a good case for testing the relative power of structural (systemic) versus domestic determinants in foreign policy making. Kenneth Waltz's "defensive realist" image of systemic constraints and socialization/selection experiences shaping a prudent defensive use of power does not predict US behavior, perhaps because the US hegemon, almost uniquely, has not experienced much of the trauma of war that socialized "Old Europe."[4] Offensive realism, predicated on the notion that one can never have enough power in an insecure world, seems more apropos, although its main proponent, John Mearsheimer, denied that the Iraq War was necessary to US security.[5] Indeed, the ability of the United States to launch a war against the opposition of most other great powers shows how little a hegemonic power faces systemic constraints (the power balance) compared to other states; the world, at least as seen by the hawks at the core of the Bush administration, seemed not to be one of neorealist material constraints or security dilemmas, but one where merely normative constraints (such as international law) on the projection of overwhelming US power should and could be swept aside. The case suggests that when the system level ceases to be the major constraint on behavior expected by neorealism, there is more scope for domestic determinants to drive policy.

Most other governments, however, were caught by the war between hegemonic power and domestic constituencies. For these, the relative impact of the (unipolar) systemic structure appears to have depended on state strength. Generally, strong states either stood with domestic opinion against the hegemon (Germany, France, and arguably Canada) or used the war for their own interests (Japan and Britain, each of which sought enhanced great power status through association with Washington); weak states needed the hegemon (albeit for diverging reasons) and hence defied or evaded accountability to domestic opinion in order to bandwagon with it (postcommunist and Middle Eastern states). Russia and China, states with certain weaknesses but also exceptional strengths (nuclear arsenals, permanent UN Security Council seats, vast size/populations) were driven less by accountability to public opinion (which nevertheless overwhelmingly opposed the war) than by conceptions of their great power interests in opposing the hegemon without actively balancing against it.

What was striking was how little regime type (democratic versus nondemocratic) made a difference for a government's stand on the war. In democracies such as Germany and France, leaders rode the crest of public opinion, and it was only the deepening of Turkey's democracy that allowed public opinion to block the government's natural tendency to bandwagon with its global patron. By contrast, in Britain, Spain, and Eastern Europe, leaders defied their publics. In the US case, checks and balances were systematically subverted and public opinion misled by "weapons of mass deception";[6] similarly, in the UK, cabinet-level checks were undermined by Tony Blair's "presidentialism." In both countries, opposition parties made little difference, while politicization of the bureaucracy distorted policy processes partly designed to prevent arbitrary decisions. Ostensibly democratic state structures could *either* transmit public wishes into decisionmaking or buffer leaders from them.

Similarly, less democratic or authoritarian states were also to be found on both sides of the issue. In the Arab world the episode consolidated the yawning cleavage between public opinion and nondemocratic regimes that bandwagon with the hegemon to contain opposition at home or are highly dependent on it for security against neighbors. The one exception, Syria, whose opposition to the war risked regime interests but reflected public opinion, was more authoritarian than most. The Arab "street" was again shown to be impotent, with much less public protest than in the Gulf War, although mass frustration is probably fueling continuing "terrorism" (see below).

Generally, the evidence on the determinants of foreign policy in the Iraq War tends to better correspond to the expectations of realism than to those of its rivals, with the crucial exception of the hegemon. Ordinary states were constrained by the system level, albeit differentially according to their strength, while regime type—democratic or nondemocratic—carried little explanatory power. But the hegemon, relatively unconstrained by the system, was overtly driven by domestic and transnational politics rather than realism's material threats. And these forces, operating through the hegemon, shaped the (systemic) situation to which other actors could only respond.

■ Iraq's Significance for Theories of Imperialism and War

The notion of the United States as an empire is becoming central to contemporary political debate, with numerous scholarly works published on the issue of whether the United States is an empire and, if so, of what kind.[7] US empire is generally thought to be *informal or indirect,* since it does not, except as a temporary expedient, involve territorial conquest: such informal empire is arguably located on a continuum somewhere between conventional territorial empire and the liberal idea of global hegemony based on consent.

Globalization theorists argue that contemporary empire is "indirect" because power and wealth no longer directly derive from physical control of territories, which, on the contrary, can entail burdensome responsibilities.[8] But the Iraq War nevertheless supports Chalmers Johnson's view of the United States as an empire of global clients and military bases that, however "informal" it may be, depends on control of strategic territories. That a strategic territory "swimming in oil" can be seen by empire-builders as a prize rather than a burden suggests that globalization has emphatically *not* put an end to geopolitics. The war also demonstrates how crucial military force remains to empire, not least to entrenching informal systems of control in the face of popular resistance.[9] Ronald Robinson's notion of empire as a system in which war puts in place largely economic instruments allowing durable exploitation of periphery states,[10] and Michael Klare's notion of resource wars in the third world,[11] both seem validated by the seizure and attempted neoliberal privatization of Iraq's oil and economy.

Theories of benign hegemony such as John Ikenberry's, critiqued in Chapter 23, or of "liberal imperialism," such as Niall Ferguson's view of US empire as a consensual one of invitation reluctantly assumed in a needed defense of world order, hardly seem compatible with the Iraq War, which was largely imposed on a skeptical or unwilling Europe and Middle East and at risk to world order.[12]

According to Benjamin Barber, a drive to empire is not inherent in the United States but a function of the Bush administration's will to power and ability to exploit Americans' fear of threat (9/11).[13] This is plausible but does not adequately settle the issue: after all, a similar combination existed under Ronald Reagan and was only constrained by the then-existence of a superpower balance, and it does not wholly explain how George W. Bush so easily ran roughshod over all the checks and balances, notably Congress, built into the US policy process. Emmanuel Todd's argument that the corruption of US democracy has enervated the domestic constraints expected by theories of democratic peace to constrain war, seems relevant here.[14] However, for "structuralists" such as Roger Burbach and Jim Tarbell, control of oil, the key to US empire and source of the superprofits that benefit its right-wing elites, is what drove Washington;[15] even those who reject this view of the motivations of, or at least the benefits for, particular economic interests within the United States do acknowledge that access to oil is essential to daily US economic well-being and the international position of the United States. Clearly the US drive to empire (if that is what Iraq exemplifies) has multiple determinants.

But is empire viable in the contemporary world? European empires were possible because of the relatively brief period when they enjoyed decisive military and technological superiority, but for much of the twentieth century, conventional warfare capacities tended to narrow as anticolonial wars of liberation made empire too costly, at least as long as countervailing Soviet power generally prevented Western powers from unrestrained use of their military capabilities. However, is imperialism again viable in a post–Cold War era, particularly as the "revolution in military affairs" promises to make war relatively cost-free for the United States and hence a usable instrument of power projection in the third world?[16]

The apparently cost-free high-tech war recently waged by dominant powers, notably in Kosovo, has been described by Michael Ignatieff as "virtual war."[17] The United States evidently did think it would fight a war in Iraq with some (certainly not all) of the features of such a virtual war, that is, one dominated from the air and with few casualties or costs for itself and requiring minimal sacrifice or commitment from its citizenry. Of course the Iraq War differs from the strategic dimensions of virtual war in the size of the deployment, the implications for society of the extensive use of reservists, and the risks inherent to all of these forces even from the underequipped Iraqi military and from guerrilla forces. But the initial tactics used suggested a desire nevertheless for limited direct engagement. This included the targeted decapitation strike against Saddam Hussein and the concept of "shock and awe" itself, which was meant to collapse the regime with a limited number of precision attacks against high-value targets.

However, the truism that war planners always plan to fight the last war, not the one they actually face, nowhere seems more apropos than in Iraq. To be sure, the Iraq campaign had little of a conventional state-to-state war, as Saddam's obsolete army could hardly stand up to US forces operating under a strategic doctrine that provided unprecedented operational integration of massive, well-armed, sophisticated air and ground forces. Despite this, what the United States ended up with was a classic case of Mary Kaldor's so-called new war, in which its role was not that of a benevolent humanitarian intervener facilitating state reconstruction but a party to a substate conflict about nationalism and identity and facing a resistance using both terror tactics and guerrilla warfare.[18] The Iraq case may signal, thus, that virtual wars are special cases and not the post–Cold War norm.

Moreover, the war may actually have been counterproductive in that it had been justified in terms of the war on terrorism; a report by a body of prestigious terrorism experts led by Paul Wilkinson concluded that the war "gave al-Qaida . . . a major propaganda, recruiting and fund-raising boost and . . . a perfect training ground for a new generation of terrorist planners and operatives."[19] More than that, Samuel Huntington's notion that the US reach for empire risks a clash of civilizations seems supported; the war was unleashed by and has fueled a clash of Muslim with Christian/Jewish fundamentalisms.[20]

If that is so, then writers such as Michael Mann[21] and Barber may be right that the neoconservatives' apparent imperial ambitions derived from an inflated idea of US power. They argue that US military muscle, unmatched by commensurate political and economic capabilities, merely increases resistance in the targeted societies. Robinson argued that nineteenth-century empire depended on not-too-asymmetrical bargains between the imperial center and local collaborators, but such collaborators cannot acquire much legitimacy in today's Muslim world and depend on constant US protection; in Iraq, the United States has not even been able to provide physical protection for those who are seen to collaborate with it. The soft underbelly of US power in Todd's view is its reluctance to take casualties and to pay the costs of rebuilding the societies that it invades; certainly Washington hoped to do Iraq on the cheap, but it has not worked out that way. Iraq is thus a test case of the neoconservatives' project of liberal empire. Specifically, it tests whether wars of regime change followed by "democratization" of a sort can be a cost-effective formula for establishing stable regimes aligned with the world hegemon. At this point, the verdict is simply not yet in.

■ Iraq's Significance for Theories of World Order

The Iraq War carries major significance for prospects that the post–Cold War world order might evolve beyond the old realist power politics. Liberals have argued that with the growth of complex interdependence and the end of the Cold War, the balance of power was, possibly, becoming obsolete as the basis of world order, replaced by the shared norms of a deepening international society, backed by checks on power inside democratic states and, at the suprastate level, by international organization and law. By contrast, realists, such as Stephen Krasner, have countered that norms could not effectively constrain power because there were so many conflicting norms or interpretations of them that (in the absence of an authoritative global judiciary) great powers would use the norms and interpretations that suited their interests and ignore others that constrained them.[22]

In fact, both of the mechanisms that liberals expect to make for a democratic peace failed to prevent US war-making. Constraints on the executive within the United States were as easily overridden as were those from without, such as the UN and international law. The Bush administration's promulgation of a new doctrine of preventive war, justified by the norm of self-defense, and its mobilization of its own international lawyers to contest the conventional presumption against war, suggest that Krasner is right about the malleability of norms. Indeed, the war-makers threw off customary legal constraints with remarkable ease.

This is not to argue that norms do not count, however; that they matter can be seen in the fact that the Iraq War was facilitated by the previous erosion of one of the main normative pillars of international order, sovereignty, by the self-assumed right of supposedly benign great powers, widely backed by liberal opinion, to undertake "humanitarian intervention" against rogue or repressive states. Whatever the merits of this argument in theory and in particular cases, by undermining the presumption against the first use of force, it weakens one of the main normative restraints against predatory great powers on which world order rests. But Krasner is surely right that the multitude of conflicting norms opens the door to their use and abuse. Thus the liberal norm of democratization, laudable in itself, can also seemingly be manipulated to brush aside other liberal norms such as international law. As many have observed, the neoconservatives are, underneath, Straussians, holding a Machiavellian view of politics in which the ends pursued by the enlightened few justify the use of violence and deception;[23] the Iraq War was a classic deployment of both such means, with liberal norms manipulated to construct an ex post facto justification for conquest and occupation: the mission, to spread democracy.

As for the role of international institutions and the expected post–Cold War empowerment of the UN, the lesson of the war for the organization was highly ambivalent. The United States failed to pressure the UN into setting aside international law or the presumption against the first use of force. On the other hand, this did not stop the US war, and not a single UN member dared sponsor a resolution condemning it; this recalls the failure of the League of Nations to restrain great powers bent on aggression against weaker states—a failure that arguably set the stage for World War II. To be sure, in the aftermath of its invasion of Iraq, the United States felt it needed UN legitimation for its occupation, but it was readily able to extract this from the Security Council without conceding its sole control over Iraq to international supervision.

The Iraq episode suggests that interstate normative and institutional constraints are most effective when they are underlain by or in congruence with material ones, specifically a *balance of power*. This long-understood basic *realist* principle of world governance has been lost sight of in the post–Cold War period of liberal optimism.

Needless to say, these short observations can constitute no more than some preliminary suggestions as to the implications of the Iraq War for our understanding of world politics. This presumably will constitute a major focus of the coming research agenda in the discipline.

■ Notes

1. Robert Keohane and Joseph Nye, *Power and Interdependence.*
2. See, for example, Alexander Wendt's seminal article "Anarchy Is What States Make of It."
3. Robert Jervis, *Perception and Misperception in International Politics;* John G. Stoessinger, *Why Nations Go to War* (various editions).
4. Kenneth Waltz, *Theory of International Politics.*
5. See John Mearsheimer and Stephen Walt, "An Unnecessary War"; see also John Mearsheimer, *The Tragedy of Great Power Politics.*
6. Sheldon Rampton and John Stauber, *Weapons of Mass Deception.*
7. John Ikenberry, "Illusions of Empire."
8. Michael Hardt and Antonio Negri, *Empire.*
9. Chalmers Johnson, *The Sorrows of Empire.*
10. Ronald Robinson, "Imperial Theory and the Question of Imperialism After Empire."
11. Michael T. Klare, *Resource Wars.*
12. John Ikenberry, "American Power and the Empire of Capitalist Democracy"; Niall Ferguson, *Colossus.*
13. Benjamin R. Barber, *Fear's Empire.*
14. Emmanuel Todd, *After the Empire.*
15. Roger Burbach and Jim Tarbell, *Imperial Overstretch.*
16. Stephen Howe, "American Empire: The History and Future of an Idea," *openDemocracy.net,* 12 June 2003.
17. Michael Ignatieff, *Virtual War.*
18. Mary Kaldor, *New and Old Wars.*
19. Centre for the Study of Terrorism and Political Violence and the Mountbatten Centre for International Studies, report of St. Andrews/Southampton Universities ESRC Project on the UK's Preparedness for Future Terrorist Attack, 2004.
20. Glenn Perry, "Huntington and His Critics."
21. Michael Mann, *Incoherent Empire.*
22. Stephen Krasner, "Rethinking the Sovereign State Model," p. 19.
23. Danny Postel, "Noble Lies and Perpetual War: Leo Strauss, the Neo-Cons, and Iraq," *openDemocracy.net,* 17 November 2003; Jim Lobe, "The Strong Must Rule the Weak: A Philosopher for an Empire," *Foreign Policy in Focus,* 12 May 2003.

Bibliography

Aarts, Paul. "The New Oil Order: Built on Sand?" *Arab Studies Quarterly* 16, no. 2 (1994).

Ajami, Fouad. *The Vanished Imam: Musa Al Sadr and the Shia of Lebanon*. Ithaca: Cornell University Press, 1986.

Aliriza, Bulent. "Turkey's Iraq Jitters." *CSIS Turkey Update*, 18 October 2002.

Allison, Graham T., and Morton H. Halpern. "Bureaucratic Politics: A Paradigm and Some Policy Implications." *World Politics* 24 (Spring 1992).

Amaki, Naoto. *Saraba Gaimusho: Watashi wa Baikoku Kanryo wo Yurusanai* [Good-bye Foreign Ministry: The Unforgivable Bureaucrats Who Sold Their Country]. Tokyo: Kodansha, 2003.

al-Angari, Haifa. *The Struggle for Power in Arabia: Ibn Saud, Hussein, and Great Britain, 1914–1924*. Reading, MA: Ithaca Press, 1998.

Augustine of Hippo. *Political Writings*. Edited by E. M. Atkins and R. J. Dodaro. Cambridge: Cambridge University Press, 2001.

Axworthy, Lloyd. *Navigating a New World: Canada's Global Future*. Toronto: Knopf Canada, 2003.

Bacevich, Andrew. *The New American Militarism: How Americans Are Seduced by War*. Oxford: Oxford University Press, 2005.

Bamford, James. *Pretext for War: 9/11, Iraq, and the Abuse of America's Intelligence Agencies*. New York: Doubleday, 2004.

Barber, Benjamin R. *Fear's Empire: War, Terrorism, and Democracy*. New York: W. W. Norton, 2003.

Barnes, Joe, Amy Jaffe, and Edward L. Morse. "The New Geopolitics of Oil." *National Interest*, Energy Supplement, 15 November 2004.

Beinin, Joel. "Pro-Israeli Hawks and the Second Gulf War." *Middle East Report Online* (April 2003), http://www.merip.org/mero.

Beltran, Jacques. *French Policy Towards Iraq*. US-France Analysis Series. Washington, DC: Brookings, September 2002.

Bennis, Phyllis. "And They Call It Peace." *Middle East Report* no. 215 (Summer 2000).

Bennis, Phillis, et al. *A Failed "Transition": The Mounting Cost of the Iraq War*. Washington, DC: Institute for Policy Studies and Foreign Policy in Focus, 2004.

Bergen, Peter L. *Holy War, Inc.: Inside the Secret World of Osama bin Laden*. London: Weidenfeld and Nicolson, 2001.

331

Betts, Richard. "The Soft Underbelly of American Primacy." *Political Science Quarterly* 117, no. 1 (2002).
———. "Striking First: A History of Thankfully Lost Opportunities." *Ethics & International Affairs* 17, no. 1 (2003).
Bichler, Shimshon, and Jonathan Nitzan. "Dominant Capital and the New Wars." *Journal of World-Systems Research* 10, no. 2 (Summer 2004).
Biddle, Stephen, et al. *Toppling Saddam: Iraq and American Military Transformation.* Carlisle Barracks, PA: Strategic Studies Institute, US Army, April 2004.
Bina, Cyrus. "The Rhetoric of Oil and the Dilemma of War and American Hegemony." *Arab Studies Quarterly* 15, no. 3 (1993).
Blix, Hans. *Disarming Iraq.* New York: Random House, 2004.
Bromley, Simon. *American Hegemony and World Oil: The Industry, the State System, and the World Economy.* Cambridge: Polity, 1991.
Brown, Chris. "Self-Defence in an Imperfect World." *Ethics & International Affairs,* 17, no. 1 (2003).
Buckley, Mary, and Rick Fawn, eds. *Global Responses to Terrorism.* London: Routledge, 2003.
Bueno de Mesquita, Bruce, et al. *The Logic of Political Survival.* Boston: MIT Press, 2003.
Burbach, Roger, and Jim Tarbell. *Imperial Overstretch: George W. Bush and the Hubris of Empire.* London: Zed, 2004.
Burke, Jason. *Al-Qaeda: Casting a Shadow of Terror.* London: I. B. Tauris, 2003.
Bush, George, and Brent Scowcroft. *A World Transformed.* New York: Vintage, 1998.
Cagaptay, Soner. "An Accident on the Road to US-Turkish Cooperation in Iraq: Implications for Turkey." *Policywatch* (Washington Institute for Near East Policy) no. 717 (3 March 2003).
———. "Enhancing the Turkish-American Alliance: The Campaign for Iraq and Other Possibilities." *Policywatch* (Washington Institute for Near East Policy) no. 665 (2 October 2002).
———. "Turkmens: The Soft Underbelly of the War in Northern Iraq." *Policywatch* (Washington Institute for Near East Policy) no. 735 (27 March 2003).
Calleo, David P. *Beyond American Hegemony: The Future of the Western Alliance.* New York: Basic, 1987.
Campbell, Colin. *The Coming Oil Crisis.* Brentwood, England: Multi-Science Publishing and Petro-Consultants, 1997.
Chalabi, Fadhil. "Iraq and the Future of World Oil." *Middle East Policy* 7, no. 4 (October 2000).
Champion, Daryl. *The Paradoxical Kingdom: Saudi Arabia and the Moment of Reform.* London: Hurst, 2003.
Chase, James. "Quixotic America." *World Policy Journal* 20, no. 3 (Fall 2003).
Chesterman, Simon. *You, the People: The United Nations, Transitional Administrations, and State-Building.* Oxford: Oxford University Press, 2004.
Chomsky, Noam. "Imperial Ambition." *Monthly Review,* 16 May 2003.
———. *On Power and Ideology.* Montreal: Black Rose, 1987.
Cirincione, Joseph. "Origins of Regime Change in Iraq." *Proliferation Brief* (Carnegie Endowment for International Peace) 6, no. 5 (19 March 2003).
Cirincione, Joseph, Jessica Mathews, and George Perkovich. *WMD in Iraq: Evidence and Implications.* Washington, DC: Carnegie Endowment for International Peace, 2004.

Clarke, Richard A. *Against All Enemies: Inside America's War on Terror.* London: Free Press, 2004.

Cook, Robin. *Point of Departure.* London: Pocket, 2004.

Cordesman, Anthony. *The Eroding US Position on Iraq.* Washington, DC: Center for Strategic and International Studies, 30 April 2004.

———. *Iraq's Evolving Insurgency.* Washington, DC: Center for Strategic and International Studies, 23 June 2005.

———. *The Iraq War: Strategy, Tactics, and Military Lessons.* Westport, CT: Greenwood, 2003.

———. *Saudi Arabia: Guarding the Desert Kingdom.* Boulder: Westview, 1997.

Dalgaard-Nielsen, Anja. "Gulf War: The German Resistance." *Survival* 45, no. 1 (2003).

Dekmejian, Hrair. "The Rise of Political Islam in Saudi Arabia." *Middle East Journal* 48, no. 4 (1994).

Dobbins, James, et al. *America's Role in Nation-Building: From Germany to Iraq.* Santa Monica: Rand, 2003.

Dodge, Toby, and Steven Simon, eds. *Iraq at the Crossroads: State and Society in the Shadow of Regime Change.* Oxford: Oxford University Press, 2003.

Drury, Shadia B. *Leo Strauss and the American Right.* New York: Palgrave, 1999.

Duffield, John S. "Oil and the Iraq War: How the United States Could Have Expected to Benefit, and Might Still." *MERIA Journal* 9, no. 2 (June 2005).

Economist Intelligence Unit. *Jordan Country Report.* London, June 2003.

Ehsane, Kaveh, and Chris Toensing. "Neo-Conservatives, Hardliner Clerics, and the Bomb." *Middle East Report* no. 233 (Winter 2004).

Ehteshami, Anoushiravan. "Iran's International Posture in the Wake of the Iraq War." *Middle East Journal* 58, no. 2 (Spring 2004).

Etherington, Mark. *Revolt on the Tigris: The Al-Sadr Uprising and the Governing of Iraq.* Ithaca: Cornell University Press, 2005.

Fandy, Mamoun. *Saudi Arabia and the Politics of Dissent.* Basingstoke: Macmillan, 1999.

Fawn, Rick. "Perceptions in Central and South-Eastern Europe." In Mary Buckley and Sally N. Cummings, eds., *Kosovo: Perceptions of War and Its Aftermath.* London: Continuum, 2001.

Ferguson, Niall. *Colossus: The Price of America's Empire.* New York: Penguin, 2004.

Fisher, Louis. "Deciding on War Against Iraq: Institutional Failures." *Political Science Quarterly* 118, no. 3 (2003).

Francke, Rend Rahim. "On the Situation in Iraq." Iraq Democracy Watch Report no. 1. September 2003, http://www.iraqfoundation.org.

Freedman, Lawrence. "War in Iraq: Selling the Threat." *Survival* 46, no. 2 (2004).

Freedman, Lawrence, and Efraim Karsh. *The Gulf Conflict, 1990–1991.* London: Faber and Faber, 1993.

Gill, Stephen. *Power and Resistance in the New World Order.* London: Palgrave Macmillan, 2003.

Gilpin, Robert. *War and Change in World Politics.* Cambridge: Cambridge University Press, 1982.

Golan, Galia. "Russia and the Iraq War: Was Putin's Policy a Failure?" *Communist and Post-Communist Studies* 37, no. 4 (December 2004).

Gordon, Philip H., and Jeremy Shapiro. *Allies at War.* Washington, DC: Brookings, 2004.

Graham-Brown, Sarah. "Sanctioning Iraq." *Middle East Report* no. 215 (Summer 2000).
———. *Sanctioning Saddam: The Politics of Intervention in Iraq.* London: I. B. Tauris, 1999.
Grunberg, Isabelle. "Exploring the 'Myth' of Hegemonic Stability." *International Organization* 44, no. 4 (Autumn 1990).
Hale, William. *Turkish Foreign Policy, 1774–2000.* London: Frank Cass, 2000.
Hansen, Birthe. *Unipolarity and the Middle East.* London: Curzon, 2000.
Hardt, Michael, and Antonio Negri. *Empire.* Cambridge: Harvard University Press, 2000.
Hashim, Ahmed S. "The Sunni Insurgency." *Middle East Institute Perspective,* August 2003.
Hendrickson, David. "Toward Universal Empire: The Dangerous Quest for Absolute Security." *World Policy Journal* 19, no. 3 (Fall 2002).
Henkin, Louis. *International Law: Cases and Materials.* 3rd ed. St. Paul, MN: West, 1993.
Hersh, Seymour. *Chain of Command: The Road from 9/11 to Abu Ghraib.* New York: HarperCollins, 2004.
Hinnebusch, Raymond. *The International Politics of the Middle East.* Manchester: Manchester University Press, 2003.
———. *Syria: Revolution from Above.* London: Routledge, 2001.
Hirano, Sadao. *Komeito-Soka Gakkai no Shinjitsu* [The Truth of Komeito and Soka Gakkai]. Tokyo: Kodansha, 2005.
Hiro, Dilip. *Secrets and Lies: The True Story of the Iraq War.* London: Politico, 2005.
Hooglund, Eric, ed. *Twenty Years of Islamic Revolution: Political and Social Transition in Iran Since 1979.* Syracuse: Syracuse University Press, 2002.
Hudson, Michael. *Super Imperialism: The Origin and Fundamentals of US World Dominance.* London: Pluto, 2003.
Hudson, Michael C. "To Play the Hegemon: Fifty Years of US Policy in the Middle East." *Middle East Journal* 50, no. 3 (1996).
———. "The United States in the Middle East." In Louise Fawcett, ed., *The International Relations of the Middle East.* Oxford: Oxford University Press, 2005.
Huntington, Samuel. "The US: Decline or Renewal?" *Foreign Affairs* (Winter 1988).
Ignatieff, Michael. *Virtual War.* New York: Vintage, 1999.
Ikenberry, John. "American Power and the Empire of Capitalist Democracy." In Michael Cox, Tim Dunne, and Ken Booth, eds., *Empires, Systems, and States.* Cambridge: Cambridge University Press, 2001.
———. "Illusions of Empire: Defining the New American Order." *Foreign Affairs* (March–April 2004).
Ivanov, Igor'. *Novaya Rossiiskaya Diplomatiya: Desyat' let Vneshnei Politiki Strany.* Moscow: Olma, 2001.
Jabar, Faleh A. "Postconflict Iraq: A Race for Stability, Reconstruction, and Legitimacy." Special Report no. 120. Washington, DC: US Institute of Peace, May 2004.
———. "Shaykhs and Ideologues: Detribalization and Retribalization in Iraq, 1968–1998." *Middle East Report* no. 215 (Summer 2000).
———. *The Shi'ite Movement in Iraq.* London: Saqi, 2003.
Jervis, Robert. *Perception and Misperception in International Politics.* Princeton: Princeton University Press, 1976.

———. "Understanding the Bush Doctrine." *Political Science Quarterly* 118, no. 3 (Fall 2003).

Johnson, Chalmers. *Blowback: The Costs and Consequences of American Empire.* New York: Time Warner, 2002.

———. *The Sorrows of Empire: Militarism, Secrecy, and the End of the Republic.* New York: Metropolitan, 2004.

Kagan, Robert. *Of Paradise and Power: America and Europe in the New World Order.* New York: Vintage, 2003.

Kaldor, Mary. *New and Old Wars: Organized Violence in a Global Era.* Cambridge: Polity, 1999.

Kampfner, John. *Blair's Wars.* London: Free Press, 2004.

Katzenstein, Peter, ed. *The Culture of National Security.* New York: Columbia University Press, 1996.

———. *Policy and Politics in West Germany: The Growth of a Semi-Sovereign State.* Philadelphia: Temple University Press, 1987.

Kaufman, Burton I. "Mideast Multinational Oil, U.S. Foreign Policy, and Antitrust: The 1950s." *Journal of American History* 63 (March 1977).

Kennedy, Paul. *The Rise and Fall of the Great Powers.* New York: Random House, 1987.

Keohane, Robert. *After Hegemony: Cooperation and Discord in the World Political Economy.* Princeton: Princeton University Press, 1984.

———. "The Theory of Hegemonic Stability and Changes in International Economic Regimes." In Ole R. Holsti et al., *Change in the International System.* Boulder: Westview, 1980.

Keohane, Robert, and Joseph Nye. *Power and Interdependence: World Politics in Transition.* Boston: Little, Brown, 1977.

Kepel, Giles. *Chronique d'une Guerre d'Orient.* Paris: Gallimard, 2002.

al-Khafaji, Isam. "A Few Days After: State and Society in a Post-Saddam Iraq." In Toby Dodge and Steven Simon, eds., *Iraq at the Crossroads: State and Society in the Shadow of Regime Change.* Oxford: Oxford University Press, 2003.

———. "The Myth of Iraqi Exceptionalism." *Middle East Policy* no. 4 (October 2000).

———. "War as a Vehicle for the Rise and Decline of a State-Controlled Society: The Case of Baathist Iraq." In Steven Heydemann, ed., *War, Institutions, and Social Change in the Middle East.* Berkeley: University of California Press, 2000.

Kharrazi, Kamal. "The View from Tehran." *Middle East Policy* 12, no. 1 (Spring 2005).

Kindleberger, Charles. "Dominance and Leadership in the International Economy." *International Studies Quarterly* 25, no. 2 (1989).

Kirisci, Kemal. "The Kurdish Question and Turkish Foreign Policy." In Lenore G. Martin and Dmitris Keridis, eds., *The Future of Turkish Foreign Policy.* Cambridge: MIT Press, 2004.

———. "Turkey and the Muslim Middle East." In Alan Makovsky and Sabri Sayari, eds., *Turkey's New World: Changing Dynamics in Turkish Foreign Policy.* Washington, DC: Washington Institute for Near East Policy, 2000.

Kirisci, Kemal, and Gareth M. Winrow. *The Kurdish Question and Turkey: An Example of a Trans-State Ethnic Conflict.* London: Frank Cass, 1997.

Klare, Michael T. "For Oil and Empire? Rethinking the War with Iraq." *Current History* 102, no. 662 (March 2003).

———. *Resource Wars.* London: Palgrave Macmillan, 2002.

Kolosov, V. A., ed. *Mir Glazami Rossiyan: Mify i Vneshnyaya Politika.* Moscow: Institut Fonda "Obshchestvennoe Mnenie," 2003.

Kramer, Heinz. *A Changing Turkey: The Challenge to Europe and the United States.* Washington, DC: Brookings Institution, 2000.

Krasner, Stephen. *Defending the National Interest.* Princeton: Princeton University Press, 1978.

———. "Rethinking the Sovereign State Model." in M. Cox, J. Dunne, and K. Booth, eds., *Empires, Systems, and States.* Cambridge: Cambridge University Press, 2001.

———. *Sovereignty: Organized Hypocrisy.* Princeton: Princeton University Press, 1999.

———. "State Power and the Structure of International Trade." *World Politics* 28 (April 1976).

Krauss, Ellis. "The Media's Role in a Changing Japanese Electorate." *Asia Program Special Report* no. 101 (February 2002).

Kritzinger, Sylvia. "Public Opinion in the Iraq Crisis: Explaining Developments in Italy, the UK, France, and Germany." *European Political Science* 3, no. 1 (Autumn 2003).

Kubursi, Atif. "Oil, Influence, and Development: The Gulf and the International Economy." *International Journal* 41, no. 2 (Spring 1986).

Kubursi, Atif, and Salim Mansur. "From Sykes Picot Through Bandung to Oslo: Whither the Arab World." *Arab Studies Quarterly* 18, no. 4 (Fall 1996).

———. "Oil and the Gulf War: An American Century or a 'New World Order'?" *Arab Studies Quarterly* 15, no. 4 (1993).

———. "The Political Economy of Middle Eastern Oil." In Richard Stubbs and Geoffrey Underhill, eds., *Political Economy and the Changing World Order.* Toronto: McClelland and Stewart, 1990.

Lang, Anthony, Jr., Albert C. Pierce, and Joel H. Rosenthal, eds. *Ethics and the Future of Conflict: Lessons from the 1990s.* Upper Saddle River, NJ: Prentice Hall, 2003.

Lawrence, Bruce B., ed. *Messages to the World: The Statements of Osama bin Laden.* London: Verso, 2005.

Leverett, Flynt. *Inheriting Syria: Bashar's Trial by Fire.* Washington, DC: Brookings, 2005.

Lieven, Anatol. *America Right or Wrong: An Anatomy of American Nationalism.* Oxford University Press, 2004.

Lind, Michael. "The Israeli Lobby." *Prospect* (April 2002).

———. *Made in Texas: George W. Bush and the Southern Takeover of American Politics.* New York: Basic, 2003.

Lochery, Neill. "Israel and Turkey: Deepening Ties and Strategic Implications." *Israel Affairs* 5, no. 1 (Autumn 1998).

Looney, Robert. "Petrodollars: A Threat to US Interests in the Gulf?" *Middle East Policy* 9, no. 1 (Spring 2004).

Luttwak, Robert. *Rogue States and U.S. Foreign Policy: Containment After the Cold War.* Baltimore: Johns Hopkins University Press, 2000.

Lynch, Marc. "Taking Arabs Seriously." *Foreign Affairs* (September–October 2003).

Mabro, Robert. *Political Dimensions of the Gulf Crisis.* Gulf and World Oil Issues no. 1. Oxford: Oxford Institute for Energy Studies, 1990.

Mandle, Jay R. "A War for Oil: Bush, the Saudis, and Iraq." *Commonweal* 129, no. 19 (8 November 2002).

Mann, James. *Rise of the Vulcans: The History of Bush's War Cabinet.* New York: Viking, 2004.

Mann, Michael. *Incoherent Empire.* New York: Verso, 2003.

Marlin, Robert O., ed. *What Does Al-Qaeda Want? Unedited Communiqués.* Berkeley: North Atlantic, 2004.

Massing, Michael. *Now They Tell Us: The American Press and Iraq.* New York: New York Review of Books, 2004.

Maull, Hanns W. "German Foreign Policy Post-Kosovo: Still a 'Civilian Power.'" *German Politics* 9, no. 2 (2000).

———. "Normalisierung oder Auszehrung? Deutsche Außenpolitik im Wandel." *Aus Politik und Zeitgeschichte* no. 11 (2004).

Mead, Walter Russell. *Special Providence: American Foreign Policy and How It Changed the World.* New York: Knopf, 2001.

Mearsheimer, John. *The Tragedy of Great Power Politics.* New York: W. W. Norton, 2001.

Mearsheimer, John, and Stephen Walt. "An Unnecessary War." *Foreign Policy* (January–February 2003).

Menoret, Pascal. *L'Enigme Saoudienne: Les Saoudiens et le Monde, 1744–2003.* Paris: Editions la Decouverte, 2003.

Migdalovitz, Carol. "Iraq: The Turkish Factor." *CRS Report for Congress,* RS 21336 (updated 31 October 2002).

Moisi, Dominique. "Reinventing the West." *Foreign Affairs* (November–December 2003).

al-Mudayris, Falah. *Al-Baathiyuun fi al-Khalij wa al-Jazirah al-Arabiyya* [The Baathists in the Gulf and Arabian Peninsula]. Kuwait: Qurtas, 2002.

Munson, Henry. "Islam, Nationalism, and Resentment of Foreign Domination." *Middle East Policy* 10, no. 2 (2003).

Muriel Mirak-Weissbach. "Arab Nations Changed, Shaken by the War." *Executive Intelligence Review* 30, no. 14 (11 April 2003).

Ninkovich, Frank A. *The Wilsonian Century: US Foreign Policy Since 1900.* Chicago: University of Chicago Press, 1999.

Noreng, Oystein. *Crude Power: Politics and the Oil Market.* London: I. B. Tauris, 2002.

Norton, Augustus R. *Amal and the Shi'a: Struggle for the Soul of Lebanon.* Austin: University of Texas Press, 1987.

Noyes, J. H. *The Clouded Lens: Persian Gulf Security and U.S. Policy.* Stanford: Hoover Institution Press, 1979.

O'Donovan, Oliver. *The Just War Revisited.* Cambridge: Cambridge University Press, 2003.

Oguzlu, H. Tarik. "The 'Turkomans' as a Factor in Turkish Foreign Policy." *Turkish Studies* 3, no. 2 (Autumn 2002).

Organski, A. F. K. *World Politics.* New York: Knopf, 1968.

Otte, Max. *A Rising Middle Power? German Foreign Policy in Transformation, 1989–1999.* London: Palgrave, 2000.

Packer, George. *The Assassin's Gate: America in Iraq.* New York: Farrar, Straus, and Giroux, 2005.

Pape, Robert Anthony. *Dying to Win: The Strategic Logic of Suicide Terrorism.* New York: Random House, 2005.

Paterson, Thomas, and Dennis Merrill, eds. *Major Problems in American Foreign Relations.* Vol. 1, *To 1920.* Lexington, MA: Heath, 1995.

Perry, Glenn. "Huntington and His Critics." *Arab Studies Quarterly* 24, no. 1 (Winter 2002).

Peterson, John, and Mark A. Pollack. "Conclusion: The End of Transatlantic Partnership?" In John Peterson and Mark A. Pollack, eds., *Europe, America, Bush: Transatlantic Relations in the 21st Century.* London: Routledge, 2003.

Pieterse, Jan Nederveen. *Globalization or Empire?* New York: Routledge, 2004.

Pollack, Kenneth M. *The Threatening Storm: The Case for Invading Iraq*. New York: Random House, 2002.

Pradetto, August. "From 'Tamed' to 'Normal' Power: A New Paradigm in German Foreign and Security Policy." In Werner Reutter, ed., *Germany on the Road to "Normalcy": Policies and Politics of the Red-Green Federal Government*. London: Palgrave, 2004.

Rampton, Sheldon, and John Stauber. *Weapons of Mass Deception: The Uses of Propaganda in Bush's War on Iraq*. New York: Tarcher Penguin, 2003.

al-Rasheed, Madawi. "La Couronne et le Turban: L'État Saoudien à la Recherche d'Une Nouvelle Légitimité." In Basma Kudmani-Darwish and Mai Chartouni-Dubarry, eds., *Les Etats Arabes Face à la Contestation Islamiste*. Paris: Armand Collin, 1997.

———. *A History of Saudi Arabia*. Cambridge: Cambridge University Press, 2002.

———. "Saudi Arabia's Islamist Opposition." *Current History* 95, no. 597 (1996).

Rengger, Nicholas. "On the Just War Tradition in the Twenty-First Century." *International Affairs* 78, no. 2 (April 2002).

Rhodes, Edward. "The Imperial Logic of Bush's Liberal Agenda." *Survival* 45, no. 1 (Spring 2003).

Ritter, Scott. *Iraq Confidential: The Untold Story of America's Intelligence Conspiracy*. London: I. B. Tauris, 2005.

Roberts, Les, Riyadh Lafta, Richard Garfield, Jamal Khudhairi, and Gilbert Burnham. "Mortality Before and After the 2003 Invasion of Iraq: Cluster Sample Survey." *The Lancet* 364, no. 9448 (2004).

Robins, Philip. "Confusion at Home, Confusion Abroad: Turkey Between Copenhagen and Iraq." *International Affairs* 79, no. 3 (May 2003).

———. *Suits and Uniforms: Turkish Foreign Policy Since the Cold War*. London: Hurst, 2003.

Robinson, Ronald. "Imperial Theory and the Question of Imperialism After Empire." In Robert F. Holland and Gowher Rizvi, eds., *Perspectives on Imperialism and Decolonization*. London: Frank Cass, 1984.

Robinson, William I. "Capitalist Globalization and the Transnationalization of the State." In Mark Rupert and Hazel Smith, eds., *Historical Materialism and Globalization*. London: Routledge, 2002.

Roth, Kenneth. "The Law of War in the War on Terror." *Foreign Affairs* (January–February 2004).

Rubin, Barry, and Judith Colp Rubin. *Anti-American Terrorism and the Middle East: A Documentary Reader*. New York: Oxford University Press, 2002.

Rupnik, Jacques. "Why Are the Eastern Europeans Pro-American?" *East European Constitutional Review* 12, pts. 2–3 (Spring–Summer 2003).

Sampson, A. *The Seven Sisters: The 100 Year Battle for the World's Oil Supply*. Rev. ed. New York: Bantam, 1991.

Scheuer, Michael. *Imperial Hubris: Why the West Is Losing the War on Terrorism*. London: Brassey's, 2004.

Schöllgen, Gregor. "Die Zukunft der Deutschen Außenpolitik Liegt in Europa." *Aus Politik und Zeitgeschichte* no. 11 (2004).

Schurr, Sam H., and Paul T. Homan, with Joel Darmstadter. *Middle Eastern Oil and the Western World*. New York: American Elsevier, 1971.

Schwarzkopf, H. Norman, and Peter Petre. *It Doesn't Take a Hero: General H. Norman Schwarzkopf—The Autobiography*. New York: Bantam Books, 1992.

Schwenninger, Sherle R. "Revamping American Grand Strategy." *World Policy Journal* 20, no. 3 (Fall 2003).

Seckinelgin, Hakan, and Hideaki Shinoda, eds. *Ethics and International Relations*. London: Palgrave, 2001.

Shadid, Anthony. *Night Draws Near: Iraq's People in the Shadow of America's War*. New York: Holt, 2005.

Shawcross, William. *Allies: The United States, Britain, and Europe in the Aftermath of the Iraqi War*. London: Atlantic Books, 2003.

Shinoda, Tomohito. *Kantei Gaiko* [Prime Minister's Office Diplomacy]. Tokyo: Asahi Shinbunsha, 2004.

Snidal, Duncan. "The Limits of Hegemonic Stability Theory." *International Organization* 39, no. 4 (Autumn 1985).

Stansfield, Gareth. "The Kurdish Dilemma: The Golden Era Threatened." In Toby Dodge and Steven Simon, eds., *Iraq at the Crossroads: State and Society in the Shadow of Regime Change*. Oxford: Oxford University Press, 2003.

Stephens, Philip. *Tony Blair: The Making of a World Leader*. New York: Viking, 2004.

Stocking, George W. *Middle East Oil*. Vanderbilt, TN: Vanderbilt University Press, 1970.

Stoessinger, John G. *Why Nations Go to War*. 6th ed. New York: St. Martin's, 1993.

Strange, Susan. *States and Markets*. London: Pinter, 1988.

Strindberg, Anders. "Iraq Crisis Threatens Syrian Reforms." *Jane's Intelligence Review* 15, no. 1 (January 2003).

Suskind, Ron. *The Price of Loyalty: George W. Bush, the White House, and the Education of Paul O'Neill*. New York: Simon and Schuster, 2004.

Taft, William H., IV, and Todd F. Buchwald. "Preemption, Iraq, and International Law." *American Journal of International Law* 97, no. 3 (July 2003).

Taras, Ray. "Poland's Diplomatic Misadventure in Iraq." *Problems in Post-Communism* 51, no. 1 (January–February 2004).

Telhami, Shibley, et al. "Does Saudi Arabia Still Matter? Differing Perspectives on the Kingdom and Its Oil." *Foreign Affairs* (November–December 2002).

Terzian, P. *OPEC: The Inside Story*. London: Zed, 1985.

Thurow, Lester C. *The Zero-Sum Society*. New York: Basic, 1980.

Todd, Emmanuel. *After the Empire: The Breakdown of the American Order*. New York: Columbia University Press, 2003.

Tripp, Charles. *A History of Iraq*. Cambridge: Cambridge University Press, 2002.

Tucker, Robert W. "Oil: The Issue of American Intervention." *Commentary* (January 1975).

Udum, Sebnem. "Missile Proliferation in the Middle East: Turkey and Missile Defense." *Turkish Studies* 4, no. 3 (Autumn 2003).

US Department of State. *Patterns of Global Terrorism, 2001*. Washington, DC: US Government Printing Office, 2002.

US National Security Council. *The National Security Strategy of the United States of America*. Washington, DC: 17 September 2002.

van der Pijl, Kees. *Transnational Classes and International Relations*. London: Routledge, 1998.

Volgy, Thomas J., and Alison Bailin. *International Politics and State Strength*. Boulder: Lynne Rienner, 2003.

Wallerstein, Immanuel. *The Politics of the World Economy*. Cambridge: Cambridge University Press, 1984.

Walt, Stephen. "Taming American Power: The Global Response to U.S. Primacy." *Foreign Affairs* (September–October 2005).

Waltz, Kenneth. "Structural Realism After the Cold War." *International Security* 25, no. 1 (Summer 2000).

————. *Theory of International Politics*. New York: McGraw-Hill, 1979.

Walzer, Michael. *Arguing About War*. New Haven: Yale University Press, 2004.

Wedgewood, Ruth. "The Fall of Saddam Hussein: Security Council Mandates and Pre-emptive Self-Defence." *American Journal of International Law* 97, no. 3 (July 2003).

Wendt, Alexander. "Anarchy Is What States Make of It: The Social Construction of Power Politics." *International Organization* 46, no. 2 (Spring 1992).

Williams, Rowan, and George Weigel. "War and Statecraft: An Exchange." *First Things* 14, no. 141 (March 2004).

Williamson, Murray, and Major General Robert H. Scales Jr. *The Iraq War: A Military History*. Cambridge: Harvard University Press, 2004.

Wohlforth, William. "The Stability of a Unipolar World." *International Security* (Summer 1999).

Woodward, Bob. *Bush at War*. New York: Simon and Schuster, 2003.

————. *Plan of Attack*. New York: Simon and Shuster, 2004.

Yergin, Daniel. *The Prize: The Epic Quest for Oil, Money, and Power*. New York: Simon and Schuster, 1991.

Zaborowski, Marcin, and Kerry Longhurst. "America's Protégé in the East? The Emergence of Poland as a Regional Leader." *International Affairs* 79, no. 5 (2003).

Zisser, Eyal. "Syria and the War in Iraq." *MERIA Journal* 7, no. 2 (June 2003).

Zuesse, Eric. *Iraq War: The Truth*. Delphic, VT: Whiting, 2004.

The Contributors

Rex Brynen is professor of political science and chair of Middle East studies at McGill University, and research director of the Interuniversity Consortium for Arab and Middle Eastern Studies, Montreal. His books include *A Very Political Economy: Peacebuilding and Foreign Aid in the West Bank and Gaza* and *Persistent Permeability: Regionalism, Localism, and Globalization in the Middle East* (with Bassel Salloukh).

Toby Dodge is lecturer in the Department of Politics, Queen Mary, University of London, and senior consulting fellow for the Middle East at the International Institute for Strategic Studies, London. His books include *Globalisation and the Middle East: Islam, Economics, Culture, and Politics* (edited with Richard Higgott); *Iraq at the Crossroads: State and Society in the Shadow of Regime Change* (edited with Steven Simon); *Iraq's Future: The Aftermath of Regime Change;* and *Inventing Iraq: The Failure of Nation Building and a History Denied.*

Rick Fawn is senior lecturer in international relations at the University of St. Andrews, Scotland, where he teaches international security and Central and East European politics. His books include *Global Responses to Terrorism: 9/11, the War in Afghanistan, and Beyond* (edited with Mary Buckley); *Ideology and National Identity in Post-Communist Foreign Policies* (editor); and *The Czech Republic: A Nation of Velvet.*

John Gee has been an executive committee member of the Palestine Solidarity Campaign, and has worked at the information office of the Council for the Advancement of Arab-British Understanding. His publications include the book *Unequal Conflict,* about the Palestine issue, and articles on Middle East–related issues, particularly Iraq and Palestine.

Raymond Hinnebusch is professor of international relations and Middle East politics at the University of St. Andrews, Scotland. He is author of *The International Politics of the Middle East; The Foreign Policies of Middle East States* (edited with A. Ehteshami); *Syria, Revolution from Above; Syria and the Middle East Peace Process* (with Alasdair Drysdale); and *Egyptian Politics Under Sadat.*

Rosemary Hollis is director of research at Chatham House, Royal Institute of International Affairs, London. Her recent publications include *The Middle East Security Agenda* (Strategic Yearbook 2005); "Europe in the Middle East," in Louise Fawcett (ed.), *The International Relations of the Middle East;* and "The U.S. Role: Helpful or Harmful?" in Lawrence Potter and Gary Sick (eds.), *Unfinished Business: Iran, Iraq, and the Aftermath of War.*

Eric Hooglund is the editor of *Critique: Critical Middle East Studies* and a consulting editor for the *Journal of Palestine Studies.* He is author or contributing editor of *Land and Revolution in Iran; Iranian Revolution and the Islamic Republic* (with Nikki Keddie); *Twenty Years of Islamic Revolution;* and *Encyclopedia of the Modern Middle East,* 2nd ed. (with Philip Mattar et al.).

Jolyon Howorth is Jean Monnet professor of European politics and professor of French civilization at the University of Bath, UK, visiting professor of political science at Yale University, and senior research associate at the Institut Français des Relations Internationales, Paris. His recent books include *Defending Europe: The EU, NATO, and the Quest for European Autonomy* (with John T. S. Keeler); *European Integration and Defence: The Ultimate Challenge?* and *The European Union and National Defence Policy* (with A. Menon).

Clive Jones is senior lecturer in Middle Eastern politics and international relations at the School of Politics and International Studies, University of Leeds. His recent publications include *Britain and the Yemen Civil War: Foreign Policy and the Limits of Covert Action* and *Between Terrorism and Civil War: The Al-Aqsa Intifada* (edited with Ami Pedahzur).

Atif Kubursi is professor of economics at McMaster University, Canada. His articles on the economy of the Middle East and the international political economy of oil have been featured in such journals as *Arab Affairs; Arab Studies Quarterly; The Beirut Review; Journal of Developing Areas; Industry and Development;* and *International Journal.*

Anthony F. Lang Jr. is lecturer at the School of International Relations, University of St. Andrews, Scotland. He is author of *Agency and Ethics: The Politics of Military Intervention* and editor of *Just Interventions* and *Ethics and the Future of Conflict.*

Yukiko Miyagi is a doctoral candidate at the School of East Asian Studies, University of Sheffield, where she is writing her thesis on Japan's policy toward the Middle East. Her master's dissertation, written at the University of St. Andrews, was titled "From Hafiz to Bashar: Authoritarian Transition, Generational Change and Foreign Policy in Syria."

Henry Munson is professor of anthropology at the University of Maine. He is author of *The House of Si Abd Allah: The Oral History of a Moroccan Family; Islam and Revolution in the Middle East;* and *Religion and Power in Morocco.*

Neil Quilliam is a senior Middle East analyst at Control Risks Group, where he is responsible for covering political and security issues in the Levant and Arabian Peninsula. He is author of *Syria and the New World Order.*

Madawi al-Rasheed is professor of anthropology of religion at King's College, University of London. Her books include *Politics in an Arabian Oasis; Iraqi Assyrian Christians in London; A History of Saudi Arabia; Counter Narratives: History, Contemporary Society, and Politics in Saudi Arabia and Yemen;* and *Transnational Connections and the Arab Gulf.*

David Romano is senior research fellow at the Interuniversity Consortium for Arab and Middle Eastern Studies, Montreal. He is author of *The Kurdish Nationalist Movement* and several articles on Middle Eastern politics.

Graham Timmins is senior lecturer and Jean Monnet professor in European integration studies at the University of Stirling. He is a specialist on German and EU politics, with numerous publications in these areas, and is completing a study on European Union–Russian relations.

Stephen White is professor of international politics and senior research associate of the School of Central and East European Studies, University of Glasgow, and visiting professor at the Institute of Applied Politics, Moscow. He is chief editor of the *Journal of Communist Studies and Transition Politics,* and author of *Russia's New Politics* and *The Soviet Elite from Lenin to Gorbachev* (with Evan Mawdsley).

Ian Williams has been covering the United Nations at UN Headquarters since before the Gulf War, for publications such as *Middle East International* and *Washington Report on Middle East Affairs.* He is currently working on a book about the US-UN relationship.

Gareth Winrow is a professor in the Department of International Relations at Istanbul Bilgi University. His books and monographs include *Turkey in Post-Soviet Central Asia; The Kurdish Question and Turkey: An Example of a Trans-State Ethnic Conflict; Turkey and Caspian Energy; Dialogue with the Mediterranean: The Role of NATO's Mediterranean Initiative;* and *Turkey and the Caucasus: Domestic Interests and Security Concerns.*

Stephen Zunes is professor of politics and chair of peace and justice studies at the University of San Francisco, senior policy analyst and Middle East editor for the Foreign Policy in Focus Project, associate editor of *Peace Review,* and principal editor of *Nonviolent Social Movements.* He is author of the highly acclaimed *Tinderbox: U.S. Middle East Policy and the Roots of Terrorism* and the forthcoming *Western Sahara: Nationalism and Conflict in Northwest Africa.*

Index

About the Book

While the war in Afghanistan saw most industrial countries back the US-led campaign, the subsequent war in Iraq has profoundly divided international opinion—and likely represents a watershed in the post–Cold War international order. *The Iraq War* examines the full range of explanations of the conflict, as well as its significance for the Middle East, for key international relationships, and for the future of the international system.

The authors critically assess the foreign policy decisions of both global and regional actors. What policies were adopted, and against what opposition? What state interests were served or compromised in the process? What are the likely longer-term consequences of each country's position? Addressing these questions, as well as broader issues of regional stability, global political economy, and the changing nature of warfare, they offer an in-depth, systematic analysis that brings clarity to this complex subject.

Rick Fawn is senior lecturer in international relations at the University of St. Andrews. His publications include *Global Responses to Terrorism: 9/11, the War in Afghanistan, and Beyond* (edited with Mary Buckley); *Ideology and National Identity in Post-Communist Foreign Policies;* and *The Czech Republic: A Nation of Velvet.* **Raymond Hinnebusch** is professor of international relations and Middle East politics at the University of St. Andrews. He is author, most recently, of *The International Politics of the Middle East* and *Syria: Revolution from Above,* and coeditor of *The Foreign Policies of Middle East States.*

357